SOVIET ECONOMIC STRUCTURE AND PERFORMANCE

Soviet Economic Structure and Performance

Paul R. Gregory
University of Houston

Robert C. Stuart
Rutgers University

Harper & Row, Publishers
New York, Evanston, San Francisco, London

Sponsoring Editor: John Greenman
Project Editor: Elizabeth Dilernia
Designer: T. R. Funderburk
Production Supervisor: Robert A. Pirrung

Library of Congress Cataloging in Publication Data
Gregory, Paul R
   Soviet economic structure and performance.
     1. Russia—Economic conditions—1918–
2. Russia—Economic policy—1917–
I. Stuart, Robert C., 1938–   joint author.
II. Title.
HC335.G723   330.9'47'085   73–8539
ISBN 0–06–042509–1

For Annemarie and Paul Mischa;
Beverly and Craig Robert

Contents

Preface

Our knowledge of the Soviet economy has grown at a near exponential rate since the early 1950s. While pioneering research in the West emphasized prevailing institutional arrangements and the reestimation of Soviet GNP and other macro measures according to Western concepts, later research has sought to answer questions of more general interest to economist and layman alike: How well has the Soviet economy performed? How does the Soviet model of economic development differ from Western experience, and is it applicable to today's underdeveloped economies? How have the Soviets coped with those problems—inflation, unemployment, pollution, etc.—that seem to confront all industrialized economies? What forces are there in the Soviet economic system that promote or retard economic integration with the capitalist world? —and so on. In addition to asking such broad questions, Western researchers have come to apply the standard tools of Western economists—ranging from elementary supply and demand analysis to sophisticated econometric and mathematical techniques—to the study of the Soviet economy. Thus today one can find econometric estimates of Soviet production functions, mathematical theories of central planning, statistical studies of Soviet structural change, and the like. An important offshoot of such efforts has been the reexamination and questioning of accepted doctrine, such as the rationale for collectivization and the heroic industrialization drive of the 1930s, the origins of the War Communism period, and the myth of perfect centralization of economic decision making.

The objective of this book is to provide an introduction to the history, operation, and performance of the Soviet economy in light of this amassed knowledge. The emphasis throughout is on these same questions with a relatively moderate amount of attention paid to institutional arrangements. Perhaps the most controversial feature of this book is the selection of institutional material to be included, which is always a difficult choice when the size must be limited to manageable proportions. Yet it is our belief that a work relying primarily upon the standard economic tools is needed at this point.

This book is developed around four central themes and is, accordingly, subdivided into four parts: (1) the evolution of the Soviet economic system (economic history), (2) the process of resource allocation in the Soviet economy, (3) reform of the Soviet command economy, and (4) the economic performance and economic development of the Soviet economy. We have attempted to make each part as self-contained as possible, which has necessitated a small amount of repetition; but in view of the length of the book, this practice seemed desirable. Throughout it is assumed that the reader has a knowledge of economic theory equal to that normally acquired in a standard introductory course. The more advanced concepts have been relegated to footnotes and appendixes.

The authors would like to acknowledge and thank a large number of scholars for their direct and indirect participation in this project. In the latter category, Professors Abram Bergson and David Granick must be singled out for their guidance during our years of graduate study, and the Harvard University Russian Research Center must be noted as having provided the intellectual stimulation that played an important role in the project's conception. In the direct participation category, thanks are due to Carl McMillan, Franklyn D. Holzman, Holland Hunter, Keith Bush and H. Peter Gray, all of whom kindly commented on some aspect of this study. For the conception, development, and presentation of this work, the authors bear sole responsibility.

P. R. G.

R. C. S.

SOVIET ECONOMIC STRUCTURE AND PERFORMANCE

Introduction

The Russian Revolution ushered into being what would become the first important experiment with centrally planned socialism. Russia in 1917 was a large, economically promising land, populated by 144 million people of diverse ethnic backgrounds engaged primarily in agrarian pursuits. Its economic development had been retarded by the social unrest, political instability, feudal vestiges, and low educational achievement of the tsarist period. Russia would provide a rigorous test of the viability of the socialist experiment.

SUCCESSES AND FAILURES OF SOVIET SOCIALISM

Russia became a socialist economy with the October Revolution of 1917 and instituted central planning in 1928 under the First Five Year Plan. Thus we have a sufficiently long time period for viewing the Soviet system in perspective. Yet unbiased evaluation of Soviet economic performance is difficult, since many in the West would be unsympathetic to the Soviet political system. Nevertheless, amidst a degree of contention, there is substantial agreement concerning the following achievements of the first 55 years of Soviet government.

Possibly the most notable achievement from the Soviet viewpoint is a political one—the expansion of communism. The magnitude of this achievement becomes evident when one compares the tenuous control exercised by the Bolshevik regime over the former Russian Empire in 1918—encircled by unfriendly capitalist countries and plagued by civil war, foreign intervention, and a shaky economy—with the current situation in which roughly one-third of the world's population lives under some form of communism. The Soviet Union is no longer encircled by unfriendly capitalist countries; rather it has fashioned a bloc of (sometimes reluctant) socialist allies in Europe to act as buffers between itself and the capitalist world. Ironically the major political threat to the Soviet Union—The People's Republic of China—comes from within the socialist world.

Second, the Soviet command economy has failed to succumb to alleged internal contradictions after more than a half century of operation, though at one time some prominent Western economists saw such a result as inevitable. We use the term "command economy" to indicate that resource allocation basically proceeds according to administrative orders rather than to market signals. The long-run ability of the Soviet system to function without private ownership of the factors of production and without profit motivation is no longer seriously questioned. The Soviet Union has established itself as the world's second largest economic power (the magnitude of which Table 1, prepared by the U.S. Department of Commerce, readily demonstrates), and it would now be foolish to question its economic viability. Instead, the performance of the Soviet command economy relative to market economies is now the subject of contention, surely a lesser question than whether the system can operate at all.

Third, the speed with which the Soviet Union transformed itself from relative economic backwardness into industrial and military strength must be listed as a major achievement. Russia in 1917 was predominantly agricultural, with high mortality rates, especially among infants. Nearly 60 percent of the population was illiterate. The industrial sector's shares of output and labor force were quite small, and the domestic machinery sector was poorly developed, requiring heavy dependence upon the capitalist world for capital equipment. By 1937 most of the above indicators had been

Table 1 **Economic Indicators—USSR and USA Comparisons, 1971**

	USSR 1971	USA 1971
GNP (billion 1970 US $)	548.6	1,000.4[a]
Population, mid-year (million persons)	245.1	207.0
Per capita GNP (1970 US $)	2,240	4,830[a]
Bread grains (million metric tons)	91.0	45.9
Feed grains (million metric tons)	58.0	186.2
Potatoes (million metric tons)	92.3	14.4
Meat[b] (million metric tons)	12.2	23.1
Total labor force (including the armed forces), adjusted annual average (million persons)	126.0	86.9
Agricultural, adjusted annual average (million persons)	36.9	4.5
Crude oil (million metric tons)	377	470
Natural gas (billion cubic meters)	212	637
Electric power (billion kilowatt-hours)	800	1,827
Petroleum products (million metric tons)	266	610
Coal (million metric tons)	592	507
Primary energy production (million metric tons of coal equivalent)	1,291	2,130
Crude steel (million metric tons)	120.9	109.1
Cement (million metric tons)	100.3	72.1[a]
Aluminum (thousand metric tons)	1,760	3,561
Refined copper (thousand metric tons)	1,190	1,745
Chromite (million metric tons)	1.4	Negl.
Manganese ore (million metric tons)	6.8	0
Iron ore (million metric tons)	203.0	83.6
Nickel, refined (thousand metric tons)	151	14
Bauxite (thousand metric tons)	5,000	2,032
Phosphate rock[c] (million metric tons)	19.5	34.5[a]
Automobiles (thousand units)	529.0	8,585
Trucks, including buses (thousand units)	613.7	2,053
Electric generators (thousand kilowatts)	13,354	36,548

Table 1 **Economic Indicators—USSR and USA Comparisons, 1971
(continued)**

	USSR 1971	USA 1971
Machine tools, metalcutting (thousand units)	206.0	32.8
Computers, digital (units)	1,000	20,000
Refrigerators (thousand units)	4,557	5,691[d]
Washing machines (thousand units)	4,052	4,608[d]
Radios (thousand units)	8,794	20,600
Television sets (thousand units)	5,814	11,200
Vacuum cleaners (thousand units)	1,720	7,973[d]
Gold production (thousand troy ounces)	6,960	1,580

[a] Preliminary.
[b] Carcass weight, bone in, includes beef, veal, mutton-lamb, goat, pork, poultry, and edible offals, but excludes lard.
[c] Estimated.
[d] Factory sales.

SOURCE: Peter G. Peterson, Secretary of Commerce, *U.S.-Soviet Commercial Relations in a New Era* (Washington, D.C.: 1972), p. 35.

reversed; the USSR had been transformed into an industrial economy without reliance upon foreign aid or extensive imports from the West (with the exception of industrial technology). Commenting on the speed of Soviet industrialization, Simon Kuznets of Harvard University, a distinguished student of modern economic growth, writes:

As in all countries, economic growth in the USSR meant a decline in the shares of national product originating in, and labor force attached to, the A [agriculture] sector. But the rapidity of this shift was far greater in the USSR than in the other developed countries . . . the shift of labor force out of agriculture of the magnitude that occurred in the USSR in the 12 years from 1928 to 1940 took from 30 to 50 years in other countries . . . and the same was true of the decline in the share of the A sector in national product.

A comparable shift took from 50 to 60 years in most other countries.[1]

Fourth, the Soviet economy has exhibited surprising strength and resiliency throughout its history, perhaps reflecting the ability of the Soviet system to direct resources to its most immediate needs. Examples are the Soviet military effort during World War II, the Soviet space program, the absolute magnitude of the Soviet gross national product (its GNP is second only to the United States), and Soviet military power. Also, the USSR has been able to generate relatively high rates of growth of GNP between 1928 and the present. These gains have slackened during short periods, but they are high by international standards. Major economic crises have been avoided, and insufficient aggregate demand remains unknown.

On the other hand, the weaknesses exhibited by the Soviet economic system are equally well known and are not seriously contested: the Soviet economy's inability to provide consistent increases in living standards, especially during the initial Five Year Plan periods, and its inability to produce an assortment of consumer items corresponding to the demands of the population for quantity and quality are serious problems. Second, in terms of absolute economic efficiency, the Soviets have tended to generate less output per unit of input than the American and most western European economies. Third, Soviet economic successes have often been achieved at the cost of human life and material deprivation, making an overall evaluation of the system extremely difficult. The most immediate cost of rapid industrialization was the establishment of dictatorial control over the population in order to implement the extreme austerity of the First Five Year Plan.

Also, the relatively neglected agricultural sector, a source of Soviet capital accumulation through a depressed peasant standard of living, has thus far failed to be an adequate and efficient supplier of meat and vegetable products. In addition, the output of the major grain crops is still subject to large annual fluctuations, and the regime has been forced in recent years to import substantial

[1] Simon Kuznets, "A Comparative Appraisal," in Abram Bergson and Simon Kuznets, eds., *Economic Trends in the Soviet Union* (Cambridge, Mass.: Harvard University Press, 1963), pp. 345, 347.

amounts of grain. While these imports do not necessarily imply a failure of Soviet agriculture (much went towards meeting export commitments to eastern Europe), they were nevertheless considered undesirable by the Soviet leadership, and have tended to reflect adversely on the organization of agriculture in collective and state farms.

RELEVANCE OF SOVIET ECONOMICS

Before proceeding further, it is necessary to ask what relevance a study of the Soviet economy has to contemporary problems and issues. A general answer to this question must suggest that examination of a Soviet command-type economy points toward the substitutions that are required if the market mechanism is to be replaced. Thus one can better understand not only the functions that the market performs without central direction, but also the gains and sacrifices involved in its abolition. This issue has considerable relevance for the growing concern over the shortcomings of capitalism: pollution, unemployment, persistent inflation, and so on. Economies cannot function in a vacuum without a guiding mechanism, be it a market, central plan, or some combination of the two. Therefore the costs and benefits of alternative guidance mechanisms are matters worthy of continuing investigation.

Traditionally economics is defined as the study of how scarce resources are allocated among competing uses. In the United States, for example, scarce resources (generally those resources that command a positive price as determined by the market) are predominantly allocated among competing uses via the interaction of supply and demand. Relative prices form the only common information required by the participants in the market (consumers and producers) to make their (consumption and production) decisions. Of course, there are major exceptions to this pattern of market allocation—such as the resources allocated by the government budget—and there are many imperfections such as monopoly, misleading advertising, ineffective government regulation, and labor immobility that may cause the market to perform its allocative function poorly.

The Soviet experience suggests that an economy can function by command without markets to allocate scarce resources. In fact, even the common method of defining "scarcity" is absent in such an economy because, with only minor exceptions, there are no market prices. There are, of course, exceptions to the rule of command allocation in the Soviet Union. Consumer goods, once produced in planned quantities, have generally been allocated among consumers by the market. Also, regional and occupational allocation of labor is generally achieved by the manipulation of wage differentials (in addition to a degree of physical planning). Nevertheless, the most important production and allocation decisions are made not by the market but by a substitute mechanism—a *central plan*—which embodies the goals of the system's directors. Prices no longer allocate resources but serve instead largely as accounting units. The party specifies the economic objectives of society and insures that they are enforced by means of party control over the economic and political hierarchy.

In sum, by showing how an economy operates in the absence of a market and by revealing the substitutions that must be made for it, the Soviet command economy provides insights into the operation of our own market system. In making such comparisons, however, one must guard against the fallacious technique of comparing the problems of planning reality with the elegance of the theoretical market model, or for that matter comparing perfect planning with market imperfections.

The relevance of alternative economic systems—private enterprise or centrally planned socialism and combinations thereof—to the problems of developing countries provides a second area of relevance to contemporary issues. Should a developing country emulate the Soviet or the Western market pattern to break out of the vicious circle of stagnation and poverty? Or, should it combine features of both models?

The USSR was able to transform itself into an industrialized economy within a short period of time largely without market forces, thus freeing central planners to maximize the speed of industrialization. Whether this rapid and comprehensive transformation could have been handled within a market context remains an open question. For it was the combination of planning and political dictatorship that permitted the realization of high investment ratios and the rapid expansion of the quantity and quality of industrial labor that, in large measure, determined its pace. The Soviet model channeled investment into selected economic sectors (neglecting domestic consumption) to develop a domestic base for heavy industry—with minimum dependence on foreign trade. The major phases of industrialization were accomplished within one decade. Would this Soviet-style industrialization "work" for developing economies in the same way, or are there crucial differences that mitigate against the use of the Soviet model and that require the adoption of the more evolutionary "aid and trade" path? Answers can emerge only from an in-depth study of Soviet economic development—a central objective of this work.

The international arms race and the general instability of world peace provide a third area of relevance. It is common to equate economic and military power, although the relationship has become more tenuous in this age of nuclear weapons and guerrilla warfare. Yet despite obvious exceptions, the equation still holds at base: for economic capacity eventually imposes limits on military capability as defense and domestic interests compete for available capital resources. These limits may take a variety of forms; for example, an inflation that the public is unwilling to accept, or the inability of the domestic economy to provide subsistence levels of living if military needs are to be met.

Thus the current and future economic potential of the Soviet Union is important as it ultimately relates to military power. Questions that are relevant in this regard are: what has the Soviet growth record been in the past, and what are the prospects for future growth relative to our own? Does the Soviet economy have a natural advantage over market economies in the areas of economic growth and expansion of military power? The observer who doubts the political importance of such issues should be reminded of the 1960 United States presidential campaign that centered around an alleged missile gap and a USA–USSR growth rate differential.

A fourth reason for studying the Soviet economy is that we perhaps have something to learn regarding the operation of our own public sector. The Russians have had more than 50 years of experience with the operation of state enterprises in which profit maximization is not the primary motivation. While the appropriate scope of government activity remains a subject of continuing debate in our economy, there is general agreement that government must supply certain goods and services, such as public health, national defense, and highway construction which will not be subjected to a "market test" but which should ideally be provided at a minimum cost of scarce resources. Can we learn from the Soviet experience in the field of public enterprises, for example, to encourage cost efficiency in nonprofit institutions and in cost-plus pricing defense industries and to allocate resources efficiently among budgetary units of the government? We would probably all agree that the problems faced by the Soviet state enterprise and by our public enterprises are similar, which suggests that we could possibly benefit from the Soviet experience in this area, especially if we accept the view of John Kenneth Galbraith that we suffer from an irrational bias against public enterprise, and that the role of public enterprises should be increased.[2]

Market economies could perhaps benefit from Soviet experience in yet another crucial area in which the unregulated market fails to provide satisfactory results. Whether we consider pollution and other environmental problems to be functions of the type of economic system, or, more likely, characteristics of the industrialization process itself, it behooves us to consider how a socialist command economy copes with ecological problems. Time may not be adequate to find answers by experimenting within a particular system, therefore, the experiences of other systems should provide invaluable data upon which to base policy decisions.

A final reason for learning about the Soviet economy relates to the growth of trade between East and West with the West supplying wheat and industrial technology in return for the natural resources (natural gas and oil) of the USSR. The development of the complex machinery for implementing trade and economic relations in general between command socialist and market economies—with their concomitants of credit mechanisms, currency valuations, and leasing arrangements—must rest upon mutual understanding of how each economic system functions.

The present study attempts to provide answers to some of these questions, more specifically: (1) How and with what level of efficiency does the Soviet command economy function? (2) What is the

---

[2] John K. Galbraith, *The Affluent Society* (Boston: Houghton Mifflin, 1958).

relevance of the Soviet development model to developing economies? (3) What has the Soviet growth record been in the past and
what are its future growth prospects? (4) How does the Soviet economy regulate and control State enterprises and handle environmental problems?

THE ROLE OF
VALUE JUDGMENTS

Discussions about the Soviet economy inevitably turn to value considerations: is a predominately private enterprise economy, such
as we have in the United States and much of western Europe, somehow superior or inferior to the Soviet economy? Although the
question is legitimate, we maintain that the answer must ultimately
reflect subjective individual biases (personal value judgments)
and cannot rest on objective grounds.

The question of the ends or goals of a society serves as an illustration. It is generally assumed that the economic goal of a private
enterprise society is the satisfaction of consumer wants concerning
the production and distribution of goods and services. In other
words, consumer satisfaction is the end of such an economy, and
consumer sovereignty is said to prevail. As a general rule, if the demand for a particular product increases, more of that commodity
will be produced, probably at a slightly higher price. The important
point is that consumers (assuming a given set of supply relationships) determine the output mix of the economy by exerting effective demand in the marketplace. This pure case must be modified,
however, to be applied to real market economies: as governments
—through their monetary and fiscal powers—can alter both the
current output mix and the distribution of present output between
current consumption and investment and as advertising can—to
some extent—mold consumer preferences directly.

The ends of society in a centrally planned socialist economy are
generally pictured quite differently. The goal of such a society is
said to be the satisfaction of *planners' preferences*. A central plan,
which administratively determines the current output mix and then
distributes it between current consumption and investment, substitutes planners' preferences for consumers' preferences. This does

not necessarily mean that consumer desires will be wholly neglected. In fact, it is theoretically possible for the planning agency to plan output to fit consumers' preferences by employing a complex market research network. In practice, however, there generally has been a dichotomy between consumers' and planners' preferences. In fact, a basic rationale for the planners' preferences system is that it enables the planners to do as they, not the consumers, see fit.

Can we judge the superiority of one economic system over the other on the basis of the goals of the two societies? The answer, we think, is no—for to do so would require a weighting system that could gauge the relative importance of the goals of each so that the aggregate achievement of one society could be compared with that of the other society. Pure objectivity in either direction is impossible, because the weighting itself implies a preference for one set of goals over the other. Insofar as value judgments differ among individuals, there is no scientific or objective basis for such a conclusion.

Using strictly economic criteria, the superiority of one economic system over another can only be demonstrated when one or more individuals feel themselves "better off" and no one feels "worse off" under the one system relative to their perceptions of their own welfare under the other system. But such cases are not likely to be found in the real world.[3] One might argue that the Soviet system involves a reduction in current welfare since Soviet planners have generally opted for high investment and low consumption ratios; therefore, the private enterprise system provides higher levels of welfare and is thus superior. The Soviets could reply to this contention that the welfare of future generations has been enhanced as a result of their investment policy, and that their system is superior. The whole argument would then hinge on whose welfare should be valued more highly, the welfare of present or of future generations, which again would involve a value judgment.

An alternative approach would be to evaluate economies ac-

[3] For a discussion of welfare criteria and their applicability to comparing economic systems, see, for example, Abram Bergson, "Market Socialism Revisited," *Journal of Political Economy,* vol. 75, no. 5 (October 1967), 655–672; and Maurice Dobb, *Welfare Economics and the Economics of Socialism* (Cambridge: Cambridge University Press, 1969).

cording to whether they derive maximum output from their limited resources. To do so would be to judge an economic system solely on the basis of its *technical efficiency*—the goals of a society accepted as givens.[4] Even this criterion can be objected to on the grounds that a technically efficient economy producing that mix of output designated either by planners or consumers can have an extremely "poor" distribution of income among the members of society and is therefore "inferior" to a less efficient economy having a "better" distribution of income. This, of course, brings us back to close the circle—in that "better" or "inferior" distributions of income can only be determined by specific value judgments.

We are not suggesting that value judgments should not be made in comparing economic systems; rather we are pointing out that such judgments must be made with the explicit understanding that they *are* value judgments and should be treated as such. For example, the substitution of planners' for consumers' preferences in the USSR was accomplished by imposing a dictatorship that subjected the Soviet population to considerable suffering and dis-

---

[4] The matter of economic priorities can be illustrated using the familiar Production Possibilities Schedule (PPS). The graph below pictures a hypothetical economy that produces two types of goods: (a) producer and defense goods, and (b) consumer goods. This economy is endowed with a fixed stock of land, labor, and capital, which producers employing the available technology convert into output. Insofar as total resources are limited, the economy cannot produce unlimited quantities of output; instead it must choose among a large number of maximum combinations of goods that the economy can produce. A technically efficient economy, which generates a maximum amount of output from its stock of inputs, is said to be operating on its "Production Possibility Schedule." Let us say that a consumer-oriented economy would choose point A and a planned socialist economy would choose point B on the PPS. One cannot say that A is superior to B or that B is superior to A because both statements would be personal value judgments, which vary according to individual preferences and prejudices.

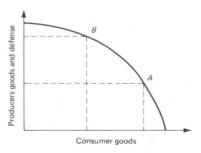

comfort during the 1930s. Any reader might find this tactic personally objectionable. Nevertheless, such an objection rests upon personal value judgments, and it should be recognized that others (Soviet planners, for example) may subjectively argue the opposite, namely, that dictatorship and deprivation were the necessary price of building a socialist society.[5] It is impossible to prove one viewpoint right or wrong on purely objective grounds.[6] Some might find this proposition difficult to accept in view of what they consider to be obvious deficiencies of the Soviet economic and political system.

PURPOSE AND SCOPE

This work is designed to serve as a basis for introductory courses in Soviet economics, comparative economic systems, and the economics of socialism—inasmuch as capitalism, centralized socialism, and decentralized socialism are compared extensively in theory and in practice throughout this book. In a comparative systems course, supplementary materials could be used if the instructor wishes to stress the various mixed systems such as France and Yugoslavia. We suggest that since the average student of economics already has some knowledge of the operation of market economies from his basic courses, a systems course should initially emphasize the difference between the two major prototype systems—the centrally planned socialism of the Soviet Union and the market economies of the United States and some western European countries—and then should turn to the variants of these prototypes, such as the decentralized market socialism of Yugoslavia or the indicative planning of France among others. In addition to a

[5] For instance, the official Soviet text, *Political Economy,* argues that such suffering and sacrifice were required to overcome the economic backwardness of Russia. *Political Economy: A Textbook,* 4th ed. (East Berlin: Dietz Verlag, 1964), p. 383.

[6] For a discussion of criteria for comparing economic systems, see Bela A. Belassa, "Success Criteria for Economic Systems," in Morris Bornstein, ed., *Comparative Economic Systems,* rev. ed. (Homewood, Ill.: Irwin, 1969), pp. 2–18; for a more detailed treatment, see Alexander Eckstein, ed., *Comparison of Economic Systems* (Berkeley: University of California Press, 1971), pp. 25–240.

detailed survey of the Soviet command economy, we also deal with the variants of socialism (the theory of socialism) to provide a theoretical foundation for the study of alternative socialist systems suggested above.

This work assumes a level of sophistication generally acquired in a one-year introductory economics course. The more rigorous theoretical concepts have been relegated to appendices and footnotes, thus providing the instructor with the option of teaching at different levels of sophistication. We emphasize the broad issues in the operation of the Soviet planned economy without lingering over its institutional aspects, which are quite complex at the introductory level and which change rather frequently. A basic understanding of the working arrangements of the Soviet economy is deemed more important: in what manner and how effectively are resources allocated by the Soviet command economy? This question can be answered only by relying extensively upon theoretical abstraction. Thus central tendencies are described without concentrating on the numerous deviations from these tendencies. This is the only way to develop an ordered framework to view the economy of the Soviet Union in its entirety.

This work consists of four parts. Part One, entitled "Origins of the Soviet Economy," focuses on the economic history of the Soviet Union from the tsarist period to the development of the central planning apparatus and collectivization during the 1930s. Chapter One recounts the nature and extent of Russian economic development prior to the Revolution of 1917. The objective of this chapter is to determine the nature of the economic base inherited from the tsars to facilitate an evaluation of the achievements of the Soviet period and to allow comparisons with the developing countries.

Chapter Two deals with the period from 1918 to 1928, that is, War Communism and the New Economic Policy. This chapter examines the two Soviet economic organizations of this period and their roles in the evolution of the Soviet planned economy.

Chapter Three describes the Soviet Industrialization Debate that preceded the adoption of the First Five Year Plan in 1928. The outcome of the debate is evinced by a discussion of the vast institutional and structural changes that occurred during the 1930s once the all-out industrialization decision had been made. The tools of aggregate economic theory and development economics are used to describe the various issues and to present the views of three different factions. In addition, special effort is made to place the issues of the debate within a general context relating to the problems of today's developing economies.

Chapter Four deals with the foundations of the Soviet planned-economy by considering the evolution of central planning in the Soviet Union during the late 1920s and early 1930s, and the introduction of collective agriculture into the Soviet countryside. In this chapter only the immediate impact of collectivization upon agricultural performance is discussed—the long-run implications are considered in later chapters.

Part Two, "How the Soviet Economy Operates," focuses on the process of resource allocation in the Soviet command economy. Chapter Five deals with the functioning of the Soviet economy in terms of institutions, industrial planning, and price setting. Chapter Six continues this topic in a discussion of decision-making by the Soviet manager, labor allocation, and the investment decision.

Chapter Seven discusses resource allocation in Soviet agriculture. First, the characteristics of Soviet collectivized agriculture are considered. Second, the role of collectivized agriculture as a part of, and contributor to, the industrialization process is analyzed. Third, the long-run performance of Soviet agriculture in terms of output growth and productivity is discussed.

In Chapter Eight attention is drawn to the Soviet foreign trade sector. The institutional planning and operation of foreign trade is first considered both in terms of the Soviet foreign trade monopoly and of the Council for Mutual Economic Assistance (*Comecon*) organization. The results of the Soviet foreign trade sector are then examined, especially as they bear upon the important question of the role of foreign trade in the course of Soviet industrialization and its impact upon economic integration within the Soviet bloc.

Part Three deals with economic theory and reform. Chapter Nine treats the various theories of socialism—ranging from the theoretical discussions in the Soviet Union during the 1920s, to the decline of economic theorizing during the Stalin years, to Western theories of socialism (the "socialist controversy"), and finally to the postwar Soviet school of mathematical economics.

Chapter Ten turns to the topic of economic reform in the Soviet Union and relates the results of economic reform to date. In par-

ticular, the Liberman reform discussions are analyzed along with
the light-industry experiments of 1964. Most attention, however,
is devoted to the September 1965 reforms and to their implementation.

Part Four is an evaluation of the performance of the Soviet
economy. Chapter Eleven considers Soviet economic performance
in terms of a series of possible performance indicators: economic
growth, static efficiency, dynamic efficiency, income distribution,
consumer welfare, and environmental quality. Chapter Twelve eval-
uates the Soviet experience as a possible model for developing countries. A summary presentation of the Soviet pattern of economic
development (based largely upon earlier chapters) is made, followed by consideration of the model's crucial components and the
preconditions necessary for its effective implementation.

Finally, Chapter Thirteen briefly summarizes Chapters One
through Eleven and considers future problems and prospects for the
Soviet economy, such as growth potential, decentralization, and
convergence.

PART ONE

Origins of the Soviet Economy

CHAPTER ONE

Economic History of Russia to 1917

The achievements of the Soviet period cannot be evaluated in proper perspective without some conception of the economic base that the Bolsheviks inherited from the tsars. If economic development during the tsarist period had been extensive, then the rapid industrialization of the 1930s becomes merely a continuation of past development. If, on the other hand, the Bolsheviks inherited a backward and stagnant economy, their achievements must be gauged differently.

Both the rate and the level of Russian economic development prior to 1917 are matters of some controversy. Lenin proclaimed tsarist Russia as the "weakest link" in the capitalist chain; current Soviet ideology argues that the economic backwardness inherited from the tsarist period made the sacrifices of the 1930s necessary; Alexander Gerschenkron stresses the discontinuous industrialization spurt of the 1890s; and W. W. Rostow dates the Russian "take-off" into sustained growth to the 1890–1914 period.[1] The resolution of these questions has been difficult without a generally accepted definition of economic development that could be verified

---

[1] *Political Economy: A Textbook*, 4th ed. (East Berlin: Dietz Verlag, 1964), p. 383; Alexander Gerschenkron, *Economic Backwardness in Historical Perspective* (Cambridge, Mass.: Harvard University Press, 1962), chap. 1; W. W. Rostow, *The Stages of Economic Growth* (Cambridge: Cambridge University Press, 1965), p. 67.

19

empirically. Even if agreement could be reached on the definition of economic development, the sketchy and unreliable prerevolutionary statistics of tsarist Russia would still present an obstacle to measurement.

Our approach to the question of Russian economic development is to consider a series of development indicators, while implicitly incorporating fairly wide margins of error into our conclusions. We first consider the development of industry and agriculture during the last half-century of tsarist rule, and then we turn to other factors, such as growth of per capita GNP, changes of industrial structure and demographic characteristics, suggested by Simon Kuznets as being indicators of "modern economic growth."[2]

INDUSTRIAL GROWTH
UNDER THE TSARS

Though it is usually difficult to trace the development of the industrial sector in a country as ancient as Russia, the reign of Peter the Great (1698–1725), an important turning point in Russian economic history, provides us with a convenient place to begin.

Peter the Great, impressed by the technology and industrial expertise he observed during his extensive early travels in western Europe, decided to industrialize Russia by importing Western technology and technicians en masse. Military considerations played an important role in this decision. Thus, the initial impetus was provided to move the backward Russian economy toward the development of an increasingly modern industrial sector, by eighteenth-century standards. As a result, eighteenth-century Russia acquired a nascent industrial capacity that, when combined with its vast natural and manpower resources, enabled it to compete militarily with the West for nearly two centuries despite a succession of less vigorous Russian tsars. After Peter the Great, however, a gap began to widen between the Russian economy and its industrializing Western European competitors, especially during the nineteenth century. In fact, during this period, industrialization came to be

[2] Simon Kuznets, *Modern Economic Growth* (New Haven, Conn.: Yale University Press, 1966), chap. 1.

regarded in Russia as a threat to the autocracy. Tsarist authorities feared that railroads would spread egalitarianism and that the growth of factory towns would spawn a rebellious proletariat.[3] One of history's great ironies was the firm entrenchment during the reign of Peter the Great of feudalism—a retrogressive social institution that later was to become a great obstacle to long-term economic development. Serfdom was used by Peter the Great to finance his military ventures and, indeed, he staffed his new factories, mines, and postal system with serf labor to implement his progressive industrial policies.

The Crimean War (1854–1856) forced Russian leaders to realize the relative industrial backwardness of Russia vis-à-vis the industrializing Western powers. The potential dangers of this gap were painfully obvious, especially to an empire-conscious country accustomed to respect as a formidable military power. As a result, the Russian government began to promote industrialization in a reversal of its earlier anti-industrialization stance, especially under the forceful leadership of Count Witte, the Minister of Finance from 1892 to 1903. Industrial development was fostered by the government in a variety of ways. The state sponsored massive railroad construction, spurred by the obvious military importance of railway transport in a land as massive as the Russian Empire. In 1860, the Russian rail network consisted of 1,600 kilometers of track. By 1917, 81,000 kilometers had been built.[4] This new transportation network opened up the iron and coal resources of the Ukraine, which soon overtook the Ural region as the metallurgical center of the Russian Empire. In addition, it opened up world markets for Russian wheat. Russian exports of wheat products increased five times between the 1860s and 1900, competing with North American wheat, which had also been made available to the world market by the railroads.[5] The state acted as guarantor of bonds, thereby promoting the widespread participation of foreign capital in industrial development. Domestic heavy industry was

---

[3] Alexander Gerschenkron, "Russian Agrarian Policies and Industrialization, 1861–1917," in *Continuity in History and Other Essays* (Cambridge, Mass.: Harvard University Press, 1968), pp. 144–147.

[4] P. A. Khromov, *Ekonomicheskoe razvitie Rossii* [The economic development of Russia] (Moscow: 1967), p. 280.

[5] *Ibid.* pp. 361–362.

promoted by a series of measures such as high protective tariffs, profit guarantees, tax reductions and exemptions, police help in labor disputes, and government orders at high prices to ensure adequate demand for domestic production. In addition, the state actively recruited foreign entrepreneurs for Russian industry. The military objectives of the state are seen in the Ministry of Finance's one-sided promotion of heavy industry at the expense of small-scale light industry during this period.[6]

The result of this state activity was a monumental spurt in Russian industrial growth during the 1880s. A prominent scholar of Russian economic history, Alexander Gerschenkron has proposed the relative backwardness hypothesis to explain this spurt.[7] He suggests that whenever the gap between economic potential and economic actuality of a nation becomes too great, that is, whenever a nation with great economic promise as measured by its total resource endowment becomes backward relative to other countries (as Russia was around 1860), tension is created, new institutions are substituted for missing preconditions, and a spurt of industrial growth occurs. In the case of Russia, the tension was great, the resulting industrial spurt was significant, and the Russian state, which acted as a substitute for missing entrepreneurial resources and deficient demand, was the instigator of industrialization.

Between 1880 and 1900, industrial production more than tripled, accelerating again between 1906 and 1914 after the depression at the turn of the century and the political instability of the 1905 revolution.[8] The extent of Russian industrial progress between 1870 and 1912 is shown in Table 2, which indicates that by 1912, Russia had risen to become the world's fifth largest industrial power behind the United States, England, Germany, and France,

[6] Alexander Gerschenkron, "The Early Phases of Industrialization in Russia: Afterthoughts and Counterthoughts," in W. W. Rostow, ed., *The Economics of Takeoff into Sustained Growth* (New York: St. Martin, 1963), pp. 152–154; and John P. McKay, *Pioneers for Profit: Foreign Entrepreneurship and Russian Industrialization, 1885–1913* (Chicago: University of Chicago Press, 1970).

[7] Gerschenkron, *Economic Backwardness in Historical Perspective, op. cit.,* chap. 1.

[8] Raymond Goldsmith, "The Rate of Growth in Tsarist Russia, 1860–1913," *Economic Development and Cultural Change,* vol. 9 (April 1961), 462–463; and Alexander Gerschenkron, "The Rate of Growth in Russia Since 1885," *Journal of Economic History* (supplement), vol. 7 (1947), 144–174.

Table 2 **Output of Selected Industrial Products: Russia and Other Countries, 1870 and 1911–1912**

	Coal (million tons)		Iron (million tons)		Steel (million tons)	Use of Raw Cotton (thousand tons)	
	1870	1911–1912	1870	1911–1912	1911–1912	1870	1911–1912
Russia	.7	24.9	.4	4.1	4.9	42	742
England	110.0	276.3	5.8	8.9	16.9	1,155	1,917
USA	32.9	450.1	1.5	27.7	31.8	470	2,415
Germany	34.0	234.5	1.4	17.8	16.9	117	805
Austria-Hungary	9.5	49.8	.4	2.6	2.7	50	208
France	13.3	39.2	1.2	4.9	4.7	86	457

SOURCES: P. A. Khromov, *Ekonomicheskoe razvitie Rossii v. 19. i 20. vekakh* [The economic development of Russia in the 19th and 20th centuries] (Moscow: 1950, pp. 452–454; A. N. Waltershausen, *Die Enstehung der Weltwirtschaft* (Jena: 1931), pp. 531–533; J. Clapham, *An Economic History of Modern Britain* (Cambridge: The University Press, 1952), pp. 47–48. *Fran-zösiche Wirtschaftsgeschichte*, Band 2 (Jena: 1936).

and had succeeded in narrowing the gap between itself and the leading producers of key industrial products.

Thus Russian industrial growth between 1870 and 1917 was rapid, and the industrial gap between Russia and the more advanced industrialized countries, although it remained significant, was narrowed. For this reason, economic historians who have concentrated on Russian industrial development prior to 1917 have traditionally taken a fairly sanguine view of Russian economic development during the last three decades of tsarist rule.

Is this conclusion justified? While significant industrial development is a necessary condition, it is not sufficient in itself to produce overall economic development. Insofar as the growth of GNP (industry, agriculture, services) and per capita GNP—not industrial growth alone—are the most generally accepted indicators of the rate of economic development, we must focus upon the performance of the second major sector, agriculture, during this period of rapid industrialization before a balanced picture of Russian economic development can be obtained.

RUSSIAN AGRICULTURE
UNDER THE TSARS

If industrialization is to generate self-sustaining long-term growth of total output, complementary developments in agriculture must occur simultaneously. This is so because part of the agricultural labor force must be transferred to the industrial sector—for this to be possible labor productivity in agriculture must be increased.[9]

[9] This assumes no surplus labor in agriculture. It could be argued that there was excess labor in Russian agriculture during this period which could have been transferred into industry without reducing agricultural output. Soviet sources place rural underemployment in the 1920s at 8 or 9 million; see L. M. Danilov and I. I. Matrozova, "Trudovye resursy i ikh ispol' zovanie," in A. P. Volkova et al., eds., *Trud i zarabotnaia plata v SSSR* [Labor and wages in the USSR] (Moscow: 1968), p. 246. The extent to which this surplus labor could be withdrawn into industry would depend upon industrial demand for labor and upon exit barriers in agriculture. The withdrawal of such surplus labor would reflect itself statistically in higher labor productivity of the remaining agricultural workers even without an increase in agricultural technology.

Thus it could perhaps be argued that increased technology in agriculture

Second, agriculture's output of raw materials must increase to meet industry's growing demand. Third, insofar as agriculture is the dominant sector initially, it must provide savings to finance industrialization, especially in the absence of foreign aid or credits. Fourth, agriculture must produce surpluses for export to pay for the machinery imports required to sustain industrial development until a domestic machinery industry is established. Finally, agriculture may be called upon to provide a market for the expanding output of industry.[10]

The agricultural revolutions that accompanied the industrialization of western Europe and England were generally preceded by the breakdown of feudalism, which prepared the way for a modern agriculture unfettered by traditional cultivation methods and restrictions. Feudalism developed rather late in Russia, at a time when this institution was declining or extinct in the more advanced Western nations. Perhaps as a result of its late emergence, feudalism in Russia embodied particularly odious forms of servitude in which serfs were bound to the soil, could be deported to Siberia, were conscripted into the army, and sold on the open market by their masters. Depending upon the region of the country, Russian serfs were either required to provide free labor services on the landlord's land (*barshchina*) or to make payments in kind from their crops (later money) for the use of their allotted land (*obrok*). In addition, peasant land was held communally and was periodically redistributed by the village elders.

Russian feudal agriculture provided little incentive for the individual peasant. Serf labor was so inefficient that it became customary to call *barshchina* "all that is done slowly, incorrectly, and

---

would not be required under such circumstances. This argument is misleading since economic development requires increased agricultural output, not stable agricultural output, for reasons noted above. For a detailed dicussion of the labor surplus economy, see John C. Fei and Gustav Ranis, *Development of the Labor Surplus Economy* (Homewood, Ill.: Irwin, 1964), chaps. 3 and 4. For a critical view of the doctrine of zero marginal product of labor, see Theodore W. Schultz, *Transforming Traditional Agriculture* (New Haven, Conn.: Yale University Press, 1964), chap. 4.

[10] For a more detailed discussion of the role of agriculture in the development process, see B. F. Johnston and R. W. Mellor, "The Role of Agriculture in Economic Development," *The American Economic Review*, vol. 51, no. 4 (September 1961), 566–593.

without incentive."[11] Mobility from the countryside to the town was limited. A peasant working in the town not only had to pay a large portion of his earnings to his master but also had to return to his village if so ordered, unlike the earlier western European practice whereby serfs could gain their freedom by living in the town.

The Emancipation Act of 1861, which freed the serfs and divided the land holdings of the landed aristocracy (the gentry) between the peasant and the gentry, was a significant watershed, for it provided a unique opportunity to establish the foundations for a modern Russian agriculture that would have then supported the industrialization drive of the 1880s. However, the primary objective of the Russian Emancipation, initiated by the tsar himself, was not to promote economic development, but to prevent further peasant revolts and preserve the autocracy while retaining a form of agriculture that could be readily controlled. The vested land interests were favored. While the peasants received their juridical freedom, they were allotted plots of gentry land to be "redeemed" by the holder. The remaining gentry land (well over 50 percent) was retained by its original owners. The peasant plots were generally too small to provide a surplus over subsistence for the redemption payments due to the state (which had purchased the land from the gentry).

Let us now consider how the principal features of the Emancipation Act of 1861 relate to the problems of economic development.[12] While the reform did contain certain positive elements—an increase in the large estates that created export surpluses, the introduction of a money economy into the countryside via redemption payments, and the psychological impact of emancipation—the overall balance remains negative: the Emancipation neither promoted productivity increases nor facilitated the transfer of labor out of agriculture into industry. Communal agriculture was retained, as a means of control over the rural population in the institution of the *mir* or *obshchina*. The agricultural communes were held responsible for the debts of their individual members; therefore, the more prosperous commune members were liable for the defaults of the poorer. Because of this, there was little incentive to accumulate

---

[11] M. V. Dovnar-Zapol'skii, *Na zare krestianskoi svobody* [At the daybreak of peasant emancipation] (Kiev: 1911), p. 179.

[12] The following discussion is based primarily upon Alexander Gerschenkron, "Russian Agrarian Policies," *op. cit.*, pp. 140–256.

wealth within the commune. The peasant could not withdraw his land from the commune until all debts on the land were met and then only with a two-thirds vote of the membership. Nor could he leave agriculture for the city until his land was free of obligations —the rigid internal passport system ensured peasant compliance with this rule. In addition, the land was to be redistributed periodically within the commune, thereby reducing incentives to improve a particular plot of land. In short, the Emancipation Act made it difficult for the peasant to develop both a sense of private property and an interest in long-term productivity improvements, factors that had proven crucial in the agricultural revolutions of other countries. Instead, productivity gains were thwarted by the small inefficient plots and the retention of communal agriculture. In fact, the per capita land allotment of the peasant declined between the time of emancipation and 1900 as peasant population expanded.

According to Gerschenkron, the guiding principles of the Russian agrarian program between 1861 and 1906 were:

> to preserve the *obshchina* [communal agriculture] until
> the liquidation of the redemption debt, to prolong the
> amortization of that debt so as to protect the *obshchina*,
> and at the same time to continue to hold the peasantry in the
> vise of ruinous aggregate taxation.[13]

Massive peasant dissatisfaction with the Emancipation Act along with the unrest of the urban worker were significant factors in the Revolution of 1905. Peasant unrest during this period bordered on spontaneous armed rebellion in the countryside, which prompted the state to enact measures to improve the lot of the peasant: joint responsibility was abolished in 1903 and 50 percent of peasant indebtedness was forgiven in 1906, and finally cancelled fully in 1907. From the point of view of long-run economic development, the Stolypin Reforms of 1906 and 1910 were the most significant government measures because they sought to weaken communal agriculture in favor of the emergence of a class of small peasant proprietors. Their principal provision facilitated the exit of individual peasants from the commune, which combined with the

[13] *Ibid*. p. 229.

reduced indebtedness of the peasantry, opened the way for private agriculture in Russia. Heads of households could demand their portion of commune land and withdraw from the commune. They could further demand consolidation of their land into a single area.

It is difficult to predict what impact the Stolypin Reforms would have had on the Russian economy had they been given sufficient time to take effect. They could have possibly strengthened Russian agriculture to the point where it would have provided strong support for the industrial sector. The relatively poor performance of Russian agriculture after the Emancipation is, however, a matter of record: the rate of growth of agricultural output between 1860 and 1913 was not more than 2 percent annually, only slightly exceeding the rate of population growth. In fact, the output of wheat and rye per capita actually declined between 1870 and 1900. The major portion of the growth of agricultural production can be accounted for by the expansion of cultivated area, not by increased output per worker. The rate of growth of labor productivity in Russian agriculture between 1880 and 1913 was a meager 3 percent per decade.[14] Thus instead of relying upon increased output per worker to feed and supply the city, the state placed substantial pressure on peasant incomes through taxes and redemption payments to generate peasant marketings. In turn, Russian industry did not rely upon growing peasant demand for industrial products, but instead turned to the state itself as a source of demand.

MODERN ECONOMIC GROWTH IN RUSSIA

Pre-Revolutionary Russia presents an ambiguous picture of the pace of economic development. Industrial growth was rapid after 1880, but the stagnation of agricultural productivity and the weakness of peasant demand acted as constraints on overall economic development. A definitive answer to the rate (or level) of Russian economic development prior to 1917 cannot be gotten from an examination of industrial or agricultural performance alone, because they provide contradictory evidence. An even more fundamental

[14] These figures have been computed from Goldsmith, *op. cit.*, 446–447; and Gerschenkron, "Russian Agrarian Policies," *op. cit.*, p. 223.

objection to basing conclusions on the performance of individual sectors is that modern economic growth is a complex phenomenon, characterized by a series of complementary events, which cannot be described in terms of a single indicator. An established authority on this point is Nobel Prize winner Simon Kuznets, who has extensively investigated the growth experience of the now industrialized countries.[15] On the basis of this study, Kuznets concludes that modern economic growth cannot be described in terms of a single indicator. Instead, he notes a series of common characteristics of modern economic growth: sustained rates of growth of per capita GNP in excess of 15 percent per decade, rapid growth of productivity as the major factor behind GNP growth, relative increases (decreases) in the industry (agriculture) shares of output and labor force, an acceleration in the rate of population growth brought about primarily by the decline in death rates (especially infant mortality), and the development of political institutions conducive to economic development. If we accept Kuznets' multidimensional approach, we may then consider the extent to which Russian trends during the late tsarist period conform to the above-noted characteristics of modern economic growth (MEG) and thus more fully evaluate Russian economic development.

Growth of Per Capita GNP

A first distinctive feature of MEG is accelerated and sustained growth of per capita GNP. This rapid growth contrasts with the secular stagnation of the premodern period. Decadal rates of growth of Russian GNP, population, and per capita GNP are given in Table 3. These figures suffer from several weaknesses, which can be seen from the notes to Table 3; yet they should be accurate within a reasonable margin of error.

If one compares the Russian growth record between 1861 and 1913 with that of countries experiencing MEG, one is struck by the relatively slow growth of Russian per capita GNP. For the period as a whole, the Russian decadal rate was 9.1 percent, much less

[15] Kuznets, *op. cit.* The modern economic growth concept is only one method of measuring economic development. The Kuznets concept has been chosen because it is based upon the historical experience of a large number of countries and because limits are defined that permit empirical comparisons.

Table 3 **Patterns of Russian Growth, Fifty European Provinces (rates in percent per decade)**

	(1) GNP	(2) Population	(3) Per Capita GNP	(4) Labor Force	(5) GNP per Worker (1–4)
1861–1863 to 1881–1883	19.6	14.5	5.1	20.5	−.9
1881–1883 to 1911–1913	28.5	16.5	12.0	18.2	10.3
1861–1863 to 1911–1913	24.5	15.4	9.1	19.4	5.1

SOURCES: Paul Gregory, "Economic Growth and Structural Change in Tsarist Russia: A Case of Modern Economic Growth?" *Soviet Studies*, vol. 23, no. 1 (January 1972), 422. The population data are from V. Zaitsev in V. G. Groman, *Vliania neuroz-haev na narodnom khoziastve Rossii* [The influence of crop failures on the national economy of Russia] (Moscow: 1927). The GNP data represent an aggregation of the Goldsmith indexes of industrial production (1900 prices, imputed weights) and crop production, a livestock index (based upon Goldsmith's suggested one percent annual growth rate), and an employment index for the service sector. The weights are Goldsmith's 1902 weights. The service sector's weight is derived by using its employment share. See Goldsmith, *op. cit.*, 446–447, 462–463; and S. Strumilin, *Statistiko-ekonomicheskiie ocherki* [Statistical-economic es-says] (Moscow: 1958), p. 678 and appendix 2.

than the 15 percent per decade MEG limit suggested by Kuznets.[16] Even during the rapid industrialization period (1881–1883 to 1911–1913), Russian growth was still only 12 percent per decade. The conclusion that Russian growth was slow by MEG standards between 1861 and 1913 is not changed by incorporating reasonable margins of error into Table 3.

If, as Kuznets suggests, the most distinctive feature of MEG is a sustained and rapid rate of growth of per capita GNP,[17] then it was not achieved in tsarist Russia.

Growth of Output
Per Unit of Input

A second distinctive feature of MEG noted by Kuznets is that the rapid growth of GNP and per capita GNP are primarily due to increased output per unit of labor and capital inputs rather than to expansion of such inputs, that is, to the increased efficiency in the use of productive resources.[18] Column 5 of Table 3 shows the decadal rates of growth of GNP per worker, which was 5.1 percent for the entire period and 10.3 percent during the rapid industrialization period from 1881–1883 to 1911–1913. If one accepts the modest assumption that Russian capital stock grew at the same rate as GNP, it follows that the growth of capital and labor inputs accounted for slightly over 80 percent of GNP growth between 1861–1863 and 1911–1913.[19] Thus Russian growth was largely extensive, relying upon increased inputs rather than upon increased efficiency, quite unlike the MEG experience.

The relatively slow growth of Russian per capita GNP has several important implications as far as other aspects of development are concerned. First, long-term increases in per capita income are

---

[16] *Ibid.*, p. 67.

[17] *Ibid.*, p. 63.

[18] *Ibid.*, pp. 72–85.

[19] To compute the rate of growth of output per unit of combined input, we use the formula:

$$\frac{dGNP}{GNP} = \frac{dT}{T} + .8\frac{dL}{L} + .2\frac{dK}{K}$$

where T denotes technology, L denotes labor force, K denotes capital stock. See E. Phelps, "Tangible Investment as an Instrument of Growth," in E. Phelps, ed., *The Goal of Economic Growth* (New York: Norton, 1962), pp. 94–105.

required to bring about the changes in demand that alter the structure of output away from agriculture toward the more dynamic industry and service sectors. Second, a steadily growing consumer market fed by rising consumer income is necessary to provide an atmosphere of growing expectations conducive to private investment. Third, as incomes rise above subsistence, the ability to save for capital and human investment (education) is enhanced. In this manner, the productivity of the economy is increased and further economic growth occurs. Fourth, a margin of income over subsistence, combined with the increased availability of preventive public health measures, drives the death rate down (especially among the younger age groups). This is generally followed by declines in birth rates as the population becomes urbanized. Thus the economy is stabilized with steady but not extensive population increase —a pattern conducive to long-term growth. Let us examine each of these factors—structural change, the domestic market, human investment, and demographic patterns—as they relate to Russian trends.

Structural Change

Rapid shifts in the relative shares of agriculture (A), industry $(M+)$, and services $(S-)$ are characteristic features of MEG. From Kuznets' survey of the MEG experience of developed countries, the decline in the A share of total labor force was from 65 percent and more in the premodern period to lows of around 10 percent in the current period. Substantial increases in the labor force shares of $M+$ and $S-$ are the corollaries of the relative decline in A.[20]

Sector labor force shares for the Russian economy in 1880 and 1913 are given in Table 4. They have been compiled from a number of different sources and probably contain moderate errors stemming from inadequate data on employment in A and $S-$. The basic trends, however, seem clear.

The decline in the Russian A labor force share between 1880 and 1913 was extremely limited in view of the MEG trends noted above. The 72 percent 1913 share was still quite comparable to the premodern shares of the now advanced countries prior to their

[20] Kuznets, *op. cit.,* pp. 86–113.

Table 4 **Russian Industrial Structure: Labor Force Shares, 1880 and 1913**

	(1) Agriculture (*A*)	(2) Nonagriculture *M* + and *S* −	(2a) Industry (*M* +)	(2b) Services (*S* −)
1880	74	26	13	13
1913	72	28	18	10

SOURCE: Gregory, *op. cit.,* 425.

economic growth. The same conclusion can be reached concerning the *M*+ share, which despite an increase of five percentage points between 1880 and 1913 was still equivalent to the premodern shares of the developed countries. The *S*− share failed to conform to the rising MEG trend and actually dropped between 1880 and 1913. We see in these figures the impact of the Emancipation Act on structural change in the Russian economy. By retaining communal agriculture, the flow of labor from agriculture into nonagricultural pursuits was limited, which explains the small relative decline in the *A* share.

The Domestic Market

A second implication of the relatively slow growth of per capita GNP was the limited development of the domestic Russian market, especially in agriculture, during the industrialization drive of the 1880s and 1890s.[21] Russian industry, lacking an adequate home market because of the relative impoverishment of the peasant,[22]

[21] Gerschenkron, "Russian Agrarian Policies," *op. cit.,* p. 247; and Roger Portal, "The Industrialization of Russia," in *The Cambridge Economic History of Europe,* vol. 6 (Cambridge: Cambridge University Press, 1965).

[22] We relate a couple examples of rural poverty in Russia during the 1870s and 1880s to illustrate how limited the rural market was. In the Kazan province, it was estimated that the yield per *desiatin* on fertile land was about 1.9 rubles. Obligations (taxes, redemption payments, etc.) per *desiatin,* however, were 2.8 rubles, which means that the peasant had to make up the difference by gainful employment either in industry or as a hired hand. Yu. Yanson, *Opyt statisticheskogo isledovaniia o krestianskikh nadelakh i platezhakh* [Experience of statistical investigations of peasant plots and payments] (St. Petersburg: 1877), pp. 75–85. A study of the Novgorod province revealed that total peasant income was 8.8 million rubles, of which 70 percent was earned outside agriculture. Bread purchases, taxes, and other obligations came to 6.3 million rubles, leaving a remainder of 2.6 million rubles, or 12

was dependent upon the world market and upon State orders to sustain industrialization. The State's interest in railroad construction and munitions, in turn, explains the heavy industry orientation of Russian industry during this period. Agricultural prices rose after the Stolypin Reforms, and a more prosperous Russian peasantry began to emerge. As a consequence, the home market became more balanced, and the "economic Malthusianism"—the limited domestic market—of the earlier period was reduced. However, the short time span between the Stolypin Reforms and World War I, and the persistence of communal agriculture lead us to conclude that the impact of this improvement was small.

Investment in Human Capital

One of the probable reasons for the slow long-term rates of growth of efficiency was the limited private and public investment in human beings during the tsarist period—both a cause and effect of low per capita income. With a low per capita income, personal investment in education must be sacrificed to maintain subsistence levels, and without an educated labor force it is difficult to raise labor productivity. Illiteracy rates for Russia in 1897 and 1913 (Table 5) indicate that despite the considerable industrial progress after 1880, 72 percent of the over-ten-year-old Russian population was still illiterate in 1897 with urban literacy being almost three times rural literacy. Between 1897 and 1913, considerable progress was made in providing education to the population, and a rough estimate places Russian illiteracy in 1913 at 60 percent of the over-ten population. For comparison we note that U.S. illiteracy in 1900 was only 11 percent of the over-ten population.

The low literacy rates of the Russian population prior to the Revolution is a fairly convincing indicator of the relative backwardness of the Russian economy. As recent studies of the development process have demonstrated, there is a close link between the quality of labor force (as measured by educational achievement) and the level of economic development.[23] In the Russian case, the

---

rubles per household for other consumption items. A. A. Kornilov, *Krestianskaia reforma* [The peasant reform] (St. Petersburg: 1905), pp. 194–195.
[23] F. Harbison and C. Myers, *Education, Manpower and Economic Growth* (New York: McGraw-Hill, 1964), chaps. 1 and 2.

Table 5 **Illiteracy Rates: Russia in 1897 and 1913—
United States in 1900 (percent of total population
over ten years of age)**

		Urban	Rural	Total
Russia	1897	55a	83a	72
	1913	—	—	60
U. S.	1900	—	—	11

a Percent of entire population.

SOURCE: A. G. Rashin, *Formirovanie rabochego klassa v Rossii* [Formation of the working class in Russia] (Moscow: 1958), pp. 579–581.

limited pool of educated workers constrained overall industrialization and may have forced Russian industry to adopt capital-intensive production techniques to utilize more efficiently the limited supply of skilled industrial laborers (some of whom were imported from abroad).[24] The extremely low rural literacy rates show that, while the pool of rural labor was substantial, it was not perhaps suited for employment in modern factory conditions without considerable training.

Demographic Patterns

MEG has characteristic demographic patterns as well. As Kuznets notes, the dominant MEG trend in birth rates is downward throughout the modern period although changes in premodern institutional practices may create initial increases in birth rates.[25] The death rate declines rapidly during MEG, being the principal factor behind the acceleration of population growth. The most conspicuous benefactors of the declining death rate are the younger age groups owing to increased control over infant mortality. Com-

---

[24] Gerschenkron writes ". . . [the] labor supply to Russian industry was inadequate in quantity and inferior in quality. . . . Therein lies the explanation for the paradoxical situation that a country, so poor in capital and holding much of its accumulated wealth in hands that would not make it available for industrial venture, contrived to build up . . . a modern industrial structure . . . [which] compared favorably with those of economically advanced countries." In Gerschenkron, "Russian Agrarian Policies," *op. cit.,* pp. 210–211. For a contrary interpretation, see Paul Gregory, "Some Empirical Comments on the Theory of Relative Backwardness: The Russian Case," *Economic Development and Cultural Change* (forthcoming).

[25] Kuznets, *op. cit.,* pp. 40–51.

paring premodern and modern rates, Kuznets notes that premodern birth rates varied substantially among countries ranging from highs of 55 per 1000 to lows of 31 per 1000. The average premodern death rate was around 30 per 1000 in western Europe and somewhat lower in the areas of European settlement in North America and Australia. From these initial levels, birth and death rates declined, the death rate approaching a lower limit of around 10 per 1000 in recent times.

Russia began the post-Emancipation development in 1861 with a demographic base like that of western Europe and North America some 75 to 100 years earlier (see Table 6). The Russian birth rates of the early 1860s were exceeded only by the U. S. rates of the 1790–1800 period. The Russian 1861 death rate was well above the eighteenth-century western Europe average of approximately 30 per 1000. The Russian death rate began to decline steadily during the late 1890s but remained high relative to western European standards. The 1913 Russian death rate of 27 per 1000 was still more than double the western European average of 13 per 1000 for that same year.

The high Russian death rate can be explained by the high rate of infant mortality—27 deaths per 100 during the 1867–1871 period

Table 6 **Birth Rates, Death Rates, and Rates of Natural Increase: 50 European Russian Provinces, 1861–1913 (per 1000)**

	Birth Rate	Death Rate	Rate of Natural Increase
1861–1865	51	37	14
1866–1870	50	37	12
1871–1875	51	37	14
1876–1880	50	36	14
1881–1885	51	36	14
1886–1890	50	35	16
1891–1895	49	36	13
1896–1900	50	32	17
1901–1905	48	31	17
1906–1910	46	30	16
1910–1913	44	27	17

SOURCE: A. G. Rashin, *Naselenie Rossii za 100 let* [The population of Russia for 100 years] (Moscow: 1956), p. 155.

and 24 deaths per 100 in 1911. This limited decline over a 40-year period indicates the meager success which tsarist Russia had in reducing infant mortality.[26]

The Russian birth rate hovered around 50 per 1000 from 1860 to 1900, after which it declined steadily, but in 1913 it was still twice the western European average of the same year. Thus, although Russian birth and death rates began to conform to MEG patterns around the turn of the century, they still roughly corresponded to premodern levels at the time of the Revolution.

RUSSIA'S DEPENDENCE UPON THE WEST FOR CAPITAL

As a final note, we consider tsarist Russia's economic dependence on the more developed countries of the West. This topic was to assume considerable importance during the Soviet industrialization debates of the 1920s (Chapter Three) in which the proper role of the Soviet Union in the world economy was discussed, and the role of foreign capital, in particular, was a central question. The extent of Russia's dependence on foreign capital bears significantly on our discussion of Russia's economic development because heavy dependence is accepted as an indicator of underdevelopment.[27] As an economy develops, it becomes able to produce domestically the capital equipment that it had been required to import earlier (import substitution) and thus to reduce its dependence on foreign capital.

To determine Russia's dependence on foreign capital, one must first consider its domestic production of capital equipment. A possible rough indicator of Russia's domestic machinery-producing capacity was the relative importance of metal products (engineering) in the tsarist Russian economy. In 1913 metal products ac-

[26] In 1886, the average life span was 29 years for males and 32 for females, which shows the marked effect of the high rate of infant mortality on age structure. See A. G. Rashin, *Naselenie Rossii za 100 let* [The population of Russia for 100 years] (Moscow: 1956), p. 205.

[27] See, in particular, Hollis Chenery, "Patterns of Industrial Growth," *American Economic Review,* vol. 50, no. 4 (September 1960), 624–653.

counted for 10 percent and 12 percent of manufacturing net output and labor force, respectively. During that same period, the average manufacturing product share of engineering in England, the United States, and Germany was 21 percent.[28] Thus, Russia in 1913 probably devoted less than half as much of her manufacturing resources to machinery as did the major industrial powers of the West. Inasmuch as Russia in 1913 devoted a much smaller proportion of her total resources to manufacturing than the three major industrial powers, the share of total resources devoted to the production of capital equipment was even smaller.

This conclusion is perhaps surprising in view of the apparent zeal with which the Russian state one-sidedly promoted the investment goods industries at the expense of consumer goods industries during the 1890s which, according to Alexander Gerschenkron, resulted "in the relative top-heaviness of the Russian industrial structure as well as its relative concentration upon producer goods."[29]

Given the weakness of the Russian machinery industry, one would expect extensive Russian dependence on foreign capital after 1880 in view of the rapid rate of growth of Russian industry during this period. Russia was, in fact, a large debtor country during the entire 1880 to 1913 period, receiving significant capital inflows from France, England, and Belgium. S. Strumilin, a prominent Soviet economist, has estimated that foreign investment in Russia accounted for some 20 percent of total investment in both 1885 and 1914.[30] Assuming a probable Russian investment ratio of between 10 percent and 20 percent of GNP, the ratio of foreign capital to Russian GNP was between 2 percent and 4 percent throughout the entire 1885 to 1914 period.

As a frame of reference, one might compare the Russian experience with that of two other large countries, the United States and

[28] Paul Gregory, *Socialist and Nonsocialist Industrialization Patterns* (New York: Praeger, 1970), pp. 28–29, 34, 171–174.

[29] Alexander Gerschenkron, "The Early Phases of Industrialization in Russia: Afterthoughts and Counterthoughts," *op. cit.,* pp. 152–154. For two studies which seek to demonstrate that Russian industry was not top-heavy in heavy industry, see Gregory, "Some Empirical Comments," *op. cit.;* and Gregory, "A Note on Relative Backwardness and Industrial Structure," *Quarterly Journal of Economics* (forthcoming).

[30] S. Strumilin, *Statistiko-ekonomicheskie ocherki* [Statistical-economic essays] (Moscow: 1958), p. 520.

Japan, both of which were debtor countries at early stages of their economic development. Foreign capital accounted for about 1 percent (10 percent) of United States GNP (investment) during the mid-1880s, when U. S. dependence on foreign capital was at its peak. They accounted for .2 percent of Japanese GNP between 1887 and 1896, rising briefly to a high of 4 percent between 1897 and 1906, after which Japan became a capital exporter.[31] This comparison suggests that tsarist Russia was much more dependent upon foreign capital in both magnitude and duration, than were either the United States or Japan during their dependency periods. The inability of the domestic economy to meet the needs of industrialization and the resulting extensive dependence on foreign capital left a deep impression on the Bolshevik leaders and was to play an important role in Stalin's industrialization and collectivization decisions of 1928 and 1929 (Chapter Three).

WAS RUSSIA UNDERDEVELOPED IN 1917?

Our survey of the Russian economy prior to 1917 indicates rather conclusively its relatively slow pace of economic development. It had failed to generate high long-term rates of growth of per capita GNP, despite rapid rates of increase of industrial output after 1880. In 1917 the structures of Russia's GNP and its labor force were still comparable to the premodern industrial structures of the developed countries. The peasant, not the industrial worker, was still the dominant figure in the Russian economy. A minority of the Russian population and, therefore, labor force was literate, indicating poorly developed human capital; illiteracy was nearly complete among the vast, underemployed peasant population. Russia's demographic pattern was still roughly comparable to those of the developed countries during their premodern periods. Birth rates, death rates, and, especially, rates of infant mortality remained stubbornly high. Industrialization remained dependent upon foreign capital, and domestic demand for products was inadequate to stimulate industrial growth; the slack was absorbed by govern-

[31] Kuznets, *op. cit.,* pp. 332–334.

ment orders and the world market. In fact, Russia in 1917 possessed many of the features of a "dual economy" so characteristic of many presently underdeveloped countries: an isolated, modern, and capital-intensive industry existing alongside a backward and tradition-oriented agriculture.[32]

It could perhaps be argued that economic development did not occur in Russia because of the general political instability of the period and that once the political problem was solved, Russia would have experienced a significant upsurge in economic development. Education would have ceased to be regarded as a threat to the monarchy, free movement of industrial and agricultural labor would have been allowed, and private investment would have been forthcoming without state guarantees. But is not a stable political environment perhaps the ultimate precondition to modern economic growth? Kuznets sums up this relationship in the following manner: "The association . . . between economic performance and growth and political structure is unmistakable. . . . One can hardly expect much economic growth under conditions of political turmoil, riots, and unpredictable changes in regimes."[33]

Thus it is more reasonable to argue that the political instability of tsarist Russia only reinforces our earlier conclusions about the backwardness of the Russian economy—insofar as the Russian political system failed to meet the minimum political requirements for MEG. This, in itself, is a strong indicator of the low level of Russian economic development.

The formidable task of creating modern economic growth still lay ahead when the Bolsheviks came to power in 1917. The Soviets directed themselves to their task in 1928, after recovery from the ravages of World War I and the civil war (1917 to 1920), and came to grips with the universal economic and political problems of economic development that the developed countries had faced before them. The Soviet response to this task was distinctive in that the Soviets chose to combine nonmarket forces with political dictatorship to generate rapid development; whereas other countries chose to rely primarily upon market forces and some form of political representation. We shall call this response the "Soviet development

[32] Benjamin Higgins, *Economic Development* (New York: Norton, 1959), pp. 325–340.
[33] Kuznets, *op. cit.,* pp. 451–452.

model." It serves as a recurring theme throughout this book and is dealt with specifically in Chapter Twelve.

It does not seem relevant at this point to debate what might have occurred in Russia had the political outcome been in favor of democracy. As the Soviet experience during the 1930s shows (Chapter Twelve), economic development can occur under a variety of political arrangements. Rather our objective is to examine the institutions and mechanisms that the Soviets used to attack the problems of economic backwardness to determine their general relevance to present problems of the less developed countries. We shall return to this issue in Chapter Twelve.

Selected Bibliography

NON-SOVIET SOURCES

Jerome Blum, *Lord and Peasant in Russia* (New York: Atheneum, 1965).

Alexander Gerschenkron, "Russian Agrarian Policies and Industrialization, 1861–1917," *The Cambridge Economic History of Europe,* vol. 6 (Cambridge: Cambridge University Press, 1965), pp. 706–800.

Alexander Gerschenkron, "The Early Phases of Industrialization in Russia: Afterthoughts and Counterthoughts," in W. W. Rostow, ed., *The Economics of Takeoff into Sustained Growth* (New York: St. Martin, 1963).

Alexander Gerschenkron, "The Rate of Growth in Russia Since 1885," *Journal of Economic History* (supplement), vol. 7 (1947), 144–174.

Raymond Goldsmith, "The Economic Growth of Tsarist Russia, 1860–1913," *Economic Development and Cultural Change,* vol. 9, no. 3 (April 1961), 441–476.

Alec Nove, *An Economic History of the USSR* (London: Penguin, 1969), chaps. 1 and 2.

Roger Portal, "The Industrialization of Russia," *The Cambridge Economic History of Europe,* vol. 6 (Cambridge: Cambridge University Press, 1965), pp. 801–872.

S. N. Prokopovic, "Über die Bedingungen der industriellen Entwicklung Russland," *Archiv für Sozialwissenschaft und Sozialpolitik,* Ergänsungsheft X, 1913.

G. T. Robinson, *Russia Under the Old Regime* (New York: Macmillan, 1949).

SOVIET SOURCES

P. A. Khromov, *Ekonomicheskoe razvitie Rossii* [The economic development of Russia] (Moscow: 1967).

P. A. Khromov, *Ekonomicheskoe razvitie Rossii v 19. i 20. vekakh* [The economic development of Russia in the 19th and 20th centuries] (Moscow: Gospolitizdat, 1950).

V. I. Lenin, *Razvitie kapitalizma v Rossii* [The development of capitalism in Russia] (Moscow: 1952).

P. I. Lyaschenko, *History of the National Economy of Russia to the 1917 Revolution* (New York: Macmillan, 1949).

A. G. Rashin, *Formirovanie rabochego klassa v Rossii* [The formation of the working class in Russia] (Moscow: 1958).

A. G. Rashin, *Naselenie Rossii za 100 let* [The population of Russia for 100 years] (Moscow: 1956).

A. G. Rashin, *Formirovanie promyshlennogo proletariata v Rossii* [The formation of the industrial proletariat in Russia] (Moscow: 1940).

CHAPTER TWO

The Economic Precedents of the Twenties: The Soviet Economy under War Communism and the New Economic Policy (1918–1928)

This chapter considers the events of the period from 1918 to 1928 and their impact upon later Soviet economic policies. During this period, the economy operated under two quite different administrative regimes—War Communism and the New Economic Policy (NEP)—that provided experience to assist in making the final choice of comprehensive central planning (1928) and collectivization of agriculture (1929).

The lessons of War Communism and the New Economic Policy provide insights into the evolution of the Soviet economic system. The Soviet planning system did not appear from a vacuum—rather it emerged gradually as a response to the practical economic problems of earlier periods. Our emphasis on the precedents of the 1920s is not meant to deny the important impact of the early Five Year Plan period (the 1930s) and World War II upon the evolution of the current system. The former topic is dealt with in Chapter Four.

WAR COMMUNISM
(1918–1921)[1]

In general terms, War Communism was an abortive attempt on the part of the inexperienced Bolshevik leadership to attain full Communism directly without going through any preparatory interme-

---

[1] The following discussions of War Communism and NEP are largely based upon the following sources: Alec Nove, *An Economic History of the USSR*

43

diate stages: the use of money was virtually eliminated, private trade was abolished, workers were paid virtually equal wages in kind, and farm output was requisitioned. Were these war measures the product of the ideological intent of the Bolshevik leadership to establish full Communism directly, or were they forced responses to the civil war? The most generally accepted view, as postulated by the well-known British authorities on War Communism, Maurice Dobb and E. H. Carr,[2] is that War Communism was forced upon the Bolshevik leadership by the Russian civil war and that the various theoretical arguments posited by the Bolshevik leadership in support of War Communism were "no more than flights of leftist fancy."[3] The opposite view, recently postulated by Paul Craig Roberts,[4] argues that Lenin originally conceived War Communism —with its elimination of market institutions and its introduction of administrative controls—as a necessary step in the socialist revolution. In Roberts's view, War Communism was adopted for ideological reasons as a product of Marxian ideas (as interpreted by Lenin), not as a forced response to the wartime emergency. We can provide no final answer to this controversy; instead we shall attempt to outline as objectively as possible the basic features of War Communism.

The roots of War Communism can be traced to the October Revolution. One of the first actions of the fledgling Bolshevik regime was to confiscate the remaining large estates (the Land Decree of November 8, 1917) and to sanction the distribution of this land among the peasants. This action legalized in part the spontaneous appropriation of land by the peasantry, a process that had already taken place to a large degree. Irrespective of its causes, this change

---

(London: Penguin, 1969), chaps. 3 and 4; Eugene Zaleski, *Planning for Economic Growth in the Soviet Union, 1918–1932* (Chapel Hill: University of North Carolina Press, 1971), chap. 2; Maurice Dobb, *Soviet Economic Development Since 1917,* 5th ed. (London: Routledge & Kegan Paul, 1960), chaps. 4–9; E. H. Carr and R. W. Davies, *Foundations of a Planned Economy, 1926–1929,* vol. One, part II (New York: Macmillan, 1969), chaps. 33–35.

[2] Dobb, *op. cit.,* chaps. 4–9.

[3] *Ibid.,* p. 122.

[4] Paul Craig Roberts, *Alienation and the Soviet Economy* (Albuquerque: University of New Mexico Press, 1971), chap. 2.

of land tenure was to have a far-reaching impact upon economic policy throughout the 1920s. In their enhanced capacity as full proprietors, the peasants were no longer obligated to deliver a prescribed portion of their output either to the landlord (as a rental payment) or to the state (as a tax or principal payment). Now they, not the state or landlord, made the basic decisions about how much to produce and what portion of this output would be sold. Thus the total agricultural output and the *marketed portion* thereof became dependent for the first time upon the Russian peasant.

The initial Bolshevik attitude towards private industry was cautious and restrained since an uneasy truce between Bolshevik and capitalist was required to prevent a drop in industrial output. Workers' Committees in privately owned enterprises were given the right to supervise management, but, at the same time, the proprietor received the executive right to give orders that could not be countermanded by the Workers' Committees. Also the Workers' Committees were denied the right to take over enterprises without permission of higher authorities. Only enterprises of key importance such as banking, grain purchasing, transportation, oil, and war industries were nationalized—establishing a form of State Capitalism based upon state control of key positions in the economy, mixed management of enterprises, and private ownership of agriculture, retail trade, and small-scale industry.

The uneasy truce between the Bolsheviks and the capitalists and the peasants did not last long. By 1918 the Bolsheviks were locked in a struggle for survival with the White Russian forces supported in part by foreign powers. The Germans were in possession of the Ukraine, while the White Russian armies occupied the Urals, Siberia, North Caucasus, and other economically important regions. Poland invaded in May of 1920. At one time, the Bolsheviks retained only 10 percent of the coal supplies, 25 percent of the iron foundries, less than 50 percent of the grain area, and less than 10 percent of the sugar beet sources of the former Russian Empire.[5]

To divert industrial and agricultural resources from private into military uses, the Bolsheviks, lacking a domestic tax base and access to foreign aid, resorted to printing money. This expansion of

[5] Dobb, *op. cit.,* p. 98.

the money supply combined with shrinking supplies of consumer goods created hyperinflation, and by 1920 the ruble had fallen to one percent of its 1917 purchasing power.

The hyperinflation resulted in the near-destruction of the market exchange economy. The state grain monopsony (grain elevators and warehouses were nationalized in 1918) acted to prevent grain prices from rising as rapidly as the prices of manufactured goods. The peasants, faced with the dearth of manufactured consumer goods that, when available, sold at inflated prices, felt no incentive to market their agricultural output. Instead, the peasant either consumed his produce or hoarded it for future use, and the central government found itself powerless to obtain through the market agricultural products it needed to fight the war.

War Communism Policies

The Bolshevik leadership under Lenin responded by introducing War Communism, a system by which the leaders attempted to substitute administrative for market allocation to marshal resources for the war. The crux of War Communism was its agricultural policy of forcibly requisitioning agricultural surpluses. Police (the *Cheka*) were sent into the countryside to collect the surpluses of the rich and middle peasantry—a policy that severed the existing market link between industry and agriculture. In theory at least, the link was to be maintained by state allocation of manufactured products to the peasants and barter transactions for the remaining agricultural output. In fact, the peasants received only from 12 to 15 percent of prewar supplies of manufactured goods.[6]

Nationalization of the nonagricultural economy was the second major policy of War Communism. The sugar industry was the first to be nationalized in the spring of 1918, and by autumn of 1920, 37,000 enterprises had been nationalized of which roughly one-half were small-scale businesses that did not use mechanical power. This pervasive nationalization of industry may be regarded in part as a crisis response, for a large number of former industrial proprietors had deserted to the White Russian side, and there was widespread fear of German takeovers of German-owned enterprises. Also, nationalization from below by workers had been pro-

[6] *Ibid.*, p. 117.

ceeding at a rapid pace despite government opposition. On the other hand, the excessive nationalization from above down to enterprises employing only one worker may perhaps be regarded as an ideological response not to be justified by the crisis situation.

The abolition of private trade was a third cornerstone of War Communism policy. Private trade was regarded as incompatible with the War Communism system of centralized requisitioning and allocation. Government trade monopolies and monopsonies (mainly the Commissariat of Supply and the Commissariat of Agriculture) were set up to replace private organizations and concentrate commodity distribution in the hands of the state. In November 1918, all private internal trade was abolished, and the state ostensibly became the sole supplier of consumer goods to the population. In fact, the black market continued to supply a significant portion of total consumption goods and was unofficially tolerated by the authorities.[7]

Semimilitary controls over industrial workers became the major means of labor allocation. The movement of industrial workers was restricted, and they could be mobilized for special work. In some cases, army personnel were used for special projects. Labor deserters received severe penalties according to a Decree of November 28, 1919, which placed the employees of state enterprises under military discipline. Insofar as the state controlled the flow of consumer goods to a large degree, money wages lost much of their meaning and were mostly paid in kind from provisions provided by the state—with little differentiation among occupations. Money was virtually eliminated as a means of exchange, and interfirm transactions were made with bookkeeping entries. Transportation and municipal services were provided free of charge.

An Evaluation of War Communism

Any evaluation of War Communism must emphasize a frequently neglected point: War Communism did enable the Bolsheviks to muster sufficient resources to win the civil war. In this sense, War Communism may be viewed as an important political and military success. It is easy to overlook this basic point and to concentrate

---

[7] Nove, *op. cit.*, p. 62. Estimates of the period suggest that in the large towns, only 31 percent of all food came through official channels (1919).

instead on its many weaknesses. We seek rather to evaluate War Communism in terms of the following question: Was War Communism a viable economic system for coping with the long-term problems of economic growth and development facing the Soviet regime during the 1920s?

As one might expect, War Communism's replacement of market exchange by administrative resource allocation created several serious problems. First, there was a sharp decline in both agricultural output and marketings to the state during the 1918 to 1921 period even after adjustment for war devastation. Peasants were holding back grain in storage, were planting less, and were selling to private traders. The area of Siberia sown in wheat was halved and in the Volga and Caucasus regions was reduced to as little as one-quarter of previous levels. Actual sowing concealed from authorities was reported as high as 20 percent of the sown area in some regions.[8] Since agricultural surpluses in excess of family subsistence were requisitioned, there was no incentive to produce a surplus. Instead, the peasant, if he could not conceal his surplus from the authorities, restricted output to the subsistence needs of his family. Thus, War Communism's agrarian policy estranged the Russian peasant from the Bolshevik regime and encouraged him to engage in dysfunctional behavior, such as restricting output and hoarding or concealing surpluses during a period of agricultural shortages.

Soviet industry was also faced with serious problems. Almost all enterprises with the exception of certain small-scale handicraft shops had been nationalized without first establishing a suitable administrative structure to coordinate their activities. The industrial census of 1920 showed over 5000 nationalized enterprises employing only one worker each.[9] The abolition of private trade, which was to be superceded by state rationing, however, removed the existing market link between consumer and producer. Producers, except those selling to the black market, therefore were no longer directed by the market in their production decisions.

Ostensibly, large-scale industry was to be coordinated by the Supreme Council of the National Economy (*Vesenkha*), which was broken up into subdepartments (*Glavki*), each of which was to di-

[8] Dobb, *op. cit.,* p. 117.
[9] Nove, *op. cit.,* p. 70.

rect a particular industry. In addition, the provincial economic councils (*Gubsovnarkhozy*) were the local organs of *Vesenkha*. This arrangement bordered on chaos. In 1920 there were over 37,000 nationalized enterprises. The *Glavki* possessed insufficient information about local enterprises to direct them effectively, to such a degree that an investigative committee of 1920 found that many *Glavki* not only "do not know what goods and in what amounts are kept in warehouses under their control, but are actually ignorant even of the numbers of such warehouses."[10] As a result, the directives that the *Glavki* issued to the local authorities rarely corresponded to local capacities and requirements, causing a prolonged struggle between central and local administrations. Often, local authorities merely gave formal compliance to directives from above and then countermanded them, knowing they could do so with impunity.

In sum, War Communism industry operated essentially without direction, either from the market or from planners. Bottlenecks were eliminated by employing "shock" methods, which meant that whenever congestion in a particular sector became alarming, it would receive top priority in the form of adequate supplies of fuels, materials, and rations. The "shock" system provided a means of establishing priorities and was beneficial in this sense. However, while the concentration of resources in the "shock" industries allowed them to surge ahead and overcome the original bottleneck, the "nonshock" industries had, in the process, fallen behind and had created new bottlenecks, which would then be attacked by additional "shock" methods. In this manner, some weak sense of general direction was supplied to the economy to replace total chaos. The "shock" system was somewhat effective as long as it remained undiluted, which meant the number of "shock" industries at one time must be limited. As time went by, the agitation for widening the "shock" categories became so intense that eventually even the manufacture of pens and pencils was included, thus destroying the whole purpose of the "shock" method—to set up a system of priorities.

Finally, the lack of an adequate system of incentive wages led to industrial labor supply problems. The government controlled the

[10] Dobb, *op. cit.*, p. 112.

legal distribution of consumer commodities among members of the industrial labor force, thereby controlling a significant portion of real industrial wages. The Bolshevik Party never officially subscribed to a utopian view of income distribution according to need; instead, it was realized that wage differentials were important in attracting labor into skilled and/or arduous jobs. For example, the Ninth Congress of the Communist Party in 1920 resolved that the food supply system should give preference to the industrious worker, and the Third Trade Union Conference of the same year proposed incentive premiums in kind to be paid to diligent workers.

The result, however, contradicted the intention, which led Trotsky to refer to War Communism wage policy as the measure of a "beseiged fortress." In fact, wages were rationed out to industrial workers on a fairly equal basis because first, shortages were so severe that local supply authorities were content to keep the working force at subsistence and, second, it proved too complex to devise a system of incentive wages to be paid in kind.

The result of this equalitarianism was an insufficient pool of qualified labor in industry. Instead of being drawn into factories, labor was flowing out of factories during War Communism. The number of townspeople declined from 2.6 million in 1917 to 1.2 million in 1920.[11] Morale was poor, worker sabotage was rampant, absenteeism was high, and the tenuous loyalty of specialists was slipping. These developments were especially ominous in view of the dearth of skilled laborers available in industry during this early period. Strikes became quite common during the latter part of 1920.

The Soviet regime had succeeded in solidifying its position by the end of 1920. A peace treaty had been signed with Poland, and the White Russian army had been driven out of the crucial industrial and agricultural regions that it had earlier occupied. The crisis under which War Communism had come into existence had been overcome, and the dangers of continuing that economic policy were growing more apparent. The still-powerful trade unions were revolting against the crippling centralization of industry and the conscription of labor. The alienated peasant population called for abolition of the state grain monopoly. Industrial workers were restive,

[11] Nove, *op. cit.,* pp. 66–67.

the military was in a rebellious mood, and the Soviet regime was in danger of falling victim to internal discontent. Factory output had fallen to less than 15 percent of its prewar level.[12] The final blow was the Kronstadt Uprising of March 1921, when the sailors of the Kronstadt naval base revolted in support of the Petrograd workers. The Soviet leadership moved quickly to dispel this discontent by replacing War Communism with the New Economic Policy in March of 1921.

THE NEW ECONOMIC POLICY (1921–1928)

Just as War Communism may have been thrust upon the Soviet regime by the civil war in 1918, the New Economic Policy (NEP) was forced upon the Soviet leadership by the excesses of War Communism. For whatever its reasons, the Soviet leadership at the time took pains to stress the temporary nature of both periods. Lenin declared that "War Communism was thrust upon us by war and ruin. It was not, nor could it be, a policy that corresponded to the economic tasks of the proletariat. It was a temporary measure."[13] In the same vein, Lenin described NEP as a temporary step backward (away from socialism) in order to later take two steps forward. From the viewpoint of the Bolshevik leadership, NEP was a transitional "step backward" because of the important roles that "antisocialist" institutions, such as private ownership, private initiative, and capitalist markets, were allowed to play during this period.

The most striking feature of NEP was its attempt to combine market and socialism: Agriculture remained in the hands of the peasant, the management of industry (with the exception of the

---

[12] *Ibid.*, p. 94.

[13] Quoted in Dobb, *op. cit.*, p. 130. According to Roberts, *op. cit.*, pp. 36–41, this quote is not reflective of Lenin's true position during War Communism. Instead, Lenin tended to view War Communism as a basically correct movement in the direction of revolutionary socialism, which he was forced to back away from by the strikes and civil unrest of 1920. Roberts points out the pains taken by Lenin during this period to justify the abandonment of War Communism on ideological grounds which would have been unnecessary if War Communism had simply been a temporary wartime measure.

"commanding heights" of industry) was decentralized. Market links between industry and agriculture and between industry and consumer replaced state control of production and distribution. On the other hand, most industrial enterprises were not nationalized. But many of the largest enterprises—the so-called commanding heights —remained nationalized and encompassed about three-quarters of industrial output. In this manner, it was thought that the state could provide general guidance by retaining direct control of the "commanding heights" of the economy—heavy industry, transportation, banking, and foreign trade, while allowing the remainder -of the economy to make its own decisions.

The political basis of NEP was the *Smychka,* or collaboration between the Soviet regime (representing the urban proletariat) and the peasant. An important political objective of NEP was to regain the political and economic support of the peasant. Thus the War Communism policy of requisitioning agricultural surpluses had to be abandoned, for the peasant would never ally himself with a regime that confiscated his surpluses. Market agriculture had to be reestablished in its place, freeing the peasant both to sell his surpluses freely and to buy industrial products freely.

The *Smychka* strategy represented a fairly significant concession from the Bolshevik leaders whose freedom of action was accordingly severely restricted because they were limited to policies that would not alienate the peasant. This at times placed them in the tenuous position of having to choose between the support of the peasantry and the attainment of basic party objectives. However, there was even a more fundamental contradiction. The reestablishment of market agriculture would serve to create a commercially minded peasantry and an environment that would reward success and penalize failure. The very success of NEP would require increasing economic differentiation among the agricultural population, and the emergence of a class of relatively prosperous peasants, who would produce the critical market surpluses. Marx had condemned the wealthy and middle peasant as adamant opponents of socialism, but NEP would serve to promote this class. Thus the ideological concession underlying NEP was apparently very great.[14]

[14] A quote from Stalin on this point (from the late 1920s after he had adopted his antipeasant stance): "What is meant by not hindering *kulak* farming? [The

NEP Policies

The cornerstone of NEP was the proportional agricultural tax introduced in March of 1921 to replace the War Communism system of requisitions. First paid in kind, and by 1924 in money, it was a single tax, based upon a *fixed proportion* of each peasant's *net produce* above his subsistence needs (subsistence being defined primarily according to the number of dependents). The state now took a fixed proportion of surplus production, and the peasant now had an incentive to aim for as a large a surplus as possible.

The agricultural tax was the first step in reestablishing a market economy that, in turn, necessitated further measures. Unless the peasant could dispose profitably of his after-tax surplus, he would have little incentive to produce above subsistence. Therefore the state granted the peasant commercial autonomy to sell his output to the buyer of his choice, be it to the state, a cooperative, or a private dealer. This measure required the legalization of private trade, which was again permitted to compete with state and cooperative trade organizations. Now the peasant could market his after-tax surplus at terms dictated by market forces, not by a state monosony. The resurgence of private trade provided a further incentive for the peasant to market his surplus, for he no longer faced a state supply monopoly, rationing out industrial products to him. Finally, peasants were allowed to lease land and to hire farm laborers, both of which had been forbidden under War Communism.

Within one year, private activity dominated Soviet retail trade and restored the market link beween consumer and producer. In 1922–1923, nine-tenths of all retail trading outlets were private, and they handled over three-quarters of the value of all retail trade turnover, with state and cooperative outlets handling the balance.[15] The private trader, or *Nepman* as he was called, was less strongly entrenched in wholesale trade, which remained dominated by state and cooperative organizations.

---

term *kulak* refers to the prosperous peasant.] It means setting the *kulak* free. And what is meant by setting the *kulak* free? It means giving him power." I. V. Stalin, *Sochinenia* [Collected works] (Moscow: 1946–1951), vol. XI, p. 275. Quoted in Alexander Erlich, *The Soviet Industrialization Debate, 1924–1928* (Cambridge, Mass.: Harvard University Press, 1960), pp. 172–173.

[15] Dobb, *op. cit.,* p. 143.

NEP also brought about significant changes in Soviet industry. The majority of industrial enterprises were permitted to make their own contracts for the purchase of raw materials and supplies and for the sale of their outputs; whereas during War Communism, the state had officially performed these functions. Small enterprises employing twenty persons or less were denationalized, and a small number of them were returned to their former owners. Others were leased to new entrepreneurs, thereby re-creating a class of small-scale capitalists. The Bolsheviks even granted a limited number of foreign concessions. Denationalization was limited to small-scale enterprises, and the overwhelming portion of industrial production during NEP was produced by nationalized enterprises. The industrial census of 1923 showed that private enterprises accounted for only 12.5 percent of total employment in "census" establishments.[16] In addition only 2 percent of the industrial output of large-scale industry was produced by the private sector in 1924–25.[17]

While much of large-scale industry remained nationalized, decision-making throughout industry was decentralized to a great extent. Nationalized enterprises were divided into two categories: the "commanding heights" of the economy—fuel, metallurgy, war industries, transportation, banking, and foreign trade—were not separated from the state budget and remained dependent upon centralized allocations of state supplies. The remaining nationalized enterprises were granted substantial financial and commercial autonomy from the state budget. The latter enterprises were instructed to operate commercially, that is, to maximize profits and to sell to the highest bidder, be it state or private trade. Most important, they were not obligated to deliver output according to production quotas to the state as under War Communism.

The nationalized enterprises of this second category were allowed to federate into trusts, which soon became the dominant form of industrial organization during NEP. By 1923, the 478 chartered trusts accounted for 75 percent of all workers employed in

---

[16] *Ibid.*, p. 142. Census establishments were those employing 16 or more persons along with mechanical power or 30 or more without it. G. W. Nutter, *The Growth of Industrial Production in the Soviet Union* (Princeton, N.J.: Princeton University Press, 1962), pp. 187–188.
[17] Nove, *op. cit.*, p. 104.

nationalized industry.[18] These trusts were given the legal authority to enter into independent contracts. They were to be supervised loosely either by *Vesenkha* (the Supreme Council of the National Economy) or by the *Gubsovnarkhozy* (the provincial economic councils) but their commercial independence was protected in that the state was not allowed to acquire the property or products of a trust except by contractual agreement. In light industry, the trusts were largely independent of state control other than the usual forms of fiscal and monetary intervention. In some key sectors of heavy industry, *Vesenkha* exercised much stricter controls over trusts in the form of specific production and delivery targets. The profits of trusts were subject to property and income taxation in the same manner as private enterprises. The monopoly State Bank controlled trust commercial credit. Although the "commanding heights" enterprises remained within the state budget, they were instructed to operate as profitably as possible to eliminate reliance on subsidies.

NEP was not a command economy. Planning authorities generally provided trusts with "control figures," which were to be used as forecasts and guides for investment decisions. Mandatory output plans were drawn up only in the case of a few key sectors in heavy industry. The limited physical planning and distribution was carried out through the Committee of State Orders (representing the commissariats), which placed orders through *Vesenkha* that, in turn, negotiated the order with the producer trusts. During the major part of NEP, the most important force of economic control and regulation was the Peoples Commissariat of Finance (*Narkomfin*), which exerted its influence through the budget and credit system (the so-called dictatorship of finance). Planning during the NEP period was carried out by a variety of organizations—*Vesenkha,* the State Planning Committee (*Gosplan,* established in 1921), the commissariats, and local authorities. Until the late 1920s, planners primarily limited themselves to forecasting trends as dictated by market conditions. Also there was a notable lack of coordination among the various planning agencies until *Gosplan* established itself as the dominant coordinating planning body after 1927.[19]

[18] Dobb, *op. cit.,* p. 135.
[19] Carr and Davies, *op. cit.,* pp. 787–836.

Use of money had been virtually eliminated during War Communism as a result of hyperinflation, and had been replaced by a system of barter and physical allocation. Such a system, however, would have been too clumsy for the new market system of NEP. To avoid this obstacle, the Soviets reintroduced the use of money with the reopening of the State Bank in 1921 for the expressed purpose of aiding the development of the economy. Both public and private enterprises were encouraged to deposit their savings in the State Bank: limitations on private bank deposits were removed and safeguards were established to protect such deposits from state confiscation. A new stabilized currency, the *chervonets,* was issued by the State Bank in 1921, a balanced budget was achieved in 1923–1924, a surplus in 1924–1925, and the old depreciated paper ruble was withdrawn from circulation in the currency reform of May 1924. Thereby a stable Soviet currency was created, which, for a time, was even quoted on international exchanges. Money transactions between state enterprises replaced earlier barter transactions.

The Economic Recovery of NEP

Just as War Communism provided the means for waging the civil war, NEP provided the means for recovery from the war, and in this sense, it was an important strategic success for the Soviet leadership. The economic recovery during NEP was impressive (Table 7).

In 1920, production statistics (Table 7) indicate the low level of economic activity that existed at the end of War Communism. Industrial production and transportation were both only one-fifth of the prewar level. The shortage of fuel threatened to paralyze in-

Table 7 **Production Indexes, USSR: 1913, 1920, 1928 (1913 = 100)**

	Industry	Agriculture	Transportation
1913a	100	100	100
1920	20	64	22
1928	102	118	106

a The 1913 figures refer to interwar territory of the USSR.

SOURCES: G. W. Nutter, "The Soviet Economy: Retrospect and Prospect," in David Abshire and Richard V. Allen, *National Security: Political, Military, and Economic Strategies in the Decade Ahead,* (New York: Praeger, 1963), p. 165.

dustry and transportation, and industry was living on dwindling reserves of pig-iron. The food shortage led to exhaustion and demoralization of the labor force. Agricultural production was 64 percent of the prewar level.

In 1928—at the eve of the First Five Year Plan and the end of NEP—the statistics provide a striking contrast: both industry and transportation had moderately surpassed their prewar levels, while agriculture was almost 20 percent above its prewar level. Although the NEP recovery was impressive, one should note that high rates of growth during recovery periods are to be expected once a suitable economic environment is established. The NEP policies provided this suitable framework for recovery.

The End of NEP

The high level of NEP is usually dated to 1926 when prewar production levels were generally surpassed, according to Soviet statistics.[20] The absolute growth of the nonagricultural private sector stopped in 1926.[21] At this time all seemed to be going well; yet two years later NEP was abandoned in favor of a radically different system of state central planning, collectivization of agriculture, and nationalization of industry and trade. This radical turn of events seems puzzling in view of the impressive NEP successes. Why was NEP abandoned? Several considerations stimulated the decision.

First, a large number of party members viewed NEP as a temporary and unwelcome compromise with class enemies. Now that the state was stronger, they argued, the offensive against class enemies could be resumed.[22] Second, the Soviet authorities feared that economic policy might become dominated by the growing numbers of prosperous peasants and Nepmen. Increasingly, policies were being dictated to suit the needs of the peasants, not the objectives of the state. A prime example of this was the "Scissors Crisis" of 1923, which forced the Soviet regime into the paradoxical

[20] Nove, *op. cit.*, p. 94. Recent recalculation of the Soviet figures for the 1913 to 1927–1928 period show that these official figures may overstate the speed of recovery during the NEP period. See on this M. E. Falkus, "Russia's National Income, 1913: A Revaluation," *Economica*, vol. 35, no. 137 (February 1968), 61.
[21] Nove, *op. cit.*, p. 137.
[22] *Ibid.*, p. 138.

stance of favoring private agriculture over socialist industry. The
Scissors Crisis merits a slight digression at this point.

According to Soviet figures, the total marketed surplus of agriculture in 1923 was 60 percent of the prewar level with grain marketings falling even below this figure. On the other hand, industrial
production was only 35 percent of the prewar level.[23] The more
rapid recovery of agriculture placed upward pressure on industrial
prices relative to agricultural prices. The different sectoral recovery
rates were not the sole determinants of relative price movements. A
portion of the already limited output of industry was being withheld
from the market by the industrial trusts, who were using their monopoly power to restrict trust sales to raise prices. The net result
was an even more rapid rise of industrial prices relative to agricultural prices. The relative price movements between early 1922 and
late 1923 (Figure 1) take on the shape of an open pair of scissors,
from whence came the term "Scissors Crisis."

The Soviet authorities viewed the opening price scissors with
alarm, for they expected the peasant to react by refusing to market
his surpluses as his terms of trade with the city fell. During the prewar period, the Russian peasant marketed (outside of the village)

Figure 1 **The Scissors Crisis**

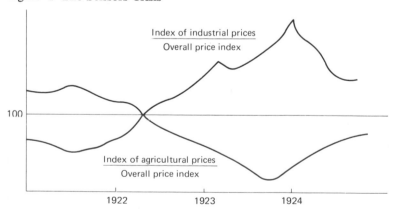

SOURCE: Maurice Dobb, *Soviet Economic Development Since 1917* (London:
Routledge & Kegan Paul, 1960), p. 164. Based on figures of S. Strumilin, in
Na khoziastvennom fronte [On the economic front].

[23] Cited in Dobb, *op. cit.*, pp. 161–162.

on the average 30 percent of his output. In early 1923 before the price scissors had opened sharply, he marketed about 25 percent, and Soviet authorities feared a further drop.[24] It is uncertain what did happen to peasant marketings as the scissors opened, since statistics for this early period are difficult to find. A student of the scissors crisis, James Millar, suggests that the Bolsheviks mistakenly *expected* peasant marketings to decline as agricultural prices fell in relative terms.[25] In fact, Millar argues, the Russian peasant had traditionally responded to a decline in the terms of trade with the city by selling more to the city in order to maintain his standard of living. Grain marketing statistics for the Ukraine do, however, suggest a reduction in peasant marketings between 1923 and 1925, but such evidence is quite fragmentary,[26] and it is difficult to determine whether Millar's or the Soviets' perception of peasant behavior is correct.

Rightly or wrongly, the Soviet government viewed this development as a threat to the NEP recovery, for the industrial worker had to be fed. The regime's reaction to a similar problem in 1918 had been to requisition agricultural surpluses, which resulted in a costly reduction of agricultural output; a return to requisitioning would jeopardize the progress made by NEP between 1920 and 1923. Further, the government feared (probably irrationally) an insufficient aggregate demand if the Scissors Crisis continued: if the peasant refused to market his output, peasant demand for industrial commodities would shrink, thereby causing an eventual glut of industrial commodities, which would also threaten the industrial recovery.

In essence, the Scissors Crisis forced the Soviet leadership to choose between two alternatives: to abandon NEP and return to requisitioning, or to retain NEP and to favor agriculture over industry to preserve the tenuous peace with the peasantry. More on this below.

A third source of dissatisfaction with NEP was the conviction

[24] *Ibid.*, p. 162.
[25] James R. Millar, "A Reformulation of A. V. Chayanov's Theory of Peasant Economy," *Economic Development and Cultural Change*, vol. 18, no. 2 (January 1970), 225–227.
[26] Jerzy Karcz, "Thoughts on the Grain Problem," *Soviet Studies*, vol. 18, no. 4 (April 1967), 407.

at that time that economic recovery had reached its limits, and that further advances could be achieved only by expanding the capacity of the economy, that is, by accumulating capital. NEP statistics revealed that much capacity had been lost as a result of World War I and the civil war: the capital stock of heavy industry as of 1924 was estimated to be 23 percent below its 1917 peak, and this capital equipment was, on the whole, old and outmoded. In 1924 the output of steel, a principal component of investment equipment, was 23 percent of 1913 output.[27] Thus industrial capacity had been lost between 1917 and 1924 and little had been done to replace it, although the building of socialism in the Soviet Union and expansion of military capacity were priority objectives of the Soviet state. After eight years of Soviet rule, investment and military commodities accounted for the same proportion of industrial output as they had prior to the revolution. For example, 28 percent of manufacturing net output was devoted to heavy industry in 1912, and this share had only risen to 29 percent by 1926.[28]

In spite of their dissatisfaction with the course of industrial development during the 1920s, the Soviet leadership viewed its hands as tied as long as NEP was retained. They feared that a drive to increase industrial capacity, that is, to increase the share of heavy industry, would reduce the availability of and consequently raise the prices of manufactured goods in the short run, and would further turn the terms of trade against agriculture, thus creating a further agricultural supply crisis that would impede industrialization.

Fourth, the NEP period demonstrated to the Soviet leadership its inability to make policy in a market environment. The handling of the Scissors Crisis described above is a classic case in point. Although the scissors probably would have closed by themselves when (and if) the peasant reduced his marketings, the Soviet government actively intervened directly to improve the peasant's terms of trade: first, maximum selling prices were set for industrial products and price cuts for selected products were ordered. Second, imports of cheaper industrial commodities were allowed to enter the country. Third, the State Bank restricted the credit of the industrial trusts to force them to unload excess stocks. The substan-

[27] Erlich, op. cit., pp. 105–106.
[28] Paul Gregory, Socialist and Nonsocialist Industrialization Patterns (New York: Praeger, 1970), p. 28.

tial closing of the scissors (Figure 1) by 1925 indicates the apparent success of these measures.

However, the setting of maximum industrial selling prices in a period of rising wage income had an important side effect: an excess demand for industrial products was soon created, which could not be eliminated through price increases as ceilings had been set. Despite this excess demand and its resulting shortages, no formal rationing system was in effect, which meant that lucrative profits could be made by the Nepmen by selling at prices in excess of ceiling prices. This general shortage of industrial commodities has been called the "goods famine," and the peasant—because of his isolation from the market—was hit especially hard.[29] Despite the efforts of the Peoples' Commissariat for Trade to sell in the village at the established ceiling prices, the peasant had to buy primarily from the Nepman, who sold at much higher prices. Thus the peasant, despite the nominal closing of the scissors, still lacked incentive to market his surplus. In fact, there is some evidence to suggest that grain marketings were falling as the scissors were closing.[30] The *net* marketings of grain in 1926-1927 were between 50 and 57 percent of prewar levels although grain output was close to the prewar level.[31]

The state's pricing policy had another serious side effect that eventually destroyed the market orientation of NEP. Initially two sets of industrial prices coexisted side by side: the higher prices of the Nepmen, who sold to a great extent in the villages, and the official state ceiling price. The Nepman soon came to be regarded as a black-marketeer and enemy of the state. Beginning in late 1923, policies were adopted to systematically drive out the Nepmen and widen the state's control over trade. This objective was pursued through the control of industrial raw materials and goods produced by state industry, surcharges on the rail transport of private goods, and taxes on profits of Nepmen. In 1926, it became a crime punishable by imprisonment and confiscation of property to make "evil-

---

[29] Karcz, *op. cit.*, 419.

[30] The marketed share of grain for the Ukraine between 1923–1924 and 1925–1926 was: 1923–1924 = 26%, 1924–1925 = 15%, 1925–1926 = 21%.

[31] R. W. Davies, "A Note on Grain Statistics," *Soviet Studies*, vol. 21, no. 3 (January 1970), 328. The controversy over grain marketings during the late 1920s will be discussed in Chapter Seven.

intentioned" increases in prices through speculation.[32] Finally in 1930, private trade was declared a crime of speculation. Similar phenomena can be noted in agriculture. After 1926–1927, the state lowered grain procurement prices (which eventually caused peasants to divert production to higher priced crops and livestock), and a gap between state procurement prices and private purchase prices developed. Again the private purchaser was systematically forced out of the agricultural market by the state. This trend culminated in 1929 when compulsory delivery quotas replaced the agricultural market system.

Such actions, however, effectively signaled the end of NEP, for the market upon which NEP primarily depended for direction was no longer functioning. Prices were set by the state and no longer reflected supply and demand. The economy was without direction, either from market or plan—a situation that was not to be tolerated long.

A final source of dissatisfaction with NEP relates to national security problems. The fear of imperialist conspiracies, England's breaking off of diplomatic relations in 1927, and concern over Japanese activities in the Far East prompted the Soviet leaders to realize that rapid industrialization would be required to meet the security needs of the Soviet Union and that NEP was not well suited to generate such rapid industrialization.[33]

THE PRECEDENTS
OF THE 1920s

During the 1920s, the economic problem of resource allocation was dealt with using two radically different economic systems. The first —War Communism—relied heavily upon command elements, whereas the second—NEP—attempted to combine market and command methods. The experiences of this early period tended to establish precedents that had a visible and lasting impact upon the eventual organizational structure of the Soviet planned economy. These precedents are introduced at this point as recurring themes throughout the ensuing chapters.

[32] Nove, *op. cit.,* pp. 137–138.
[33] *Ibid.,* pp. 121–122.

First, we emphasize the Soviet experiences with central planning during the 1920s. War Communism indicated that the market cannot be eliminated by fiat, for, unless an enforceable plan is introduced in its place, the economy will be without direction other than that provided by the "sleepless, leather-jacketed commissars working round the clock in vain effort to replace the market."[34] The "paper" planning of War Communism was shown to be virtually no plan at all, and unless planners have detailed and coordinated information from the enterprise level and up, and the political and economic muscle to ensure compliance, planning will be ineffective. A further precedent in the area of planning was the importance of "shock" tactics in a world of deficient information and imperfect control. Thus the concentration of resources on priority projects to eliminate bottlenecks was seen as a way to give guidance to the planned economy in accordance with politically determined priorities. It was also noted that the success of "shock" tactics depended upon their limited application. This precedent can be seen in the "storming" tactics and the practice of singling out a few key branches for preferential treatment that persist until today. The 1920s also introduced the issue of central versus regional direction, which was to become a recurring theme throughout later periods. The friction between central and regional planning authorities (the *Glavki* and the *Gubsovnarkhozy*) throughout the 1920s revealed an imperfect harmony of national and regional interests that persists to the present period. Thus the vacillation between ministerial and regional planning, a particularly important issue during the Khrushchev years, had its roots in the 1920s.

Second, the Soviet leadership's experiences with peasant agriculture during the 1920s also set important precedents. It was widely feared that peasant agriculture could be a thorn in the side of rapid industrialization, for the success of industrialization was seen as being dependent upon peasant marketings. It was thought that attempts on the part of the state to extract surpluses from the peasantry without offering economic incentives in return would be met by reductions in agricultural output and/or marketings. The Soviet leaders' apprehension was the impetus for the introduction of force into the countryside with the collectivization of agriculture

[34] *Ibid.*, p. 74.

in 1929 and provides an explanation for the continuing reluctance of the leadership to reinstate individual peasant farming (other than the small household plot) despite the often disappointing performance of collective agriculture.

A third important precedent of this early period was the development of an ingrained mistrust of the market that persists to the present. Most of the experiences with the market during the late NEP period were negative. The predominant trusts utilized their monopoly positions to restrict output and withhold stocks. The Nepmen sold at high market prices despite the efforts of state pricing authorities to set limits on industrial prices. The peasant withheld his output whenever he deemed market incentives insufficient. For these and other reasons, the market was virtually abolished after 1929 with only minor exceptions such as the collective farm market and, in part, the labor market. It is in this context that one can better understand the Soviet leadership's inbred opposition to fluctuating prices, output and input decisions based on profit maximization, and other market phenomena that persists to the present.

Viewing this antimarket bias in perspective, one could perhaps argue that it was irrational and stemmed from an insufficient understanding of the forces of supply and demand. On the other hand, the bias might be viewed as a rather keen perception of a development problem not always realized: Often during periods of rapid industrialization the interests of the state may conflict with the interests of individual consumers and producers—especially if the state lacks the means and expertise to manipulate the market; the individual wishes to consume, while the state wishes to save, for example. Could one not then argue that the most rational course of action is to eliminate, or at a minimum, substantially modify the market during early phases of development?

A fourth precedent, which can be related directly to the experiences of War Communism labor policies, was the evident necessity of freedom of choice of occupation. If the worker is to be productive, he must be allowed to choose his occupation on the basis of economic incentives. The militarization of labor that was attempted under War Communism proved to be an ineffective tool for allocating labor. Not only must wages be differentiated, but the resultant money income must have meaning in terms of real purchasing power; i.e., a consumer goods market must exist. The labor experiences of War Communism set an important precedent in favor of free occupational choice—a precedent followed in subsequent periods except when temporarily abandoned during the late 1930s and 1940s in response to the tremendous turnover of the inexperienced factory labor force and wartime emergency.

The year 1928 found the Soviet Union on the eve of the Five Year Plan period—about to embark on an ambitious program of forced industrialization. It was during this period that the Soviet command system evolved in large part to its present form. The period that we have just discussed—from the Revolution to the First Five Year Plan—is important because of its impact on this Soviet command system. One might in fact argue that War Communism and NEP represented a practical learning experience for the Soviet leadership. The next chapter describes another (more theoretical) learning experience that also had a significant impact on the evolution of the Soviet command system—the Soviet Industrialization Debate.

Selected Bibliography

E. H. Carr and R. W. Davies, *Foundations of a Planned Economy, 1926–1929,* vol. I, parts 1, 2 (London: Macmillan, 1969).

Maurice Dobb, *Soviet Economic Development Since 1917,* 5th ed. (London: Routledge & Kegan Paul, 1960), chaps. 4–7.

Alexander Erlich, *The Soviet Industrialization Debate, 1924–1928* (Cambridge, Mass.: Harvard University Press, 1960).

M. Lewin, *Russian Peasants and Soviet Power* (London: Allen & Unwin, 1968).

Alec Nove, *An Economic History of the USSR* (London: Penguin, 1969), chaps. 3–6.

Paul Craig Roberts, *Alienation and the Soviet Economy* (Albuquerque: University of New Mexico Press, 1971).

Eugene Zaleski, *Planning for Economic Growth in the Soviet Union* (Chapel Hill: University of North Carolina Press: 1971), chaps. 1 and 2.

CHAPTER THREE

The Soviet Industrialization Debate (1924-1928)[1]

An extraordinary debate on how to initiate economic development took place in the Soviet Union between 1924 and 1928 that antici-pated Western discussion on the same topic by some twenty-five years. Its participants ranged from leading party theoreticians to nonparty economists, and its audience included almost everyone of political and intellectual importance in the Soviet Union. The most remarkable feature of this debate was that it raised a multitude of questions concerning development strategy—issues of balanced growth versus unbalanced growth, agricultural savings, the proper scope of planning, taxation, and inflation to promote development —which are still widely debated among Western students of eco-nomic development.[2] The debate focused upon the alternative devel-opment strategies open to the Soviet economy in the late 1920s. An

---

[1] Our discussion of the Soviet Industrialization Debate is drawn primarily from the following sources: Alexander Erlich, *The Soviet Industrialization Debate, 1924–1928* (Cambridge, Mass.: Harvard University Press, 1960); Nicolas Spulber, *Soviet Strategy for Economic Growth* (Bloomington: In-diana University Press, 1964); Nicolas Spulber, ed., *Foundations of Soviet Strategy for Economic Growth* (Bloomington: Indiana University Press, 1964); Alexander Erlich, "Stalin's Views on Economic Development" in Ernest Simmons, ed., *Continuity and Change in Russian and Soviet Thought* (Cambridge, Mass.: Harvard University Press, 1955), pp. 81–99.
[2] Erlich, *Soviet Industrialization Debate, op. cit.,* p. xv.

important point to note is that Stalin, who actually made the eventual choices of central planning and collectivization in 1928 and 1929, respectively, was an observer of and participant in this debate.

In the present chapter, we consider the major issues of the Soviet Industrialization Debate, without undue emphasis on details and biographical information. The debate on the scope and objectives of planning will be considered in the next chapter. Here, we limit ourselves to the views of spokesmen for three important factions: Lev Shanin and N. I. Bukharin representing different views within the right wing of the Bolshevik party, and E. A. Preobrazhensky, the economic spokesman of the left wing of the party. We omit mention of significant contributors such as Bazarov, Rykov, Sokolnikov, and many others not because they are unimportant but because of space limitations and because the three views presented cover a broad spectrum of the debate subsuming many of the ideas of other participants. A mathematical appendix at the end of the chapter summarizes the three programs and supplements the textual exposition.

THE SETTING OF THE SOVIET INDUSTRIALIZATION DEBATE

The economic recovery of NEP reached its peak in 1926. The extensive loss of industrial capacity during World War I had not been recovered by the limited industrial investment during NEP. Therefore, industrial capacity during the late 1920s was probably below prewar levels. The economic instability of the 1920s—the "scissors crisis" and the "goods famine," the desire for rapid industrialization, and concern with defense all pointed to the need for massive capital accumulation in industry.[3] Yet could this capital accumula-

[3] The growth models developed during this period by V. A. Bazarov and V. G. Groman predicted a declining growth rate as the Soviet economy approached its prewar equilibrium. For a discussion of these models, see Leon Smolinski, "The Origins of Soviet Mathematical Economics," in Hans Raupach et al., eds., *Yearbook of East-European Economics,* Band 2 (Munich: Gunter Olzog Verlag, 1971) p. 144.

tion occur without ruinous inflation? This was the inflationary imbalance dilemma that initially sparked the Soviet Industrialization Debate.

The Soviet inflationary imbalance of the 1920s can be described in terms of some elementary macroeconomic concepts: the rapid NEP recovery had brought aggregate demand back close to the capacity limits of the economy. In fact, given the loss of industrial capital stock and the limited net investment of the 1920s, the fact that industrial output had regained prewar levels indicates that industrial capacity was probably already being overtaxed by the recovery of the mid-1920s. If, in this situation, considerable industrial investment was undertaken to raise industrial capacity, additional income would be created through the investment multiplier thereby generating severe inflationary pressures. This was the Soviet inflationary imbalance in a nutshell: industrial investment was required to raise industrial capacity; yet the capacity-creating effect of investment would be felt only after a period of time. The income-generating effect of investment, however, would be felt almost immediately, thus creating an inflationary problem.

If this inflation were to occur, the peasant would again be alienated by the increasing prices of manufactured goods, which would rise rapidly as capacity was diverted to producing investment goods. The terms of trade would again move against agriculture and another scissors crisis would ensue. The *smychka* basis of NEP would be jeopardized, and some alternative system would have to be substituted to feed the industrial workers.

A second alternative, a slow rate of capital accumulation, would avoid excessive inflation and preserve the alliance with the peasant. On the other hand, the basic problem—the low capacity of the economy—would not be met, thereby keeping the economy on the brink of inflation without achieving long-run objectives.

This inflationary-imbalance dilemma was the spark that ignited the Soviet Industrialization Debate in 1924. The scope of the debate then broadened to include far-reaching discussions of the long-run development alternatives available to a growing economy. The fact that the relevance of the issues raised by the Soviet Industrialization Debate is not limited to the Soviet Union of the 1920s strengthens our conviction that the problems facing developing economies are similar irrespective of the nature of the economic system utilized during the development process.

SECTOR PRIORITIES AND MARXIAN DYNAMICS

The participants in the Soviet Industrialization Debate addressed themselves to the proper way to industrialize the Soviet economy. The debate centered to a great extent on sectoral growth strategies, that is, on whether industry or agriculture should be favored or whether sectoral growth should be balanced. This same question has been widely discussed by Western economists in the postwar period and has been called the "balanced versus unbalanced growth controversy."[4]

In view of the pervasive ideological impact that Marxian economics had upon the Soviet Industrialization Debate—all figures involved were interested in "building socialism," all agreed that the state should own the means of production at least in industry, and all used a Marxist framework to support their programs—we begin our discussion of the Soviet debate by considering Marx's views on sectoral priorities. As it turns out, they are fairly general: If one subdivides the total economy into two broad sectors—the investment goods sector (which roughly corresponds to heavy industry) and the consumer goods sector (which roughly corresponds to agriculture and handicraft), Marx concludes that the economy will expand (grow) only if the output of investment goods exceeds the capital replacement needs of both sectors. According to Marx, this is the minimum condition that a growing economy must meet. Once it is met, growth can occur along a variety of sectoral expansion paths. However, net investment (upon which the economy depends for growth) would depend upon the capacity of the investment goods sector relative to the overall economy. Thus the higher the relative share of the investment goods sector in overall output, the higher the growth rate of the economy.[5]

---

[4] Benjamin Higgins, *Economic Development* (New York: Norton 1959), pp. 396–408.
[5] Erlich, *Soviet Industrialization Debate, op. cit.,* pp. 147–148.

PREOBRAZHENSKY—
UNBALANCED GROWTH
OF INDUSTRY

E. A. Preobrazhensky, the vocal spokesman of the left wing of the Bolshevik Party, took up where Marxian dynamics left off and argued that a discontinuous spurt in the output of investment goods was required in order to attain rapid industrialization.[6] Preobrazhensky envisioned two possible courses of action at the end of the 1920s: The Soviet economy could either continue to stagnate or even retrogress to lower levels of capacity, or a "big push" to expand capacity could be undertaken. In taking this latter step which he supported, halfway measures would not be advisable, for a spurt below the crucial minimum effort of investment would be self-defeating.

Preobrazhensky based this conclusion upon several factors. It was his opinion that the inflationary imbalance had two causes: the low capacity of the industrial sector, and a loss of saving ability—the latter being a consequence of institutional change in agriculture. Prior to the Revolution, the peasant had been forced to "save" in real terms a substantial portion of his output, which was delivered either to the state or to the landlord.[7] This saving limited his capacity to purchase industrial products. The Revolution, however, established him as a free proprietor. Rent payments were eliminated and agricultural taxes (in 1924–1925) were less than one-third of prewar obligations.[8] The peasant became accustomed to receiving industrial commodities in return for the sale of his agricultural surplus. This caused, according to Preobrazhensky, a "drastic disturbance of the equilibrium between the effective demand of the village and the marketable output of the town."[9] That is, the effective demand of the peasant had increased substantially

---

[6] Preobrazhensky's views are outlined in his famous work: *Novaia Ekonomika* [The new economics], which is available in English translation. See E. Preobrazhensky, *The New Economics*, Brian Pierce, trans. (Oxford: Oxford University Press, 1964).

[7] This view is supported by Gerschenkron's analysis of the objectives of the 1861 Emancipation Act (see Chapter 1).

[8] Erlich, *Soviet Industrialization Debate, op. cit.*, p. 35.

[9] *Ibid.*, p. 35.

without a substantial increase in industrial capacity—thus creating an inflationary gap.

Preobrazhensky suggested that net investment in industry must be raised significantly to close the gap between effective demand and capacity and that the inflationary effects of this action must be neutralized by altering the structure of demand significantly away from consumption and toward saving. Once the new industrial capacity had been created, private consumption could again be free to approach its previous position.

As far as the sectoral allocation of this net investment was concerned, Preobrazhensky argued for unbalanced growth to favor industry in general and heavy industry in particular on the grounds that the short-run benefits of investment in agriculture and light industry would be well outweighed by the long-run benefits of investment in capacity-expanding heavy industry. Thus he emphasized that investment-goods and consumer-goods industries must be arranged in "marching combat order" in keeping with the Marxian theory of economic dynamics.[10]

[10] This conclusion follows the Fel'dman growth model of 1928. Employing Marxian definitions and accepting Marx's division into an investment goods sector (Department A) and a consumption goods sector (Department B), G. A. Fel'dman developed a mathematical model for the USSR State Planning Commission that made a stronger case for unbalanced growth in favor of Department A than the original Marxian model of expanded reproduction outlined above. Fel'dman made several implicit and explicit assumptions in deriving his model: (1) that the state had the power to control the division of total investment between Department A and Department B; (2) that once investment had been made in one sector, this capital could not be shifted later for use in the other sector; (3) that the economy was closed to trade with the outside world; (4) (implicitly) that the state controlled aggregate consumption and savings rather than individuals (given a particular aggregate investment goal, the state could make saving equal that amount); and (5) that capital was the sole limiting factor of production, and that labor was overabundant.

Given these assumptions, Fel'dman concluded that the rate of growth of GNP in the long-run depends upon the proportion of output of the investment goods sector that is ploughed back into that sector. If a substantial portion of the Department A output goes into the consumer goods sector, then the rate of growth of total output will be small. The long-term rate of growth of consumption also depends upon reinvestment in the investment goods sector. A high reinvestment ratio will yield high rates of growth of consumption in the long-run; whereas a low reinvestment ratio will yield a relatively high short-term rate and a relatively low long-term rate of growth of consumption. That is, current consumption must be sacrificed in order to

In arguing in favor of a "big-push," Preobrazhensky stressed that moderate increases in the capacity of the capital goods sector would be self-defeating: the technological gap between the USSR and the advanced capitalist powers had become so wide that it was now impossible to adopt advanced technology gradually. Second, he echoed a view widely held at the time that the replacement arrears of the Soviet economy had become so immense that a significant increase in investment was required just to keep industrial capacity from falling.

Foreign trade, according to Preobrazhensky could, to some extent, act as a substitute for domestic capital production by importing foreign capital. However, the Soviets' capacity to import was limited by the lack of foreign credits (which would probably not be offered by the capitalist foes of the USSR) and by the small size of

---

obtain a maximum rate of growth of both output and consumption in the long-run. In sum, Fel'dman's model concludes that the bulk of investment must flow into the capital goods sector at the expense of consumer goods sectors if the growth rate of consumption and GNP is to be maximized in the long run. The partial derivation of the Fel'dman model is given below:

Symbols:

I:	total investment
I^1:	investment allocated to A
C:	total consumption
α:	portion of I allocated to A
V_1:	capital coefficient of A
V_2:	capital coefficient of B
t:	time subscript

Model:

$$I_t^1 = \alpha I_t \tag{1}$$

$$I_t - I_{t-1} = \frac{\alpha I_{t-1}}{V_1} \tag{2}$$

$$I_t = \left(1 + \frac{\alpha}{V_1}\right) I_{t-1} \tag{3}$$

$$= I_0 \left(1 + \frac{\alpha}{V_1}\right)^{t-1} \tag{4}$$

$$C_t - C_{t-1} = \frac{(1 - \alpha) I_{t-1}}{V_2} \tag{5}$$

$$C_t - C_{t-1} = \frac{I_0(1 - \alpha)\left(1 + \frac{\alpha}{V_1}\right)^{t-2}}{V_2} \tag{6}$$

See Evsey Domar, "A Soviet Model of Growth," in *Essays in the Theory of Economic Growth* (New York: Oxford University Press, 1957), pp. 223–261.

the exportable agricultural surplus. However feasible, he argued that a foreign trade monopoly would be essential to insure that machinery and not luxuries would be imported. In any case, considering the massive capital requirements of the Soviet economy in the 1920s, Preobrazhensky felt that the foreign sector could only play a limited role in the Soviet capacity build-up.

The long-run payoff of Preobrazhensky's policy of one-sided reinvestment in the capital-goods sector would be an enhanced capacity to produce manufactured consumer goods and industrial farm machinery. Yet he recognized that it would take years for this to happen:

> . . . a discontinuous reconstruction of fixed capital involves a shift of so much means of production towards the production of means of production, which will yield output only after a few years, that thereby the increase of the consumption funds of the society will be stopped.[11]

To dampen the interim inflationary pressures, Preobrazhensky proposed a system of "primitive socialist accumulation," which was to replace the market so as to force the economy to save more for capital investment than it would have had the market prevailed. Instead of the market, state trade monopolies would set prices. By purchasing at low delivery prices and then selling at higher retail prices, the state would be able to generate a form of profit or forced saving (affecting a downward shift in the consumpton function in real terms) that would reduce inflationary pressures. Preobrazhensky further suggested that during the period of primitive socialist accumulation, the main burden of industrialization should be placed on the peasantry in the form of low state purchase prices and high manufactured consumer goods prices, thereby extracting forced savings through a reduced peasant living standard.

In addition to his ideological preference for industry, Preobrazhensky chose to burden the peasants because of the high potential of their saving capacity as exhibited prior to the Revolution, and because of peasant agriculture's ability to be independent of industry. The overall purpose of primitive socialist accumulation was

[11] Quoted in Erlich, *Soviet Industrialization Debate, op. cit.,* pp. 56–57.

to let the state, not private individuals, decide how much would be saved. In doing so, the state would try to equate real savings (composed of both voluntary and involuntary savings) with the output of the capital goods sector (real investment).

Preobrazhensky clearly recognized the dangers inherent in primitive socialist accumulation. Given the large volume of savings that had to be extracted from agriculture, extremely low agricultural purchase prices would have to be set. The peasant would again be faced with deteriorating terms of trade and would withdraw from the market, alienated from the Soviet regime. This was the weakest point of his program and proved the focus for strong attacks by Preobrazhensky's opponents. How was the industrialization drive to be sustained if agricultural supplies were not available?[12]

SHANIN—UNBALANCED GROWTH OF AGRICULTURE

Lev Shanin, a representative of the extreme right wing of the Bolshevik Party, favored a program of unbalanced growth emphasizing agriculture within an essentially free market environment. The inflationary imbalance of the mid-1920s also provided the point of departure for Shanin. In view of this imbalance, Shanin thought that the Soviet economy should adopt a short-term horizon in planning policy. If massive investments were made in heavy industry with its long gestation periods, demand-creating income would be released without a parallel increase in capacity except in the long run, and by that time it would be too late. Thus, Shanin empha-

---

[12] Stalin's solution to this dilemma—collectivization of the peasantry, which eliminated the peasant's freedom to dispose of surpluses—did not occur to Preobrazhensky. Several years after the collectivization decision, Preobrazhensky declared in a speech: "Collectivization—this is the crux of the matter! Did I have this prognosis of the collectivization? I did not." Quoted in Erlich, *Soviet Industrialization Debate, op. cit.,* p. 177. Erlich adds to this: "He [Preobrazhensky] was careful not to add that neither did Stalin at the time when the industrialization debate was in full swing. And he was wise not to point out that the decision to collectivize hinged not on superior intellectual perspicacity but on the incomparably higher degree of resolve to crush the opponent. . . ."

sized the income-generating side of capital investment, whereas Preobrazhensky emphasized its capacity-creating aspect.

The difficult transition from NEP recovery to new construction of capacity could be smoothed, according to Shanin, by adopting an agriculture-first policy. There were several reasons for this conclusion.

First, Shanin argued that the short-term increment in real output to be derived from an additional ruble of investment (the marginal output-capital ratio) in agriculture far exceeded that of industry, especially in view of agriculture's surplus population and its low capital-intensity.[13]

Second, Shanin believed that there was a higher propensity to save in agriculture than in industry. According to this assumption, aggregate savings (a crucial factor in an inflation-prone economy) would be enhanced by a redistribution of money income in favor of agriculture.[14] Using these two assumptions, Shanin derived his agriculture-first policy.

Shanin presented his arguments by contrasting two alternative investment programs: one channeling investment into industry, the other channeling investment into agriculture. By investing a given amount in agriculture, a relatively large increase in capacity would be generated because of agriculture's low marginal capital-output ratio. In addition, the increased investment in agriculture would increase agricultural incomes, and because of the high marginal propensity to save in agriculture, this increase in income would create a relatively large amount of incremental saving and inflationary pressures would be reduced. On the other hand, an equivalent amount of investment in industry would not only generate a smaller increase in capacity but would also fail to create as large an increase in saving because of the high marginal propensity to consume of the industrial worker.[15]

---

[13] Lev Shanin, "Questions of the Economic Course," in Spulber, ed., *Foundations of Soviet Strategy, op. cit.,* p. 219.

[14] *Ibid.*

[15] The accompanying graphs illustrate Shanin's argument: Part A shows the consumption function of industrial workers (C_I) with a high marginal and average propensity to consume out of personal income. Industrial personal income in the mid-1920s is represented by IY^0, which yields a consumption level of IC^0 for industry. The consumption function of agriculture (C_A) in Part B is drawn to have a low marginal but high average propensity to con-

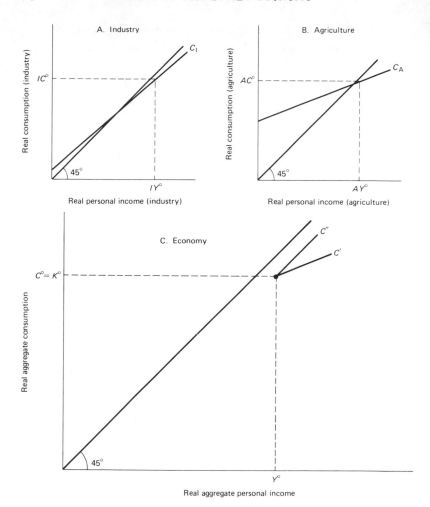

sume at the initial agricultural income level (AY^o) of the mid-1920s. The agricultural consumption level is AC^o.

The aggregate personal income of the economy in the mid-1920s is Y^o (in Part C), which is the sum of IY^o and AY^o (from Parts A and B). Aggregate consumption is C^o, which is the sum of IC^o and AC^o (from Parts A and B). This consumption level is assumed to equal the real output of consumer goods of the two sectors operating at full capacity, which is denoted by K^o.

The graphs can be used to support Shanin's invest-in-agriculture policy: Because of agriculture's smaller marginal capital-output ratio, agricultural investment would tend to raise capacity (K) more than would industrial investment. In this manner, inflationary pressures in the consumption goods sector would be eased, for the additional investment would raise personal income and consequently consumption—hence the necessity to raise capacity. Second, because of the lower marginal propensity to consume within the agricultural sec-

According to Shanin, two benefits would be derived from investment in agriculture. First, the capacity of the economy would be increased by a larger amount, in a shorter period of time, thereby ameliorating the short-term inflationary imbalance. Second, the creation of additional income in agriculture would generate a larger amount of incremental saving that could be used to finance additional investment without inflation.

Finally, Shanin emphasized the benefits to be gained from foreign trade. By trading according to its comparative advantage in agriculture, the Soviet Union could exchange agricultural products for industrial capital equipment thereby building up the capital stock of industry while at the same time avoiding the inflation that would have occurred had the investment initially been in industry.[16]

Shanin envisioned that his policies would have to be carried out within an essentially free market environment to insure the support of the peasantry and thereby the efficient utilization of investment in agriculture. He was sufficiently realistic to see that his proposals would have to be altered in the case of an imminent military threat, which would require the short-run enhancement of industrial capacity irrespective of the economic consequences. He also saw that certain industrial investments such as in transportation would be required in order to carry out his agricultural programs.[17] Therefore, industrial investment could not be neglected entirely. Another circumstance mitigating against the full-scale adoption of his agriculture-first program would be the exhaustion of foreign markets for Soviet agricultural products. Nevertheless, he minimized the importance of these exceptions, and did not allow them to materially alter his main conclusions.

In the long run, after the initial inflationary imbalance had been eliminated, Shanin proposed a shift in emphasis toward industry,

---

tor, more savings could be generated by investing in agriculture, thereby raising agricultural income. As agricultural income rises, the economy would expand along the C' consumption function (which tends towards the marginal propensity to consume of agriculture). If investment had been in industry, the economy would have expanded along C'', which tends toward the higher marginal propensity to consume of industry. In this manner, Shanin's invest-in-agriculture policies allow the economy to expand through additional investment without inflation.

[16] Erlich, *Soviet Industrialization Debate, op. cit.,* pp. 140–141.
[17] *Ibid.,* p. 132.

a shift toward reinvesting in capital goods that could be now accomplished free of inflationary pressures. At this time, the "building of socialism" could begin in earnest unhindered by short-term inflationary problems.

BUKHARIN—BALANCED GROWTH

According to N. I. Bukharin, the official spokesman of the right wing of the Bolshevik Party, any investment policy that one-sidedly favors agriculture over industry or vice versa, or one branch of industry over another, will fail because of the interdependence of economic sectors.[18] First, industry cannot function successfully without agricultural supplies: the productivity of the industrial worker depends upon the availability of marketed agricultural foodstuffs. Further, industrial capacity will be reduced greatly if agricultural raw materials are not available for sale. Industry requires sophisticated capital equipment, which it initially cannot produce domestically, and which cannot be purchased abroad if agricultural surpluses are not exported to finance such imports. Agricultural producers, on the other hand, depend upon industry for hand tools and agricultural machinery and manufactured consumer goods. If these goods are not forthcoming, the peasants will retaliate by not supplying agricultural products for industry.

Bukharin recognized the need for capital accumulation, but argued that it should be kept within manageable proportions. The overextension of one sector or subsector of the economy at the expense of other sectors would create critical bottlenecks—steel shortages, deficits of vital agricultural raw materials, insufficient foreign exchange earnings—that would inevitably retard overall economic development. According to Bukharin, any formula calling for maximum investment in heavy industry without a corresponding expansion of light industry would not only aggravate the "goods famine"—owing to the channeling of investment resources into time-consuming capital goods industries—but would also threaten to undermine the NEP recovery.

[18] *Ibid.,* pp. 82–83.

Because he emphasized economic interrelationships, Bukharin's economic program called for a gradual expansion of all sectors simultaneously. The critical link between agriculture and industry would be maintained by creating a favorable atmosphere for peasant agriculture. Instead of setting low agricultural delivery prices and high industrial prices, the state should do the opposite: first, to provide an incentive for the peasant to produce and market a larger output, and second, to pressure state enterprises to lower costs. It would not be necessary to force saving from agriculture as Preobrazhensky proposed; instead, only a stable economic environment free of the uncertainties of War Communism and NEP would be needed. In such a situation, the peasant would return to his traditional frugality, creating the savings to finance the further expansion of capacity.[19]

To resolve the incongruency between limited industrial capacity and his call for moderate capital investment spread fairly evenly among economic sectors, Bukharin proposed a series of measures to economize and utilize the available capital more fully. Small-scale manufacturing and handicraft were to undergo a technological "rationalization" and be transformed into supposedly more efficient producers' cooperatives. Large-scale investment projects were to be made more efficient by better planning and more efficient construction work. Maximum attention was to be accorded to the speedy completion of investment projects. The available capital equipment was to be used more exhaustively by employing multiple shifts. Attention was to be given to appropriate factor proportions, that is, capital was not to be invested in areas where labor could do the job as efficiently. The state pricing policy should stimulate cost economies and more efficient use of available resources by eliminating monopoly profits.[20]

In sum, Bukharin favored the balanced expansion of both industry and agriculture under a general policy of moderate capital accumulation financed by the voluntary savings of the peasantry. This balanced growth was to be fostered by an environment that would encourage the peasantry to produce and sell their surpluses to the city. State pricing policy would be used to gain the favor of the

[19] *Ibid.*, pp. 86–87.
[20] *Ibid.*, pp. 84–86.

peasants by setting low industrial and high agricultural prices. By fostering methods to increase the efficiency of capital utilization, a return to the "goods famine" of the 1920s could be avoided without resorting to the massive industrialization drive favored by the superindustrialists of the left wing. The foreign sector would play an important role in that it would provide the foreign machinery to sustain the growing capacity of industry.

THE OUTCOME OF THE SOVIET INDUSTRIALIZATION DEBATE

In a series of adroit political maneuvers, Stalin consolidated his power within a rather brief period of time after Lenin's death in 1924. First, he allied himself with the right wing of the party (Bukharin) to purge the leftist opposition led by Trotsky from positions of power—a phase completed in late 1927. Then Stalin turned his attention to the "right deviationist" Bukharinites, who were denounced by the Central Committee of the Communist Party in November of 1928. This occurred just one month after Stalin's adoption of the more ambitious alternative draft of the First Five Year Plan, which was supportive of the original left-wing industrialization program.[21]

The variant of the First Five Year Plan adopted in 1928 would have staggered the imagination of even the superindustrialists. The low capacity of the Soviet industrial sector was to be subjected to an all-out attack: the Soviet fixed capital stock was to double within five years to provide the industrial base for building socialism. The First Five Year Plan also called for a 70 percent expansion of light industry which was quite unrealistic in view of the limited industrial capacity in 1928.[22]

The First Five Year Plan was adopted in October of 1928 amidst a new grain collection crisis that was to have a crucial impact

---

[21] *Ibid.,* chap. 9. It was not until the Stalin purges in the late 1930s that this political process was complete. Preobrazhensky, Shanin, and Bukharin all lost their lives in the purges.

[22] *Ibid.,* p. 166.

upon subsequent events. According to Stalin, the very success of the industrialization program was clearly jeopardized, for it was dependent upon an increasing supply of food products and agricultural raw materials from the countryside. As long as the peasants refused to turn over such deliveries to the city, they held the power to halt the entire industrialization program.[23]

Stalin's answer to the crisis he perceived was to mount a counteroffensive designed to break once-and-for-all the peasants' hold over the pace of industrialization. In the autumn of 1929, he ordered the wholesale collectivization of agriculture. Peasant landholdings and livestock were forcibly amalgamated into collective farms, which were obligated to deliver to the state planned quotas of farm products at terms dictated by the state.

The ensuing turmoil was great not only in the countryside, which burst into open rebellion, but also in Soviet cities, which received a vast influx of workers from the countryside and saw a significant redistribution of labor among industrial branches as enterprises attempted to fulfill their taut production targets.

The actual Soviet industrialization pattern that emerged after 1928 (Panels A, B, and C, Table 8) bears a close resemblance to Preobrazhensky's industrialization program: Soviet economic growth between 1928 and 1940 was heavily biased in favor of industry in general and in favor of heavy industry in particular. Industrial production grew at an annual rate of 11 percent, whereas agricultural production grew at an annual rate of only 1 percent between 1928 and 1937 (Panels C–3, C–4). The negative rate of growth of livestock graphically indicates the impact of collectivization upon agricultural performance. The same trends are apparent

---

[23] According to Jerzy Karcz, there was no real agricultural crisis during this period. The grain collection "crisis" was precipitated by the lowering of state grain procurement prices in 1926–1927, while procurement prices for animal products were raised. Peasants shifted their attention to animal products, fed grain to livestock, and held grain in stock, waiting for grain prices to be increased. Total agricultural sales did not fall during this period. Thus the "crisis" was caused not by the weakness of peasant agriculture but by the ineptitude of state pricing policy. In addition, Karcz raises the question of deliberate falsification of grain statistics by Stalin to gain support for collectivization. Jerzy Karcz, "Thoughts on the Grain Problem," *Soviet Studies,* vol. 18, no. 4 (April 1967), 399–434. For a different view, see R. W. Davies, "A Note on Grain Statistics," *Soviet Studies,* vol. 21, no. 3 (January 1970), 314–329. This controversy will be discussed in detail in Chapter Four.

Table 8 **Outcome of the Soviet Industrialization Debate:
The Industrialization Drive of 1928–1940**

	1928	1933	1937	1940
A. Changes in manufacturing				
1. heavy manufacturing ÷ overall manufacturing				
a. net product share (1928 prices)	31	51	63	—
b. labor force share	28	43	—	—
2. light manufacturing ÷ overall manufacturing				
a. net product share (1928 prices)	68	47	36	—
b. labor force share	71	56	—	—
3. net product per worker in heavy ÷ net product per worker in light manufacturing (1928 prices)	.94	1.40	—	—
B. Changes in major economic sectors, structure of output				
1. share in net national product (1937 prices)				
agriculture	49	—	31	29
industry	28	—	45	45
services	23	—	24	26
2. share in labor force				
agriculture	71	—	—	51
industry	18	—	—	29
services	12	—	—	20
3. net product per worker in industry ÷ net product per worker in agriculture (1937 prices)	2.3	—	—	2.7
C. Rates of growth (1928–1937) and capital stock				
1. GNP (1937 prices)			4.8%	
2. labor force				
a. nonagricultural labor force			8.7%	
b. agricultural labor force			−2.5%	
3. industrial production (1937 prices)			11.3%	
4. agriculture production (1958 prices)			1.1%	
a. livestock			−1.2%	
5. gross industrial capital stock (1937 prices, billion rubles)	34.8	75.7	119	170

Table 8 (Continued)

	1928	1933	1937	1940
D. Changes in the structure of GNP by end use (1937 prices)				
1. household consumption ÷ GNP	80	—	53	49
annual growth rate (1928–1937)			.8%	
2. communal services ÷ GNP	5	—	11	10
annual growth rate (1928–1937)			15.7%	
3. government administration and defense ÷ GNP	3	—	11	21
annual growth rate (1928–1937)			15.6%	
4. gross capital investment ÷ GNP	13	—	26	19
annual growth rate (1928–1937)			14.4%	
E. Foreign trade proportions				
1. exports + imports ÷ GNP	6%[a]	4%	1%	—
F. Shares of the socialist sector in				
1. capital stock	65.7%	—	99.6%	—
2. gross production of industry	82.4%	—	99.8%	—
3. gross production of agriculture	3.3%	—	98.5%	—
4. value of trade turnover	76.4%	—	100.0%	—
G. Prices				
1. consumer goods prices (state and cooperative stores, 1928 = 100)	100	400	700	1000
2. average realized prices of farm products (1928 = 100)	100	—	539	—

[a] 1929.

SOURCES: Panel A.: Paul Gregory, *Socialist and Nonsocialist Industrialization Patterns* (New York: Praeger, 1970), pp. 28–29, 36. Heavy manufacturing is defined according to the International System of Industrial Classification as ISIC 30–38. Light manufacturing is defined as ISIC 20–29. Panel B: Simon Kuznets, "A Comparative Appraisal," in Abram Bergson and Simon Kuznets, eds., *Economic Trends in the Soviet Union* (Cambridge, Mass.: Harvard University Press, 1963), pp. 342–360. Panel C: Bergson and Kuznets, *op. cit.*, pp. 36, 77, 187, 190, 209. Panel D: Abram Bergson, *Real Soviet National Income and Product Since 1928* (Cambridge, Mass.: Harvard University Press, 1961), pp. 217, 237. Panel E: Bergson and Kuznets, *op. cit.*, pp. 288–290. Panel F: *Narodnoe khoziastvo SSSR v 1958 g.* [The national economy of the USSR in 1958], p. 57. Panel G: Franklyn Holzman, "Soviet Inflationary Pressures, 1928–57," *Quarterly Journal of Economics*, vol. 74, no. 2 (May 1960), 168–169.

in the differential rates of growth of the agricultural and nonagricultural labor forces between 1928 and 1937 (C–2): The former actually declined, while the latter expanded rapidly at an annual rate of almost 9 percent.

The structural transformations resulting from these differential sector growth rates are impressive (Panel B). Agriculture's shares of net national product and labor force declined from 49 percent and 71 percent, respectively, in 1928 to 29 percent and 51 percent, respectively, in 1940; whereas the increase in industry's product and labor force shares was from 28 percent and 18 percent, respectively, to 45 percent and 29 percent, respectively, during the same period.

The most remarkable feature of the 1930s was the extent to which the pro-heavy-industry bias asserted itself (as Preobrazhensky said it should). Between 1928 and 1937, heavy manufacturing's net product share of total manufacturing more than doubled from 31 percent to 63 percent; whereas light manufacturing's product share fell from 68 percent to 36 percent. The sharp increase in output per worker in heavy manufacturing relative to light manufacturing, from .94 to 1.40 between 1928 and 1933, indicates the pro-heavy-industry bias of investment allocation (Panel A).

The impact of this production program upon real consumption levels in the absence of significant foreign trade (the ratio of imports plus exports to GNP sank to one percent by 1937, Panel E) had already been foreseen by Preobrazhensky. Between 1928 and 1937 household consumption scarcely grew (at an annual rate of .8 percent), and the share of consumption in GNP (in 1937 prices) declined markedly from 80 percent to 53 percent. During the same period, gross capital investment grew at an annual rate of 14 percent and the ratio of gross investment to GNP doubled from 13 percent to 26 percent. If we define total consumption expenditures to include both private consumption and communal services, and nonconsumption expenditures to include investment, government administration, and defense, then total consumption fell between 1928 and 1937 from 85 percent of GNP to 64 percent of GNP (Panel D).

The changing institutional setting within which these transformations were occurring should also be noted (Panel F): between 1928 and 1937 the share of the socialist sector of total capital stock, industry, agriculture, and trade expanded sharply so that by 1937 the socialist sector totally dominated all economic activity.

Panel G has special relevance to the outcome of the industrialization debate. Consumer prices rose by 700 percent between 1928 and 1937 and probably would have risen even faster without the

Figure 2 **Correlation of State Wholesale Prices for Objects of Mass Consumption and Purchase Price of Wheat (USSR 1929 = 100)**

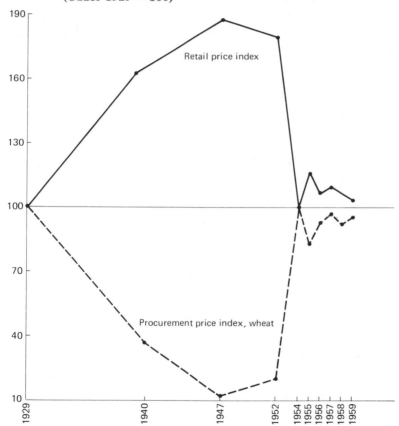

SOURCES: A. N. Malafeev, *Istoriia tsenoobrazovaniia v SSSR,* [The history of price formation in the USSR] (Moscow: 1964), p. 286. These figures are not directly comparable to those in Fig. 1, which relate an index of agricultural prices to an index of all prices, because of the vast change in agricultural prices after 1929 when procurement prices began to diverge significantly from the retail prices of agricultural commodities, and because Figure 2 refers only to wheat prices, not to a more general farm price index.

extensive formal and informal rationing of the period. Average realized prices of farm products, which are weighted averages of the extremely low state procurement prices, the above-quota state delivery prices, and collective farm market prices, on the other hand, rose by 539 percent, which indicates a reopening of the price scissors against agriculture between 1928 and 1937. An examination of some partial data (Figure 2) suggests that, in fact, the scissors did reopen and were not closed again until the mid-1950s, with a resultant squeeze upon the agricultural sector in terms of low procurement prices.

In sum, the left opposition program was apparently the model for the Soviet industrialization drive. The pro-industry and pro-heavy industry bias of the first two Five Year Plans is clearly shown in Table 8 and was implemented at the expense of the agricultural sector and the consumer. The expected deterioration in the agricultural terms of trade occurred, but did not halt the industrialization drive possibly owing to the forced collectivization of agriculture.

In retrospect, the Soviet industrialization drive must be seen as a remarkable and rapid shift of the Soviet economic structure. However, as we examine this process in greater detail, it will become even more apparent that the "Soviet development model," like any approach to economic development, is not without cost. Thus, the costs and benefits of alternative development models must always be carefully considered. We shall return to this issue in Chapter Twelve.

Appendix 3

Mathematical Models of the Soviet Industrialization Debate

Introduction. The models of Preobrazhensky, Shanin, and Bukharin, which have been described verbally in the text, can also be shown in terms of a fairly basic mathematical growth model. Such a model is developed in this appendix, which shows how, by varying the assumptions, the policy conclusions of all three were derived.

In keeping with the original debate, the model consists of two sectors—industry and agriculture—and allows for differences in sectoral capital-output ratios and savings functions. The allocation of investment between industry and agriculture is treated as the principal policy variable of the model. The initial assumptions are: (a) the economy is closed; (b) capital is the sole limiting factor of production in both sectors; and (c) all variables are in real terms. Other less crucial assumptions are: (d) the average and marginal capital-output ratios are equal; (e) the average and marginal propensities to save are equal; (f) the initial allocation of investment does not change over the planning period; and (g) the initial sector capital ratio is equal to the constant investment allocation factor.

List of Symbols:

m marginal capital-output ratio of agriculture (assumed equal to the average capital-output ratio), e.g., $m = dka/dYa = Ka/Ya$

bm marginal capital-output ratio of industry (assumed equal to the average capital-output ratio), e.g., $bm = dKi/dYi = Ki/Yi$

s marginal propensity to save of agriculture (assumed equal to the average propensity), e.g., $s = dSa/dYa = Sa/Ya$

$s-e$ marginal propensity to save of industry (assumed equal to the average propensity), e.g., $s - e = dSi/dYi = Si/Yi$

S savings (real)

I investment (real)

Y real income (output)

K capital stock (real)

g ratio of income allocated to industry

$1 - g$ ratio of income allocated to agriculture

a subscripts refer to agriculture
i subscripts refer to industry
f ratio of investment allocated to agriculture
$1-f$ ratio of investment allocated to industry
$DY = dY/dt$

Derivation of the Model. The derivation of the model begins with the allocation of investment between industry and agriculture, from which an investment equation is developed. The equilibrium condition requires equality of savings and investment. The savings equation is derived by starting with a particular allocation of income between industry and agriculture (how this allocation is determined will be considered later). In the familiar Harrod–Domar manner, the savings equation is set equal to the investment equation, and then solved for the growth rate of the economy. The steps are as follows.

Investment is allocated by the state between agriculture and industry:

1. $I_a = f \cdot I$
2. $I_i = (1 - f)I$

Investment sector

3. $DY = fI/m + (1 - f)\,I/bm$
4. $I = [bm/(bf - f + 1)]\,DY$

Savings sector

5. $Y_a = (1 - g)Y$
6. $Y_i = gY$
7. $S = s(1 - g)Y + (s - e)gY$
   $= (s - eg)Y$

Equilibrium of savings and investment

8. $S = I$
9. $bm/(bf - f + 1) = (s - eg)Y$
10. $DY/Y = (bf - f + 1)(s - eg)/bm$

It is now necessary to determine how the allocation of income between industry and agriculture (the factor g) relates to the allocation of investment between industry and agriculture (the factor f). Because capital is the sole scarce factor of production, one would expect intuitively that the allocation of investment between sectors will determine the allocation of income between sectors. By equating the income of each sector with the output of that sector (as determined by the sector capital stock and the average sector capital-output ratio), the model can be completed with the following steps:

Determination of g

11. $Y_a = (1 - g)Y$

12. $Y_a = K_a/m$
     $= fK/m$

13. $(1 - g)Y = fK/m$

14. $g = 1 - (f/m)(K/Y)$

15. $K/Y = m/f + bm/(1 - f)$

16. $g = -fb/(1 - f)$

This new expression of g (equation #16) is then substituted into the growth equation (#10):

17. $$DY/Y = (s/m)\left[\frac{f(b - 1) + 1}{b} + \frac{ef[fb(b - 1) + 1]}{(1 - f)}\right]$$

Thus the growth rate of the economy has been related to the structural parameters (s, b, m, e) which are taken as given, and to the policy variable f. As one might expect, the growth equation (#17) reduces to the familiar Harrod–Domar equation ($DY/Y = s/m$) if the sector capital-output ratios and savings propensities are equal ($b = 1, e = 0$).

Policy Implications. Shanin's policy conclusions can be derived easily from equation #17. His crucial assumptions were: (a) the industry capital-output ratio was larger than in agriculture ($b>1$), and (b) the marginal propensity to save in agriculture was greater than in industry ($e>0$). Differentiating the growth equation #17 with respect to the policy variable f, we get:

18. $$\frac{\partial (DY/Y)}{\partial f} = (s/m)(1 - 1/b)$$
     $$+ \frac{em[f(b - 1)(2 - f) + 1]}{(m - fm)^2}$$

Under Shanin's two assumptions, the expression (#18) is *positive,* and the higher the allocation of investment to agriculture, the higher the growth rate of the economy.

To derive Preobrazhensky's policy conclusions from the above model, we follow his assumptions that (a) the state can control the aggregate real saving rate by "primitive socialist accumulation" and that (b) the industry capital-output ratio (after a big push) is smaller than in agriculture ($b<1$). Thus a different savings equation must be substituted:

19. $S = wY$

for equations #5-#7, where *w is the state controlled saving rate*. The growth equation now becomes:

20. $DY/Y = (w/bm)(bf - f + 1)$

Taking the partial derivative of the growth rate with respect to f, one gets:

21. $\dfrac{\partial(DY/Y)}{\partial f} = w/m - w/bm$

which is *negative* under Preobrazhensky's assumptions, and the higher the allocation of investment to agriculture, the lower the growth rate of the economy. Thus Preobrazhensky's conclusions.

Bukharin's policy conclusions are even easier to derive from the model. If one accepts Bukharin's assumption that, owing to the rigid interrelationships between industry and agriculture, investment must be allocated between them in roughly fixed proportions, f is no longer a policy variable but is, instead, a constant determined by technology. The growth rate of the economy can now be raised either (a) by more efficient utilization of sector capital (reducing m) or (b) by raising the marginal propensity to save (raising s), which is exactly what Bukharin proposed: to create a stable environment in agriculture, to promote peasant saving, and to lower capital-output ratios in industry by amalgamation, multishift operations, and industrial price setting.

Further Evaluation of the Soviet Industrialization Debate.
To the extent that the models of Shanin, Preobrazhensky, and Bukharin are logically consistent yet arrive at different policy conclusions, we are led to examine the different assumptions upon which each model is based. The logical consistency of the three models has been demonstrated above; let us now turn to the assumptions of each to further evaluate the Soviet debate.

First, Preobrazhensky's model requires that the state, not individuals and enterprises, determine the portion of output saved. The substitution of the state's time preferences for those of individuals was, in fact, the objective of his system of primitive socialist accumulation. Preobrazhensky was thus able to assume away the savings constraint that played such an important role in Shanin's and Bukharin's models.

Preobrazhensky's plan to place the savings decision in the state's hands illustrates the dangers of ignoring omitted variables in the growth equation. For inherent in his scheme is the assumption that those variables will not be affected by manipulation of the savings rate—a rather tenuous assumption in view of the disincentive effects that would follow. Both Shanin and Bukharin paid more attention to secondary impacts upon incentives, especially in agriculture, which caused them to favor lower rates of capital accumulation within a market context.

Second, many of the differences between Shanin, Bukharin, and Preobrazhensky can be explained by variations in planning *time horizons*. The Fel'dman model (p. 71 above), which Preobrazhensky implicitly accepted by stressing the long gestation period of the capital goods sector, clearly indicates that if planners have a short planning horizon they should invest in light industry and agriculture. A long time horizon, however, would require them to invest in heavy industry.

Even Shanin's model might favor investment in industry if the time horizon were changed. If we define sector marginal capital-output ratios as the ratios of the *present discounted values* of the present and future increments in output attributable to current net investments, the sector marginal capital-output ratios would then depend on the social discount rate. A high rate (Shanin and Bukharin) would yield low marginal capital-output ratios in consumer goods sectors ($b > 1$, in the model) and a low discount rate (Preobrazhensky) would yield a low ratio in the industry sector ($b < 1$ in the model).

The general model outlined above assumes a closed economy. Once the economy is opened to the world market, the policy differences can be explained more fully. Thus a third major difference in assumptions concerned the exhaustibility of foreign demand. Preobrazhensky was skeptical about the Soviet Union's ability to transform indefinitely agricultural exports into machinery imports at fairly constant terms of trade. Not only was the USSR surrounded by belligerent capitalist countries in his view, but also the foreign demand for Soviet agriculture was in danger of imminent exhaustion (which did occur during the 1930s). Thus he proposed a rapid build-up of domestic heavy industry in spite of comparative advantage in agriculture. Shanin and Bukharin held more sanguine views of the world market, which seemed to them to offer almost unlimited expansion possibilities at constant terms of trade. They stressed the obvious point that the USSR could "have its cake" (build industrial capacity) and "eat it too" (produce consumer goods) by investing in agriculture and exporting its surplus for machinery.

A fourth difference concerned the question of shifting fixed capital between sectors. Preobrazhensky's model (in its strict form) requires that once capital is invested in one sector it cannot be shifted to another sector. If a factory is built to mill wheat, it cannot be used later to produce cement. If fixed capital could be shifted, however, then one might first invest in low marginal capital-output ratio consumer goods sectors for the short-run return and then shift this fixed capital to heavy industry for the long-run return. In this manner, the degree to which fixed capital is shiftable between various sectors has a profound impact upon proper investment allocation.

A fifth difference concerned sector interrelationships. Of the three participants, only Bukharin emphasized sectoral interdependence. By proposing the one-sided expansion of either agriculture or industry, Preobrazhensky and Shanin were assuming a decomposable economy, that is, an economy in which one sector can expand independently of others without negative effects. Of the two, Shanin better recognized that in certain obvious cases, such as transportation, the expansion of agriculture would be limited by the lack of investment in nonagricultural sectors. Shanin failed, however, to realize that such cases are not isolated and that many industrial products not obtainable through trade—electricity, gas and construction—are crucial to the long-run development of agriculture. Yet if one were to invest according to capital-output ratios, such products would not be developed. Preobrazhensky, on the other hand, thought that agriculture could subsist (as it did before the Revolution) independent of industry, but not vice versa. His program therefore called for investment in heavy industry without a simultaneous expansion of agriculture, extracting sufficient surpluses from the latter by administrative means (primitive socialist accumulation) to finance this investment.

Bukharin emphasized the interdependence of economic sectors and thus disavowed unbalanced growth. The weakness of Bukharin's model is the weakness of all balanced growth models: given the limited amount of resources that will be available, to spread it evenly among sectors means that it will be diluted and ineffective. While the concept of balanced growth is sound, it requires more resources than will be available. Instead Bukharin unrealistically called for spontaneous increases in the efficiency of factor utilization to surmount this problem.

Finally, all three assumed that the availability of labor was not an effective constraint on economic growth because of the surplus labor in Soviet agriculture. This assumption can be questioned on two counts. First, the overwhelming portion of the Russian rural population was illiterate during the 1920s. Thus the number of skilled industrial workers that could be drawn immediately from this vast reservoir of rural manpower was limited. Preobrazhensky's one-sided concern with the expansion of heavy industry via massive investment in that sector was perhaps misplaced and should possibly have been directed toward investment in human capital. The same conclusion holds for Shanin's model. Shanin assumed that the economy would encounter no structural difficulties in transforming savings into real investment either via domestic production or foreign trade. He therefore concluded that investment should be allocated to maximize voluntary savings. On the other hand, Western development economists[1] have concluded that a "skill constraint" limits the investment capacity of the economy even with an unlimited savings capacity or foreign aid. Thus the growth rate of skilled labor must also be included in the planning model.

[1] H. Chenery and A. Stroud, "Foreign Assistance and Economic Development," *American Economic Review,* vol. 56, no. 4 (September 1966), 679–733.

Selected Bibliography

Maurice Dobb, *Soviet Economic Development Since 1917,* 5th ed. (London: Routledge & Kegan Paul, 1960), chap. 8.

Evsey Domar, *Essays in the Theory of Economic Growth* (New York: Oxford University Press, 1957).

Alexander Erlich, *The Soviet Industrialization Debate, 1924–1928* (Cambridge, Mass.: Harvard University Press, 1960).

Alexander Erlich, "Stalin's Views on Soviet Economic Development," in Ernest Simmons, ed., *Continuity and Change in Russian and Soviet Thought* (Cambridge, Mass.: Harvard University Press, 1955), pp. 81–99.

Alec Nove, *An Economic History of the USSR* (London: Penguin, 1969), chap. 5.

Nicolas Spulber, ed., *Foundations of Soviet Strategy for Economic Growth* (Bloomington: Indiana University Press, 1964).

Nicolas Spulber, *Soviet Strategy for Economic Growth* (Bloomington: Indiana University Press, 1964), chaps. 1–4.

CHAPTER FOUR

The Foundation of the Soviet Planned Economy: Planning and Collectivization (1928-1940)

We have already described the precedents of the 1920s and the impact of the Soviet Industrialization Debate upon the course of Soviet industrialization during the 1930s. Our focus of attention now turns to the historical evolution of the Soviet command economic system during the early plan era, specifically to the development of a coordinated central planning apparatus and to the introduction of forced collectivization into the countryside. This brief chapter concludes our historical survey of the Soviet economy. Part Two will describe in detail how the Soviet command economic system allocates resources.

The 1920s witnessed two significant struggles over the nature of economic planning in the Soviet Union. The first was the debate over the theory of planning in a socialist economy—the debate between the so-called *genetic* and *teleological* schools of planning. The second was the struggle among the various planning bodies in existence during the 1920s for ascendancy in the planning hierarchy—a battle eventually won by *Gosplan* (the State Planning Committee). Let us first turn to the planning debate.

95

THE PLANNING DEBATE:
THE GENETICISTS
VERSUS THE
TELEOLOGISTS[1]

During NEP, an important controversy arose in the course of the industrialization debate concerning the proper role of economic planning in the Soviet Union. The debate centered largely around the issue of whether planning was to be directed (and limited) by market forces or molded by the will of planners, unconstrained by market forces and limited only by the physical constraints of the economy. The so-called *geneticists* advocated the first approach to planning, the most notable being N. D. Kondratiev (the prominent Russian authority on business cycles), V. A. Bazarov, and V. G. Groman, the lattter two being *Gosplan* economists. The geneticists basically argued that economic planning should be directed by consumer demand, which would dictate to planners the needed direction of change in the economy. Thus, the principal function of the planner would be to forecast and project market trends to aid central and local administrators in their decision-making; i.e., the geneticists envisioned a form of *indicative* planning, as it is called today. In drawing up such plans, authorities should always make sure of their internal consistency, for the geneticists viewed the economy as a vast complex of interrelated sectors (a general equilibrium system), the balance of which would be severely disturbed if planners neglected sectoral interrelationships. For example, to expand the heavy industry sector without concern for the resulting impact on the general equilibrium of other interrelated sectors would create serious disproportions that would impede overall development. Thus the geneticists advocated a form of planning that was largely consistent with the precepts of NEP in view of the dominant role that market forces would be allowed to play in the planning process.

[1] Our discussion of the planning debate of the 1920s is based on the following sources: E. H. Carr and R. W. Davies, *Foundations of a Planned Economy, 1926–1929*, vol. I, part 2 (London: Macmillan, 1969), pp. 787–801; Nicolas Spulber, *Soviet Strategy for Economic Growth* (Bloomington: Indiana University Press, 1964), pp. 101–111.

The *teleological* approach to planning, as advocated by S. Strumilin, G. L. Pyatakov, V. V. Kuibyshev, and P. A. Fel'dman, stated that the economic plan should be consciously formulated by social engineers and shaped by national goals established by the state. Such planning should seek to *overcome* market forces, rather than be directed by them as the geneticists argued. The market and finance, according to the teleologists, should *follow* the plan rather than dictate the plan. Planning should begin only after national economic goals have been set by the political authorities. Then the planners should form economic strategy, largely in terms of binding targets for basic industries, limited only by the availability of investment, and such investment should be allocated to meet the needs of industry independently of market forces.

In drawing up output and investment plans, the teleologists argued that planners need not be constrained by the need to preserve the general equilibrium of the economy, for to do so would be to subject the growth of the economy to the spontaneous forces of the market. Instead, the concept of equilibrium should be denounced as an unnecessarily severe constraint on the flexibility of planners. As stated by one teleologist, to accept the direction of the market meant acceptance of the "genetical inheritance" of 300 years of tsarism.[2]

According to the teleologists, the actual process of plan construction should proceed according to a system of "successive approximations," that is, first plans for the leading branches (namely, heavy industry) were to be drawn up; then the plans for other sectors (light industry, agriculture, trade, etc.) would have to be molded into the framework of the first set of plans. In this manner, the plans of lower priority sectors would be predetermined by the plan for heavy industry, not by the market.

The late 1920s witnessed the conclusive victory of the teleological viewpoint. As the NEP system was gradually abandoned, the advocates of the genetic approach, tied as it was to a market-directed system of planning, saw their support within the party deteriorate. From the summer of 1927, actual planning paid little attention to market equilibrium and financial stability as advocated

[2] Statement of P. Vaisburg in *Planovoe Khoziastvo* [The planned economy], no. 4 (1928), p. 167. Quoted in Carr and Davies, *op. cit.,* p. 793.

by the geneticists. Instead, attention turned to physical planning involving a "ferocious straining of effort," the outcome of which would be "decided by struggle."[3] Eventually, the geneticists came to be accused of counterrevolution and right-wing Menshevism. The advocates of the teleological approach, namely Strumilin and Krzhizhanovsky and others remained prominent in the *Gosplan* apparatus during the 1930s and played a guiding role in the planning for rapid industrialization.

THE EVOLUTION OF THE PLANNING STRUCTURE[4]

A variety of agencies dealt with planning problems throughout the 1920s—*Vesenkha* (the Supreme Council of the National Economy), the Peoples Commissariat of Finance, the Peoples Commissariat of Transportation, *Gosplan* USSR (State Planning Committee of the USSR), the regional *Gosplans,* local authorities, and many others. However, of these agencies only *Gosplan* was explicitly and exclusively concerned with economic planning. *Gosplan's* duties (according to a 1922 decree) were "the preparation not only of a long-range plan but also of an operational plan for the current year."[5]

From modest beginnings in February of 1921 (in 1925, *Gosplan* employed only around 50 economists and statisticians[6]), *Gosplan* gradually came to be accepted by the late 1920s as the planning agency in charge of coordinating economic planning for the entire economy. Much of this recognition emerged as a consequence of *Gosplan's* work on the annual *control figures* or tentative output targets for the various branches of the economy. The first control

---

[3] *Pravda,* September 14, 1927. Quoted in Carr and Davies, *op. cit.,* p. 818.
[4] Our discussion is based on the following sources: Carr and Davies, *op. cit.,* chaps. 33–35; Alec Nove, *An Economic History of the USSR* (London: Penguin, 1969), pp. 212–215, 263–267; Maurice Dobb, *Soviet Economic Development Since 1917,* 5th ed. (London: Routledge & Kegan Paul, 1960), chap. 13; Eugene Zaleski, *Planning for Economic Growth in the Soviet Union* (Chapel Hill: University of North Carolina Press, 1971), pp. 40–73.
[5] Zaleski, *op. cit.,* p. 41.
[6] Carr and Davies, *op. cit.,* p. 802.

figures were prepared covering the year 1925–1926, and while they did not initially prove important in directing economic activity, the 1925–1926 figures were used to establish the principle that economic policy should be guided on an annual basis by control figures prepared by *Gosplan*. In this manner, *Gosplan* came to play a supervisory role in the preparation of plans by other administrative bodies. The growing importance of *Gosplan's* control figures is clear: by 1926 the control figures were the first order of business of the Central Committee meeting of the party.

While *Gosplan's* role as the coordinator of all planning was developing, it had little to do with the actual operational planning of the economy, especially at the enterprise and trust level. Such work was primarily performed by the central planning staff of *Vesenkha* and by the *Glavki* planning offices of *Vesenkha*. In this manner, annual plans including production and financial targets, known as *promfinplans,* were drawn up. Gradually, the *promfinplans* drawn up by *Vesenkha* were merged into the control figures compiled by *Gosplan*. Beginning in 1925, *Vesenkha* was instructed to prepare its *promfinplans* on the basis of *Gosplan's* 1925–1926 control figures. By 1926–1927 *Vesenkha* was in the habit of compiling a comprehensive *promfinplan* for all industry, to be scrutinized by *Gosplan* and the Peoples Commissariat of Finance, and it was established that the *promfinplan* was clearly dependent upon the control figures.

During this period, the machinery for physical planning was also being developed—the system of *material balances.* As certain basic industrial commodities grew scarce as early as 1925 and the administrative allocation of commodities increased, planning bodies began compiling balances for critical industrial materials. In 1925, a balance for the production and uses of iron and steel was compiled, and in 1927 an energy balance of fuel and power consumption was drawn up. The balance system was extended to building materials in 1928.[7] In charge of coordinating these balances through the *promfinplan* and control figure system were *Vesenkha* and *Gosplan,* but initially this coordination proved too complex in the absence of detailed statistical information, and most of these early material balances were poorly prepared.

Thus the plan period began with the adoption of the First Five

[7] Carr and Davies, *op. cit.,* pp. 830–831.

Year Plan in 1928, with the following planning principles established: *Gosplan* was to be the central coordinating planning body to which all other planning bodies were to submit their proposals. Second, the annual control figures prepared by *Gosplan* were to provide the general direction for the economy on an annual basis. Third, the actual detailed operational plans for industries and for enterprises (the *promfinplans*) were to conform to the control figures prepared by *Gosplan*. Fourth, materials were to be allocated through a system of balances, compiled from the control figures and *promfinplans*, which would elaborate the supplies and uses of basic industrial materials.

Gosplan's elevation to full planning authority came in 1932 with the development of the ministerial system. Between 1928 and 1932, the functions of *Vesenkha* had grown increasingly complex and confused, and in 1932, *Vesenkha* was in effect dissolved as a central coordinating agency for industry. Its chief departments, the *glavki,* which later became ministries, were allowed to take direct power over planning and administering their enterprises. Earlier, *Vesenkha* had served to coordinate the activities of the industrial departments—a role that *Gosplan* now inherited.

This period also witnessed the evolution of a centralized administration for the setting of prices. Extensive centralized price setting and regulation, introduced during the early plan era, proved to be a complex task involving issues well beyond the setting of prices per se and requiring the expansion of administrative arrangements.[8] Although the setting of prices was largely decentralized during the NEP period (typically reflecting cost-price relationships of the pre-Soviet period), the Commission for Internal Trade and *Vesenkha* gained increasing authority toward the end of NEP. This tendency towards the centralization of price formation and related functions was greatly enhanced after the introduction of comprehensive central planning in 1928. Not only were internal prices subsequently shielded from world prices through the creation of a state monopoly in foreign trade, but also, a series of decrees in the late 1920s and early 1930s harnessed the price system toward the achievement of state goals; price dis-

[8] The discussion here is based upon Raymond Hutchings, "The Origin of the Soviet Industrial Price System," *Soviet Studies,* vol. 13, no. 1 (July 1961), 1–22.

crimination in state purchases (buying the same product at different prices determined by factory costs of production and then selling at one set price) was introduced, as was the system of multiple pricing (charging different retail prices for the same product), profit margin controls, and differentiated sales taxes (the so-called turnover tax), the latter serving as a primary mechanism for generating state revenues.

As might be expected, the early 1930s witnessed a significant expansion of the number of administrative organs concerned directly or indirectly with price formation, although during the 1930s there was a measure of consolidation with *Vesenkha* and later the ministries becoming the main price setting bodies.[9]

Our foregoing discussion of the evolution of the Soviet planning structure stressed the growing role of *Gosplan* and its emergence from the confusing maze of local, regional, and national agencies engaging in planning and economic coordination during the late 1920s and early 1930s to become the dominant figure in Soviet economic planning.

THE DECISION TO COLLECTIVIZE

Developments in agricultural sector during the late 1920s were as significant in the evolution of the Soviet planned economy as the formation of the centralized planning structure. Our examination of War Communism and NEP pointed, above all, to the crucial nature of the relationship between the peasant and the state. This relationship, the subject of continuing discussion in the 1920s, was abruptly formalized by the Communist Party under Stalin's leadership when the historic collectivization movement (the introduction of the collective farm, the *kolkhoz,* into the countryside) was begun in 1929.

Our purpose here is to examine the decision to collectivize (i.e., the decision to introduce a significant command element into the Soviet countryside) and in particular to understand the reasons for collectivization as perceived by the Soviet leadership at that time.

[9] For details of the organizational arrangements, see *ibid.,* 13–14.

In addition, it is important that we examine the process of collectivization as it was in fact carried out, and finally, the impact of this process upon immediate postcollectivization agricultural performance. With this background, we will be in a position to consider long-run agricultural organization and the nature of the *kolkhoz* and its performance in Chapter Seven and finally, in Chapter Twelve, the role of agriculture in the Soviet development model.

The reader should be aware that the collectivization decision and the forces underlying that decision have only recently been the subject of in-depth research. A full understanding, therefore, must await further investigation when, hopefully, our presently limited picture can be significantly expanded.[10]

UNDERPINNINGS OF THE COLLECTIVIZATION DECISION

It will be recalled that the focus of the Soviet Industrialization Debate of the 1920s was the strategy of industrialization; the desire to industrialize not being a matter of contention among the participants. From this discussion and the fact that the Soviet Union was in the 1920s primarily an agricultural economy, it is not surprising that alternative roles for the agricultural sector in the development process would be a point of focus for the participants.

Recall that Preobrazhensky had argued that the rate of saving

[10] In the present section, we rely heavily upon the following sources: Jerzy F. Karcz, "From Stalin to Brezhnev: Soviet Agricultural Policy in Historical Perspective," in James R. Millar, ed., *The Soviet Rural Community* (Urbana: University of Illinois Press, 1971), pp. 36–70; Jerzy F. Karcz, "Thoughts on the Grain Problem," *Soviet Studies,* vol. 18, no. 4 (April 1967), 399–434; M. Lewin, *Russian Peasants and Soviet Power* (London: Allen & Unwin, 1968); James R. Millar and Corinne A. Guntzel, "The Economics and Politics of Mass Collectivization Reconsidered: A Review Article," *Explorations in Economic History,* vol. 8, no. 1 (Fall 1970), 103–116; Alec Nove, "The Decision to Collectivize," in W. A. Douglas Jackson, ed., *Agrarian Policies and Problems in Communist and Non-Communist Countries* (Seattle: University of Washington Press, 1971), pp. 69–97; Erich Strauss, *Soviet Agriculture in Perspective* (London: Allen & Unwin, 1969), chaps. 5–6; Lazar Volin, *A Century of Russian Agriculture* (Cambridge, Mass.: Harvard University Press, 1970), chaps. 10–11; R. W. Davies, "A Note on Grain Statistics," *Soviet Studies,* vol. 21, no. 3 (January 1970), 314–329.

had to be increased as industrial investment rose. The peasant, according to Preobrazhensky, should bear the burden of this increase in the savings rate through the system of primitive socialist accumulation, whereby savings would be extracted from the countryside by setting low agricultural prices. How to insure the critically needed peasant marketings under such a system was a question that Preobrazhensky was unable to answer. Bukharin, on the other hand, argued that any system designed to extract involuntary savings from the peasants would destroy any positive relationship between peasant and state and lead to active peasant resistance in the form of reduced peasant marketings. Instead, Bukharin argued, it would be better to adopt a slower rate of economic growth and set prices to favor the peasant. The perceived behavior of the peasants during the Scissors Crisis was thought to underscore this view—that is, the falling trend in peasant marketings as relative agricultural prices dropped.[11]

Against this background, it should be pointed out that Lenin had long stressed the need to take advantage of economies of scale in agricultural production. Although there was some experimentation with various forms of agricultural collectives in the pre-plan era, these were largely unsuccessful.[12] At the same time, and under the prevailing institutional arrangements, improvements in the performance of NEP peasant agriculture must have appeared ideologically unpalatable to the regime insofar as the NEP arrangements would imply the use of market forces and the enrichment of certain segments of the peasant population.[13]

Collectivization of agriculture, therefore, to the extent that it

[11] As was pointed out above (footnote 25, Chapter Two), there is some controversy surrounding the Scissors Crisis and the traditional interpretation of the Russian peasant's response to falling agricultural prices.

[12] The reader interested in the agricultural collectives of the 1920s should consult D. J. Male, *Russian Peasant Organization Before Collectivization* (Cambridge: Cambridge University Press, 1971); and Robert G. Wesson, *Soviet Communes* (New Brunswick, N.J.: Rutgers University Press, 1963).

[13] Class stratification played an important role in the thinking about collectivization and its actual implementation. Although census data from the 1920s suggests that the wealthy peasants (*kulaks*) were a very small proportion of the total peasant population, they were nevertheless seen as politically unreliable at best and enemies of the Soviet industrialization program at worst. For a detailed discussion of the problems of class stratification in this case, see Lewin, *op. cit.*, chaps. 2 and 3.

might provide a mechanism for effective control of the country-side, might have appeared both ideologically and practically a rather ingenious solution to the complex problem of Soviet agriculture, yet more difficulties were to arise.

To what extent Stalin was personally responsible for the collectivization decision and all its ramifications is unclear and to some extent uninteresting.[14] He did, however, use as a major justification for instigating collectivization the *grain procurement crisis* of 1928, a matter that merits further attention.

Although the output of the Soviet agricultural sector had declined sharply during the Revolution and World War I, prerevolutionary output levels were generally met or exceeded by 1928, although yields remained poor and fluctuations from year to year in major crops made agricultural performance uncertain (see Table 9). Indeed by 1928, gross agricultural production had reached 124

Table 9 **Gross Production of Major Agricultural Products, 1913–1929 (millions of metric tons)**

Year	Grain	Raw Cotton	Sugar Beets	Sunflower Seeds	Flax	Potatoes	Meat[b]	Milk	Eggs[c]
1913[a]	76.5	0.74	10.9	0.74	0.33	23.3	4.1	24.8	10.2
1923	56.9	0.14	2.6	—	0.22	—	—	—	—
1924	51.8	0.36	3.4	—	0.30	—	—	—	—
1925	72.5	0.54	9.1	2.22	0.30	38.6	—	—	—
1926	76.8	0.54	6.4	1.54	0.27	43.0	—	—	—
1927	72.3	0.72	10.4	2.13	0.24	41.2	—	—	—
1928	73.3	0.82	10.1	2.13	0.32	46.4	4.9	31.0	10.8
1929	71.7	0.86	6.3	1.76	0.36	45.6	5.8	29.8	10.1
1930	83.5	1.11	14.0	1.63	0.44	49.4	4.3	27.0	8.0
1931	69.5	1.29	12.0	2.51	0.55	44.8	3.9	23.4	6.7
1932	69.9	1.27	6,6	2.27	0.50	43.1	2.8	20.6	4.4
1933	89.8	1.32	9.0	—	0.56	—	2.3	19.2	3.5

[a] All data apply to pre-1939 boundaries.
[b] Meat and milk production in millions of tons.
[c] Eggs in billion units.

SOURCE: Erich Strauss, *Soviet Agriculture in Perspective* (London: Allen & Unwin, 1969), pp. 304–305.

[14] Millar and Guntzel, *op. cit.,* 112.

(1913 = 100) while crop production had reached 117 and live-stock products 137.[15]

Stalin, however, in a now-famous presentation made in May 1928 put forward data to suggest that *grain* output (considered a critical indicator by the Soviet leadership) had declined between 1913 and 1926-1927, but most important, that the *marketed share* of grain had declined much more rapidly.[16] According to the data presented by Stalin, between 1913 and 1926–1927 gross output of grain declined slightly but the marketed share declined by roughly 50 percent. In addition, while grain production and marketings by the *kulaks* fell back sharply (both had declined to less than one-third of prewar levels), output and marketings of the middle and poor peasants had both expanded. For Stalin, this was evidence of the need for a move against the *kulaks*.

There are, however, two important considerations. First, as Jerzy Karcz has pointed out, Stalin's grain data was ". . . completely misleading and presents an exceedingly distorted picture of the relation between 1913 and 1926–1927 grain marketings."[17] According to Karcz, these data, when appropriately reconstructed as grain balances for these years, suggest that in fact gross grain output had, by 1928, all but recovered prewar levels and that the problem was the definition of marketings. Thus in the data brought forth by Stalin, *gross marketings* were presented for 1913 while *net marketings* were given for 1926–1927.[18] With two sets of data, quite incomparable, Stalin's case for collectivization as the answer to the marketing problem appeared to be strong.

A second and related factor, according to Karcz, was the role of government policy in bringing about the grain procurement "crisis." In the few years immediately preceding collectivization, net grain marketings did decline precisely because the state lowered grain procurement prices in 1926–1927, naturally encouraging peasants to market their grain through other than state channels where prices were relatively more attractive. At the same time, peasant taxes

---

[15] Strauss, *op. cit.,* p. 303.
[16] For details of Stalin's argument and related data, see Karcz, "Thoughts on the Grain Problem," *op. cit.,* 399–402.
[17] *Ibid.,* 403.
[18] *Ibid.,* 403–409.

were lowered as were the prices of manufactured goods, thus stimulating peasant demand. Also, in the face of lower state grain procurement prices, peasants were encouraged to shift into the production of meat and related products, the prices of which were generally rising. Thus, although peasant marketings of grain were falling, output and marketings of *other* farm products were rising in response to the more favorable prices and offsetting the declining grain marketings.

The immediate justification for collectivization may, therefore, have been based upon inadequate statistical information and adverse state policy against the peasants, in addition to ideological underpinnings and the drive for large-scale production units.[19]

THE COLLECTIVIZATION PROCESS

While the discussion of collectivization and Stalin's arguments on its behalf were well underway in 1928, it was not until mid-1929 that central control over existing cooperatives was substantially strengthened, and the system of grain procurements changed—in short, the beginning of the process of mass collectivization.[20] By the latter part of 1929 an all-out drive for collectivization had been initiated by the Communist Party, becoming in large measure an organized movement against the *kulaks*.

There were, of course, significant regional differences in the speed of collectivization and also a continuing debate over the precise organizational form to be utilized. The data in Table 10 suggest, however, that the overall speed of collectivization was rapid. Between July 1, 1929, and March 1, 1930, for example, the number of peasant households in collective farms increased from 4 to 56 percent.[21]

[19] Karcz's analysis of grain marketings and agricultural performance during the late 1920s has been disputed by R. W. Davies. Thus we cannot know for sure whether Stalin's analysis of the agricultural "crisis" was erroneous. For example, Davies estimates that the 1926–1927 net grain marketings were slightly more than one half of prewar marketings—a figure close to the Stalin figure. See Davies, *op. cit.,* 328.

[20] Lewin, *op. cit.,* p. 409.

[21] Volin, *op. cit.,* p. 222.

Although Stalin, in a famous speech in March 1930, warned against proceeding too rapidly and blamed local party leaders for the excesses that had occurred—in fact the pace of collectivization remained rapid and by the mid-1930s the collectivization process was basically completed.[22] The role of the Communist Party in the countryside was formally strengthened when in 1933 political departments (*Politotdely*) were established in the machine tractor stations. The machine tractor stations (MTS) had themselves been established earlier, and in addition to serving as a mechanism for supplying machinery and equipment to the collective farms (for which payment in kind would be made to the state), they were to play a significant role in the management of collective farms.[23] Informal party control in the countryside had also been strengthened considerably by collectivization through the party's placing of "reliable" men in the posts of collective farm chairman.

Table 10 **Expansion of the Collective Farm Sector, 1918–1938 (selected years)**

Year	Collective Farms (in thousands)	Households in Collectives (in thousands)	Peasant Households Collectivized (percentage)
1918	1.6	16.4	0.1
1928	33.3	416.7	1.7
1929	57.0	1,007.7	3.9
1930	85.9	5,998.1	23.6
1931	211.1	13,033.2	52.7
1932	211.1	14,918.7	61.5
1935	245.4	17,334.9	83.2
1938	242.4	18,847.6	93.5

SOURCE: Lazar Volin, *A Century of Russian Agriculture* (Cambridge, Mass.: Harvard University Press, 1970), p. 211.

[22] *Ibid.*, pp. 228–229.
[23] For a detailed account of the history and functions of the MTS, see Robert F. Miller, *One Hundred Thousand Tractors* (Cambridge, Mass.: Harvard University Press, 1970), especially chap. 2.

THE IMMEDIATE IMPACT
OF COLLECTIVIZATION

In Chapter Twelve we will examine the role of collectivization and the collective farm system in the Soviet development model. At this juncture, our interest is in the immediate impact of the collectivization process upon agricultural output, human lives in the rural sector, and the agricultural capital stock.

The most immediate result of collectivization was a decline in agricultural output. Although there were year to year fluctuations, the general decline is unmistakable (see Table 9). The index of gross agricultural production (1913 = 100) declined from a precollectivization high of 124 in 1928 to an immediate postcollectivization low of 101 in 1933.[24] In large part this can be accounted for by a sharp decline in gross production of livestock products from 137 in 1928 (1913 = 100) to 65 in 1933.[25] Although grain output declined in the initial years of collectivization (1928 through 1932, with the exception of 1930), both gross and net marketings of grain increased between 1928–1929 and 1931–1932, to some extent due to a sharp decline in the number of cattle for which grains would now not be necessary as fodder.[26] The worsening of agricultural performance during the First Five Year Plan (1928–1932) plus the losses from state reserves were major factors contributing to the famine that reached a peak in 1932–1933.

The loss of lives (especially severe in grain-producing regions) from both the collectivization process *per se* and the famine thereafter (the famine being the major factor) has been the subject of considerable discussion, but very little hard data is available by which to assess its severity. The most frequently quoted estimate of lives lost is 5 million, although the reader should be cautioned that other estimates vary from 1 to 10 million.[27]

In addition to the loss of life and the decline in agricultural pro-

---

[24] Strauss, *op. cit.,* p. 303.
[25] *Ibid.*
[26] Jerzy F. Karcz, "From Stalin to Brezhnev: Soviet Agricultural Policy in Historical Perspective," *op. cit.,* p. 42.
[27] For detailed discussion of various estimates, see Dana G. Dalrymple, "The Soviet Famine of 1932–1934," *Soviet Studies,* vol. 15, no. 3 (January 1964), 250–284.

duction, there was a sharp decline in agricultural capital stock, most notably caused by the mass destruction of animal herds as the peasants vented their hostility toward the colectivization process by slaughtering their livestock rather than bringing them into the collective farms. The impact of this development can be observed in Table 11. In addition, Naum Jasny, one of the research pioneers in this area, has indicated that other forms of capital stock—notably buildings and machinery, simply disappeared during the turmoil of collectivization.[28] The impact of collectivization upon per capita incomes of the farm population was predictable: they fell sharply.[29]

Collectivization was indeed a unique "solution" to what Soviet leaders apparently viewed as an intractable problem. In Chapter 7 we shall examine the organizational structure of the collective farm and the means by which it was to extract a "surplus" from the

Table 11 **Numbers of Livestock in the Soviet Union, 1928–1935 (in millions of head)**

Year	Cattle (total)	Cows	Pigs	Sheep	Goats	Horses
1918[a]	60.1	29.3	22.0	97.3	9.7	32.1
1929	58.2	29.2	19.4	97.4	9.7	32.6
1930	50.6	28.5	14.2	85.5	7.8	31.0
1931	42.5	24.5	11.7	62.5	5.6	27.0
1932	38.3	22.3	10.9	43.8	3.8	21.7
1933	33.5	19.4	9.9	34.0	3.3	17.3
1934	33.5	19.0	11.5	32.9	3.6	15.4
1935	38.9	19.0	17.1	36.4	4.4	14.9

[a] Borders of the Soviet Union as of 1939.

SOURCE: Erich Strauss, *Soviet Agriculture in Perspective* (London: Allen & Unwin, 1969), p. 307.

[28] Naum Jasny, *The Socialized Agriculture of the USSR* (Stanford, Calif.: Food Research Institute, 1949), p. 323.
[29] Naum Jasny, *Essays on the Soviet Economy* (New York: Praeger, 1962), p. 107. Jasny's figures on per capita income of the Soviet farm population in constant prices reveal the following picture:

1928	100
1932–33	53
1936	60
1937	81
1938	63

countryside. It did, of course, have both costs and benefits, and a proper evaluation of collectivization can only be cast in a long-term framework with due consideration for potential alternatives. These matters we leave for further discussion in Chapter Twelve.

CONCLUSIONS: SOVIET ECONOMIC HISTORY TO 1940

We have outlined in capsule form the events between the Revolution and World War II that played an influencing role in the evolution of the Soviet command economic system. Beginning with the economic heritage that the Bolsheviks inherited from the tsars, to the War Communism and NEP periods preceding the plan era, and finally to the evolution of the Soviet planning structure and collectivization during the early plan era, we sought to relate the early economic history of the Soviet Union to the broad issues of Soviet resource allocation and Soviet economic development dealt with in this work. Of course, certain events that likely had a large impact upon the contemporary Soviet economic structure, such as World War II, have not been dealt with. In this instance, the amount of independent Western research of the Soviet economy during World War II was deemed insufficient to warrant its inclusion. Also other events, such as labor policy during the 1930s and the evolution of investment allocation rules during the same period, will be dealt with in Part Two.

Selected Bibliography

E. H. Carr and R. W. Davies, *Foundations of a Planned Economy, 1926–1929* (London: Macmillan, 1969), vol. 1, parts 1, 2.

Maurice Dobb, *Soviet Economic Development Since 1917,* 5th ed. (London: Routledge & Kegan Paul, 1960).

Alexander Erlich, *The Soviet Industrialization Debate, 1924–1928* (Cambridge, Mass.: Harvard University Press, 1960).

Jerzy F. Karcz, "Thoughts on the Grain Problem," *Soviet Studies,*
vol. 18, no. 4 (April 1967), 399–434.

M. Lewin, "The Immediate Background of Soviet Collectivization,"
Soviet Studies, vol. 17, no. 2 (October 1965), 162–197.

M. Lewin, *Russian Peasants and Soviet Power* (London: Allen &
Unwin, 1968).

Alec Nove, *An Economic History of the USSR* (London: Penguin,
1969), chap. 7.

Leon Smolinski, "Soviet Planning: How It Really Began," *Survey,*
no. 64 (April 1968), 100–115.

Leon Smolinski, "Planning Without Theory, 1917–1967," *Survey,*
no. 64 (July 1967), 108–128.

Nicolas Spulber, ed., *Foundations of Soviet Strategy for Economic
Growth* (Bloomington: Indiana University Press, 1964).

Nicolas Spulber, *Soviet Strategy for Economic Growth* (Bloomington: Indiana University Press, 1964).

Lazar Volin, *A Century of Russian Agriculture* (Cambridge, Mass.:
Harvard University Press, 1970), chaps. 9 and 10.

How the Soviet Economy Operates

CHAPTER FIVE

How the Soviet Economy Operates: Planning and Pricing

INTRODUCTION TO SOVIET RESOURCE ALLOCATION

In this chapter, we turn from the origins of the Soviet planned economy to its actual operation. Although arrangements for allocating resources in the Soviet Union have changed over time, we shall concentrate on the Soviet economy between the First Five Year Plan (1928) and the economic reform of 1965. The pre-1928 period was discussed in Chapter Two and the reforms of 1965 and thereafter are discussed in Chapter Ten. The 1928 to 1965 period warrants special emphasis since it illustrates the basic working principles used to industrialize the Soviet economy. In addition, it appears that the various Soviet economic reforms have brought about, at best, relatively minor changes in basic Soviet working arrangements—although this view might be subject to challenge. Nevertheless, the reader should be aware that some changes, primarily in the areas of industrial planning and criteria for managerial success, have occurred since 1965 as will be discussed in Chapter Ten on economic reform.

Our foremost concern in the next two chapters is to elaborate how resources are allocated in the Soviet Union, in particular by what arrangements goods and services are produced and distributed and how the major factors of production (labor and capital)

115

are allocated. To analyze the matter of goods production, we consider in this chapter the planning apparatus, the relationship between the planners and enterprises, and the process of price formation. We approach the latter question of factor allocation in Chapter Six by examining the Soviet manager, the labor market, and the allocation of scarce capital among competing uses.

First, however, it is necessary to outline the institutional framework in which the Soviet economy operates, since these institutions —the state economic hierarchy and the Communist Party—provide much of the direction and control generally exerted by the market in capitalist economies.

POLITICAL INSTITUTIONS AND CONTROL OF THE ECONOMY[1]

In the Soviet Union, the crucial economic decisions—the allocation of output among consumption, investment, and defense, and the rates of expansion of different sectors are made administratively, not by the market. Whereas in the United States about one-quarter of GNP is allocated by administrative decisions through the public sector, in the Soviet Union almost all output is allocated administratively. In this manner, *planners' preferences* supplant *consumer sovereignty* by taking resource allocation out of the hands of the market and placing it under the control of an administrative apparatus.[2] In this section, we consider the political apparatus, the planning apparatus, and the intertwining of the two.

[1] Our discussion relates to institutions in the postwar period. It is based on the following sources: Alec Nove, *The Soviet Economy,* rev. ed. (New York: Praeger, 1969), introduction and chap. 2; Merle Fainsod, *How Russia Is Ruled,* rev. ed. (Cambridge, Mass.: Harvard University Press, 1963); Abram Bergson, *The Economics of Soviet Planning* (New Haven, Conn.: Yale University Press, 1964), chap. 3; Paul Cook, "The Political Setting," in Joint Economic Committee, *Soviet Economic Prospects for the Seventies* (Washington, D.C.: U.S. Government Printing Office, 1973), pp. 2–10.

[2] By a system of *planners' preferences* we mean a mechanism for guiding the economic system so that the decisions as to what to produce, how to produce, and who gets the output are made by central planners rather than by the dollar (and political) votes of consumers in the marketplace. Although

Nominally, the Soviet Union is governed by an elected government that is subject to the Soviet constitution. The highest organ of the state is the *Supreme Soviet,* which is comprised of directly elected deputies. Because the Supreme Soviet meets infrequently, the *Praesidium* appointed by the Supreme Soviet carries on the work of the Supreme Soviet between sessions. The *Council of Ministers* is the government bureaucracy of the USSR and is elected by the Supreme Soviet. The Soviet Union is a republic, composed of 15 union republics, and each union republic has a state apparatus that parallels the national apparatus. Beneath the union republican governments are the provincial (*oblast'*) governments and the local governments.

Parallel to the state apparatus is the Communist Party of the Soviet Union (CPSU).[3] The supreme authority over the party organization is exercised nominally by the Party Congress, made up of delegates from all levels of the party hierarchy. Party congresses are held only at infrequent intervals and they serve to elect (often perfunctorily) the *Central Committee* of the CPSU that, in turn, appoints the *Praesidium* of the CPSU (or *Politburo,* as it has also been called), which is the most important policy-setting body in the Soviet Union.

At the republican, regional, and local levels, departments of the CPSU duplicate the various state agencies; thus for each state agency there is a parallel party branch. This applies even to the lowest administrative echelons. At the enterprise level, a party branch supervises enterprise operations. Unlike the state apparatus, where lines of authority generally run from the local to the provincial to the republican to the national level, all lines in the

---

theoretically under such a system planners may take full account of consumers' wishes, historically this has not typically been the case in the Soviet Union.

[3] The Communist Party is, of course, a crucial mechanism in Soviet society. For a detailed treatment of party structure and functions, see Leonard Shapiro, *The Communist Party of the Soviet Union* (New York: Random House, 1971); and T. H. Rigby, *Communist Party Membership in the U.S.S.R., 1917–1967* (Princeton, N.J.: Princeton University Press, 1968). For the official Soviet view (subject to change in different editions), see *History of the Communist Party of the Soviet Union* (Moscow: Foreign Languages Publishing House, 1960).

party apparatus run directly to Moscow, suggesting a significant centralization of power.

One of the principal functions of all branches of the CPSU is the control and supervision of the economy. This control is exercised in several ways. Many branches of government report directly to the party. The State Planning Committee, for example, reports directly to the Praesidium (Politburo) of the CPSU. At lower levels, building projects are first submitted to the party before being submitted to the appropriate government office. At the enterprise level, the party organization serves two functions—one, to mobilize the workers to fulfill the plan (often through the enterprise trade union that the party dominates); and the other, to check on the enterprise manager. These are just isolated examples of party supervision.

Perhaps the most potent tool used by the CPSU to direct the economy is the *nomenklatura* system.[4] The *nomenklatura* is a comprehensive list of appointments that are controlled by the party. It is the party that nominates individuals for all important posts in the CPSU, state, industry, and army. At the national level, the Central Committee Cadres Department exercises this function. Party control over *nomenklatura* is crucial insofar as it is party nominees who run for elective office and become enterprise directors and farm managers. It is not surprising to find that while roughly ten percent of the Soviet population belongs to the CPSU, very few agricultural or industrial managers are *not* members of the party. A noted observer of the Soviet scene, Alec Nove, sums up the pervasive influence of the party as follows:

> Party control over policy and over its execution is an essential,
> if not always visible, fact of Soviet life, and affects not only
> basic planning decisions or the appointment and behavior of
> a minister, but also the choices between alternatives which a
> factory director or a *kolkhoz* chairman may wish to make.
> This is why . . . it [the party organization] affects all
> aspects of economic life.[5]

---

[4] Paul K. Cook, "The Administration and Distribution of Soviet Industry," in *Dimensions of Soviet Economic Power* (Washington, D.C.: U.S. Government Printing Office, 1962), pp. 185–186.
[5] Nove, *op. cit.*, p. 109.

We turn now from the party apparatus to the state apparatus to consider the planning and organization of the economy. Throughout most of the plan period (1928 to present), the Soviet economy has operated under a ministerial system in which individual enterprises belonging to a particular branch of the economy (aviation, chemicals, metallurgy, etc.) are subordinated to a single ministry. There are three types of ministries: the *all-union ministry* runs the enterprises under its control directly from Moscow and its enterprises are not answerable to regional authorities. The *union-republican ministry* has offices both in Moscow and in the various republics, and the enterprises under its control are subject to the dual authority of Moscow and the republican Councils of Ministers. The *republican ministry* directs enterprises within the republic and has no direct superior in Moscow. The heads of these ministries are members of the Council of Ministers of the USSR and of the republican Councils of Ministers, respectively.

The ministerial system was introduced in 1932 to replace *Vesenkha*. Initially three ministries were created, for heavy, light, and timber industries. Since then the number has fluctuated from a high of 32 in the late Stalin years, to 11 immediately after Stalin's death, to around 40 in the late 1960s. In April of 1973 there were 39 industrial ministries.[6] The ministries have, at times, possessed considerable power: they control a network of productive enterprises and have tended to develop their own supply and disposal agencies. Although various superior agencies have been established at different times to coordinate the activities of the ministries, this has principally been done by *Gosplan* (the State Planning Committee), which has derived much of its authority from its close association with the Praesidium (Politburo) of the CPSU.

Gosplan was established in 1921 and engaged primarily in nonoperational long-term planning during the 1920s. During the 1920s, the role of *Gosplan* as a central coordinator of national planning was challenged by the People's Commissariat of Finance (*Narkomfin*), by *Vesenkha,* and the ministerial planning bodies, but by the late 1920s *Gosplan* was fairly well recognized as the principal planning body in the Soviet Union.[7] After its reorganization in 1928,

[6] Nove, *op. cit.,* pp. 69, 110; Cook, *The Political Setting, op. cit.,* Fig. 2.
[7] E. H. Carr and R. W. Davies, *Foundations of a Planned Economy, 1926–1929,* vol. I, part 2 (New York: Macmillan, 1969), pp. 802–836.

Figure 3 **Central Economic Administrative Structure of the USSR**[a] **(June 1972)**

AUTHORIZED SOURCE: Central Intelligence Agency, *Central Economic Administrative Structure of the USSR* (Washington, D.C., 1972).

A-U: All-Union Ministry. All-Union ministries administer branches of the economy having national importance and requiring centralized direction from Moscow.

U-R: Union-Republic ministry. Union-Republic ministries administer branches of the economy with important regional differences. Direction is exercised at the republic level subject to guidance and review by the ministries' headquarters in Moscow.

ADMINISTRATIVE ORGANS

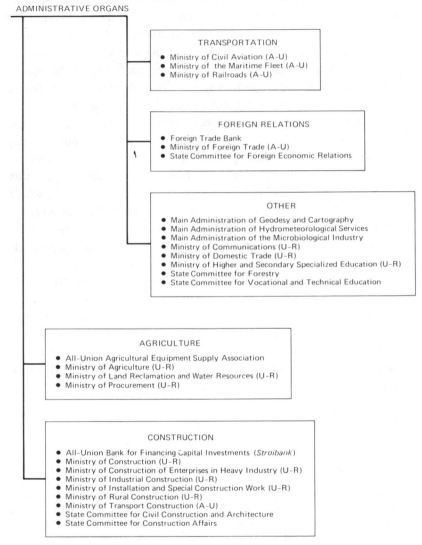

TRANSPORTATION
- Ministry of Civil Aviation (A-U)
- Ministry of the Maritime Fleet (A-U)
- Ministry of Railroads (A-U)

FOREIGN RELATIONS
- Foreign Trade Bank
- Ministry of Foreign Trade (A-U)
- State Committee for Foreign Economic Relations

OTHER
- Main Administration of Geodesy and Cartography
- Main Administration of Hydrometeorological Services
- Main Administration of the Microbiological Industry
- Ministry of Communications (U-R)
- Ministry of Domestic Trade (U-R)
- Ministry of Higher and Secondary Specialized Education (U-R)
- State Committee for Forestry
- State Committee for Vocational and Technical Education

AGRICULTURE
- All-Union Agricultural Equipment Supply Association
- Ministry of Agriculture (U-R)
- Ministry of Land Reclamation and Water Resources (U-R)
- Ministry of Procurement (U-R)

CONSTRUCTION
- All-Union Bank for Financing Capital Investments (*Stroibank*)
- Ministry of Construction (U-R)
- Ministry of Construction of Enterprises in Heavy Industry (U-R)
- Ministry of Industrial Construction (U-R)
- Ministry of Installation and Special Construction Work (U-R)
- Ministry of Rural Construction (U-R)
- Ministry of Transport Construction (A-U)
- State Committee for Civil Construction and Architecture
- State Committee for Construction Affairs

[a] Economic organizations below the union-republic level of administration are not included.

[b] Industrial defense ministries are concerned primarily with the production of military and space machinery and equipment, but they also supply products to civilian clients. Industrial nondefense ministries, while largely serving the civilian economy, also produce items for the military and space sector.

121

it came to play an important coordinating function, especially after the ministerial system was introduced in 1932. Although the ministries themselves performed most of the current planning within the ministry, *Gosplan* was given the task of coordinating these ministerial plans by drawing up *material balances,* the basic planning system to be discussed shortly. The structure and functions of *Gosplan* have changed quite significantly during the plan period, though to relate these changes in detail would be confusing to the reader and would not add significantly to our understanding of Soviet planning.[8] The important point to note is that in spite of continuing changes in the organizational structure of planning agencies, *Gosplan* has played a central coordinating role throughout the plan period especially with the application of material balance planning.

The one major organizational change in the planning apparatus that deserves mentioning is the *Sovnarkhoz* reform of 1957, which was in effect until 1965.[9] It was argued by then Premier Khrushchev that the ministerial system had certain deficiencies—empire building within the ministry, lack of regional coordination, and bureaucratic delays—that could be corrected by reorganizing the economy along regional lines. Thus in 1957 the ministries were abolished (with the exceptions of the ministries supervising nuclear industries and electricity) and a system of 105 *Sovnarkhozy* (Regional Economic Councils) was introduced. Enterprises were now to be subordinated to the *Sovnarkhozy* (rather than to a ministry), which was in turn subject to the republican government, which, in turn, was subject to the all-union government. In fact, throughout

[8] In 1948–1949, *Gosplan* was weakened by the establishment of what had formerly been its material allocation department, technical department, and Central Statistical Agency as separate agencies. After Stalin's death, these departments (with the exception of the Central Statistical Agency) were returned to *Gosplan.* In 1955, *Gosplan* was split into two agencies: *Gosplan,* which was to concentrate on long-term planning, and the State Economic Commission, which was to be concerned with short-term plans. As a result of the regionalization reforms (the *Sovnarkhozy*) of 1957, *Gosplan* took on new responsibilities. *Gosplan* absorbed the planning functions of the defunct ministries and was the crucial coordinating agency at the all-union level. In 1960, *Gosplan* was again split into the State Economic-Science Council in charge of long-range planning and *Gosplan* in charge of current planning. On these organization changes, see Nove, *op. cit.,* pp. 71–85.

[9] Nove, *op. cit.,* pp. 78–81. Also, Oleg Hoeffding, "The Soviet Industrial Reorganization of 1957," *American Economic Review* (proceedings), vol. 49, no. 2 (May 1959), 65–77.

this period *Gosplan* generally bypassed the republican governments and the *Sovnarkhozy* and dealt directly with the enterprise.[10]

In 1965, after the fall of Khrushchev, who had engineered the 1957 *Sovnarkhoz* reform in the first place, Kosygin and Brezhnev replaced regional planning with the former ministerial system. The failure of the regional system was blamed on the growing "localism" of the various *Sovnarkhozy,* which placed the needs of the region above that of the national economy, and on the difficulties of coordinating a regionally operated planning apparatus. Both of these problems had led since 1957 to the growth of national supervisory agencies. However, the return to the ministerial system in 1965 was not a complete return to the *status quo*. The *Sovnarkhoz* supply agencies were retained and placed under the control of the State Committee on Material-Technical Supplies (*Gossnab*), which had, prior to 1957, been a branch of *Gosplan*.

A recent organization chart (1972) of the Soviet economic-administrative structure is provided in Figure 3 to illustrate the organization of the Soviet economy according to its ministerial system.

SUPPLY AND OUTPUT PLANNING — MATERIAL BALANCE PLANNING [11]

In the Soviet Union, the most basic economic decisions are made by the Communist Party. The planning apparatus, which is a branch of the state government, must then draw up plans for all levels of the economy that implement these basic political and economic de-

[10] Nove, *op. cit.*, p. 76.

[11] We avoid detailed footnoting of sources in this section. The material presented here is largely based on the following sources: Bergson, *op. cit.*, chap. 7; Nove, *op. cit.*, pp. 87–96; R. W. Davies, "Soviet Planning for Rapid Industrialization," *Economics of Planning*, vol. 6, no. 1 (1966), and "Planning a Mature Economy in the USSR," *Economics of Planning*, vol. 6, no. 2 (1966); Michael Ellman, "The Consistency of Soviet Plans," *Scottish Journal of Political Economy*, vol. 16, no. 1 (February 1969). These last three are reprinted in M. Bornstein and D. Fusfeld, eds., *The Soviet Economy*, 3rd. ed. (Homewood, Ill.: Irwin, 1970). See also Herbert Levine, "The Centralized Planning of Supply in Soviet Industry," in *Comparisons of the United States and Soviet Economies* (Washington, D. C.: U. S. Government Printing

cisions. After the plan is formulated and each ministry, region, and enterprise receives its input and output targets, a complex control organization swings into action. The planners themselves have their own control system (described below), but the party also plays a significant role in this area. From the various national party control commissions to the enterprise party committee, party officials are given the task of making sure that all levels of the economy are observing plan directives. In this manner the party attempts to insure that planners' preferences are actually being fulfilled.

The Soviet planning apparatus must translate party directives into actual operational plans. As the reader might imagine, this is an extremely complicated task in view of the complexity of the Soviet economy, which produces millions of distinct commodities and encompasses a vast territory. Yet the Soviet economy has been directed by a comprehensive central plan since 1928, indicating that the actual Soviet planning system has somehow been able to direct the economy in spite of its complexity. Our discussion of the Soviet planning system begins with an account of industrial supply and output planning—the so-called system of material balances.

Material Balance Planning. Soviet material balance planning defies a simplified description.[12] First, the fairly frequent administrative changes in the Soviet planning apparatus complicate description, and, second, there is the problem of differentiating between the idealized version of Soviet planning described in Soviet texts on planning and its actual operation.[13] In discussing Soviet material balance planning, we avoid further reference to administrative changes and describe Soviet planning under the ministerial system prior to the economic reforms of 1965. In our later evaluation of

---

Office, pp. 151–176, reprinted in M. Bornstein and D. Fusfeld, *The Soviet Economy,* rev. ed. (Homewood, Ill.: Irwin, 1965), pp. 49–65; Michael Ellman, *Soviet Planning Today: Proposals for an Optimally Functioning Economic System* (Cambridge: Cambridge University Press, 1971); Gertrude Schroeder, "The 'Reform' of the Supply System in Soviet Industry," *Soviet Studies,* vol. 24, no. 1 (July 1972), 97–119, and "Recent Developments in Soviet Planning and Incentives," in Joint Economic Committee, *Soviet Economic Prospects for the Seventies, op. cit.,* pp. 11–38.

[12] For a discussion of the historical development of material balance planning in the late 1920s, see Carr and Davies, *op. cit.,* pp. 829–836.

[13] As an example, see A. N. Efimov et al., *Ekonomicheskoe planirovanie v SSSR* (Economic planning in the USSR) (Moscow: 1967).

Soviet planning, the problem of theory versus practice will be given further scrutiny.

Our discussion begins with the construction of the annual plan.[14] The key to Soviet success in dealing with the enormous complexities of planning is that only a limited number of commodities are centrally planned and distributed by *Gosplan USSR*. Even then industrial supply and distribution plans compiled by *Gosplan* have been known to total 70 volumes of almost 12,000 pages and deal with well over 30,000 commodities.

The most important industrial products—such as steel, cement, machinery, building materials—are called *funded commodities.* *Gosplan USSR* is in charge of drawing up output and distribution plans for these funded commodities, which are specifically approved by the USSR Council of Ministers. Between 1928 and the present, *Gosplan* has developed annual balances for between 277 (1971) and 2,390 (1953) separate funded product groups. Output and distribution plans are also drawn up for two other categories of industrial products. *Planned commodities* are those industrial products jointly planned and distributed by *Gosplan,* the State Committee for Material-Technical Supply and the All-Union Main Supply and Sales Administrations under the approval of the heads of these organizations. In recent years, several thousand commodities have been planned according to this system. Finally, *decentrally planned* commodities are planned and distributed by the territorial

[14] This chapter deals only with annual plans, which are the operational plans in the Soviet economy, and omits long-term "perspective planning," since historically there seems to have been little relationship between perspective and annual plans. See Naum Jasny, *Essays on the Soviet Economy* (New York: Praeger, 1962), essay 6. In theory, at least, annual plans should be compiled on the basis of the five or seven year perspective plans in such a manner that at the end of five (or seven) annual plans the perspective plan targets are met. This has not generally been the case for the first eight Five (Seven) Year Plans. The Ninth Five Year Plan (1971–1975) apparently seeks to remedy this situation by upgrading the role of the long-range plan by requiring more conformity between it and the annual operational plans. For more on this point, see Schroeder, *Recent Developments in Soviet Planning, op. cit.,* pp. 13–15. The reader interested in perspective plans is referred to the U.S. Department of Commerce's translation of the 1971–1975 Soviet Ninth Five Year Plan: Joint Publications Research Service, Department of Commerce, *State Five-Year Plan for the Development of the USSR National Economy for the Period 1971–1975,* Part II (Springfield, Va.: National Technical Information Service, 1972).

administrations of the State Committee for Material-Technical Supply and by the ministries without the explicit approval of higher organs. In recent years, over 10,000 industrial products have been planned according to this system.

In addition to these three categories, the ministries plan and allocate "nonplanned" industrial commodities, largely for internal use. In 1970, for example, the ministries allocated 26,000 products in this category.

A somewhat idealized version of *Gosplan's* planning of funded commodities through the industrial supply and output planning system would appear as follows (the following breakdown into distinct steps is somewhat arbitrary, for there is considerable overlapping).

1. The first step in the planning process is for the party (the Praesidium or the Central Committee) to establish its own priorities for the forthcoming planning period. This is usually done in the spring preceding the planning period. The party expresses its priorities by setting output targets (generally in the form of desired rates of growth) for a number of crucial funded commodities.

2. These output targets are sent down through the state apparatus to *Gosplan,* which has been active gathering data on past plan fulfillment and bottlenecks. *Gosplan* then formulates a preliminary set of *control figures* (tentative output targets) for 200 to 300 product groups that fulfills the priorities set by the party. *Gosplan* also tentatively estimates, on the basis of past performance, the inputs required to achieve the control figures. At this stage, the planning departments of the ministries aid *Gosplan* in the formulation of the full set of control figures and project input requirements —a process that involves some negotiation and friction as the ministries bargain for reasonable targets and sufficient resources.

3. These control figures are then sent down through the planning hierarchy via the ministerial organizations until they reach the individual enterprises. As the control figures progress through the planning hierarchy, they are disaggregated into specific tasks. For example, the all-union ministry will receive its control targets, which are then disaggregated by branches within the ministry, and so on, until each enterprise under the purview of the ministry receives its own control figures. At this stage, the planning branch of the ministry will prepare a list of tentative input requirements,

based on the ministry's control figures, for internal use by each enterprise.

4. Now information begins to flow up the planning hierarchy from the enterprise to *Gosplan*. The enterprise will relate to its immediate superior its input requirements, which, in turn, will aggregate the requirements of all enterprises under its control, which will be related to its superior, and so on, up to the ministry and then on to *Gosplan*. At each stage in this process, the requested inputs are compared with earlier estimated input needs and the so-called correction principle is used to adjust for differences between the two (after considerable bargaining among the various levels).

5. At this point in the planning process, *Gosplan* must check the *consistency* of the control figures, that is, determine whether a *material balance* exists. A material balance is achieved when the planned supplies of each commodity equal its targeted material input requirements and final uses. Assuming a total of 2000 funded commodities to be balanced, a material balance is achieved when:

$$Exhibit\ 1$$
$$S_1 = D_1$$
$$S_2 = D_2$$
$$\cdot$$
$$\cdot$$
$$\cdot$$
$$S_{2000} = D_{2000}$$

where the Ss refer to the planned supplies and the Ds refer to the estimated demands for the (2000) materials.

The planned supply of the first commodity (S_1), for example, is the sum of its planned output (the control figure), which is denoted as X_1, available stocks (V_1), and planned imports (M_1). The total demand for the first commodity (D_1) is the sum of its intermediate (interindustry) demands (X_{11}, X_{12}, X_{13}, . . . $X_{1\ 2000}$)[15] and its final demand (investment, household demand, and exports),

[15] The X_{ij} refer to interindustry demands. For example, X_{13} would refer to the quantity of commodity 1 required to produce the planned output of commodity 3. In more general terms, X_{ij} would refer to the quantity of commodity i required to produce the planned output of commodity j. Such input requirements are also called *intermediate* inputs.

which is denoted as Y_1. From Exhibit 1, it is noted that a consistent set of control figures requires that:

Exhibit 2

Sources   Distribution

$$X_1 + V_1 + M_1 = X_{11} + X_{12} + \cdots + X_{1,2000} + Y_1$$
$$X_2 + V_2 + M_2 = X_{21} + X_{22} + \cdots + X_{2,2000} + Y_2$$

$$X_{2000} + V_{2000} + M_{2000} = X_{2000,1} + X_{2000,2} + \cdots$$
$$+ X_{2000,2000} + Y_{2000}$$

In most cases, planned production (the X_i) is the most important supply source, accounting for as high as 95 percent of the total supply of funded materials. On the other hand, imports are usually an insignificant source of supply. It is *Gosplan's* task to ensure that a material balance exists.

A simplified hypothetical material balance consisting of four product categories—coal, steel, machinery, and consumer goods —is provided here (Exhibit 3) to illustrate the concepts of inter-mediate demand, final demand, balance, and so on.

Usually when *Gosplan* first compares supplies and demands, it finds a tendency for demands to exceed supplies because of large inter-industry requirements and taut planning in general. *Gosplan* must then equate supplies and demands by adjusting their different components (Exhibit 2). To illustrate this process in the simplest possible manner, assume that a material balance has been achieved with the exception of the first commodity, which is, say, steel— that is, the supplies of all other commodities equal their demands, but the demand for steel exceeds its supply. This material imbalance can be equilibrated in five different ways:

a. *Gosplan could order an increase in the planned output of the deficit commodity (raise X_1).* This approach, however, could throw the remaining sectors out of balance because additional coal, electricity, and other inputs used to make steel would be required, and their targets would have to be increased accordingly, which would, in turn, require increased outputs of commodities used in producing them, and so on. If an output target is changed to achieve a material balance, a chain of secondary effects is set off that affects balances in other sectors. For this reason, Soviet planners have

Exhibit 3 **A Sample Material Balance**

| | Sources | | | Intermediate Inputs Required by: | | | | Final Uses | |
	Output	Stocks	Imports	Coal Industry	Steel Industry	Machinery Industry	Consumer Goods Industry	Exports	Domestic Uses
Coal (tons)	1000	10	0	100	500	50	50	100	210
Steel (tons)	2000	0	20	200	400	1000	300	100	20
Machinery (units)	100	5	5	20	40	10	20	10	10
Consumer goods (units)	400	10	20	0	0	0	100	100	230

Demonstration that a balance exists:

sources of coal: 1010 tons = uses of coal: 1010 tons
sources of steel: 2020 tons = uses of steel: 2020 tons
sources of machinery: 110 units = uses of machinery: 110 units
sources of consumer goods: 430 units = uses of consumer goods: 430 units

generally been reluctant to use this first approach to achieve a balance, finding it difficult to adjust for the secondary impacts of such changes. When Soviet planners have used this approach, they have tended to adjust only for secondary effects in obvious cases.[16] A more common approach has been to call for increased production without raising planned inputs thus pressuring enterprises to economize on inputs and increasing the tautness of planning.

b. *Gosplan could increase imports* (M_1) *of the deficit commodity.* The major drawback of this approach is that it would make the consistency of the material balance dependent on foreign suppliers and would require use of essential foreign exchange reserves (if imported from the West). Even utilizing trade connections within the communist bloc would be an uncertain alternative because of the risk of delivery deadlines not being met. This second equilibrating approach has in fact generally been of limited importance in Soviet material balance planning, although during the First Five Year Plan (1928–1933) it was used to make up deficits of certain types of machinery, and during the postwar period it has been used to import grain and, in recent years, advanced-technology products from the West.

c. *Gosplan could reduce interindustry demands for the deficit commodity* (*the* $X_{1j}s$). This could be done by directing enterprises to use substitutes not in short supply or by reducing their overall inputs. The danger inherent in this approach is that by reducing planned intermediate inputs or by forcing enterprises to use inferior substitutes the affected enterprises may not be able to meet their own output targets, thus creating further bottlenecks.

d. *Gosplan could reduce final demands for the deficit commodity* (Y_1). This could be done by reducing either exports, household demand, or investment demand. The positive feature of this approach is that household demand (such as for coal for home heating), in particular, can be treated as residuals in the planning

[16] In practice, Soviet planners have generally adjusted only for *first-order relationships* when output targets are changed because of the tremendous amount of time required to make the necessary computations. By first-order changes, we mean the additional coal, electricity, ore, and other commodities required to produce the additional steel in our example above. No account is taken of the additional resources required to produce the extra coal, electricity, and ore. For a detailed discussion of this point, see Levine, in Bornstein and Fusfeld, rev. ed., *op. cit.*, pp. 55–57.

process that have little impact upon the interindustry balances. Its negative feature is that such final demands are required to meet the material needs of the populace and could tend to be too readily sacrificed simply to achieve a balance of interindustry demands.

e. *Gosplan could draw upon stocks of the deficit commodity* (V_1). This approach is generally impractical because of either the lack of adequate stockpiles or the unwillingness of planners to draw down strategic supplies, and has been used only rarely.

Gosplan has historically favored the third and fourth balancing techniques, and has generally applied them within the context of a priority system, which has limited the flow of inputs to low-priority industrial branches (generally consumer goods) and has restricted the availability of final consumer goods. In the former case, planners have assumed that the neglect of low-priority consumer goods branches will not jeopardize plan fulfillment in the high-priority heavy industry branches, which tend to be fairly independent of the consumer good branches. For example, if a garment-producing enterprise were to fall short of its output goal owing to inadequate materials, this failure would not jeopardize plan fulfillment in the steel industry. In the latter case, if coal, for example, was in deficit, a simple balancing method would be to reduce coal available for household heating, which would have little immediate impact on the crucial interindustry balance. Over time (especially during the 1930s), the consumer sector has tended to be neglected for the sake of achieving a material balance, so much so that it has been called at times the "buffer" sector of the Soviet economy.[17]

After *Gosplan* achieves (or approximates) the material balance, the final version of the plan is submitted to the Council of Min-

[17] This neglect is seen rather clearly by looking at the record of plan fulfillment between 1933 and 1955. Ignoring the First Five Year Plan (1928–1933) when unachievable targets were set in all sectors, we see (Table 12) especially during the Second (1933–1937) and Fourth (1945–1950) Five Year Plans that the major shortfalls in plan fulfillment occurred in the consumer goods branches, which indicates how this buffer mechanism works. In addition, the heavy industry targets tend to be more ambitious in the first place. The buffer status of light industry is by no means a thing of the past. Owing to the worst performance of the economy in 25 years in 1972, most major economic indicators had to be reduced in the 1973 plan; but the planned growth of consumer goods was cut back 44 percent, whereas producer goods were cut back only 17 percent. Cook, *The Political Setting, op. cit.*, p. 4.

Table 12 **Five Year Plans: Targets and Fulfillments**
(base year of the Five Year Plan = 100)

	Second 5 YP (1933–1937)		Fourth 5 YP (1945–1950)		Fifth 5 YP (1950–1955)	
	Target 1937	Actual 1937	Target 1950	Actual 1950	Target 1955	Actual 1955
Electric power	282	267	170	189	182	187
Coal	237	199	157	157	143	150
Petroleum	210	133	114	122	185	187
Steel	289	299	139	129	162	166
Consumer goods	234	160	126	102	160	165
Cotton fabric	187	128	118	99	161	115
Retail trade	251	135	128	110	170	185

SOURCE: Naum Jasny, *Essays on the Soviet Economy* (New York: Praeger, 1962), p. 266.

isters for approval (and sometimes modification), after which the finalized targets are sent down the hierarchy to the individual firm. In its final form, the enterprise plan is called the *techpromfinplan* (the technical-industrial-financial plan) and establishes enterprise output targets as well as input allocations, supply plans, delivery-plans, financial flows, wage bills, and many other targets.

The final stage of material balance planning occurs during the actual operation of the finalized plan. During this stage, *Gosplan* checks plan fulfillment at the various levels and gathers information upon which next year's plan will be based. An important element of the plan fulfillment stage is the response of *Gosplan* and the ministries to bottlenecks, that is, their manipulation of available resources to insure fulfillment of priority targets. It would be a mistake to think that the process of resource allocation is completed with the approval of the finalized version of the plan. Rather, important shifts of resources occur during the very course of plan fulfillment as the planning agencies respond in a pragmatic manner to the various crises and bottlenecks that arise.

An Evaluation of Material Balance Planning. It is difficult to evaluate Soviet material balance planning because it combines both positive and negative features. On the positive side, Soviet supply planning, by placing severe pressure on enterprises in the form of taut targets designed to strain enterprise capacity, has brought about rapid growth of industrial output in selected priority sectors and has presided over a vast and rapid transformation of the Soviet economy. Thus the major strength of Soviet planning seems to be its ability to direct resources into areas selected by planners with more speed and force than a market-directed economy.

The material balance system does work, in an indirect sense, to equate supply and demand within the priority system. That is, although taut output targets do often exceed enterprise capacities and create supply shortages, ultimately the administration can equate supplies and demands by directing available resources into higher priority enterprises. The Soviets themselves stress this very point: Their planning system is seen to replace the "anarchy of the market" by rational direction of resources into socially necessary ends.[18] In fact, Soviet planners recognized from the very outset of the industrialization drive that taut planning would result in severe strains and pressures on the economy, but considered the risks well worth taking. Taut (*naprazhennye*) plans continue to be demanded by the Soviet leadership and remain a basic fact of industrial planning up to the present. For example, *Gosplan* was directed by the Central Committee of the CPSU to undertake three separate revisions of the Ninth Five Year Plan (1971–1975) so as to uncover further "hidden reserves" of the economy—a euphemism for increasing the tautness of the plan.

One reason for taut planning was its role in helping to maintain plan discipline. As has been pointed out by Western students of Soviet planning,[19] the greater the degree of slack in the economy, the greater the flexibility exercised by managers at the local level and the greater the likelihood that production may stray from strict adherance to the priority system. In other words, taut planning is required to enable central authorities to maintain strict control over the economy.

[18]*Political Economy, A Textbook* (East Berlin: Dietz Verlag, 1964), pp. 496–499.
[19] Richard D. Portes, "The Enterprise Under Central Planning," *Review of Economic Studies,* vol. 36, no. 106 (April 1969), 197–212. Also see Michael Keren, "On the Tautness of Plans," *Review of Economic Studies,* vol. 39, no. 4 (October 1972), 469–486.

Second, fairly convincing arguments can be made for Soviet-style taut industrial planning on other grounds, using the theories of Western development economics. The argument here is that by setting taut (often unattainable) targets rather than setting moderate targets that avoid bottlenecks, enterprises will be forced to expand to the limits of their production possibilities and the economy will be pulled up to higher production levels in the process. This pressure, combined with an appropriate degree of administrative flexibility, could lead to more rapid economic development than would have occurred under more "rational" balanced planning.[20]

On the negative side, it is also recognized that excesses result from the Soviet material balance system.[21] First, the pressurized Soviet system often forces the Soviet manager to engage in dysfunctional forms of behavior. Faced with overambitious targets while lacking flexible access to supplies, the manager has frequently engaged in excessive stockpiling. He strives to build up emergency stocks as "safety factors," which he can use for future plan fulfillment or for trading, by overstating input requirements to his immediate superiors. As a result of such actions which are often required to make the system work, the economy loses on two counts: scarce materials tend to stand idle (resources are wasted) and planners receive inaccurate information. On another score, the overtaut planning system has created a definite sellers' market, which has meant that the manager can generally unload his output

[20] Holland Hunter, "Optimum Tautness in Developmental Planning," *Economic Development and Cultural Change,* vol. 9, no. 4, part I (July 1961), 561–572. A similar argument has been made by Albert Hirschman, *The Strategy of Economic Development* (New Haven, Conn.: Yale University Press, 1958), pp. 29–33. Hunter is careful to recognize that there is a level of "optimal tautness" and that Soviet planning may have exceeded this optimal limit. Western experts have concluded that the Ninth Five Year Plan, for example, goes well beyond this optimal limit and that serious shortfalls in metals, timber, and electricity will hinder its implementation. On this, see J. Noren and F. Whitehouse, "Soviet Industry in the 1971–75 Plan," in *Soviet Economic Prospects for the Seventies, op. cit.,* pp. 207, 239–242.

[21] Hunter, *op. cit.,* 567–571; and Levine, "Pressure and Planning in the Soviet Economy," in Henry Rosovsky, ed., *Industrialization in Two Systems: Essays in Honor of Alexander Gerschenkron* (New York: Wiley, 1966), pp. 266–285. Reprinted in Bornstein and Fusfeld, 3rd ed., *op. cit.,* pp. 64–82.

irrespective of its quality and design. This feature has been an important source of the quality problems so widely noted in the Soviet press. The economic reforms of the 1960s with their emphasis on profitability, sales, and interest charges have aimed at correcting these problems.

A second weakness of Soviet planning is that as long as the consumer sector is used as a buffer, personal incentives and productivity suffer, and productivity increases are most important as the major source of growth as the economy becomes more mature. The Soviets have relied heavily on using material incentives to promote labor productivity, but if consumer goods are not available in the desired quantities and qualities (because they have been sacrificed for heavy industry), the incentive system will be less effective. The consumer sector definitely was used as a buffer sector during the Stalin years, but since the early 1950s the growth of real per capita consumption has been rapid. Also the 1965 reforms have seemed to favor light industry more than the previous system. Nevertheless Soviet living standards still tend to lag far behind countries having equal per capita income levels (such as Italy), which seems to indicate that the Soviet consumer is still relatively deprived (relative to Soviet industrial capacity) in terms of private consumption goods, and that industrial priorities have not been notably reversed from the Stalin years.

Third, material balance planning is quite cumbersome and slow. Enterprises invariably get their finalized targets well into the operating year (often as late as March) and must work without clear knowledge of what their targets actually are. When the targets are received, enterprises often desperately attempt to meet production targets at the end of each period by engaging in what the Soviets called *Shturmovshchina*—"storming"—a fairly inefficient method of scheduling production. Informal methods have been developed to get around this problem. One, the "correction principle," involves the use of advance estimates at each stage of the planning process prior to receipt of the information on the current production targets. Another device is the "advance fund allotment" that gives enterprises about one-quarter of the previous period's input allotments to tide them over until the final plan is received. A further device used by the ministries is "reserving" whereby ministries reserve for themselves a portion of enterprise material allotments to aid in combatting bottlenecks.[22] With the tendency towards planning delays and the use of informal methods, Soviet administrators have found that planning is less of a problem when targets change only marginally from year to year. Thus there is a built-in tendency in the Soviet planning system to avoid dramatic change. At the enterprise level, the manager is reluctant to introduce new technologies that require a restructuring of established supply channels. In general, the introduction of new technology and new ways of doing things are retarded by the material balance system.[23]

Fourth, the Soviet planning system, with its stress on output goals, generates dysfunctional behavior at various planning levels. The ministry, for example, tends to be primarily concerned with the success of enterprises under its own control and places the input needs of its own enterprises over those of enterprises outside its control.[24] The same was true under the *Sovnarkhoz* reforms (1957–1964), when the regional authorities were concerned primarily with the success of regional enterprises. The planning system is also responsible for a lack of concern for the environment, because enterprise managers are judged on the basis of output target fulfillment, not on the basis of how well the environment is protected from air and water pollution and depletion of natural resources. Also, the uncertainties of the material supply system have caused enterprises to adopt peculiar production patterns. Soviet

[22] Levine, "Pressure and Planning in the Soviet Economy," in Bornstein and Fusfeld, 3rd ed., *op. cit.,* p. 73.

[23] One finds frequent complaints in the Soviet press from enterprises that have attempted to introduce new products and new technologies but were unable to obtain necessary supplies. *Pravda* (December 25, 1971, p. 2) reports on the tribulations of two electrical engineers, attempting to produce new torch lamps, whose efforts were foiled by their inability to obtain detailed parts. *The Economic Gazette* [*Ekonomicheskaia gazeta*], no. 39 (1969) reports on the problems of a plant processing motor vehicle transmissions unable to obtain the necessary measuring instruments to produce a new design.

[24] For example, *The Economic Gazette,* no. 30 (1969) reports that the ministry in charge of castings and forgings had cut back on deliveries to outside enterprises, thus creating shortages—especially in all-union enterprises not subordinated to a particular ministry. Such examples are to be found in almost every issue of the economic press.

enterprises have been known to integrate vertically as many operations as possible to provide their own material inputs—it is not rare in the Soviet Union for machinery producing enterprises to fabricate their own steel.[25] Thus vital specialization of production is limited by the planning system. In this light, one may ultimately come to recognize the frequent organizational shuffling of the Soviet planning system as attempts to solve such problems of supply and specialization by finding an "optimal" Soviet planning structure.

A fifth criticism of the Soviet planning system is that it requires the maintenance of an immense bureaucracy that tends to be counterproductive. For example, the industrial supply network alone employed almost half a million people in 1969. Cases of bureaucratic excesses are easy to find. For example, the Soviet newspaper *The Economic Gazette* of March 30, 1963, noted that requisitions for ball bearings by one auto factory alone were processed in all by fourteen agencies, and some 430 pounds of documents were generated.[26] Another example of this bureaucratic red tape is the 91 volumes of engineering data generated in the planning of a new steel mill.[27] Despite such examples, it is surprising to note that the Soviet bureaucracy is relatively small when compared with those of other industrialized countries.[28] It remains for future research to resolve this apparent paradox.

Finally, one can evaluate Soviet material balance planning in terms of its *consistency* and *optimality*. A consistent plan is one in which supplies and demands of funded commodities are equal. It is obvious that consistency is one of the main objectives of the Soviet material balance system. From the point of view of Soviet planners, consistency is a desirable goal: if the plan were highly inconsistent, that is, if targeted material requirements were allowed generally to exceed available supplies, plan fulfillment would become a com-

[25] David Granick, *Soviet Metal Fabricating and Economic Development* (Madison: University of Wisconsin Press, 1967), pp. 159–160. Forgings and castings were also produced internally to avoid supply uncertainty.
[26] Cited in Bergson, *op. cit.,* p. 150.
[27] Leon Smolinski, "What Next in Soviet Planning?" *Foreign Affairs,* vol. 42, no. 4 (July 1964), 604.
[28] Gur Ofer, *The Service Sector in Soviet Economic Growth* (Cambridge, Mass.: Harvard University Press, 1973).

petitive struggle for deficit inputs that the planner would have difficulty in controlling, even with the priority system. Instead, connections, prestige, and ability to maneuver (already important factors in plan fulfillment) would primarily determine who is able to fulfill his target—a definitely undesirable situation in a controlled economy.

On the other hand, *optimality* should also be a desirable goal in a planned economy. To illustrate the concept of optimality, consider a situation where five different sets of control figures are consistent. From the point of view of the state, it would be desirable to be able to choose the "best," or optimal figures; to do otherwise would be to misallocate scarce resources.[29] This kind of choice is usually beyond the reach of Soviet planners, however, because the Soviet material balance system works so slowly that planners are fortunate if they approximate just one consistent plan variant in the allotted planning period. Current Soviet balancing techniques, time, and manpower are inadequate to find several consistent plan variants from which to choose the optimal one, and the Soviets' disregard of the importance of optimality must be seen as a major weakness of material balance planning.[30]

Our evaluation of the Soviet industrial planning reveals an apparent paradox to which we shall return in Part Four, namely: the material balance system has been effective in generating rapid growth of industrial output and military power. In fact, it has presided over the elevation of the Soviet Union to the world's second most powerful nation. On the other hand, the deficiencies of the Soviet planning system are striking: the excessive stockbuilding, the quality problems, the consumer sector buffer, the lack of emphasis on optimality, and so on. Which view of Soviet planning is correct? We will come back to this question later.

---

[29] The optimal set of control figures could be defined in technical terms as the one that yields the maximum value of all consistent sets when entered into the planners' objective function, that is, the consistent set of control figures that the planners regard as the "best" in terms of their preferences and biases. See Appendix 5-A for a further discussion of this point.

[30] It has been suggested that increased use of input-output economics in planning might resolve this problem by enabling Soviet planners to compute a series of consistent plans. For a discussion of this issue see Appendix 5-A at the end of this chapter.

THE ENTERPRISE PLAN
AND FINANCIAL
CONTROLS

Our previous discussion of material balance planning emphasized supply planning in physical terms. Let us now turn to the financial side of the enterprise. The enterprise *techpromfinplan* (technical-industrial-financial plan) includes, as its name suggests, a pervasive financial plan as well as physical input and output indicators. This financial plan parallels the physical section of the industrial supply and output plans and acts as a check on enterprise performance. The financial plan consists of a wage bill, planned cost reductions, credit plans for purchasing inputs, along with many other targets. The amount of detail contained in the financial plan has varied over the years, with recent reforms reducing the number and specificity of financial controls, but financial targets continue to serve as the monetary counterparts of enterprise's output and input targets.

Soviet managers have tended to regard the fulfillment of financial plans (cost reduction targets, wage bills, credit plans, etc.) as less important than output plans (especially prior to 1965) and have tended to sacrifice the former as a result. Despite this, financial targets have remained important to the planners because they serve to enhance the planners' control over enterprise operations. In the Soviet terminology, this is called *ruble control (kontrol' rublem)*, a system that works as follows: because the financial plan is the monetary counterpart of the firm's input and output plans, deviations from the financial plan should signal deviations from the physical plan. If a firm's labor input plan calls for the employment of 500 workers, the enterprise can draw only enough cash from its bank account to pay that number. If the input plan calls for ten tons of steel, the enterprise can draw upon its funded input account only enough for that particular transaction, nothing in excess. If the firm is in need of working capital, short-term credit will be granted only if the transaction is called for in the plan. Reinforcing the system of ruble control is the fact that all (legal) interfirm transactions are handled by *Gosbank* (the State Bank), which supervises all such transactions and is the sole center for the settling of accounts.

The Soviet manager, in response to this system of financial supervision, has developed informal sources of supply that do not require bank clearing operations, and other informal devices to circumvent many financial controls. Also, successful firms are often not strictly held to their financial plans. Financial controls are used primarily to detect significant deviations from planned activities, and desired corrections are normally made administratively. Despite the flexibility of and circumventions of financial controls, ruble control remains an important monitoring device in the Soviet planning system.

PUBLIC FINANCE AND
FINANCIAL PLANNING
IN THE SOVIET UNION

The major allocation decisions in the Soviet Union are reflected in the annual budget of the USSR, which determines the allocation of total output by end use among private consumption, investment, public consumption, defense, and administration. The annual budget of the USSR is a consolidated budget, which encompasses the all-union budget, the state budgets of the republics, and the local budgets of provinces, regions, and districts.[31] It is a much more comprehensive system of accounts than the budget of the United States, which encompasses only federal receipts and expenditures.

As one might expect, a much larger portion of the Soviet GNP flows through its state budget than is the case with the American GNP. Between 1929 and the present, 10 to 20 percent of American GNP has been channeled through government budgets (including state and local government). In the Soviet Union, the cumulative average for the postwar period has been about 45 percent.[32] The relatively greater importance of the state budget in the Soviet economy derives from the financing of most investment directly from the state budget and because communal consumption

[31] M. V. Condoide, *The Soviet Financial System* (Columbus: Bureau of Business Research of Ohio State University, 1951), pp. 78–79.
[32] Abraham Becker, *Soviet National Income, 1958–1964* (Berkeley: University of California Press, 1969), pp. 92–93. The measure used in both cases is the ratio of expenditures (plus budget surplus) to GNP.

(public health, education, and welfare) represents a larger share of total consumption in the Soviet Union. Thus the scope of *public* goods is broader in the USSR than in the United States. In a sense, one could argue that all products produced by the Soviet economy are public because they are produced by state or collective enterprises with land and capital provided by the state. However, in dealing with the Soviet economy, a convention is normally observed that if the enterprise operates independently of the state budget on its own accounting system, it is not considered as a public enterprise.

The budget of the USSR directs resources into consumption, investment, defense, and administration in the following manner: The state collects revenues from sales taxes (the so-called turnover tax), deductions from enterprise profits, direct taxes on the population, and from social insurance contributions (Table 13). The first two alone have consistently accounted for over 65 percent of total revenues throughout most of the plan period. These revenues are then directed through the national budget, the republican budgets, and through provincial and local budgets to various

Table 13 **The Budget of the USSR, 1931–1970 (selected years)**

	Receipts (percent of total)						
	1931	1934	1937	1940	1950	1960	1970
Turnover tax	46	64	69	59	56	41	32
Deductions from profits	8	5	9	12	10	24	35
Social insurance	9	10	6	5	5	5	5
Taxes on population	4	7	4	5	9	7	8
Other revenue	33	14	12	19	20	23	20
	Expenditures (percent of total)						
National economy	64	56	41	33	38	47	48
Social and cultural undertakings	14	15	24	24	28	34	36
Defense	5	9	17	33	20	13	12
Administration and justice	4	4	4	4	3	2	1
Other expenditures	13	16	14	6	11	4	3

SOURCES: *Narodnoe khoziaistvo SSSR v 1970 g.* [The national economy of the USSR in 1970], p. 731; M. V. Condoide, *The Soviet Financial System* (Columbus: Bureau of Business Research of Ohio State University, 1951), pp. 84–87.

uses: to finance investment in the form of grants, which at various times has accounted for between 33 percent and 64 percent of total expenditures (the "National economy" category in Table 13); to finance communal consumption (called "social and cultural undertakings"), which has accounted for from 14 to 36 percent of the total; and to finance defense and administration.

Once the overall allocation of budget resources into nonprivate consumption uses (investment, communal consumption, defense, and administration) is made and the physical outputs of consumer goods are specified by *Gosplan,* financial authorities (the State Bank and the Ministry of Finance) must insure that a macro-equilibrium of supply and demand exists.

The objective of Soviet financial planning at the macro level is to balance the aggregate money demand for consumer goods with the aggregate supply at established prices. This is done centrally, because planning authorities must insure the compatibility of the output of consumer goods at established prices with employment levels and wage rates. The smaller the planned output of consumer goods and the larger the number employed and the higher the wages, the more likely that aggregate money demand will exceed available supply at established prices.

A simple algebraic example illustrates this relationship.[33] Assume that the output plan calls for enterprises to produce Q_1 "units" of consumer goods and Q_2 "units" of producer goods. The planners determine through the use of labor input coefficients that L_1 man-years of labor are required to produce Q_1 and L_2 man-years are required to produce Q_2, and these employment levels are accordingly targeted by *Gosplan*. These workers are paid the prevailing wage rates in the consumer and producer goods sectors, respectively, and average annual wages are denoted in the two sectors as W_1 and W_2 respectively. In this manner, an annual wage income of $W_1L_1 + W_2L_2$ is created (we consider only wage income and ignore the income earned by collective farmers and others).

The total demand for consumer goods, therefore, is that portion of total wage income that is not taxed away or saved. If personal

[33] This algebraic approach is a modification of the model used by Howard Sherman, *The Soviet Economy* (Boston: Little, Brown, 1969), chap. 10, appendix A.

taxes are denoted by T and personal savings by R, the total money demand (D) for consumer goods is:

$$D = W_1L_1 + W_2L_2 - T - R$$

The total supply of consumer goods at established prices (S) is total value of all consumer goods (denoted as P_1Q_1):

$$S = P_1Q_1$$

where P_1 denotes the existing consumer price level.

The task of the financial authorities is to strike an appropriate balance between consumer demand and supply at prevailing prices, that is, between $W_1L_1 + W_2L_2 - T - R$ and P_1Q_1.

Financial Planning During the 1930s. We illustrate the various balancing techniques used by Soviet planners by reviewing their handling of the inflationary pressures of the 1930s. The setting was as follows: The industrialization drive of the early 1930s had created severe inflationary pressures on both the supply and demand sides of the consumer market. On the supply side, the structure of the economy had shifted drastically during this period in favor of producer goods and away from consumer goods, and the output of consumer goods had declined in real terms.[34] At the same time, Soviet planners were practicing "overfull" employment planning by confronting enterprises with output goals that were obviously unattainable with the targeted enterprise labor force. This forced enterprise managers to compete vigorously among themselves for labor, and average wages were bid up in the process. Although wage rates were centrally determined, managers could still offer higher wages by upward reclassification of workers and by setting low piece rate norms. During the First Five Year Plan, for example, average annual industrial wages were initially planned to increase from 690 rubles to 934 rubles (an already substantial increase). In fact, they rose to 1427 rubles. For the 1928 to 1937 period as a whole, average industrial wages rose at an annual rate of 17.7 percent.

---

[34] Per capita real consumption (not including communal services) declined at an annual rate of $-.3$ percent between 1928 and 1937. Janet Chapman, "Consumption," in Abram Bergson and Simon Kuznets, eds., *Economic Trends in the Soviet Union* (Cambrbidge, Mass.: Harvard University Press, 1963), pp. 238–239.

This wage inflation exerted upward pressure on industrial whole-sale prices and was a major factor in forcing up retail prices to an index of 200 (1928 = 100) in 1933 and 700 in 1937.[35]

The rising industrial wages were only one inflationary force driving up the demand for consumer goods. Labor was also being drawn at rapid rates out of agriculture into higher paying industrial jobs thereby raising average wages for the entire economy as well—a further inflationary factor on the demand side.[36] A further complication was the rapid expansion of the full-time labor force mainly due to the rising participation rates of women and to the de-cline in part-time agricultural employment. Thus while the supply of consumer goods was declining and producer goods prices were rising, both average wages and employment were rising, generating substantial increases in money incomes. An indication of the scope of the rise in money wages was the increase in currency in cir-culation (used almost exclusively for wage payments) from 3 bil-lion rubles in 1930 to about 16 billion rubles in 1940.[37] The infla-tionary implications of these trends are obvious.

As the algebraic example shows, several methods could have been used to deal with the growing inflationary problem.[38] One ob-vious approach would have been a wage freeze (the Ws in the equation) enforced by strict limitations on the amount of cash that an enterprise could draw for wage payments. On the other hand, a system of flexible wages was required to attract labor into high priority sectors and to maintain incentives. The above cited figures on industrial wage increases during the 1930s show clearly that this approach was not followed, for these very reasons. A second ap-proach would have been to increase personal taxes (T) thereby re-ducing personal disposable income, but high tax rates also would have reduced labor incentives and retarded industrialization. How-ever, increasing taxes would not have stopped the Soviet inflation of the 1930s since it largely originated in the labor market through

[35] Franklyn Holzman, "Soviet Inflationary Pressures, 1928–1957," *Quarterly Journal of Economics,* vol. 74, no. 2 (May 1960), 177.
[36] *Ibid.,* 176.
[37] *Ibid.,* 180.
[38] For a detailed discussion of the alternative methods of financing Soviet economic development, see Franklyn Holzman, "Financing Soviet Economic Development," in Moses Abramovitz, ed., *Capital Formation and Economic Growth* (Princeton: Princeton University Press, 1955), pp. 229–287.

excessive expenditures of managers. The increased taxes could at best merely mop up the excess purchasing power after it had already done its damage. A further complication was that inflationary pressures were so great during the early 1930s that extremely high tax rates (perhaps as high as 60 percent of personal income) would have been required, and such high rates would have had a demoralizing impact on work incentives.

A third alternative would have been to encourage personal savings (R)—a difficult feat during a period of rapid inflation. The Soviets did make government bond purchases compulsory (as automatic payroll deductions) between 1930 and 1957—a policy which did create some resentment and tended to reduce work incentives. The Soviets also established a network of savings banks to encourage voluntary savings, but it proved difficult to persuade people to save during the inflationary 1930s.[39]

Inflation and Rationing During the 1930s. A fourth method for balancing supply and demand was to raise consumer retail prices (P_1) to soak up the excess consumer demand, and this is exactly what the Soviets did in large measure. The *turnover tax* was the formal device used: The turnover tax was a differentiated sales tax levied primarily on consumer products and will be discussed in detail in the following section on prices. This tax was the difference (after wholesale and retail trade margins) between the average cost of production (plus a planned profit margin) and the retail sales price. As the state determined retail prices, excess demand for a commodity could be eliminated quite simply by raising the turnover tax and hence the retail price. The extent to which this method was used can be seen from the much more rapid increase of retail prices between 1928 and 1937 than average costs of production, as measured by material costs (wholesale prices of industrial commodities) and wage costs. For example, wholesale prices of basic industrial commodities increased 75 percent. Average industrial wages increased 430 percent, but retail prices of consumer goods rose 700 percent between 1928 and 1937. These differential rates illustrate the increasing role of the turnover tax, which averaged 22 percent of the retail price in 1928–1929 and 64 percent in 1935.[40] For example, in 1934 the state sold rye for 84

[39] *Ibid.*, pp. 230–238.
[40] Holzman, "Soviet Inflationary Pressures," *op. cit.*, 168, 173.

rubles per centner, of which 66 rubles was turnover tax, and wheat for 104 rubles per centner, of which 89 rubles were turnover tax.[41]

Thus inflation via increased indirect taxation was used to soak up excess consumer demand during the 1930s. A prominent authority on Soviet taxation, Franklyn Holzman, postulates that Soviet tax authorities preferred indirect commodity taxes (the turnover tax) over direct income taxes because the former would have less of a disincentive effect on workers. It was hoped that industrial workers would pay more attention to increases in their money wages than to the reduction in their real wages resulting as retail prices rose faster than money wages (the so-called money illusion) and that incentives would be maintained. In addition, the turnover tax was administratively easier to collect and administer than direct taxation in a populous, semi-literate agricultural country.[42] To this day, the turnover tax remains an important source of government revenue in the Soviet Union.

The final balancing method employed heavily by the Soviets in the 1930s was *repressed inflation*. What this means is that Soviet authorities simply allowed some of the excess consumer demand to persist. Despite rapidly rising retail prices during the 1930s, consumer demand still exceeded supply with the possible exception of 1937, which was a good crop year with relatively abundant food supplies for purchase. Soviet authorities were therefore called upon to ration consumer goods either formally or indirectly during most of the 1930s. Such rationing proved necessary because Soviet financial authorities found it difficult to keep prices high enough to eliminate inflationary pressures in the face of the numerous unplanned wage increases and shortfalls in plan fulfillment in the consumer sector.

Rationing of essential consumer goods was introduced in the winter of 1928–1929, first on foodstuffs and then on manufactured consumer goods. To maintain labor incentives, to preserve the effectiveness of wage differentials, and to reward special groups, Soviet pricing authorities sanctioned a complex system of multiple prices during the early 1930s. They consisted of: (a) retail prices of ra-

[41] Alec Nove, *An Economic History of the USSR* (London: Penguin, 1969), p. 210.
[42] Holzman, "Financing Soviet Economic Development," *op. cit.*, pp. 231–237.

tioned goods sold in state and cooperative stores ("normal-fund" prices), (b) the so-called prices of the "commercial fund" which were higher than the "normal fund" prices (yet even these were often available only in "closed shops" open only to special groups), (c) *Torgsin* shop prices of items which could only be bought with precious metals and foreign currency, (d) free market prices (primarily on the collective farm markets), and (e) several other prices including inflated black market prices.[43] The collective farm markets where peasants could sell their private produce were especially useful in siphoning off the excess purchasing power of industrial workers and in preserving industrial incentives, for extra earned income could be used to buy scarce food products in these markets.

While prices in state and cooperative stores doubled between 1928 and 1932, collective farm market prices, the only free market prices in the Soviet Union, rose 30 times, a clear indication of the extent of repressed inflation during this period. After 1932, this differential was reduced and nearly closed in 1937 but was opened again by the outbreak of World War II. Because of the complex multiple price system, it is difficult to gauge trends in the general price level during the 1930s. What is known for sure, however, is that retail prices rose substantially but not by enough to eliminate the excess consumer demand entirely as is witnessed by the long queues and the multiple prices of the 1930s.

The Soviets' use of inflation during the industrialization drive of the 1930s provides a case study of how inflation can be used to allocate resources out of consumer goods into investment goods while seeking to preserve industrial incentives. We shall return to the Soviet inflation model in our discussion of the relevance of the Soviet development model to other developing economies (Part Four).

Financial Planning
in the Postwar Period

Inflationary pressures have been much less severe in the Soviet Union throughout the postwar period. The most visible sign of this has been the relative stability of retail prices since 1950. In fact,

[43] Nove, *An Economic History of the USSR, op. cit.,* pp. 203–207.

retail prices in state and cooperative stores were lower in 1970 than in 1950, according to official price indices,[44] which is noteworthy in view of the upward revisions of wholesale prices in 1966. Thus the stability of retail prices has occurred largely at the expense of the turnover tax, which now averages about 23 percent of the retail price (from a high of over 60 percent during the 1930s).[45] The stability of retail prices since 1950, however, conceals a degree of repressed inflation that persists to the present day. This was especially true of the early 1950s when queues in front of most shops were the order of the day. Nevertheless, the inflationary pressures of even the early 1950s were slight relative to the 1930s.

Soviet financial authorities have been better able to control inflation during the postwar period for two reasons. First, the supply of consumer goods has been increased markedly, especially between 1953 and 1958,[46] thus alleviating one of the sources of inflationary pressure. The per capita availabilities of consumer goods have roughly kept pace with wage increases throughout the postwar period.[47] Second, wage inflation, which was the major source of inflation during the 1930s, has been better controlled by *Gosbank's* stricter management of wage payments in excess of the planned allotment for an enterprise, and by a decreased emphasis on overfull employment planning. As a result, average wage increases in industry have been kept close to an annual rate of 3 percent between 1950 and 1968 as compared with the 18 percent rate of the 1928 to 1937 period.[48] This rate has generally not exceeded increases in labor productivity.

Nevertheless, some repressed inflationary pressures persist. One cause of this is the state's policy of holding down prices of im-

---

[44] *Narodnoe khoziastvo SSSR v 1970 g.* [The national economy of the USSR in 1970], p. 601.

[45] *Ibid.,* p. 178.

[46] Janet Chapman, "Consumption," in A. Bergson and S. Kuznets, eds., *Economic Trends in the Soviet Union* (Cambridge, Mass.: Harvard University Press, 1963), pp. 238–239; David W. Bronson and Barbara Severin, "Consumer Welfare," in Joint Economic Committee, *Economic Performance and the Military Burden in the Soviet Union* (Washington, D.C.: U.S. Government Printing Office, 1970), p. 97.

[47] Bronson and Severin, *op. cit.,* p. 99.

[48] Holzman, "Soviet Inflationary Pressures," *op. cit.,* 168; Murray Feshbach and Stephen Rapawy, "Labor and Wages," in *Economic Performance and the Military Burden in the Soviet Union, op. cit.,* pp. 82–83.

portant foodstuffs such as meat and dairy products, which has led to some excess demand for these products. Thus the Soviet consumer in 1972 paid, on the average, 60 percent more for food products in collective farm markets than in state and cooperative stores—down from 75 percent in 1955 but up from 35 percent in 1960—figures that indicate the state's failure to absorb the excess purchasing power for food products.[49] Also the limited supplies of certain consumer durables such as automobiles have often led to waiting lists and informal rationing. In recent years, the Soviet population has tended to accumulate large savings deposits for purchasing scarce consumer durables, which has made financial planning difficult as pent-up purchasing power accumulates. To some extent, the degree of repressed inflation can be gauged by the frequent wide fluctuations in the marginal propensity to save. In 1969, for example, 67 percent of the annual increase in disposable income was deposited in state savings banks—whereas only one year before it was much lower—but still high at 39 percent.[50] In 1966–1968, savings bank deposits rose by 14 billion rubles, whereas between 1961 and 1963, they rose by only 3 billion rubles.[51]

Although Soviet authorities prefer to interpret these large increases in savings deposits as evidence of a rising standard of living (such statistics are found in the "growth of material welfare" sections of Soviet statistical compilations), this may be only partly true. First-hand accounts (possibly biased) stress that the Soviet consumer of today is now familiar with higher-quality imports and simply refuses to purchase inferior domestic products. This results in an over-production of low-quality domestic goods and a shortage of high-quality goods, the latter being sold often under the counter. While the Soviet consumer waits for the opportunity to purchase high-quality goods, his savings grow.[52]

[49] David Bronson and Barbara Severin, "Soviet Consumer Welfare: The Brezhnev Era," in *Soviet Economic Prospects for the Seventies, op. cit.,* p. 381.
[50] Bronson and Severin, "Consumer Welfare," *op. cit.,* p. 99.
[51] *Narodnoe khoziastvo SSSR v 1970 g.* [The national economy of the USSR in 1970], p. 563.
[52] Anonymous, "The Soviet Economy Today," *Radio Liberty Dispatch* (September 28, 1972), p. 2; Zev Katz, "Insights from Emigres and Sociological Studies in the Soviet Union," in *Soviet Economic Prospects for the Seventies, op. cit.,* pp. 91–93.

THE SOVIET
BANKING SYSTEM

The Soviet banking system plays an integral role in the planning process. Soviet banking is quite unlike its Western counterpart, for it is dominated by a single bank, *Gosbank* (the State Bank), which is a monopoly bank in its purest form. As a monopoly bank, *Gosbank* combines the functions of central and commercial banking, but owing to the absence of money and capital markets, some traditional banking functions (open market operations, commercial paper transactions, etc.) are not performed by *Gosbank*.

The tremendous scope of *Gosbank's* organization is difficult to conceptualize: it has more than 150,000 employees and more than 300 main offices, about 3,500 local branches, and 2,000 collection offices. *Gosbank's* customers include approximately 250,000 enterprises, 40,000 collective farm accounts, and nearly one-half million government organizations. Since 1954, *Gosbank* has been independent of the Ministry of Finance, and its director has ministerial status in the government. Since 1963, the savings bank system (with over 70,000 branches) has been incorporated into *Gosbank*'s operations. The only other banks in the Soviet Union are the specialized banks—the Investment Bank (*Stroibank*) and the Foreign Trade Bank (*Vneshtorgbank*). The former is concerned with the disbursing of funds budgeted for capital investment, and the latter handles international transactions; neither competes with *Gosbank*.[53]

Throughout its history, *Gosbank* has had two primary functions: First, to make short-term loans for the working capital needs of enterprises. In the process it creates money (it is the only money-creating institution in the Soviet Union) by creating cash for consumers and workers as firms draw on cash accounts for wage payments and noncash accounts for interenterprise transactions. Its second purpose is to oversee enterprise plan fulfillment and to mon-

---

[53] George Garvy, *Money, Banking, and Credit in Eastern Europe* (New York: Federal Reserve Bank of New York, 1966); Paul Gekker, "The Banking System of the USSR," *Journal of the Institute of Bankers*, vol. 84, part 3, (June 1963), 189–197; Condoide, *op. cit.*, chap. 2. Prior to 1959 there were other specialized banks such as the *Sel'khozbank*, which served agriculture.

itor payments to the population by acting as the center of all accounts in the Soviet Union. Let us now consider how these two
objectives are pursued.

Each Soviet enterprise deals directly with a local *Gosbank*
branch. It is dependent upon *Gosbank* for short-term credit to
finance inventories and working capital. Its receipts are automatically deposited at *Gosbank* and it draws cash for wage payments
at the discretion of the branch bank. In addition, the portion of its
own profits that the enterprise is allowed to retain (a factor that has
increased in importance since the 1965 reforms) remains on deposit at, and under the supervision of, *Gosbank*. *Gosbank* is the sole
legal grantor of short-term credit. Interfirm credit is forbidden, and
a strict discipline on payments is enforced in interfirm transactions
to prevent spontaneous interfirm lending. In addition, all transactions between firms involving funds in enterprise accounts are
handled by, and are subject to, the supervision of *Gosbank* (with
the exception of small payments).

As far as the control function of *Gosbank* is concerned, its supervision of enterprise accounts and its short-term lending operations are important. As the single clearing agent for the economy
and the sole source of short-term credit, *Gosbank* is in a unique
position to monitor the activities of enterprises. In drawing up
short-term credit plans and in controlling enterprise accounts, *Gosbank* plays a largely passive role in the planning process by providing the monetary resources required to implement the physical
plan. In making short-term loans for working capital, *Gosbank* has
tended to grant production credit for specific purposes: if a particular transaction is called for in the input plan, the firm is automatically granted credit for this specific purpose. Not only is credit
granted for specific purposes, but all interfirm transactions are
cleared by *Gosbank,* and *Gosbank* must receive evidence of the
transaction such as a lading bill before the clearing operation is
completed.[54] In this way, as the enterprise financial plan is the
monetary counterpart of the physical plan, deviations from the
physical plan will reveal themselves as deviations from the financial
plan. This is a further extension of *ruble control.* Even if an enter-

---

[54] Recent reforms have resulted in the granting of credit for more general
purposes rather than restricting the use of credit for very specific purposes.

prise builds up excess balances at *Gosbank,* this liquidity still does not represent a command over producer goods unless they are specifically called for in the plan.[55]

As the social accounting center monitoring cash payments to the population, *Gosbank* plays a role in the macroeconomic planning described above. It provides financial authorities with data on disposable income—information that is vital in macroplanning. In case of a projected imbalance, *Gosbank* will act to limit the flow of wage payments to the population as much as possible within the limits of the plan. This is accomplished primarily by restricting the convertibility of enterprise accounts into cash for wage payments, and by permitting wage payments in excess of the planned wage bill only if the output target is overfulfilled.

The monopoly powers of *Gosbank* are seldom used to influence the flow of production. Instead, *Gosbank*'s audit operations serve primarily to reveal to planning authorities deviations from planned tasks, which are then corrected by the planners. Throughout its history, *Gosbank* has tended to automatically meet the credit needs of the economy (as specified in the plan) instead of regulating the flow of money and credit on a discretionary basis to direct the level of economic activity. Recent reforms (1965) have changed *Gosbank*'s credit operations somewhat, and this development will be discussed in Chapter Ten.

THE SOVIET PRICE SYSTEM

In our discussion of Soviet central planning, it was noted that the planning hierarchy is responsible for the allocation and distribution of resources in the Soviet Union. One may be rightly puzzled over the role that prices play insofar as they, not central planners, carry the primary allocative responsibilities in market economies.

At this juncture, a warning set forth in the Introduction is worth restating: namely, one must avoid comparing the ideal form of one economic system with the real-world form of another. This is especially true of prices, where the tendency is to contrast price for-

---

[55] Garvy, *op. cit.,* pp. 122–136.

mation in an abstract, competitive market system with the realities of price formation in the Soviet Union—a temptation we shall try to avoid.

In this section, we consider the Soviet price system. First, the actual Soviet system of industrial wholesale, retail, and agricultural price setting is discussed. Second, the role that prices are supposed to play in the Soviet economic system—allocation, control, measurement, and income distribution—are considered. Last, we provide an evaluation of the Soviet price system.

Price Setting in
the Soviet Union

Most prices in the Soviet Union are fixed by central authorities, rather than by the interaction of supply and demand. Price setting responsibilities have at various times been shared by the Price Bureau of *Gosplan USSR*, the Ministry of Trade, the Ministry of Finance, the Union-Republican Councils of Ministers and various republican and *oblast'* authorities.[56] The only important prices established by the forces of supply and demand have been the collective farm market prices. It is useful to discuss price setting in the Soviet Union in terms of four different types of prices, for the principles observed in each case are quite different: (1) industrial wholesale prices, (2) retail prices, (3) agricultural procurement prices, and (4) collective farm market prices.[57]

1. *Industrial Wholesale Prices.* Industrial wholesale prices perform less of an allocative function than other Soviet prices. Contrary to retail price setting, where an attempt is generally made to set market-clearing prices, industrial wholesale prices tend to serve primarily as accounting prices used to add together heterogeneous inputs and outputs. That industrial wholesale prices play no real al-

[56] Philip Hanson, *The Consumer Sector in the Soviet Economy* (Evanston, Ill.: Northwestern University Press, 1968), pp. 175–176.

[57] For general treatments of Soviet pricing policies, the reader is referred to the following sources: Morris Bornstein, "Soviet Price Theory and Policy," *New Directions in the Soviet Economy,* part I, reprinted in Bornstein and Fusfeld, 3rd ed., *op. cit.,* pp. 106–137; Hanson, *op. cit.,* chap. 8; Morris Bornstein, "The Soviet Price Reform Discussion," *Quarterly Journal of Economics,* vol. 78, no. 1 (February 1964), 15–48; Bergson, *op. cit.,* chap. 8; Morris Bornstein, "The Soviet Debate on Agricultural Prices and Procurement Reforms," *Soviet Studies,* vol. 21, no. 1 (July 1969), 1–20.

locative role should come as no surprise in view of our earlier discussion of industrial supply planning.

At the wholesale level, there are two important types of prices. First, the *factory wholesale price* is the price at which the industrial enterprise sells its product to the wholesale trade network. Second, the *industry wholesale price* is the price at which goods are sold to buyers outside the industry. In the latter case, a turnover tax will likely be included (on the average about 5 percent of the industry wholesale price in heavy industry)[58] whereas in the former case, there is with only rare exceptions no turnover tax. Although the rules of price setting have changed somewhat over time—generally speaking, this function has tended to remain centralized. Thus agencies in the planning hierarchy establish wholesale prices on the basis of *average branch cost* of production plus a small profit markup (generally 5–10 percent). Included in enterprise costs are wage payments, costs of intermediate materials, depreciation, insurance, and payments to overhead. Interest and rental charges are not normally included in costs, and depreciation charges do not include charges for obsolescence. While market prices in a competitive market system tend toward marginal costs, they are, in the Soviet case, average cost prices. Using average branch costs means that many enterprises will in fact make losses at the established prices because the cost figures are averages of low and high cost producers, and historically such has been the case. The consequences of such losses in the Soviet system have generally been minimal.

During the early years of planning, the prices of important industrial inputs were purposely kept low, and many industrial enterprises were operated under state subsidies. Since enterprise survival is not based on profits or losses as in a market system, such losses are of little particular importance since subsidies are granted almost automatically to enterprises to cover operating losses. In these cases, minimization of losses (which might be a short-run objective for a capitalist firm) becomes a long-run criterion of operation and price setting in the Soviet Union.

In the context of recent reform discussions about the role of

[58] Bornstein, "Soviet Price Theory and Policy," *op. cit.,* p. 110; *Narodnoe khoziaistvo SSSR v 1969 g.* [The national economy of the USSR in 1969], *op. cit.,* p. 191.

profits in the Soviet Union, the important point is this: profit calculations have always existed in the Soviet schema; they simply have not been an important criterion of enterprise performance—at least not until 1965—and the presence or absence of profits has not, therefore, been the basis for action by Soviet planning authorities. Of course, a fundamental reason for this is the inability of pricing authorities to establish "fair" prices under which the level of profits serves as a true indication of enterprise performance.[59]

In some cases, especially the extractive industries in which marked cost variations among producers occur, so-called accounting prices have been used where, in effect, producers receive different prices (depending upon cost differences) while all buyers pay the same price, with the state providing the intermediate cushion. Thus, the low-cost producers are in effect paying a differential rent to the state.

In rare cases, attempts have been made by pricing authorities to adjust prices of close substitutes for differences in "use value," the most notable cases being the pricing of fuel oil and coal, and nonferrous metals and ferrous metals. In both instances, it was determined that the "use values" of fuel oil and nonferrous metals were higher than that of coal and ferrous metals, respectively, therefore prices in excess of average branch costs were set for fuel oil and nonferrous metals (the difference between average branch costs and the wholesale prices being the turnover tax). Nevertheless, such instances are rare because generally it is difficult to distinguish among industrial commodities according to their "use values."

A further problem of industrial price setting is that, owing to the administrative complexities of price reform, industrial prices have seldom conformed to average branch costs. It has proven too difficult to change prices regularly along with costs. Instead, industrial prices have tended to remain rigid over long periods. As a result, general subsidies have often been required as the wholesale prices of many commodities gradually fell below rising costs. Indus-

---

[59] The 1965 reforms attempted to enhance the role of profits (Chapter 10) as an indicator of enterprise performance. But it has proven especially difficult to convert those enterprises making planned losses to the new system, primarily food processing enterprises, because they cannot operate without automatic subsidies. Hanson, *op. cit.,* p. 177.

trial wholesale prices remained roughly constant between 1929 and 1936, despite rapidly rising wage costs, and by 1936 subsidies were the rule rather than the exception. A price reform in spring of 1936 sharply increased prices to cover costs, while in 1949 another large general price increase was required to eliminate subsidies. Despite the general rule that prices should cover costs, industrial prices remained virtually unchanged from the 1955 price reform to the 1966–1967 price reform despite changing wage costs and changing technology.[60]

2. *Retail Prices.* At the retail level, prices are also formed by state planning authorities. They are basically designed to *clear the market* (to equate supply and demand), although this standard is often not met. This basic policy is in line with the Soviet policy of market distribution of consumer goods to preserve the incentive to work: for wage differentials to be meaningful, it is essential that they represent a differential command over consumer goods. In reality, retail prices have often tended to be somewhat below market clearing levels, and thus queues have often served in part as a rationing device.

The retail price is simply the industry wholesale price plus the retail margin (and costs, where additions to the product are generated at the retail level), plus the turnover tax. Unlike Western sales taxes where the consumer is generally aware of the tax rate he is paying, the Soviet turnover tax is included in the retail price without the purchaser knowing how large it is. The level of the tax is a function of supply and demand conditions in the given market and of the prevailing industry wholesale price. Where the price without turnover tax is below the market clearing level, a tax sufficient to raise the retail price to the clearing level is added. In Figure 4 below, if the industry wholesale price is OP and the resulting equilibrium price OP', the turnover tax will be PP' (or slightly below if the price is set below clearing levels).[61] Thus

---

[60] Abram Bergson, Roman Bernaut, Lynn Turgeon, "Basic Industrial Prices in the USSR, 1928–1950," The Rand Corporation, Research Memorandum RM-1522, August 1, 1955; *Narodnoe khoziastvo SSSR v 1969 g.* [The national economy of the USSR in 1969], *op. cit.,* p. 190.

[61] The supply schedule in Figure 4 is drawn to be perfectly inelastic. This is done under the assumption that the quantity of output is determined by the state plan, irrespective of price. This would apply largely to enterprises

the level of taxation is price determined rather than price determining.

At this point, the reader might well ask, what happens if the industry wholesale price is greater than *OP'*? Obviously in such a case there will be no turnover tax, and unless there is a subsidy that permits the setting of the retail price *below* the industry wholesale price, surplus unsold stocks will result. Two comments are in order. First, throughout much of the plan period, a sellers' market has prevailed—obviating the subsidy problem at the retail level. Second, the matter of unsold stocks is more fundamental than simply a question of price setting. In particular, as economic development proceeds and greater attention is given to consumer goods in the Soviet Union, one would expect the sellers' market to subside. Indeed such has been the case to a limited degree, for example, in the clothing industry and more recently even in the consumer durables area.[62] In these cases, there have been unsold stocks in recent years, unlike the old sellers' market where producers could be unresponsive to consumers without losing sales. Thus the current problem is a combination of matching output to consumer tastes and setting appropriate prices. In recent years, the simultaneous existence of surpluses of some commodities and shortages of others has demonstrated the magnitude of this structural problem. There are also financial implications involved: if stocks are unsold, the state is not able to collect the turnover tax—an important source of revenue. A fundamental problem of economic reform revolves around this question: When the sellers' market subsides, how can

---

producing a single homogeneous product. For a multiproduct firm attempting to fulfill a gross output target, the supply schedule would likely be less than perfectly inelastic, that is, would have a positive slope.

[62] For example, sales of clothing and leather footwear grew at an annual rate of around 8 percent between 1968 and 1971. During the same period, clothing and footwear stocks grew at an annual rate of around 19 percent largely because the types of goods produced failed to correspond to the wishes of the consumer. *Planovoe khoziastvo* [The planned economy], no. 10 (1972), pp. 5–7. This growing selectivity also applies to consumer durables. For example, the "Baku" refrigerator proved to be of such low quality that Azerbaijan SSR consumers refused to buy it. The quick-witted manager in charge of its production then changed the name and appearance and released it as a new model. For an account of this, see *Sotsialisticheskaia industria* [Socialist industry] no. 14, 1969, p. 2.

Figure 4 **The Soviet Turnover Tax**

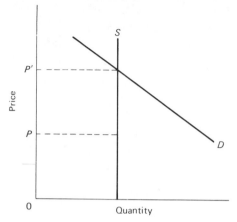

producers be made responsive to the consumer if the price system fails to provide effective information concerning consumer wants? What was not so much a problem in the past may well be an increasing problem in the future.

If retail prices are to serve as mechanisms to transmit consumer preferences to producers, fundamental changes will be necessary. In this regard, the current two-tiered price system shown in Figure 4 is an obstacle. Because retail prices are essentially demand determined and factory wholesale prices are cost determined, it may happen that *relative* retail prices diverge significantly from *relative* factory wholesale prices. Yet the producer will be more responsive to the relative wholesale prices which he receives rather than to the retail prices paid by consumers, which reflect consumer preferences. Thus, the signal sent by the consumer in the form of a market-clearing retail price is not received by the producer, who is paid a different factory wholesale price. For some products, the two-tiered system is being gradually and automatically eliminated—namely, in food processing and in clothing and textiles. Their retail prices have been held roughly constant in recent years whereas their factory wholesale prices have risen along with rising wage and material costs, thus squeezing out the turnover tax.[63]

[63] Hanson, *op. cit.,* p. 177.

Although there has been a continuing effort to vary prices on a zonal basis and to change them over time, this sort of variability has been highly restricted given the magnitude of the administrative task involved. One can expect this problem to become more difficult in the future as the economy grows more complex and the product range widens. Finally, it might be noted that the level of turnover tax (as one would expect) has varied widely among products and is as high as 80 percent of price on some products. The average light industry turnover tax (1970) was 23 percent of wholesale price.[64] As we have seen, the revenue from this tax accounts for a substantial portion of state budgetary revenues, and therefore remains an important consideration in both financial planning and price setting.

3. *Agricultural Procurement Prices.* Turning finally to agricultural pricing, we note that until 1958 (and again after 1965 for grain), there existed a two-level pricing system for state purchases of agricultural products from collective farms. For compulsory deliveries, a low fixed price was paid, while for sales to the state above the compulsory level, a higher fixed price was established. Unlike pricing in the industrial sector, these prices until recently bore little relation to the production costs of the collective farm. There was no cost accounting whatsoever on collective farms until the mid-1950s, at which time initial cost studies revealed that for most collective farms, production costs were substantially above even the above-quota prices. In this manner, state pricing policy was placing the collective farms in a most difficult financial position by purchasing output at less than cost. At the same time, the state farms operating essentially as industrial enterprises were receiving subsidies from the state to compensate them for the low procurement prices and were not financing their own capital investment as were the collective farms.

The two-level system was abandoned in 1958 and, although revived in 1965 for grain, the differential between the below- and above-quota grain prices has been small relative to earlier differentials. Most notably, however, throughout the 1950s and 1960s

[64] *Narodnoe khoziastvo SSSR v 1970 g.* [The national economy of the USSR in 1970], *op. cit.,* p. 178.

purchase prices have been raised substantially, so that, for many products, average purchase prices now cover production costs.[65] This latter development is in line with the agricultural policy of recent years, namely: that collective farm production should be "profitable" in the general sense of revenues covering costs. This policy remains in a state of active debate since the problem of agricultural land rental charges remains unresolved. Finally, there has been a preliminary effort to revise agricultural purchase prices not only in terms of their levels, but also their flexibility over time and regions.

4. *Collective Farm Market Prices.* The most significant example of a true market price in the Soviet economy is the collective farm market price. In these markets, the collective farmers sell their produce (from private plots and after meeting state targets) at prices determined by demand and supply. While these prices fluctuate, they have generally been substantially above the level of state food prices, a phenomenon explained in part by quality differentials and by the maintenance of state prices at artificially low (below equilibrium) levels. For example, collective farm market prices were, on the average, more than double state retail prices in 1940. After considerable variation throughout the postwar period, collective farm market prices were 63 percent greater than state retail prices in 1972.[66] The collective farm markets have been especially important in large cities where standard sources of supply, for example the state trade network, have been inadequate. How important are these markets? Although measurement is rather complex, collective farm markets accounted for 13.9 percent of aggregate food sales in 1960, and for 8.6 percent in 1968. However, for certain products, these markets are of much greater significance. In 1957, for example, when the aggregate collective farm market share of food sales was 18.2 percent, they accounted for 63 percent of potato sales, 48 percent of egg sales, and 35 percent of meat sales. In 1970, they accounted for 67 percent, 54 percent, and 35 percent, respectively, of sales of these products.[67]

[65] Thus a squeeze is put on food processing establishments, which are forced to make planned losses as the line is held on retail food prices.

[66] Bronson and Severin "Soviet Consumer Welfare," *op. cit.,* p. 381.

[67] Data from *Narodnoe khozastvo SSSR v 1968 g.* [The national economy of the USSR in 1968], p. 613; Jerzy F. Karcz, "Quantitative Analysis of the

The Functions of Soviet Prices

Our discussion of the Soviet price system suggests that Soviet prices are formed quite differently from their market economy counterparts. However, to evaluate Soviet prices we must consider them in the context of the various roles that prices are supposed to play in the Soviet command economy. To judge the Soviet price system exclusively as an instrument for allocating resources (as is sometimes done) would be a mistake, for Soviet authorities have generally not intended it to be used as such. Instead, industrial supply and output planning are supposed to allocate resources with prices playing other roles. Soviet prices can be considered in terms of four possible functions: (1) allocation, (2) control, (3) measurement, and (4) income distribution. A biased picture of Soviet prices would inevitably be drawn if one were to concentrate only on the first function.

1. *Allocation.* In any economic system, prices can reflect relative scarcities on the basis of which economic decisions are made. As any standard economics textbook will explain, the profit maximizing producer will employ inputs so as to equate marginal factor outlays and marginal revenue products. The utility maximizing consumer will purchase goods and services so as to equate marginal utilities per dollar, and so on. In this manner, supply and demand schedules arise, and prices that reflect *relative scarcities* are determined. Such an arrangement, under ideal conditions, will result in a maximum output produced at a minimum cost irrespective of the economic system and is, in this sense, optimal.[68] It is only necessary for the consumer and producer to be aware of relative prices to respond correctly in such a system; no planner is required to tell either how to behave.

Such price allocation is scarcely to be found in the real world either in planned or market economies; since imperfect competi-

---

Collective Farm Market," *American Economic Review,* vol. 54, no. 4, part I (June 1964), 315–333, see especially the discussion on page 315; *The Christian Science Monitor,* March 27, 1972, p. 6.

[68] See, for example, F. Bator, "The Simple Analytics of Welfare Maximization," *American Economic Review,* vol. 47, no. 1 (February 1957) 22–59. Of course, this definition of optimality (called Pareto Optimality) does not take the optimality of the distribution of income into consideration.

tion, price controls, public goods, government regulations, and so on prevail almost everywhere.

What we have in the real world is a mixture of price allocation and administrative allocation. In the United States, for example, resource allocation is accomplished primarily through the price mechanism, though not necessarily in the optimal manner described above. In the Soviet Union, administrative planning bears the primary responsibility for allocation, although prices do play a limited role. Thus, while both systems have scarce resources to be marshaled towards the achievement of given (although different) goals—for which the price system might be utilized—the fundamental difference is, first, the extent to which prices are utilized for these purposes and, second, the manner in which price formation is executed.

Soviet industrial wholesale prices, being centrally determined and based on the ideological definition of average branch costs, do not represent relative scarcities—as Soviet planners are well aware. This is one of the reasons why the administrative planning structure remains so much in charge of resource allocation and why there is so little price allocation in the Soviet Union. Like any generalization, there are exceptions. In the labor sector, differential wages are largely used to allocate labor. Also, retail prices are largely used to distribute *available* consumer goods among the population, although such prices generally play an unimportant role in the decision to produce such goods. The most striking feature of the Soviet economic system remains the minor role that prices play in the allocative process.

That Soviet prices generally fail to reflect relative scarcities is important despite their lack of use as allocative instruments, since Soviet prices do play other roles. This may sound rather abstract but it is important. The Soviets have chosen administrative allocation over price allocation. Yet it is difficult to administratively allocate resources on a day-to-day basis without knowing relative scarcities, and even more difficult to relegate decision making to lower echelons without scarcity prices. How to introduce a degree of price allocation into such a system and how to make the prices themselves more "rational" are recurrent themes in the reform discussions in the Soviet Union and Eastern Europe.

To determine what functions Soviet prices are designed to perform if not allocation, one must consider the control, measurement, and income distribution functions of prices in the Soviet Union.

2. *Control.* The control function of prices is perhaps the most important in the Soviet context. Even in a centralized economy, some delegation of authority and responsibility is required, ranging from the central planning agencies to the enterprises. This necessitates a mechanism for control of subordinates. In market economies, the profit mechanism and variants thereof can act as a control device as well as an allocative device. In the Soviet case, however, profits have played virtually no allocative role in the industrial enterprise (at least prior to 1965). However, many of the directives of higher planning authorities must be stated and verified in value terms, for example, rubles of steel output rather than tons. Thus the extensive use of value categories—the most famous being *valovaia produktsia* or *val* (enterprise gross production)—in Soviet planning means that prices have been used in a control function to evaluate and assess performance at all levels. However, value indicators have been largely used to indicate *deviations* from planned activities. Actual control has been carried out mainly through physical controls and directives.

3. *Measurement.* The measurement role of Soviet prices is also important and is similar to the control function in various aspects. Prices are required to measure the results of economic activity, especially if one's scope extends beyond individual products: the measurement of economic activity requires the aggregation of dissimilar products, and aggregation requires valuation. Without prices, one cannot determine at what rate the economy is growing, whether the capital-output ratio is rising or falling, and so on, and these are important variables in the planning process. For example, the total output of the economy ("gross material product" as the Soviets call it) must be valued to be measured, and in an important sense, the results of this measurement will depend upon the nature of the prices used. For example, the Soviets used 1926–1927 "constant" prices until the 1950s to measure Soviet total output. Over such a long period of time, these prices came to reflect less and less prevailing prices and costs, and eventually because of their questionable economic significance they were abandoned for a more up-to-date price base.

This illustration points out an important potential conflict among the various roles that a price system can play in the Soviet command economy, and this applies both to the control and measurement functions. Control and measurement are more easily carried out when prices are not changed frequently. However if prices remain unchanged, after awhile they will not reflect current cost relationships and therefore will be even less useful as a guide to allocation. Soviet authorities have been reluctant to change prices for two basic reasons. First, it is administratively difficult to gather the mass of wage and cost data required for a reform of prices. Second, it has proven a complex task to plan and evaluate when prices are in the process of change. In such a case, value targets must be stated in two variants—one for the old, the other for the new prices —and general confusion tends to reign until the new prices are firmly established.

4. *Distribution of Income.* Finally, Soviet prices play an important role in the distribution of income. In addition to the centrally determined wage scales that, of course, affect the distribution of income, pricing authorities can influence the distribution of real income through retail prices. In fact some Soviet pricing policies can be partially explained in terms of their impact on income distribution. For example, low housing rents have been charged (despite a severe housing shortage) throughout the plan period, and below equilibrium prices have generally been charged in state and cooperative shops for basic food products.[69] In line with these price setting policies has been the practice of charging nothing or only nominal prices for health care and education.[70]

One can view the Soviet policy of setting low prices for necessities such as basic food products and health and education as an

[69] Political factors have also been important in maintaining low prices on basic foods such as meat and dairy products. In the post-Stalin era, the Soviet leadership risks popular discontent and sometimes civil unrest when such prices are raised. An example of this was the 30 percent increase in meat and butter prices in 1962. On this see: Hanson, *op. cit.,* pp. 171–177.

[70] While charges for such services are generally very low, they do appear as more substantial when considered as a portion of family income. Also, it is possible to contract some services, for example, that of a doctor, privately. In these cases, charges will be higher. For a discussion of this point, see Robert J. Osborn, *Soviet Social Policies: Welfare, Equality, and Community* (Homewood, Ill.: Dorsey Press, 1970), pp. 89–94.

attempt to improve the distribution of real income. It is note-worthy that the most direct method of equalizing the distribution of income—the leveling of wage income—has not been used on the grounds that this would weaken the incentive system.

An Evaluation of Soviet Prices

Thus far we have described the operation and functions of the So-viet price system. We now turn to a partial evaluation of Soviet pricing. Is the Soviet price system really unsatisfactory and "ir-rational" as many Western observers claim?[71] It is, of course, dif-ficult to answer this question because the response depends to a great extent upon the criteria used to judge Soviet prices. If one accepts the criterion that "good" prices should smoothly allocate scarce resources among competing goals by equating supply and demand, then the Soviet price system will show up poorly. If, on the other hand, one judges the price system on the basis of how well it leads to the accomplishment of goals desired by leaders (say, Soviet planners), then the judgement may be quite different. While we cannot hope to provide conclusive answers to the rela-tive "goodness" of Soviet prices, some plausible generalizations are in order.

First, it is probably true that many Western economists tend to idealize the price system as it is supposed to operate in perfectly competitive markets. However, the conditions of perfect competi-tion are rarely met in the real world. What is worse, the competi-tive pricing model tells us little about the relative merits of market pricing when the conditions of perfect competition are only par-tially met.[72] In addition, there are cases where even the perfectly competitive model fails to provide a "good" system of prices—the cases of public goods, such as national defense and highways, and externalities (air and water pollution, for example). Thus it is dif-ficult to evaluate the "goodness" or "badness" of Soviet prices in *relative* terms, for what are being compared are imperfect real-world alternatives. Can one, for example, say that the administered oligopoly prices of much of U.S. industry are "better" or "worse"

[71] For this view, see Bergson, *op. cit.*, pp. 166–170.
[72] The standard reference here is R. G. Lipsey and K. Lancaster, "The Gen-eral Theory of Second Best," *Review of Economic Studies,* vol. 24, no. 63 (1956), 11–32.

than Soviet industrial wholesale prices? We would imagine that, in terms of reflecting relative scarcities, the oligopoly prices are more accurate, but this is merely an intuitive judgment on our part.[73]

Second, we must recognize that when one judges the Soviet price system in absolute terms it has become apparent to both Soviet and Western observers that the Soviet price system does not perform its postulated functions especially well. This dissatisfaction among observers on both sides is reflected in the long-standing Western criticisms of the lack of scarcity pricing and price inflexibility, and in the Soviets' own criticisms along these same lines. In particular, the conflict between the price flexibility required for scarcity pricing and smooth distribution of goods, and the price inflexibility required for effective control and measurement has led to numerous problems. The absence of an interest charge on capital (prior to 1965) caused managers to treat capital as a free good, with ensuing capital wastage. For many years natural gas was allowed to disappear into the air as a by-product of oil production. There are many more examples. Perhaps most disturbing have been the strict limitations imposed by the inflexible Soviet price system on the devolution of decision making through decentralization.

Third, to truly evaluate Soviet prices, one must determine to what extent the Soviet price system has promoted or retarded the attainment of the long-run economic, military, and political goals of the Soviet leadership. For example, has the Soviet price system furthered the Soviet economic goal of rapid industrialization? In this regard, we encounter a controversy that will be discussed in Part Four, namely: are the traditional microeconomic concepts of economic rationality—scarcity prices, cost minimization, internal rates of return, etc.—short-run static concepts that have little meaning during the course of economic development? In other words, is economic development perhaps to be promoted by not

[73] On this point, Philip Hanson, *op. cit.,* in a study of the Soviet consumer sector, writes:

> Nowadays the Soviet press provides lists of defects in the Soviet economic system ready-made for Western commentators. The description that has been given of the difficulties in the working of feedbacks from demand to supply is a compilation of the grumbles that are aired by Soviet reform-mongers. So what? Anyone who made a study of . . . the distributive trade press in the U. K. could make a long list of faults in British arrangements . . . (p. 193).

observing static rules of efficiency as dictated by current scarcity prices? Soviet planners' refusal to allow the price system to play an important role in the resource allocation process and their relegation of prices primarily to control, measurement, and income distribution roles may be viewed in this light as entirely rational.

Appendix 5-A

Soviet Planning and Input-Output Economics

Introduction: One of the criticisms of Soviet material balance planning is that it is so cumbersome and time consuming that it is impossible to choose an optimal plan variant from among the various possible consistent plans. The use of input-output analysis for planning purposes would seem to present a more flexible alternative to Soviet material balance planning. In this appendix, the possible applications of input-output economics to Soviet planning are considered. Our discussion assumes a basic knowledge of input-output economics and will utilize matrix notation.

Input-Output Economics in the Soviet Union: Despite impressive Soviet pioneering efforts (for example, *Gosplan's* 1923–1924 balance of the national economy)[1] and its obvious relevance to planning problems, the first real use of input-output techniques was the Central Statistical Administration's 1959 input-output table for the Soviet economy (a 73×73 matrix published in *Narodnoe khoziastvo SSSR v 1960 g.*) [The national economy of the USSR in 1960]. The principal reason for this long delay was Stalin's repression of mathematical economics during his rule. Since 1959, a series of national and regional input-output tables has been developed, one of the latest efforts being the 1966 national input-output table.[2]

---

[1] The 1923–1924 balance is discussed by V. S. Nemchinov, "The Use of Mathematical Methods in Economics," in V. S. Nemchinov, ed., *The Use of Mathematics in Economics* (Cambridge, Mass.: MIT Press, 1964), pp. 3–10.

[2] Vladimir Treml, "Input-Output Analysis and Soviet Planning," in John Hardt et al., *Mathematics and Computers in Soviet Planning* (New Haven, Conn.: Yale University Press, 1967), pp. 68–120; Herbert Levine, "Input-Output Analysis and Soviet Planning," *American Economic Review,* vol. 52, no. 2 (May 1962); J. M. Montias, "On the Consistency and Efficiency of Central Planning," *Review of Economic Studies,* vol. 29, no. 81 (October 1962); Benjamin N. Ward, *The Socialist Economy* (New York: Random House, 1967), chap. 3; V. G. Treml et al., "Interindustry Structure of the Soviet Economy," in *Soviet Economic Prospects for the Seventies, op. cit.,* pp. 246–269.

In this appendix, we discuss the actual and possible uses of input-output economics in Soviet planning.

For those familiar with input-output techniques,[3] their applicability to Soviet planning seems obvious. If the matrix of technical coefficients is known,[4] and the input-output table is entirely in physical units, then the consistency of a set of control figures can be checked almost immediately by using the formula:

$$(I - A)X = Y \qquad (1)$$

where X is the proposed vector of control figures (in gross output terms), A is the familiar Leontief matrix of technical coefficients, I is the identity matrix, and Y is the vector of final outputs. An inconsistency in the proposed control figures would be indicated by a negative Y element, or by a Y element that is unacceptably small in light of planned investment, consumption, and exports. Thus the internal consistency of alternative vectors of control figures could be readily determined simply by matrix multiplication.

If, on the other hand, Soviet planners desired to compute the vector of gross outputs (X) required to produce a proposed vector of final output targets (Y), then the following formula can be used:

$$(I - A)^{-1}Y = X \qquad (2)$$

where $(I - A)^{-1}$ is the inverse of $(I - A)$ and X is the set of required gross outputs. The feasibility of producing Y would be determined by considering the primary factor requirements (such as labor, capital, etc.) of the various programs relative to their availabilities.

A further useful property of such input-output matrices is that product prices can be derived as by-products of such computations. If the matrix B represents a matrix of primary resource coefficients, where b_{kj} represents the amount of the k_{th} primary factor

---

[3] The reader is referred to R. Dorfman, P. Samuelson, and R. Solow, *Linear Programming and Economic Analysis* (New York: McGraw-Hill, 1958), chaps. 8–10.

[4] The matrix of technical coefficients can be related to Exhibit 2 (p. 128) in the following manner:

$$a_{ij} = X_{ij}/X_j,$$

where a_{ij} denotes the amount of commodity i required to produce one unit of commodity j.

(land, labor, capital, etc.) required to produce one unit of output of commodity j, then:

$$B(I - A)^{-1} = T \qquad (3)$$

is the matrix of full primary resource coefficients.[5] Each element of T (t_{kj}) indicates the amount of primary factor k required *both directly and indirectly* to produce one unit of commodity j. The price of j would therefore be computed by multiplying the p_k by the t_{kj} where p_k is the price of the k_{th} primary factor and summing over the k's:

$$p_j = \sum_{k=1}^{n} p_k t_{kj}$$

(assuming n primary factors).

The "optimality" problem could be solved by determining all the Y vectors that meet the following condition:

$$TY = Z \qquad (4)$$

where Z is the vector of primary resource availabilities. These Y vectors would represent a "production possibilities schedule" from which the *optimal* vector could be chosen as defined by the planners' objective function.[6]

Thus in theory, it would seem as if input-output analysis would solve most of the problems of Soviet planners—consistency, optimality, and pricing. In fact, "after eight to nine years of experimentation and exploration . . . input-output techniques have neither replaced the planning apparatus nor been integrated with it."[7] Or, to quote a Soviet economist writing in 1968: "It would be no exaggeration to say that not a single important decision in current or long-range plans has been taken on the basis . . . of I-O [input-output] balances. . . ."[8] There are numerous reasons for this. First, the use of input-output tables with their stress on final output planning as opposed to gross output planning has run into political

---

[5] On this see Treml, *op. cit.*, p. 93.
[6] *Ibid.*, p. 93.
[7] *Ibid.*, p. 102.
[8] *Voprosy ekonomiki* [Problems of economics], no. 2 (1968), p. 20. Quoted in Treml et al., *op. cit.*, p. 27.

opposition.[9] The material balance system begins with the planning of gross output targets (the X vector) and to do otherwise (to plan on the basis of the Y vector), it is argued, is to abandon the growth goal in favor of a consumption orientation.[10]

Second, the present Soviet system of data gathering does not adapt itself well to input-output technology. Data is gathered on an administrative basis rather than on the product basis required to compute input-output tables. Material balances are prepared on an industrial branch basis and result in concrete plans for the various industrial ministries. Yet these ministries tend to produce internally a broad range of products (steel, machinery, and consumer goods in one ministry, for example) that should show up in different commodity categories in an input-output table. A far more serious data problem is the generally poor and unreliable data base underlying both the construction of input-output balances and industrial planning. This tends to result in what one Soviet economist has termed "natural calamities"[11] when the technological coefficients are actually estimated.

Third, it has proven difficult to compute complete input-output tables in physical terms. As one might expect, certain products are heterogeneous and must be aggregated in value terms. This leads to further problems. Because of the distortive impact of the turnover tax (different users pay different prices), it is difficult to convert from the value figures, (for example, rubles of steel) to the physical figures, (for example, tons of steel), of primary concern to supply planners. Also, the computed input-output tables in value terms reflect the existing nonscarcity industrial prices and are therefore of dubious value.

Fourth, material balance planners have traditionally derived balances for between 300 and 2,000 materials. At the distribution stage, they have planned around ten times the higher figure. Yet the Central Statistical Agency's 1959 national input-output table is a 73 by 73 matrix and the later 1966 table is 110 by 110.[12] Cur-

---

[9] Herbert S. Levine, "The Centralized Planning of Supply in the Soviet Union," in *Comparisons of the United States and Soviet Economies* (Washington, D.C.: U.S. Government Printing Office, 1959), pp. 171–173.

[10] Treml, *op. cit.,* p. 124.

[11] Statement of S. Shatalin quoted in Treml et al., *op. cit.,* p. 29.

[12] *Narodnoe khoziastvo SSSR v 1969 g.* [The national economy of the USSR in 1969], pp. 50–75.

rently work is being done on a 600 branch national table by the Academy of Sciences (Siberian branch).[13] Thus input-output tables of much larger dimensions would have to be developed to preserve the current level of disaggregation of the material balance system. Given the current data gathering capacity and computational sophistication of the Soviet Union, this would probably prove to be too complicated a task. Thus, the input-output tables used for planning would have to be at a higher level of aggregation than the material balance and industrial supply system. This aggregation would be done in value terms and the technical coefficients would be weighted averages of disaggregated coefficients. To be useful for Soviet planning purposes, some method of meaningful disaggregation would have to be devised, which is an extremely thorny problem.

[13] F. Baturin and P. Shemetov, "Activities of Siberian Economists," *Problems of Economics: A Journal of Translations,* vol. 7, no. 7 (November 1969), p. 69. Translated from *Voprosy ekonomiki* [Problems of economics], no. 5, (1969).

Appendix 5-B

The Soviet Price System—Reform

Most present day Soviet economists would probably argue in favor of some sort of reform of the price system. There are, however, substantial differences among the reform advocates. These differences reflect more than simple differences over the mechanics of price formation—in large part they imply substantially different roles for prices. Let us consider three broad schools of thought among Soviet economists:

1. Prices should be based upon value as defined in an appropriate Marxian framework.
2. Prices should be based upon scarcity and should be derived as the logical result of an optimizing mathematical model.
3. Prices should reflect scarcity and should be determined by the forces of supply and demand.

1. For those who adhere to the Marxian framework, there are several schools of thought on price formation, the details of which need not detain us here.[1] The question revolves around the law of value and its operation in a socialist society. While Stalin's view of a restricted role for the law of value in socialist societies left little room for discussion during the 1930s, such has not been the case in the post-Stalin era. In general, Soviet economists define value as the sum of labor expenditure (v), materials used in the productive process (c), and surplus product (m) as in the traditional Marxian formula:[2]

$$Value = c + v + m$$

[1] In addition to sources already cited, see Robert W. Campbell, "Marx, Kantrovich and Novozhilov: Stoimost' Versus Reality," *Slavic Review,* vol. 20, no. 3 (October 1961), 402–418.

[2] For a discussion of the Marxian position, see, for example, Alexander Balinky, *Marx's Economics* (Lexington, Mass.: Heath, 1970).

In terms of traditional Marxian theory, the principles of price formation are clear. The problem arises, however, in the use of this formula as a practical guide to price setting. *If price is to equal value,* then for each commodity it is necessary that price $= c + v + m$. How is each component to be determined? The problem here is basically one of circularity. Even if we assume that c and v are known, m will not be known since surplus product in the socialist economy would be indicated by gross national product less the aggregate wages bill. To derive gross national product, however, valuation is involved. If we assume such a valuation and derive surplus product for the entire economy, how will it be distributed among individual commodities? Those Soviet economists adhering to this general line of price formation have differed as to how this distribution should take place; some have suggested that it should be distributed in proportion to c, others have said in proportion to v, and some have argued for proportionality to $c + v$. In the past, it has been collected almost entirely on consumer goods (the turnover tax) leading to the two-tiered price system discussed earlier.

The critics of this approach to price setting have concentrated on several points. These formulas are all *cost* oriented and neglect demand as an element in the creation of value. However, those advocating this sort of price formation are not arguing in favor of an allocative role for prices and thus are willing to neglect demand, for allocation would generally remain the responsibility of the central planning agencies. Another problem for those pursuing the Marxian framework concerns the measurement of costs. According to Marx, labor (either in its direct or congealed form) is the sole source of value; therefore the elements that should enter into costs are only those that require or have required labor expenditures: wages, intermediate materials, overhead, and depreciation (the amount of previously expended labor being used up in the production process with the wear and tear on capital). There is no room for a rental charge on capital or land. In addition, it is difficult to include a charge for obsolescence.[3]

[3] There are numerous representatives of this cost-oriented approach to be found largely among the ranks of planners. For examples, see V. Batyrev, "Voprosy teorii stoimosti pri sotsializme" [Question of the theory of value under socialism], *Voprosy ekonomiki* [Problems of economics], no. 2 (February 1967), 36–47; and A. Gusarev, "Tsena-Instrument plana" [Prices-

2. The scarcity approach to pricing is of a fundamentally different nature. The main advocates of scarcity type pricing are the mathematical economists, the most notable of whom are V. S. Nemchinov, V. V. Novozhilov, and L. V. Kantorovich, the latter being one of the originators of linear programming techniques in 1938.[4] According to a representative scheme proposed by Kantorovich, a set of relative prices would be generated by the dual of a linear programming model in which the final bill of goods (determined by the state, presumably) would be produced with a cost minimizing combination of inputs with existing factor endowments and technology.[5] There are several variants of this basic approach. Their unifying feature is the maximization of an objective function (often the "consumption fund" of the economy) with the scarce factors of production (which are fixed in the short-run) acting as the principal constraints. Factor prices are then computed as "shadow prices" (the ratio of the change in the value of the objective function to the change in the factor).[6] In theory, such a set of prices would parallel those generated in a competitive market model (they would be scarcity prices) and would, therefore, be capable of performing an allocative role in the economy. While there are tremendous practical problems in the generation and continuing utilization of such a set of prices, Soviet criticism of this approach has more typically been on the basis of its apparently non-

---

Instrument of the Plan], *Ekonomicheskaia gazeta* [The economic gazette], no. 40 (October 1969), 5–6.

[4] These three mathematical economists were awarded the coveted Lenin Prize in 1965. Kantorovich's original contribution to linear programming techniques can be found in a monograph entitled *Matematicheskie metody organizatsii i planirovaniia proizvodstva* (Leningrad, 1939), translated as "Mathematical Methods of Organizing and Planning Production," *Management Science,* vol. 4, no. 4 (July 1960), 366–422.

[5] This schema can be found in L. V. Kantorovich, *Ekonomicheskii raschet nailucheskogo ispol'zovaniia resursov* (Moscow, 1959). This volume was translated by P. K. Knightsfield, and under the editorship of G. Morton published as *The Best Use of Economic Resources* (Cambridge, Mass.: Harvard University Press, 1965).

[6] One can find numerous examples of this approach in current Soviet economic literature. See for example the translation of the N. Fedorenko and S. Shatalin survey, "The Problem of Optimal Planning of the Socialist Economy," *Problems of Economics: A Journal of Translations,* vol. 7, no. 7 (November 1968), 3–29.

Marxian character (its reliance on bourgeois theories of marginal utility).[7]

From a theoretical standpoint, the Soviet mathematical school has demonstrated that such a system of price formation would lead to optimization since these prices do represent relative scarcities. Apart from the ideological problems, however, the data requirements, necessary computational facilities, and the need for spatial and temporal price flexibility would create significant problems if prices were actually set in this manner. Nevertheless, as a direction of change, the notion of scarcity prices derived from mathematical models may be of great importance to future changes in the Soviet economy.

3. The proponents of the third approach argue that prices should be determined by the forces of supply and demand and that prices should be allowed to fluctuate without central direction as socialist industrial enterprises engage in microeconomic competition among themselves for supplies. Thus the market (presumably a viable wholesale market for producer goods) would determine prices, not a mathematical model as proposed by the mathematical school. The two approaches are similar, however, in that they both propose that prices should reflect scarcity.[8]

An economic system is a mechanism for the allocation of resources to achieve socially desired ends. In any such system, prices play an important role and accordingly it is essential that these prices be formulated in such a manner that they do in fact serve the ends to which they are devoted. Indeed, one can argue that the price system as a means of transmitting information becomes increasingly important as the economic system grows and becomes more complex. If this is the case, we can expect the discussion of price formation to continue in the future.

---

[7] Batyrev, *op. cit.*, 36–37.

[8] The Soviets refer to this approach as "market socialism" and attribute such views to less orthodox East bloc (primarily Czech) economists. Judging from the vehemence of Soviet attacks on market socialism, it is apparent that such unorthodox views are also shared by some Soviet economists. For a fairly typical critique of market socialism, see A. Eremin, "On the Concept of 'Market Socialism,' " *Problems of Economics: A Journal of Translations,* vol. 13, no. 4 (August 1970), 3–20.

Selected Bibliography

POLITICAL INSTITUTIONS AND CONTROL OF THE ECONOMY

Merle Fainsod, *How Russia Is Ruled,* rev. ed. (Cambridge, Mass.: Harvard University Press, 1964).

Alec Nove, *The Soviet Economy,* 2nd rev. ed. (New York: Praeger, 1969), introduction and chap. 2.

Leonard Shapiro, *The Communist Party of the Soviet Union,* 2nd ed. (New York: Random House, 1970).

SUPPLY AND OUTPUT PLANNING

Abram Bergson, *The Economics of Soviet Planning* (New Haven, Conn.: Yale University Press, 1964), chap. 7.

R. W. Davies, "Planning A Mature Economy," *Economics of Planning,* vol. 6, no. 2 (1966), 138–153.

R. W. Davies, "Soviet Planning for Rapid Industrialization," *Economics of Planning,* vol. 6, no. 1 (1966), 53–67.

Michael Ellman, "The Consistency of Soviet Plans," *Scottish Journal of Political Economy,* vol. 16, no. 1 (February 1969), 50–74.

Herbert Levine, "The Centralized Planning of Supply in Soviet Industry," *Comparisons of the United States and Soviet Economies* (Washington, D.C.: U.S. Government Printing Office, 1959).

Michael Manove, "A Model of Soviet-Type Economic Planning," *American Economic Review,* vol. 61, no. 3, part I (June 1971), 390–406.

J. M. Montias, "Planning with Material Balances in Soviet-Type Economies," *American Economic Review,* vol. 49, no. 5 (December 1959), 963–985.

Gertrude Schroeder, "Recent Developments in Soviet Planning and Managerial Incentives," in Joint Economic Committee, *Soviet Economic Prospects for the Seventies* (Washington, D.C.: U.S. Government Printing Office, 1973), pp. 11–38.

Gertrude Schroeder, "The 'Reform' of the Supply System in Soviet Industry," *Soviet Studies,* vol. 24, no. 1 (July 1972), 97–119.

PUBLIC FINANCE AND FINANCIAL PLANNING IN THE SOVIET UNION

Franklyn Holzman, "Soviet Inflationary Pressures, 1928–1957: Causes and Cures," *Quarterly Journal of Economics,* vol. 74, no. 2 (May 1960), 167–188.

Franklyn Holzman, "Financing Soviet Economic Development," in Moses Abramovitz, ed., *Capital Formation and Economic Growth* (Princeton, N.J.: Princeton University Press, 1955), pp. 229–274.

Franklyn Holzman, *Soviet Taxation: The Fiscal and Monetary Problems of a Planned Economy* (Cambridge, Mass.: Harvard University Press, 1955).

THE SOVIET PRICE SYSTEM

Abram Bergson, *The Economics of Soviet Planning* (New Haven, Conn.: Yale University Press, 1964), chap. 8.

Morris Bornstein, "Soviet Price Theory and Policy," in M. Bornstein and D. Fusfeld, eds., *The Soviet Economy,* 3rd ed. (Homewood, Ill.: Irwin, 1970), pp. 106–137.

Morris Bornstein, "The Soviet Debate on Agricultural Price and Procurement Reforms," *Soviet Studies,* vol. 21, no. 1 (July 1969), 1–20.

Morris Bornstein, "The Soviet Price Reform Discussion," *Quarterly Journal of Economics,* vol. 78, no. 1 (February 1964), 15–48.

Morris Bornstein, "The 1963 Soviet Industrial Price Revision," *Soviet Studies,* vol. 15, no. 1, (July 1963), 43–52.

Robert W. Campbell, "Marx, Kantrovich and Novozhilov: Stoimost' Versus Reality," *Slavic Review,* vol. 20, no. 3 (October 1961), 402–418.

Philip Hanson, *The Consumer Sector in the Soviet Economy* (Evanston, Ill.: Northwestern University Press, 1968), chaps. 7 and 8.

Raymond Hutchings, "The Origins of the Soviet Industrial Price System," *Soviet Studies,* vol. 13, no. 1 (July 1961), 1–22.

Gertrude E. Schroeder, "The 1966–67 Soviet Industrial Price Reform: A Study in Complications," *Soviet Studies,* vol. 20, no. 4 (April 1969), 462–477.

CHAPTER SIX

How Resources Are Allocated in the Soviet Union—The Soviet Manager, Labor, and Capital

THE SOVIET MANAGER

In market economies there is much "automaticity" to the managerial system: the manager, in attempting to maximize profits (or some variant thereof), will automatically respond to changing prices and technology without the prompting of central directives. In the Soviet Union where such automaticity has not generally existed, the question may be asked: How can one construct an appropriate managerial environment so that desired social ends (as formulated by party and state authorities) will be achieved?

The attention that we devote to the managerial structure of the Soviet command economy is to be justified on two grounds, and, indeed, it is these two grounds that largely distinguish the Soviet planned system from the market-oriented system of, for example, the United States.

First, managers in a market system tend to take their instructions from the signals of the market—generally in the form of price information—upon which they base their actual production and distribution decisions (plans). Under Soviet planning, such instructions derive directly from the *plan*. A plan is in fact a set of instructions telling a manager how to behave—often irrespective of market signals—hence our focus upon the variables that tell the manager what the enterprise goals are (as stated in the plan) and how the manager's behavior is oriented by the incentive system toward the achievement of those goals.

Second, in market economies capacity expansion of the enterprise (capital investment) is largely a function of planning within the firm in response to market phenomena (discount rates, anticipated returns, risk, etc.). In the Soviet planned system, capacity changes are decided by plan directives, emanating from agencies outside of the firm. At the same time, the past performance of the enterprise and the external authorities' appraisal of its future capabilities are the basis of plan formation, thus making information from the firm important in both the formulation and execution stages of planning.

In this chapter, we deal explicitly with the Soviet managerial system—the parametric framework in which the manager operates, the managerial personnel, and the managers' responses to enterprise goals under the established system of incentive and behavioral constraints. Our comments apply to the situation prior to 1965; post-1965 changes are discussed in Chapter Ten.

Enterprise Planning
and the Soviet Manager

The operation of the Soviet industrial enterprise is governed in most every respect by the *techpromfinplan* (technical-industrial-financial plan). This plan is the annual (semiannual, quarterly, monthly) subplan of long-term (five to seven year) "perspective" plans (although we have noted the link between the two is often difficult to find) and is itself composed of subplans, each comprising a number of appropriate indicators or targets pertaining to the operation of the enterprise. In its broadest sense, the *techpromfinplan* sets forth the social goals—in the Soviet case, planners preferences—that the enterprise is to implement. In a narrow sense, the *techpromfinplan* specifies output levels (in quantity and value terms), output assortment, labor and other inputs, productivity indexes, profit norms, and so on, which the enterprise is expected to observe.

The most important component of the *techpromfinplan* has been the production plan. Based upon capacity of the enterprise (normally defined as past performance plus some increment to incorporate planned capacity expansion), expected resource utilization, and estimated productivity increases, the production plan has typically specified the ruble value of output [*valovaia produktsia*], the commodity assortment, and the delivery schedule of this output.[1]

In addition to the production plan, the *techpromfinplan* includes a number of other component plans, the most important of which are the financial plan (the monetary expression of the physical plan), the plan of material and technical supply, the delivery plan, the plan of plant and equipment utilization, the plan of labor and wages, and finally, indexes of labor productivity.

In the above plans, state goals and the means for their achievement are elaborated, and within the plan framework, the enterprise is exhorted by the state and party to perform all these tasks at the best possible levels.

One might conclude from this formal version of Soviet planning that the Soviet manager's freedom to make decisions is severely restricted. The *techpromfinplan* governs his choice of enterprise inputs and outputs, and he is morally and legally obligated to implement the plan, with bonuses geared to motivate him in this direction. Looking beneath the surface, however, one unearths a significant area of managerial flexibility. Due in large part to the inability of central organs to specify and control all details of local enterprise operation, Soviet managers do have a sphere of decision-making freedom. To understand management in the Soviet context, one must first understand the nature of this flexibility; second, the manner in which it is executed; and third, its consequences.

Plan Execution
by the Soviet Manager

Both formally and informally, one of the most important functions of the factory manager is the translation of state goals into daily tasks. If one considers the enterprise plan, it is readily apparent that the Soviet manager is confronted with both multiple targets (outputs, cost reduction, innovation, deliveries, etc.) and multiple constraints. Yet the enterprise plan fails to specify formally either the nature of the maximand (enterprise goal) or, for that matter,

---

[1] Enterprises producing homogeneous products often have their output targets stated in physical units rather than value terms—such as tons of cement, square meters of textiles, or tons of plastic—with a specified assortment.

the nature of the trade-offs among possibly competing goals; i.e., the plan does not tell the manager which goals are more important than others, except informally—through party campaigns, bonuses, word of mouth, and other means. The manager is thus faced with a peculiar dilemma. If all plan indicators cannot be simultaneously and harmoniously achieved,[2] which ones should be met and which sacrificed and to what degree in each case?[3] This question is resolved, at least in theory, in the capitalist enterprise by the use of profit as an enterprise goal and a set of scarcity prices such that the trade-offs among various objectives are readily apparent.

While profits have always formally been a part of the economic calculus of the Soviet enterprise, their maximization has generally not been an important enterprise goal either in theory or practice.[4] In fact, quite apart from the meaning of profit in the light of Soviet prices, profits have tended to be of minimal importance in the operation of the enterprise. What then replaces profits in the Soviet managerial calculus? In essence, the plan, the formal and informal constraints, and the managerial incentive structure have made

[2] A common conflict under conditions of ambitious output targets occurs between profit maximization and output target fulfillment. The graph below illustrates how this conflict may arise. The enterprise's output target is Q', which it produces at an average cost above the price that it receives (and thus makes losses denoted by the area of the loss rectangle). To maximize enterprise profits, the enterprise would restrict its output to Q (and fail to fulfill its output target) but would maximize profits denoted by the profit rectangle.

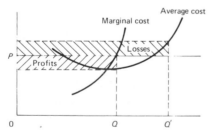

[3] For a discussion of the "success indicator" problem in Soviet industry, see Alec Nove, "The Problem of Success Indicators in Soviet Industry," in *Economic Rationality and Soviet Politics* (New York: Praeger, 1964), pp. 83–98.
[4] The enhanced role of profits in the Soviet enterprise after 1965 as a consequence of the September 1965 economic reform will be discussed in Chapter Ten. The reform theoretically established two performance indicators: first and most important, "realized" output (sales), and second, enterprise profits.

gross output—and more recently, refinements such as "realized" gross output, in other words sales—the most important indicator of enterprise performance. In short, managers have been rewarded primarily for the achievement of output targets, and accordingly those targets not directly related to output have tended to be of secondary importance.

A frequent misconception should be cleared up at this point. Soviet enterprises do operate on an independent "economic accounting" (*khozraschet*) system, which is often taken to mean that Soviet enterprises operate to maximize profits. The *khozraschet* or official managerial accounting system of the Soviet industrial enterprise cannot, however, be understood to imply that profit and other monetary variables are of prime importance. Enterprise profits are calculated, but the *khozraschet* system simply guarantees that enterprises have financial relations with external organs such as *Gosbank,* and further, that their operations are elaborated and evaluated in terms of value indicators using official prices. The minimal practical significance of *khozraschet* to the Soviet economy must be understood, for in the first instance, the structure of Soviet prices makes such calculations suspect, and second, the results of such value calculations have had little impact upon the present and future direction of enterprise activities. Future production targets are not a function of the presence or absence of current profits. This aspect of the Soviet managerial system should be emphasized in view of the crucial role of profits in market economies.

The Success Indicator Problem

The choice of gross output instead of profits as the crucial "success indicator" of managerial performance generates a series of problems. In most cases, maximands relating to output (whether in value or quantity terms) cannot be defined in perfect detail by central authorities, and in the Soviet case—in particular—gross production "success indicators" have led to considerable managerial freedom and, often, distortion. Where weight of output has been the success indicator, for example, in the production of castings, castings tend to be made heavier than necessary, thus wasting scarce inputs. Where size had been the indicator, as for example in the production of cloth, managers favor large sizes and largely ignore assortment goals. These distortions are only a part, however, of what has been described as the problem of "success indicators" in Soviet industry.[5]

We noted that the planners estimate plant capacity—a crucial aspect of plan formulation—as a direct function of past performance plus allowances for productivity improvements. At the enterprise level, however, the manager faces a dilemma: if he significantly overfulfills output targets in the current year, he may receive a sizeable bonus, but in subsequent years, targets will be substantially increased (the "ratchet effect"), thereby diminishing the likelihood of bonus earnings in the immediate future. As a result, he will tend to be cautious about overfulfilling plan targets even if overfulfillment is well within his grasp. Another problem arises from the stress upon the expansion of output in combination with a bonus system that reinforce this narrow production-oriented conception of performance. A rapid expansion of physical output this year is unambiguously "good" according to the success indicator, irrespective of poor performance in other areas. Thus technological change, cost reduction, and on-time deliveries, all very important indicators for the Soviet economy as a whole, tend to be secondary considerations as far as the manager is concerned.

In addition to these basic structural difficulties, there are dysfunctional characteristics of the managerial system. Soviet managers are faced by continual pressure from above in the form of taut production targets. Therefore management must rely heavily on the efficient functioning of the material and technical supply system, a system over which management has little formal control. Yet enterprise output depends to a great extent upon the availability of appropriate inputs in the proper quantity, quality, and at the appropriate time. In the absence of a genuine wholesale market, the enterprise must rely upon all other supplier enterprises to meet their plan obligations, and a failure by a single enter-

---

[5] Nove, *Economic Rationality, op. cit.,* p. 88. A striking example of the possible distortion as pictured by the Soviet humor magazine *Krokodil* and cited by Alec Nove is the nail factory whose gross output target is specified in *weight*. The month's output is one gigantic nail being hauled away with a crane. See Alec Nove, *The Soviet Economy,* 2nd rev. ed. (New York: Praeger, 1969), p. 174.

prise can cause continuing reverberations throughout the system.[6] The supply system is crucial to enterprise plan fulfillment; yet its manifold weaknesses outlined above continue to impede enterprise target fulfillment.[7]

Informal Behavior Patterns

The emphasis on taut production targets has led to certain informal behavior patterns by enterprise management, some of which have had negative economic consequences. First, there has been an inevitable tendency for the enterprise manager to resurrect a practice utilized under War Communism—namely, *priorities*—using plan directives, the bonus system, informal and formal communications from the party, and simple intuition as indicators of the nature of the priority structure.

On the one hand, the priority system indicates the predominance of output performance over other plan targets. The priority awareness of Soviet managers relates to two aspects of enterprise operations. First, the priority system directs him to emphasize output performance over other plan targets, with the resulting neglect of costs, innovations, quality, and so on, as described above. Second,

---

[6] Enterprise failures to meet delivery targets are generally not severely punished. Fines tend to be nominal and difficult to collect, and generally enterprises do not bother to pursue those who break contracts. Because of the lack of coordination of supply plans between the State Committee for Material-Technical Supply (*Gossnab*), *Gosplan* and the ministries, no particular agency has been willing to take the responsibility for contract violations. For Soviet discussions of these problems, see *Ekonomicheskaia gazeta* [The economic gazette], no. 30 (1969), 8, and no. 1 (1970), 8.

[7] In recent years, attempts have been made to develop *direct supply links* between enterprises to make the supply system more reliable. Also so-called free sales of some commodities are being allowed. Nevertheless, most material supplies are still centrally allocated and often the central supply organs seek to disrupt the direct supply links and force a return to centralized allocation. For a discussion of the direct links system, see for example V. Dymshits, "Sluzhba snabzheniia segodnia i zavtra" [Supply services, today and tomorrow], *Ekonomicheskaia gazeta* [The economic gazette], no. 28 (1969), 4–5; V. Ivanov, "Material'notekhnicheskoe snabzhenie v novykh usloviiakh khoziaistvovaniia" [Material-technical supply under new circumstances of management], *Vorposy ekonomiki* [Problems of economics], no. 5 (May 1969), 40–47; Getrude Schroeder, "The 'Reform' of the Supply System in Soviet Industry," *Soviet Studies,* vol. 24, no. 1 (July 1972), 105–107.

the priority system relates to managers the relative importance of the various enterprises with whom he conducts business. If the manager finds himself unable to meet delivery obligations to both enterprises X and Y, he must rely on his priority awareness to make his choice.

The major reason for the important role of priorities in the world of the Soviet manager is the existence of supply uncertainty, which itself is due to the tautness of planning and to planning errors. The priority system does have its positive aspects because in an imperfect system it insures that planners get their high-priority targets irrespective of planning errors and supply deficiencies; yet it does force managers to seek informal sources of supply and to engage in dysfunctional practices.

A second informal behavior pattern is the *safety factor* phenomenon. The combination of ambitious targets, uncertain supply, and substantial rewards for fulfillment of priority targets causes the manager to search for organizational slack or a *safety factor*, as it is called in the Soviet parlance. This search leads the manager into patterns of dysfunctional behavior, for example the hoarding of material supplies (especially those most likely to be in short supply) thus immobilizing scarce resources. This stockpiling is not totally dysfunctional, for the Soviet manager will use his *tolkach*[8] (expediter) to barter and exchange stockpiled materials with other enterprises. Nevertheless, this informal supply system operated by the *tolkach* (and tolerated by planning and legal authorities) results in a weakening of centralized control over material allocation —a definitely undesirable feature from the planning authorities' point of view. Yet the toleration of the informal supply system indicates that the authorities have reluctantly accepted it as a necessary evil required by the frequent breakdowns in the official supply system.

Third, under the existing priority system there is a tendency for managers to avoid change, for the manager tends to expect a nega-

[8] The figure of the *tolkach* has become a commonplace of Soviet life. They travel around the country at factory expense on factory assignments, often vacationing at government expense. A recent article describes the crowding of Soviet hotels on weekends by the *tolkachi,* leaving no rooms for vacationing families. See V. Varvarka, "Otpusk v kommandirovke" [Vacation during a business trip], *Ekonomichesksaia gazeta* [The economic gazette], no. 14 (1969), 16.

tive impact from innovation in both process and product innovation. Such innovations are considered risky because they might endanger plan fulfillment during the current period, and they carry little potential reward because output targets will simply be ratcheted upward if the innovations are successful. At the same time, quality, which is typically very difficult to incorporate effectively into quantitative indicators, has tended to be of secondary importance to the manager, who—at least prior to 1965—was judged on the basis of *production*, not sales. Also, in a sellers' market, those searching for supplies will be less likely to complain about inferior quality. In this case, the economic facts of life dictate against the use of legal and other channels to seek redress of supply grievances pertaining to quality or quantity.

Fourth, the bonus structure has tended to produce no rewards for 99 percent fulfillment, but substantial rewards for 101 percent fulfillment. This discontinuous aspect of the bonus system, plus the other characteristics outlined above (especially supply inadequacy), lead to *storming* or the production of a substantial portion of the monthly output in the final few days of the month. The result of *storming* is a reinforcement of other dysfunctional features—irregular delivery on supply contracts, improper utilization of capacity, poor quality, and so forth.

From what we have said, it is apparent that the reward system for enterprise managers influences both the selection of priority targets, and further, attainment of these targets. Let us now examine the managerial incentive structure in greater detail to determine how this comes about.

Soviet Management and Incentives[9]

The basic problems of management are not peculiar to the Soviet industrial enterprise; their counterparts can be found, for the most part, in capitalist industrial enterprises. Given a set of goals

---

[9] The discussion of Soviet management is based primarily upon the following works: Joseph Berliner, *Factory and Manager in the USSR* (Cambridge, Mass.: Harvard University Press, 1957) is a study of the early years of Soviet management experience based primarily upon émigré interviews; David Granick, *Management of the Industrial Firm in the USSR* (New York: Columbia University Press, 1954) is an in-depth study of industrial man-

(whether from a board of directors or a central planner), and given that appropriate information for both plan formulation and execution is held largely at local levels (in the branch plant of a capitalist enterprise, for example), how is a managerial environment and incentive structure to be constructed such that (1) managers know precisely what is expected from them, and (2) they are motivated to fulfill these expectations?

The Soviet answer to these questions is a peculiar managerial framework, in the sense that it combines a relatively high degree of centralization of decision-making within a rather formal bureaucratic structure on the one hand, with a significant degree of managerial freedom through informal decentralization on the other. Thus the hierarchical centralized planning structure implies that managers respond to "rules" while, at the same time, the *khozraschet* enterprise system implies that managers have a degree of local freedom and initiative in the operation of the enterprise.[10]

It must be recognized that in almost any organization, there will exist both a formal and an informal sphere of managerial decision authority. In a sense, the latter oils the operation of the former. In the Soviet case, to the degree that the latter does not smooth the operation of the former, there exists a myriad of internal and external enterprise controls to reorient enterprise behavior along desirable paths. These controls will be examined as we consider both the positive and negative aspects of the Soviet managerial reward structure.

Managerial Personnel and Rewards

Before considering the Soviet managerial reward system, let us consider the profile of a Soviet industrial manager. From the evi-

---

agement of the 1930s based primarily upon a detailed reading of the Soviet local and specialized press; Barry Richman, *Soviet Industrial Management* (Englewood Cliffs, N.J.; Prentice-Hall, 1964) is a general survey of material similar to that discussed by Berliner and Granick. More recent material on the Soviet as compared with other industrial managers can be found in David Granick, *Managerial Comparisons of Four Developed Countries: France, Britain, United States and Russia* (Cambridge, Mass.: MIT Press, 1972).

[10] For treatment of the Soviet managerial system in the language of organization theory, see David Granick, *Soviet Metal Fabricating and Economic Development* (Madison: University of Wisconsin Press, 1967), chap. 7.

dence gathered by Western authorities on Soviet management,[11] we know that the typical Soviet manager is probably well-educated (usually at the college level)—most likely in the field of engineering, with minimal emphasis on finance and what we would describe as "business" courses. This is an interesting deviation from the American pattern where, for example, the manager has to be primarily conversant with financial and sales matters. Instead, the Soviet manager's engineering training prepares him more for technological production problems. While the Soviet manager is typically not from a working-class background, he will during the course of his educational experience, and also throughout the period of managerial advancement, receive more practical training than his American counterpart.

The rewards for successful managerial performance can be significant. Although data in this area are limited, it is probably safe to generalize that the typical Soviet manager earns a base pay substantially higher than the average Soviet worker, and further, that monetary bonuses are a significant portion of his total earnings. In the latter respect, it is important to realize that bonus payments vary substantially both over time and by regions, and while much of our evidence on this point comes from bonus specifications, it should be apparent that actual earnings can differ substantially from the specifications. With this warning, we note that potential managerial bonuses range from 40 to 60 percent of base pay, while actual bonus payments probably range from 25 to 30 percent.[12] Thus bonus earnings are potentially important for the Soviet factory manager, although as a portion of aggregate managerial earnings, they are of no greater importance in the Soviet Union than in the United States in recent years.[13] It should be noted, however, that while participation in bonus schemes is generally universal for Soviet managerial personnel, such is not the case in the United States.

As important as the magnitude, however, is the structure of the

---

[11] Notably, Berliner, *op. cit.;* Granick, *Management of the Industrial Firm, op. cit.;* Granick, *Managerial Comparisons of Four Developed Countries, op. cit.;* Richman, *op. cit.*

[12] Richman, *op. cit.*, pp. 134–135.

[13] Granick, *Managerial Comparisons of Four Developed Countries, op. cit.,* chap. 9.

bonus payments. While the relative magnitude of bonuses is important for the typical American manager (bonuses are difficult to measure in the United States, in large part due to the special payment arrangements to minimize taxation), one must note that executive bonuses in the United States tend to be paid for achievement of both short- and long-run objectives. For example, the American manager is expected to strike a proper balance between short-run and long-run profitability, and thus enterprise performance is, for the American case, defined much more broadly than it is in the Soviet Union. In addition, bonus arrangements in the United States are more likely to be based on subjective evaluations of the performance of managers.[14] In the Soviet Union, however, bonus payments tend to be for short-run, rather clearly defined tasks, such as the quantitative fulfillment of a specific output target, or specific cost reductions. The short-run nature of Soviet bonuses tends to create an environment of pressure, and this in itself becomes a mechanism through which short-run priorities can readily be identified by managers. It is in this sense that some longer-run targets, such as quality, innovation, and so forth, may well be set aside in favor of more rewarding short-run achievements.

In the Soviet case the monetary bonus awards are normally awarded on a short-run basis (i.e. monthly), while the nonmonetary rewards are in greater measure long-run rewards, although they too can be thought of as defining priority goals and delineating the sphere of informal managerial behavior. Enterprises may, for example, provide the manager with living quarters and an automobile, the latter most likely with a driver. Both are significant amenities in present-day Soviet society when one considers the shortage of housing space (and the lack of a formal market for the purchase of same) and the prestige and convenience of an automobile. Finally, the enterprise manager can anticipate partipation in local, state, and party organs, adulation in the press for particularly good performance, and also upward mobility to positions of greater prestige and reward.

While the Soviet manager's position is one of potentially significant monetary rewards, it is also one of significant risk. First, in an environment of uncertainty where the manager lacks decisive

[14] *Ibid.*

control over all inputs (for example, the delivery of material supplies to his enterprise on time), the manager is clearly in danger of not being able to meet his priority targets. There are two possible consequences of such failure: he may lose his bonus, which represents a substantial portion of his total income, or, he may lose his job. A third consequence, execution or imprisonment, was widespread during the 1930s when failures to fulfill targets were seen to be the work of saboteurs. Fortunately, Soviet managers no longer work under this threat.[15] Executive turnover was very high in the 1930s, although it is clear that this pattern has changed significantly in recent years. Thus for the postwar years, turnover of Soviet managerial personnel at both the middle and upper levels has been substantially less than that of comparable managerial personnel in American corporations. This represents significantly increased job security for Soviet managers of the 1960s and 1970s as opposed to those of the 1930s.[16]

External Constraints
upon Soviet Managers

Numerous internal and external constraints upon managerial flexibility make the job of the Soviet manager even more difficult. The planning and administrative bodies external to the firm also have targets to meet, which depend upon the performance of subordinate enterprises. Regional and ministerial authorities are therefore interested in forcing enterprises under their control to exert themselves to the maximum. This relationship is significant, whether industry is arranged on a territorial or ministerial basis, for higher bodies will place pressure upon the subordinate enterprises to insure fulfillment of their own targets. The ministry practice of holding back enterprise supply allotments ("reserving") and of planning enterprise targets to exceed the aggregate ministry target are part of this pressure. In this manner, the manager is subjected to increased pressure from his immediate supervisors. In addition,

---

[15] One can better understand the dysfunctional behavior of the Soviet manager and his search for the "safety factor" by remembering that these practices originated during the 1930s when managers faced severe consequences if they failed to meet plan obligations.
[16] David Granick, *Managerial Comparisons of Four Developed Countries, op. cit.,* chap. 8.

while the *khozraschet* system of management implies a degree of autonomy for the enterprise, it also suggests the establishment of financial rewards and connections with the State Bank—a further form of external control. The system of "ruble control" implies that the funds of the enterprise must be deposited in the bank, and the bank will exercise control over the correct establishment and utilization of funds.

While the trade union does not play an important role in wage scale determination, it may be of importance in nonwage matters —for example, in overseeing working conditions, sick leave, vacation benefits, and the manager's authority to fire workers—which in turn, limits managerial flexibility. Finally, the Communist Party may, on the one hand, serve to define priorities in the industrial sector for the manager and, on the other hand, may serve to limit managerial decision-making freedom by the elaboration of "inadequacies," revelation of deceptive statistical reporting and other undesirable behavior patterns of managers. While the precise role of the party in managerial affairs remains to be fully understood, its influence would seem to be pervasive within the enterprise and most likely could be described as an alter ego to the manager.

Conclusions

At the outset, we noted that the industrial management system in the Soviet Union is an important component of the general system of plan formation and execution. Hence, the achievement of planners' goals is in large measure a function of managerial action. Moreover, while managerial behavior is a complex function of many economic and noneconomic variables, we have identified two especially important aspects of it: the parametric framework in which managers operate, and the managerial input to that framework. For the most part, the important information required for managerial decision making is located at the enterprise level, while goals are generated at the top of the planning hierarchy, thus necessitating a system of information flows in both directions and a managerial system that insures efficient execution of goals once spelled out at the local levels.

The problem of elaborating the appropriate managerial framework is frequently characterized as the problem of finding the appropriate level of centralization or decentralization of decision-making. Although such a concept is difficult to measure, the frequent organizational shifts in past years would indicate a degree of dissatisfaction within the Soviet leadership with most arrangements in recent use. The Soviet press abounds with reports of dissatisfaction over the operation of the managerial system. The system operates to allocate resources as directed by planning authorities, but it is generally conceived to work inefficiently in terms of resource utilization. Poor quality, lack of innovative activity, and the continuation of illegal activities in the performance of enterprise duties are evidence of a system characterized by a good deal of dysfunctional (in terms of goal achievement) behavior.

Soviet leaders have long been aware of the problem of inefficient performance of their industrial enterprises. In fact, most of the problems noted in this section—excessive stockpiling, informal supply arrangements, inflated material requests—were already apparent to the planning authorities as early as 1929.[17] It is only recently that Soviet authorities have attempted to correct deficiencies in the planning structure and the managerial incentive system through the process of economic reform, a topic dealt with in Chapter Ten. Why have Soviet administrators waited so long to deal with these problems? Largely because the existing system tends to respond relatively well to the priority goals of planners and, in this manner, the planners are assured that they control the direction of the economy. Whether alternative arrangements can guarantee the same degree of control is questionable, hence the willingness to bear the obvious deficiencies of the existing system for so long.

LABOR ALLOCATION IN THE SOVIET UNION

Labor Planning in the Soviet Union

We now consider the allocation of labor in the Soviet economy, which is accomplished through a combination of administrative controls and market forces. The latter, in the form of voluntary responses to wage differentials, primarily affect the supply of labor

[17] E. H. Carr and R. W. Davies, *Foundations of a Planned Economy, 1926–1929* (London: Macmillan, 1969), pp. 833–834.

in various occupations and regions; whereas administrative controls have been used to affect both the supply and demand sides of the Soviet labor market with the mix of market forces and administrative controls changing over time. In describing labor allocation, we first concentrate on general long-run trends, after which consideration will be given to periods when labor allocation has diverged distinctly from the central tendency. Given the important role played by the market in labor allocation, we shall consider both the demand and supply of labor in the Soviet economy. Let us consider first the determination of enterprise demand for labor through the planning system.

In the Soviet Union, the amount of labor required by the industrial enterprise is decided largely outside of the firm by superior authorities. In fact, the determination of enterprise labor staffing is an integral part of the general planning process. The enterprise *techpromfinplan* contains not only enterprise output and material input targets but also instructions on enterprise labor inputs. The amount of detail on labor staffing has varied over the years—recent reforms have reduced the number of external labor staffing directives—however, throughout most of the plan era, *techpromfinplan* labor staffing instructions have tended to be quite detailed, specifying the enterprise wage bills, the distribution of enterprise labor force by wage classes, average wages, planned increases in labor productivity, and so on. As one might recognize from our discussion of the Soviet manager, the manager has tended to exercise some discretion in the area of labor staffing within the constraints of the *techpromfinplan*; nevertheless, enterprise labor staffing is basically a decision made by planning authorities in accordance with production plans that they also determine.

Gosplan derives a balance for the Soviet labor force just as it derives balances for material inputs. The most important part of such Soviet manpower balancing is the estimation of available manpower resources, which is carried out by *Gosplan* with the help of regional and local government and planning authorities. This is not an easy task, for the reserve labor force in agriculture must be estimated along with the potential reserves among the female population, in addition to existing urban labor resources. Also, demographic factors such as birth and death rates and migration rates between regions and between the countryside and towns must be considered.

Once the available supply (both actual and potential) of labor resources has been estimated, *Gosplan* must estimate the demands for labor resources. The labor requirements of the various economic branches are determined in much the same manner as material input requirements. The planning authorities estimate in detail (after considerable bargaining and consultation with lower echelons) on the basis of coefficients (norms) relating labor inputs to outputs the labor staffing required to produce the given output targets. As in the case of material inputs, enterprises and lower planning echelons have commonly exaggerated their labor staffing needs for the purpose of adding to their safety factor, and planning authorities have had to allocate labor resources below enterprise requests to balance supplies and demands. Another complication is the fact that labor productivity tends to increase over time, meaning that the relationship between enterprise outputs and labor inputs varies over time—adding another variable to the problem of estimating required labor inputs.[18]

Once the planning authorities draw up the balance of labor resources, a second problem arises: how are they to bring the appropriate amount of labor into the various enterprises as planned or, to use the Soviet terminology, how are they to "guarantee the labor requirements of the national economy"?[19]

There are several possible alternative means of regulating supply. One would be to have the state conscript labor to be assigned administratively to enterprises. A second alternative would be to use differential wages as a means to attract labor into enterprises in planned proportions. A final alternative would be to manipulate the long-run supply of labor in various occupations through manpower training, education, and organized recruitment. In the Soviet

[18] A detailed discussion of Gosplan's labor balances can be found in A. N. Efimov et al., eds., *Ekonomicheskoe planirovanie v SSSR* [Economic planning in the USSR] (Moscow: 1967), chap. 6. For a discussion of the construction of the labor balance for the 1971–1975 plan, see M. Feshbach and S. Rapawy, "Labor Constraints in the Five-Year Plan," in Joint Economic Committee, *Soviet Economic Prospects for the Seventies* (Washington, D.C.: U.S. Government Printing Office, 1973), pp. 485–507.

[19] Efimov, *op. cit.*, p. 171.

Union, all three alternatives have been used in varying proportions; yet in more normal periods (other than during collectivization, war and so on), primary reliance has been placed on wage differentials to allocate labor, supplemented by long-run controls, as exerted through selective education. This is not to deny that the Soviet authorities have on several occasions relied heavily on strict administrative allocation of labor (especially during War Communism and World War II).

Differential Wages in the Soviet Union

Industrial wages[20] are set by central authorities in the Soviet Union. Various agencies have over time participated in wage scale determination—the ministries, the Council of Ministers, the Central Council of Trade Unions, the State Committee on Labor and Wages, and many others—but the recent trend has been towards uniformity in regulating wages by increasing centralization and standardization. A nationwide reform of industrial wages ongoing from 1956 to 1965, but largely completed between 1958 and 1960, has established a more simplified uniform system of industrial wages for the Soviet labor force.[21]

Industrial wage rates are set in the following manner: in each industrial branch, base rates are established (*stavka*) that specify the absolute wage of the lowest paid occupation. Then for each branch, a schedule (*setka*) is designated, which gives the wages of higher grade occupations as percentages of the lowest grade rate.[22]

[20] Our comments refer to wages in the noncollective farm sector. Collective-farm arrangements are discussed in Chapter Seven.

[21] Leonard J. Kirsch, *Soviet Wages: Changes in Structure and Administration Since 1956* (Cambridge, Mass.: MIT Press, 1972), pp. 1–8; Janet Chapman, "Labor Mobility and Labor Allocation in the USSR," paper presented at the joint meeting of The Association for The Study of Soviet-Type Economics and The Association for Comparative Economics (Detroit: December 1970), p. 3.

[22] Prior to 1956, this system was extremely complex. In all, there existed around 1,900 different *setka* schedules and about 1,000 different *stavka* assignments. In the new uniform system there are 10 *setka* schedules and 50 different *stavka* assignments. On this, see B. M. Sukharevsky, "Zarabotnaia plata i material'naia zainteresovannost" [The wage and material incentives] in A. P. Volkova et al., eds., *Trud i zarabotnaia plata v SSSR* [Labor and wages in the USSR] (Moscow: 1968), p. 302; see also Kirsch, *op. cit.*, table 4–2, p. 75.

By altering the base rate, the state can direct labor into and out of branches according to the plan. In this manner, high average wages in high priority sectors such as machinery, metallurgy, electricity, and coal were used to effect the dramatic shifts of labor out of agriculture and light industry into heavy industry during the early plan era. During NEP, average wages in the consumer goods sector exceeded those in heavy industry. Beginning with the First Five Year Plan, average wages in heavy industry grew more rapidly than in light industry, with a resulting shift of labor.[23] In the postwar period, a close correlation still persists between average branch wages and the national importance of the branch,[24] although recent statements suggest that wage authorities are now attempting to reduce differentials between light and heavy industry.[25]

By manipulating the *setka,* the state can encourage workers to acquire the skills that it requires. Thus, Stalin established schedules in 1931 that heavily favored skilled workers, to encourage the then untrained labor force to acquire industrial skills. As a result of the Stalin wage policy, large differentials arose between the earnings of skilled and nonskilled industrial workers. In fact, some evidence suggests that industrial wage differentials during the 1930s were larger than in the United States.[26] With the growing level of education of the labor force, the extreme differentials of the 1930s have been gradually reduced during the postwar period especially after 1956, and between 1956 and 1965 new ratios were established that set the rates of the most skilled categories at a maximum of two-and-one-half times that of unskilled categories as opposed to the

[23] Emily C. Brown, "The Soviet Labor Market," reprinted from *Soviet Trade Unions and Labor Relations* (Cambridge, Mass.: Harvard University Press, 1966), pp. 11–37, in M. Bornstein and D. Fusfeld, eds., *The Soviet Economy,* 3rd ed. (Homewood, Ill.: Irwin, 1970), pp. 217–220.

[24] Abram Bergson, *The Economics of Soviet Planning* (New Haven, Conn.: Yale University Press, 1964), p. 115. Soviet labor experts have noted in recent years that this system tends to create excessive turnover problems in branches having low base rates. In the eastern regions, during the 1960s, turnover was highest in the food industry where wages were lowest, and turnover was lowest in ferrous metals where wages were highest. Attempts are being made to reduce the turnover problem in consumer branches. On this, see Chapman, *op. cit.,* p. 13.

[25] Sukharevsky, *op. cit.,* p. 292.

[26] Abram Bergson, *The Structure of Soviet Wages* (Cambridge, Mass.: Harvard University Press, 1944), chap. 8; Sukharevsky, *op. cit.,* p. 291.

4:1-8:1 ratios of the 1930s and 1950s. Two other factors have contributed to the leveling of industrial wages in the postwar period: Minimum wage rates have been increased dramatically (they doubled between 1957 and 1968), and also the number (and percentage) of workers making low wages have declined markedly during this period.[27]

Industrial wages are also differentiated by region to encourage labor mobility into rapidly growing areas such as Siberia, Kazakstan, Central Asia, and the Far North, which have harsh climates and lack the cultural amenities of European Russia. Such regional differentials are computed by means of a uniform system of coefficients, which are multiplied by the standard wage rates to yield regionally differentiated wages. For example, the coefficients used to compute wages in the Far North range from 1.5–1.7;[28] that is, wages between 50 percent and 70 percent higher than the standard rates are paid to workers in the Far North for performing the same basic tasks. Supplements are also used, which bring the basic wage rate in the Far North to as high as 2.8 times that in European Russia.[29] As of 1968, there were ten regional coefficients used to establish regional wage differentials—a much simplified system from the ninety regional coefficients that existed prior to 1956.[30] In addition to regional differentiation, some higher rates are provided in cases of dangerous work and work performed under arduous conditions. For example, underground mining occupations receive basic monthly wages 14 to 33 percent higher than those for above-ground occupations. In the chemicals industry, work performed under especially hot, heavy, and unhealthy conditions re-

---

[27] Kirsch, *op. cit.,* chap. 4; Murray Yanowitch, "The Soviet Income Revolution," *Slavic Review,* vol. 22, no. 4 (December 1963), reprinted in M. Bornstein and D. Fusfeld, *The Soviet Economy,* 2nd ed. (Homewood, Ill.: Irwin, 1966), pp. 228–241. See also Sukharevsky, *op. cit.,* p. 196; and Kirsch, *op. cit.,* pp. 174–179.

[28] Brown, *op. cit.,* p. 219; Sukharevsky, *op cit.,* p. 302.

[29] Chapman, *op. cit.,* p. 23. Even these differentials have not proven sufficient to maintain an adequate labor force in the Far North and Siberia. Recent Soviet studies have suggested that the established regional differentials are not sufficient to compensate for cost of living differentials, not to mention the low level of services (child care, health, education) available in these regions. On this, see *ibid.,* pp. 13–16.

[30] Sukharevsky, *op cit.,* p. 302.

ceives payment 33 percent above the payment for work performed under normal conditions.[31]

The *total* wage of Soviet industrial workers is actually the sum of two components. On the one hand, the worker receives the basic wage computed according to the *setka* and *stavka* system described above. This component does not vary relative to the performance of the individual or his enterprise, and is guaranteed him by the state. In addition to the above, the worker receives a variety of supplementary bonus and incentive payments that vary with performance. These supplementary payments are in the form of bonuses for overfulfillment of plan norms, as premia paid from the wage fund or material incentive fund of the enterprise, and as supplements for special working conditions. For example in 1967, two-thirds of the average industrial worker's full wage was the basic wage, the remaining one third being from incentive payments. Of the latter, about 16 percent was for overfulfillment of norms, 10 percent was from premia payments, and 6 percent for supplements for special working conditions.

Prior to the general reform of wages beginning in 1956, bonuses and incentive payments made up a larger share of industrial wages owing to the greater importance of piece rates and incentive schemes. During the early 1950s, such payments accounted for slightly more than 40 percent of average industrial incomes. As a result of the 1956–1965 wage reform, bonuses and supplements now account for around 30 percent of industrial wage income. This decrease is a consequence of the substantial decline in the percentage of workers paid according to piece rates, which dropped from two-thirds to one-third of all industrial workers between 1957 and 1961.[32]

The common current in the Soviet wage policy has been that wage rates should be set to equate supply and demand for labor. If the state wants an increase of employment in metallurgy, for example, wage rates should be raised to attract additional labor into metallurgy. If the state wants to develop the Far North, it must take labor supply factors into account and set a highly differentiated

[31] Sukharevsky, *op. cit.,* p. 292; Kirsch, *op. cit.,* table 6–1, p. 125.
[32] Sukharevsky, *op. cit.,* pp. 297–302; Kirsch, *op. cit.,* chap. 2.

wage to overcome the workers' aversion to the region. As Leonard Kirsch has pointed out, in actual practice, the equation of supply and demand has been accomplished by combining centralized wage setting with enterprise flexibility in the area of incentive payments.[33] Thus if the basic wage rates established by central authorities create labor shortages or surpluses at the enterprise level, managers have made needed adjustments at the local level by raising or lowering incentive payments. According to Kirsch, the trend toward more simplicity and national uniformity in wage rates may therefore result in a loss of flexibility and a weakening of central control over labor allocation, compounded by the inflexibility of centrally determined basic wage rates that have remained essentially unchanged between 1960 and 1970.

Extramarket Controls
over Labor Allocation

That wage setting authorities have attempted to establish market-clearing wage rates through the system of basic and incentive wage payments does not imply that they have been content to rely entirely on the market to allocate labor. Instead, planning authorities have actively sought to influence supply conditions in labor markets within this context of voluntarism through education, organized recruitment, controls, and the *nomenklatura* procedure.

Education. In the Soviet Union, one of the most important sources of control over labor allocation in the long-run is the education system. It is important to note that the avowed objective of Soviet education is to meet the needs of the national economy.[34] In this regard, *Gosplan,* the Council of Ministers, and recently the All-Union Ministry of Education (since 1966) plan the numbers of students to enter particular areas of study, and types of educational

[33] Kirsch, *op. cit.,* chap. 8.
[34] Nicholas DeWitt, "Education and the Development of Human Resources: Soviet and American Effort," in *Dimensions of Soviet Economic Power* (Washington, D.C.: U.S. Government Printing Office, 1962), pp. 235–236. Because Soviet leaders see a direct and planned link between, say, higher education and the needs of the economy, the Soviet perception of higher education and the absence of the "liberal arts" notion differs significantly from that in the United States. For more recent developments in Soviet education, see David Carey, "Developments in Soviet Education," in *Soviet Economic Prospects for the Seventies, op. cit.,* pp. 594–637.

facilities to be provided. Such decisions are supposedly made to accord with the manpower needs of the country as stated in the economic plan. The close relationship between education and the economy is maintained at the regional and local level as well as at the national level. At the local level, educational authorities work with planning authorities and local enterprises to relate their activities to the needs of the local economy. Of course, the coordination is less than perfect, and one often finds complaints of a lack of coordination of labor and education planning.[35]

Graduates of secondary schools are often placed in local enterprises by local authorities on a quota basis. Local military commisariats are entrusted with placement of discharged military personnel in the local economy. Graduates of vocational schools are directed to positions by regional authorities, and graduates of specialized secondary and higher education are directed by special commissions to jobs in accordance with plans approved by *Gosplan* and the Council of Ministers. By placing new entrants into the labor market in this fashion, planning authorities influence the allocation of labor within the economy. There seems to be little official compulsion forcing graduates to accept their assigned jobs, although graduates of specialized and higher education are obligated to work for three years where the state places them.[36]

Organized Recruitment. A second source of state control over labor allocation is organized recruitment, which was a more important factor during the 1930s than in the postwar period. During the 1930s, *Orgnabor*—the Administration for Organized Recruitment of Labor—greatly facilitated the vast transfer of labor from the countryside to the city by supplying industrial enterprises with new laborers from collective and private farms. In this manner, some three million peasants were transferred from the village to the city through *Orgnabor* contracts. After World War II, *Orgnabor* became more involved in the transfer of workers among industrial enterprises than from agriculture to industry, and by the late 1950s *Orgnabor's* role in supplying industrial labor was a limited one. Its major role, instead, became the recruiting of labor

[35] Chapman, *op. cit.,* p. 4.
[36] Brown, *op. cit.,* pp. 206–210; and F. D. Romma and K. P. Urzhinsky, *Pravovye voprosy podbora rasstanovki kadrov* [Legal questions concerning the selection and arrangement of cadres] (Moscow: 1971).

for vast construction projects and new industries in the East and North. In this task, *Orgnabor's* efforts were supplemented by appeals of the *Komsomol* organization, designed to recruit younger workers.[37]

Controls over Labor Mobility. The competitive bidding for industrial workers plus the vast influx of untrained peasants from the countryside created excessive job turnover during the 1930s that forced the state and the enterprises to adopt additional extramarket controls over labor mobility. To take one example, the average worker in the food industry changed jobs on the average of three times a year in 1930 and 1931 and, for the economy as a whole, the average industrial worker changed jobs more than once per year.[38] One can imagine the negative impact that such high turnover had on labor productivity. In fact, labor productivity remained well below planned levels during the First Five Year Plan, a factor that contributed to the wage inflation of the period.

During the 1930s, a series of measures were adopted to reduce the excessive turnover: Absentceism was deterred by severe penalties (eviction from factory housing and loss of social insurance benefits), "closed shops" were used to reward select groups of reliable workers, and enterprise control over limited housing was used as leverage to promote labor stability. After 1938 such controls became even more severe: labor books (in which would be recorded a person's work record) were issued to all employed persons, an internal passport system was used to monitor the movements of population, and permission was required to change jobs (failure to comply being a criminal offense). These were only a few of the administrative measures employed. Such measures can perhaps be viewed as preparation for war, but they were also a part of the purges of the late 1930s. Administrative controls over labor increased during the war with the mobilization of specialists, the lengthening of the work day, the making of absenteeism a criminal offense, and the establishment of labor reserve schools. Most of the laws pertaining to labor control during the war were passed in 1940. They were quite severe and resulted in numerous instances

[37] Brown, *op. cit.,* pp. 210–212.
[38] Chapman, *op. cit.,* p. 8.

of criminal prosecution and imprisonment.[39] They remained on the books until their full repeal in 1956, although they had actually fallen into disuse during the early 1950s. In 1956, the work day was shortened, criminal liability for leaving work without permission and for absenteeism was abandoned, and social benefits were raised. As an immediate response to this liberalization, turnover in industry rose to 38 percent in 1956, after which it declined to a fairly steady 20–22 percent, which is below comparable turnover rates in manufacturing in the United States.[40] Nevertheless, the problem of "rolling stones" (workers who change jobs too frequently) remains a source of official concern especially in the outlying republics where labor is quite scarce. This concern has been sufficiently serious for the state to introduce a series of measures—special bonuses for uninterrupted employment (1965), a new labor code giving reliable workers special privileges and priority in job advancement (1971), and experimental programs in various urban areas to reduce job turnover—designed to combat what the state perceives as excessive job turnover.

Party Nomenklatura Controls. A final source of extramarket control over labor is the control over appointments, promotions, and dismissals exercised by the Communist Party through the *nomenklatura* procedure. As was pointed out in Chapter Five, the *nomenklatura* is a list from which the party nominates responsible individuals for posts in industry, agriculture, the state apparatus, and the army. In this manner, the party is able to control the staffing of important managerial and other administrative positions.

An Evaluation of
Soviet Labor Policy

One way to evaluate Soviet labor policy would be to consider its role in the process of resource allocation. How well have Soviet authorities utilized available labor resources? Are there notable labor shortages or surpluses either by occupation or by region? Has aggregate unemployment been avoided? How well does the

---

[39] For a detailed discussion of labor controls from the mid-1930s to 1956, see Alec Nove, *An Economic History of the USSR* (London: Penguin, 1969), pp. 195–198, 260–263.

[40] Chapman, *op. cit.,* pp. 7–8; Feshbach and Rapawy, *op. cit.,* p. 539.

system correct structural unemployment? This is the criterion of *allocative efficiency*.[41] Although the allocative efficiency of the Soviet labor market is an important criterion, a broader criterion may also be in order. The effectiveness of Soviet labor policy may also be evaluated in light of its contribution to the economic and social goals of the state, which we denote as *goal-achievement efficiency*.[42] Although these two efficiency measures are not necessarily incompatible, they may be in some cases. The restrictive labor policies during War Communism, the late 1930s, and World War II, for instance, definitely reduced the allocative efficiency of the Soviet labor market in order to achieve the political, economic, and military objectives of the state. On the other hand, the labor mobility of the early 1930s may have promoted allocative efficiency, yet been detrimental to goal-achievement efficiency—namely, rapid industrialization. A final criterion—the equity of Soviet wage policy is discussed in Part Four.

Let us consider first the contribution of Soviet labor policy to the major economic goal of the Soviet state between 1928 and the present, namely the achievement of rapid industrial growth. The discussion here will concentrate on the initial industrialization period of the 1930s. To achieve the long-run objective of rapid industrialization, labor policy had to accomplish several things: (1) The industrial labor force had to expand at a rapid rate; (2) within the industrial sector, a transfer of labor out of light industry into heavy industry was required; (3) the quality of the industrial labor force had to be improved to enable it to work with modern technology; and (4) a regional distribution of labor compatible with the distribution of natural resources had to be achieved. Soviet labor policy seems to have performed these functions reasonably well, with the possible exception of the last function.

Quantitative and Structural Changes. Despite the very slow population growth after the Revolution, the Soviets were able to expand their total labor force at an annual rate of 2.5 percent be-

---

[41] Our approach to allocative efficiency is quite intuitive and should not be confused with a formal development of Pareto optimality. The optimality of Soviet labor policy in terms of the Pareto conditions is discussed by Abram Bergson in *The Economics of Soviet Planning, op. cit.,* pp. 118–126.
[42] A similar standard is suggested by Kirsch, *op. cit.,* chap. 8.

tween 1928 and 1937,[43] a quite respectable rate by international standards.[44] Even more important than the overall rate of growth in employment was its sectoral distribution. In keeping with the state policy of rapid industrial transformation, the nonagricultural labor force expanded at an annual rate of nearly 9 percent while the agricultural labor force contracted at an annual rate of −2.5 percent (Table 8, Chapter Three). Commonly in the course of industrialization, agriculture suffers a *relative* decline in labor force with the *absolute* decline coming much later. In the Soviet case, there was an immediate sharp absolute decline and this transfer of labor out of the rural sector was a significant "contribution" of agriculture to development (discussed in Chapter Twelve). The trends within the industrial subsectors were in keeping with the state policy of industrial expansion in favor of heavy industry. Light industry suffered a decline in its labor force between 1928 and 1937 that was equally dramatic as the shift of labor out of agriculture (Table 8, Chapter Three).

How did Soviet labor policy affect these shifts? The rapid growth of the total labor force can in part be explained by the large rise in the participation rate (the percentage of total population employed on a full-time basis).[45] Without such an increase in participation rates, the rapid rate of expansion of the Soviet labor force would have been difficult to achieve in view of the slow overall population growth. During the First Five Year Plan alone (1928–1932), the number of workers and employees more than doubled according to official Soviet figures.[46]

[43] R. Moorsteen and R. Powell, *The Soviet Capital Stock, 1928–1962* (Homewood, Ill.: Irwin, 1966), pp. 643, 648.

[44] Simon Kuznets, *Economic Growth of Nations* (Cambridge, Mass.: Harvard University Press, 1971), p. 74.

[45] One finds varying estimates of trends in the Soviet labor participation rate. The reason is that prior to 1928, the major portion of the Soviet labor force was engaged in agriculture and, by definition, just about everyone in agriculture is considered employed, even if they only work part-time. Thus the measure cited here is for full time labor equivalents. See Warren Eason, "Labor Force," in Bergson and Kuznets, *op. cit.*, pp. 53–56.

[46] L. M. Danilov and I. I. Matrozova, *Trudovye resursy i ikh ispol'zovanie* [Labor resources and their utilization], in Volkova et al., eds., *Trud i zarabotnaia plata v SSSR* [Labor and wages in the USSR] (Moscow: 1968), p. 247.

Which particular labor policies contributed to the high participation rate? First, the policy of establishing subsistence or below subsistence wages in agriculture, coupled with the organized recruitment of able-bodied workers in agriculture (*Orgnabor*), resulted in the wholesale transfer of labor out of agriculture, where days worked per year were few relative to industry (owing to seasonal and other factors). Second, in the city the authorities introduced moral and legal, as well as economic, inducements for all able-bodied individuals to work.[47] Parasitism was subject to severe penalties and only women with young children were exempt from work obligations, with young mothers being encouraged to work where day-care facilities were available. Such pressures increased throughout the 1930s and peaked in the late 1930s (during the Stalin purges) when cases are recorded of nonworking mothers with newborn infants being criminally prosecuted for parasitism.[48] In addition to moral and legal incentives, economic incentives also contributed to the rising participation rate. The low real wages of the 1930s made it necessary for both husband and wife to work to make ends meet.[49] Thus in 1939, 71 percent of all women between the ages of 16 and 59 were members of the labor force.[50]

This increase in the overall participation rate is even more remarkable in view of the significant decline in the participation rate of the younger and older age groups during the 1930s. In 1926, 59 percent of the young people between ages of 10 and 15 worked. In 1939, this number had been reduced to 24 percent and by 1959, it was 12 percent. This decline was the result of the spread of universal education in the Soviet Union. Not only did the participation rate of the younger age groups decline, but also the participation rates of the older age groups fell during the 1930s. In 1926, 54 percent of the Soviet population over 60 years of age participated

---

[47] The Soviet Constitution (Article 12) reads "Work in the USSR is a duty and a matter of honor for every able-bodied citizen, in accordance with the principle: 'He who does not work, neither shall he eat.'" Quoted in E. Nash, "Recent Changes In Labor Controls in the Soviet Union," *New Directions in the Soviet Economy*, part III (Washington, D.C.: U.S. Government Printing Office, 1966), p. 854.

[48] Nove, *An Economic History of the USSR, op. cit.,* p. 262.

[49] Chapman, *op. cit.,* p. 31.

[50] Eason, *op. cit.,* p. 57.

in the labor force; by 1939, this number had been reduced to 49 percent.[51]

Soviet wage policy was also used to affect the distribution of labor within industry. In particular, the setting of higher relative wages in heavy industry than in light industry, the use of "closed shop" privileges to reward workers in high priority branches, and the setting of low piece-rate norms to allow large supplemental earnings in heavy industry encouraged the rapid transfer of labor into priority branches. As far as the trends in intersectoral wage differentials during the rapid industrialization period are concerned, of seventeen industrial branches, average wages in coal and in iron and steel ranked tenth and thirteenth, respectively, in 1924. By 1940, they ranked first and second, respectively.[52] On the other hand, the rankings of the consumer goods branches declined generally. These dramatic shifts in relative wages go a long way toward explaining the radical shift of labor within industry.

The Regional Distribution of Labor. In recent years, regional differentiation in wage rates has come to play an increasingly important role in the development of Siberia and the Far East. This is an important aspect of overall Soviet development policy in view of the vast oil and gas, timber, and hydroelectric power resources of these regions. Despite generally higher nominal wages and income supplements in these areas, Soviet authorities have been hard pressed to keep these regional economies supplied with highly mobile, skilled, and younger workers owing to the low real standard of living in these areas. To counter this trend, additional fringe benefits have been granted, such as longer paid vacations, earlier retirement programs, improved child care facilities, etc. Nevertheless, recent studies show that despite all these added benefits, per capita real family income in the eastern regions scarcely differed from the average level in the Russian Republic owing to higher prices, harsher climate, inadequate housing, and lack of cultural facilities.[53] Thus it seems as if the regional distribution of labor in the Soviet Union remains one of the most problematic areas of

[51] *Ibid.,* p. 57.
[52] Bergson, *The Economics of Soviet Planning, op. cit.,* p. 115.
[53] Chapman, *op. cit.,* pp. 14–28; Feshbach and Rapawy, *op. cit.,* pp. 539–541.

Soviet labor policy, and the Soviet state, despite all its efforts to the contrary, is still unable to achieve a net increase in population beyond the Urals.

Qualitative Changes. Not only was Soviet labor policy successful in bringing about significant quantitative and structural (if not regional) changes in the Soviet labor force, but, in addition, the qualitative changes were equally dramatic. Any evaluation of Soviet labor policy would be incomplete without mention of the successes of Soviet manpower policy.

A cursory examination of the educational level of the Russian population prior to the Soviet period indicates how poorly equipped the Soviet labor force was to meet the needs of all-out industrialization. The last major census of the tsarist period in 1897 showed 78 percent of the over 15 population as illiterate, with only 1.4 million having education beyond the seventh grade out of a population of 126 million, and only 93,000 with completed higher education. The immediate preindustrialization figures of the 1926 census show considerable improvement preparatory to the industrialization drive: the illiteracy rate had dropped to 56 percent, six million had received education beyond the seventh grade, and roughly half a million had completed higher eduaction.[54]

The major spurt in educational achievement, however, occurred during the industrialization drive of the 1930s. By 1939, the illiteracy rate had dropped to 20 percent, 14 million had completed education beyond the seventh grade, and more than one million had completed higher education.[55] Thus, the Soviet educational system did a very significant job in meeting the manpower needs of a modernizing economy.

Soviet labor policy contributed to this modernization of Soviet manpower in several ways: first, labor codes were put into effect forbidding the employment of younger people, a factor that enhanced the effectiveness of the universal education decrees. Most important, large wage differentials were established between the skilled and unskilled laborers, providing positive incentives for laborers to acquire highly rewarded skills. Stalin in 1931 cast aside

[54] DeWitt, *op. cit.*, p. 244.
[55] *Ibid.*, p. 243.

"left equalitarianism" and introduced large incentives for skilled occupations. Wage differentials widened substantially between 1928 and 1934 and continued to increase throughout the 1930s.[56] The wage revision beginning in 1956 narrowed wage differentials, a policy made possible by the vast increases of skilled labor during the prewar period. For example, the number of graduates of specialized secondary institutions (*technicum*) increased from 1.3 million in 1926 to 3.3 million in 1939, whereas the total population had only increased by 17 percent. By 1959, the number had risen to 7.9 million.[57]

Further Evaluation
of Soviet Labor Policies

So far we have evaluated Soviet labor policy on the basis of its contribution to the long-run objective of rapid industrialization. Our conclusion is that its contribution was considerable. Thus far the evaluation has been primarily on the basis of the goal-achievement efficiency of Soviet labor policy. Now we turn to some aspects of its allocative efficiency.

Soviet Full Employment Policies. As one might expect, aggregate unemployment has probably not been high in the Soviet Union throughout the plan period. Insufficient aggregate demand should not be a problem in a centrally planned economy where investment, public consumption, defense, and administration are supposedly balanced so as to fully utilize available labor. In this manner, the demand for labor as determined in the national balances has generally been sufficient or more than sufficient to employ fully all those willing to work at established wage rates. This was not always so: immediately prior to the First Five Year Plan (1927–1928), unemployment averaged over 8 percent of the nonfarm labor force.[58] The overfull employment planning of the 1930s actually created an excess demand for labor that reduced unemployment to minimal proportions. Unfortunately, unemployment data

[56] Bergson, *The Structure of Soviet Wages, op. cit.,* chaps. 8 and 14. Also see Sukharevsky, *op. cit.,* pp. 291–292; and Kirsch, *op. cit.,* pp. 174–179.
[57] DeWitt, *op. cit.,* p. 244. For a survey of Soviet discussion, see Kirsch, *op. cit.,* pp. 98–103.
[58] Bergson, *The Economics of Soviet Planning, op. cit.,* p. 105.

were no longer gathered during the 1930s, with the official Soviet claim that unemployment had been liquidated.[59] One can assume with some degree of safety that unemployment owing to insufficient aggregate demand has not been a serious problem during the plan period.

The lack of published unemployment figures signals both a strength and weakness of Soviet labor policy. It could indicate the absence of large-scale aggregate unemployment; yet it raises questions about the existence of significant frictional and structural unemployment in view of the official lack of attention to unemployment problems. Underemployment also seems to be a growing problem as managers are reluctant to let unneeded workers go. Thus it is probably safe to assume that unemployment, while not a pressing national problem, has not been liquidiated entirely as a social problem. For instance, younger people are reported to have difficulties in finding jobs. There has tended to be little coordinated job information, and job placement services have only been recently established. Local employment exchanges were abolished during the 1930s with the "liquidation" of unemployment. Although numerous agencies have been known to aid in the placement of workers—local government, the trade unions, the *Sovnarkozy*—unemployed workers have been forced to find new jobs primarily through informal means such as word of mouth, bulletin boards, newspaper and radio ads, and "open-door days" at factories. A 1962 survey of the chemicals industry showed that 84 percent of jobs were obtained as hires at the factory gates.[60] This is an area where ideology has seemed to lead to a less efficient solution than

---

[59] The Soviet figures on the liquidation of unemployment are:

Year	Unemployed (in thousands)
1922	407
1924	1344
1929	1741
April 1930	1081
October 1930	240
December 1930	no unemployment

SOURCE: Danilov and Matrozova, *op. cit.*, pp. 245–248.

[60] Murray Feshbach, "Manpower in the USSR," in *New Directions in the Soviet Economy, part III, op. cit.*, pp. 724–725.

possible. In 1967, a national employment service was established —being located within *Gosplan*—called the State Committee on Labor Resource Utilization. Also regional and local employment offices have been established in larger cities. In addition, vocational guidance programs are now being emphasized in the schools.[61] Thus the period since 1967 has witnessed something of a turnabout in Soviet attitudes toward labor exchanges, which were originally viewed as necessary only under capitalism. Now such agencies seem to be well accepted instruments of labor allocation with roughly one-half of all industrial jobs mediated by an employment agency.[62]

Labor Unions in the Soviet Union.[63] In the labor market of the Soviet Union, there should be little monopolistic behavior—often said to be a major source of allocative inefficiency in market economies. Enterprise managers must take the basic wage rates determined by superior planning agencies as given and must respond to them accordingly, although they do have some flexibility in determining actual wages paid through their controls over bonuses and job classifications. In turn, trade unions play no real role in the wage setting function. Therefore, the workers themselves cannot directly affect wage rates via collective bargaining with the state. Instead of acting as bargaining agents for their memberships, Soviet trade unions concern themselves primarily with encouraging the membership to meet their planned tasks, enforcing labor discipline, protecting workers from dismissals, and enforcing labor codes.

Thus, the major inefficiencies resulting from monopolistic behavior in labor markets on the part of employers and employee organizations have been avoided for the most part in the Soviet Union. This does not mean, however, that one should expect perfectly efficient behavior on the part of management in labor staffing problems. First, management is highly restricted by its wage bill and employment staffing plans and therefore lacks necessary flexibility. Second, the pressure to fulfill output targets causes management to ignore potential ways to economize on labor cost in many cases. Instead, managers are inclined to keep superfluous workers

[61] Chapman, *op. cit.,* p. 4.
[62] Chapman, *op. cit.,* p. 4; Romma and Urzhinsky, *op. cit.,* chaps. 1 and 2.
[63] For a more detailed discussion of this issue, see Bergson, *The Economics of Soviet Planning, op. cit.,* pp. 116–118.

in case they are needed later.[64] Finally, managers have often lacked the authority to fire unneeded laborers, who are protected by the trade union under the labor codes. Experiments are being undertaken to change the rules and thus to encourage management to fire superfluous workers.[65]

Third, the tremendous administrative complexity of centrally administering wage rates has tended to create anomalies throughout the plan period. Especially during the period when ministries administered wage rates, the Soviet wage structure had certain peculiarities; piece-rate earnings were often allowed to dwarf basic rates thus rendering the basic rate differentials meaningless. Also, workers in different branches performing the same work tended to be rewarded quite differently. In 1956, a cashier in nonferrous metals earned roughly twice as much as a cashier in metal processing. Such differentials were in keeping with the priority system but tended to be less than efficient—a lower wage would probably have been sufficient to attract the correct number of cashiers into the priority sector.[66] This is a further example of the sacrifice of allocative efficiency to ensure target fulfillment in priority sectors. In Siberia, wage rates in heavy industry were allowed to get far out of line with corresponding rates in light industry, thereby causing severe consumer goods supply problems that have retarded the overall development of the region.[67] In addition, the growing standardization and centralization of basic wage rates during the wage reform has tended to add inflexibility to the system, with resulting

[64] Chapman, *op. cit.*, p. 5.

[65] In this regard, the so-called *Shchekino experiment* is worthy of mention. It was introduced on an experimental basis in the Shchekino Chemical Combine in October of 1967 and allowed the enterprise to use cost savings from reduced employment to raise wages of the remaining workers. In this manner, it was hoped to encourage managers to eliminate excess staff. The results were (as of 1969) that the number employed fell by 800 and average wages rose sharply. So far, the results of the Shchekino experiment are impressive, but, as of 1972, the experiment had only been extended to 300 enterprises, and there are still significant pressures on management ("storming," variable production targets, need for volunteers for harvesting, and so on) to retain redundant workers. See Chapman, *op. cit.*, p. 5; *Ekonomicheskaia gazeta* [The economic gazette], no. 4 (1968), 11–14; Feshbach and Rapawy, *op. cit.*, p. 489.

[66] Bergson, *The Economics of Soviet Planning, op. cit.*, pp. 117–118.

[67] Chapman, *op. cit.*, pp. 23–25.

surpluses and shortages of workers in various occupations (the shortage of machine operators, for example).[68]

Discrimination by Sex in the Soviet Union. An evaluation of Soviet labor and manpower policy would not be complete without positive reference to the notable lack of discrimination by sex in the Soviet labor market—a source of allocative inefficiency in most Western market economies. In the Soviet Union, there is a relatively long tradition of free access for women to most occupations and professions, a tradition that grew out of the extreme labor shortages of the 1930s and possibly out of the more enlightened attitudes of the Soviet leadership toward women. In fact, throughout most of the plan era, especially before 1957 when women were no longer permitted to do manual work in mines, women performed heavy manual labor.[69] This practice still persists with women employed as street cleaners in urban areas and with women performing a large portion of the physical labor in Soviet agriculture.[70] The utilization of women in heavy manual labor jobs is only one side of the coin, for Soviet women have had relatively free access to the professions and state bureaucracy as well. Women have, however, tended to cluster in certain professions and sectors. For example, in 1970, while accounting for 51 percent of all workers and employees, women accounted for 85 percent of health service, 78 percent of credit and banking, 75 percent of trade, 68 percent of communication, and 61 percent of government employment.[71] Women tend to particularly dominate the medical and teaching professions, accounting for over 70 percent of all doctors (1970) and for over 70 percent of all teachers (1970) in the Soviet Union.[72] The women's access to the professions is guaranteed by their relatively free admission to higher and specialized secondary

---

[68] Kirsch, *op. cit.,* chap. 8.

[69] The basic source on the role of women in the Soviet economy is Norton T. Dodge, *Women in the Soviet Economy* (Baltimore: Johns Hopkins Press, 1966).

[70] Norton, T. Dodge, "Recruitment and Quality of the Soviet Agricultural Labor Force," in J. R. Millar, ed., *The Soviet Rural Community* (Urbana: University of Illinois Press, 1971), p. 183.

[71] *Narodnoe khoziastvo SSSR v 1970 g.* [The national economy of the USSR in 1970], p. 516.

[72] *Ibid.,* pp. 632, 691.

education, with women accounting for 49 percent of all enrollment in higher education (1970–1971) and for 54 percent of all enrollment in specialized secondary education (1970–1971). It is noteworthy that women tend to predominate in all categories of higher and specialized secondary education (education, health, law, and economics) except agriculture and industry-construction-transportation.[73] An important factor contributing to the high rates of participation of Soviet women in the labor force has been the state policy of providing kindergarten and nursery school care for their preschool children. In 1970, for example, 8.1 million preschool children were enrolled in such centers, which is slightly under one-half of all preschool children in the entire Soviet Union.[74] Thus the Soviet woman does seem to have fairly smooth access to most occupations and professions. On the other hand, there is little evidence of free access of women to important positions in agriculture, industrial management, and the party. Female industrial managers and collective farm chairwomen are indeed quite rare.

THE ALLOCATION OF CAPITAL IN THE SOVIET ECONOMY: THE INVESTMENT DECISION

Investment Planning

By designating the physical outputs of the economy in the process of material balance planning, authorities must plan at the same time the expansion of enterprise capacity, that is, capital investment in plant and equipment.[75] In order to meet the expansion of

---

[73] *Narodnoe obrazovanie, nauka i kul'tura v SSSR; statisticheskii sbornik* [Education, science and culture in the USSR; a statistical collection] (Moscow: 1971), p. 186.

[74] *Narodnoe khoziastvo v 1970 g., op. cit.,* p. 634.

[75] Investment choice in the Soviet Union has been discussed in a number of articles and books: Abram Bergson, *The Economics of Soviet Planning, op. cit.,* chap. 11; Gregory Grossman, "Scarce Capital and Soviet Doctrine," *Quarterly Journal of Economics,* vol. 67, no. 3 (August 1953); Alfred Zauberman, *Aspects of Planometrics* (New Haven, Conn.: Yale University Press, 1967), chaps. 13 and 14; Alan Abouchar, "The New Soviet Standard

output called for by either current or perspective plans, the capacity of the enterprise must be expanded accordingly to insure the consistency of the output plan. Earlier it was noted that enterprise output plans are based upon past performance plus projected increases from additional plant and equipment. Although there has at times been an imperfect meshing of output and investment plans, the latter has been primarily determined by the former.

In the Soviet Union, so-called *project-making organizations* are in charge of actual investment planning at the enterprise level. They are staffed primarily by engineers and are generally attached to the ministries. Thus, an institution external to the enterprise plans and executes investment projects for the enterprise, which explains in part the reluctance of Soviet managers to risk introducing new technology. The task of the project-making organization is first to elaborate and then to choose among alternative projects that yield the expansion of enterprise capacity specified by higher planning authorities. In this section, we deal with how project-making organizations choose among alternative investment projects. In a broad sense, they actually have little to do with the basic allocation of capital among competing ends, for they are concerned primarily with allocating fixed amounts of investment in accordance with centralized directives within their own administrative unit. The allocation of capital *among* administrative units, which, after all, is the decision most basic to the allocation of capital, remains in the hands of higher planning authorities.[76]

In the Soviet Union, an annual investment plan for the entire economy that has been formulated by *Gosplan,* the ministries, and various state committees, is submitted to the Council of Ministers.

Methodology for Investment Allocation," *Soviet Studies,* vol. 24, no. 3 (January 1973), 402–410.

[76] Prior to the adoption of the new investment rules of 1969, the basic sectoral and regional allocation of capital through the investment plan was largely a political rather than an economic decision. The 1969 rules propose that such decisions now be made on the basis of an "effectiveness coefficient." One may wonder whether this aspect of the 1969 rules will be observed, because the new rules also state that the "effectiveness coefficient" be applied subject to the planned output mix. This implies a contradiction, because once the outputs of the economy are planned, investment allocation must proceed accordingly and will not be dictated by other criteria. For a more detailed discussion, see Abouchar, *op. cit.,* 407.

Once approved, the various planning organizations including *Gosplan* and the ministries supervise its implementation by the project-making organizations. Just as the material balance plan has its financial counterpart, so does the investment plan. The Ministry of Finance provides a portion of the funds required to finance the various projects directly from the state budget—the financial institution directly in charge of disbursing such investment funds is the Investment Bank (*Stroibank*), with *Gosbank* providing the funds for general repairs.[77] In this manner, the financial counterpart of the investment plan is used to locate deviations from the investment plan in much the same manner as it is used to monitor other enterprise operations. An overcommitment of investment resources (a situation where the materials and equipment required for approved projects exceed available supplies) will usually result in financial authorities providing insufficient financial resources to complete the project as scheduled. This practice tends to bring investment supplies and demands into balance, but builds costly delays into underfinanced investment projects. One important source of this tendency to overcommit investment resources has been the ministries' desire to get as many projects started as early as possible so as to establish a priority claim on future investment supplies. This problem had become so serious that by 1971 85 percent of investment projects begun the previous year were still unfinished.[78]

Problems of Investment Choice in the Soviet Economy

The choice among alternative investment projects, all of which yield the same increase in capacity, is not easy to resolve in the Soviet context. How is the project-making enterprise to choose among them? Ideally, the choice should be made that will minimize the

[77] One of the features of the general reform introduced in 1965 was to give enterprises more control over internally generated investment funds by allowing for some decentralized investment decisions. See our discussion in Chapter 10 on the implementation of this aspect of the reform. Prior to the reform (1964), internally generated investment funds accounted for 39 percent of enterprise capital investment. By 1968, this figure had risen to 45 percent. See *Finansy SSSR* [Finances of the USSR], no. 10 (1968), pp. 22–23. It should be noted that even these internally generated funds are strictly controlled by higher financial authorities.

[78] *Voprosy ekonomiki* [Problems of economics], no. 9 and no. 11 (1972). Also see Nove, *The Soviet Economy, op. cit.,* pp. 97–98, 231–240.

consumption of scarce capital resources while achieving the required capacity expansion. On the surface, this seems like a simple criterion; yet for Soviet investment planners it can be very complex.

First, there is an ideological constraint. The Marxian labor theory of value attributes all value to current and past labor that has gone into the production of a commodity. From this, Soviet ideologists concluded during the early plan period that capital does not create value; therefore enterprises should not pay interest charges for its use—a view that prevailed until the 1965 economic reform. Thus, using interest-like calculations to rank investment alternatives seemed out of line with Marxian ideology. As the English authority Alfred Zauberman has expressed it, "where yield on capital is rejected as the motive force of the economy, its maximization could not serve as a guide for investment decisions."[79] In line with this reasoning, fixed capital from 1930 through 1965 was allocated to enterprises as an interest-free grant. Enterprises therefore came to regard capital as a free factor of production to be sought after as long as its marginal productivity remained positive. The only legitimate capital cost definitely allowable by Marxian value theory is depreciation that supposedly compensates the state for the past labor being used up in production. There is no room in this strict Marxian framework, however, for technological obsolescence that does not represent a using up of past labor. As a result, the sole capital cost to enterprises, depreciation, has generally been small because of the omission of charges for obsolescence.[80]

The conflict between the strict interpretation of the labor theory of value and Soviet growth strategy is obvious. Whereas Marxian value theory dictates that capital does not create value, the basis of Soviet growth strategy has been to direct as much additional capital as possible into growth producing sectors such as electricity, machinery, and metallurgy. Rapid industrial growth is the objective of the system; yet the instrument crucial to generating this growth was said to create no value of itself and carried a zero price. In practice, this conflict between ideology and growth strategy was resolved by having Soviet planners allocate capital administratively

[79] Alfred Zauberman, *op. cit.*, p. 139.
[80] Gert Leptin, *Methode und Efficienz der Investitions-Finanzierung durch Abschreibungen in der Sowjetwirtschaft* (Berlin: Osteuropa-Institut, 1961), part II.

according to a strict set of priorities without reference to relative rates of return.[81]

The Soviet industrial price system represents a second problem. If more than one project yields the planned capacity increase, the project-making organization must generally evaluate the costs and benefits of alternative projects in value terms. If, of two equally expensive investment projects, one project economizes on coal inputs while the other project saves natural gas, the final choice will depend to a great extent on the relative prices of coal and gas. If these prices fail to reflect relative scarcities, then the "wrong" choice can be made. Because of the inconsistencies of the Soviet price system, one can understand the reluctance of Soviet planners to rely exclusively on value criteria in making investment decisions. Instead, most official guidelines suggest that value criteria be combined with physical indicators such as labor productivity and savings of specific material inputs, rather than relying exclusively on single value indicators.[82]

A third problem, closely related to the first, has been the lack of recognition of the importance of the time factor in capital investment decisions—a consequence of the absence of a recognized *time discount factor* or interest rate. In market economies, investment projects that promise to yield large returns in the distant future will be ranked against projects yielding smaller but quicker returns by computing the present discounted value of each project using the interest rate as a common discount factor. A high interest rate (that supposedly reflects both society's time preferences and the scarcity of capital) will discourage long-term projects with delayed returns.

In the Soviet Union, there has historically been little recogni-

[81] For a detailed discussion of these points, see Grossman, *op. cit.,* 311–314, reprinted in Franklyn Holzman, *Readings on the Soviet Economy* (Skokie, Ill.: Rand McNally, 1962).
[82] "Recommendations of the All-Union Scientific-Technical Conference on Problems of Determining the Economic Effectiveness of Capital Investment and New Techniques in the USSR National Economy," *Problems of Economics: A Journal of Translations,* vol. 1, no. 9 (January 1959), 86–90, reprinted in Holzman, *op. cit.,* pp. 383–392. Also see "Standard Methodology for Determining the Economic Effectiveness of Capital Investments," *Ekonomicheskaia gazeta* [The Economic Gazette]), no. 39 (1969), 11–12. Translated in *The ASTE Bulletin,* vol. 13, no. 3 (Fall 1971), 25–36.

tion (at least until recently) of the time factor in choosing among alternative investment projects, and the perceived opportunity cost —either to the Soviet enterprise or to the ministry—of tying scarce resources down in long-term projects has been small. The lack of a time discount factor explains, to a great extent, the undue delays in the completion of investment projects (a problem frequently referred to in the Soviet press), and the tendency to select projects with long gestation periods (the gigantomania of the early thirties) despite the considerable scarcity of capital resources. Such behavior can be attributed, in part, to the expansion of planners' time horizons beyond sight during the "heroic phase of growth" during the 1930s.[83]

The Development of
Investment Choice Criteria

Beginning in 1930, interest was outlawed as a capitalistic vestige no longer required when capital is the property of the state. In keeping with the general sentiment of the early 1930s, it was argued that the economic laws of capitalism were no longer operative and that capital should be allocated administratively without resort to the economic criteria of the old capitalist order. Thus, Stalin argued that the allocation of investment according to rates of return or other profitability measures would be contrary to the interests of the state, for resources would then be directed away from heavy industry into light industry where profit rates would be higher. In addition, it was argued in some quarters that the liberation from economic rules would permit planners to choose more advanced technology than would be justified if standard economic rules were strictly observed, and the rapid industrial transformation of the Soviet Union would be promoted.[84]

The intersectoral allocation of investment became an administrative decision of higher planning authorities after 1930 and open discussion of investment choice criteria at the economywide level disappeared. The practical problem of allocating investment funds within specific sectors led, however, even during the barren Stalin years, to the development of informal investment allocation rules

[83] Zauberman, *op. cit.,* p. 139.
[84] Nove, *The Soviet Economy, op. cit.,* p. 233.

that were eventually officially formalized between 1958 and 1960. During this early period, ministerial project-making organizations were forced to develop more specific rules for making decisions than simply choosing the investment variant yielding the lowest operating costs (the only rule officially sanctioned), since the ministry had a limited capital allotment that had to be stretched as far as possible. This problem was especially troublesome in the railroad and electrical power industries where continuous substitutions between ever-increasing capital outlays and ever-lower operating costs were possible. Thus, project-making engineers and industry officials began to develop investment rules for internal use that implicitly introduced rates of return and other capital profitability criteria into the investment decision. Disguised under acceptable terminology such as "effectiveness of investment" and "periods of recoupment," such investment criteria came into fairly wide use within selected ministries by the late 1930s.[85]

The use of such interest-like calculations was officially sanctioned in 1958 by an all-Union conference on capital effectiveness after roughly three decades of pioneering work by engineers and economists.[86] The appearance of the USSR Academy of Science publication, *Typical Method of Determining the Economic Effectiveness of Capital Investment and New Technology* (*Typical Method*) in 1960 further substantiated the official acceptance of interest-like criteria for allocating investment within administrative units. Let us turn to the rules suggested by this 1960 publication.

Investment Decision Rules,
1960–1969

The most important decision rule suggested by the *Typical Method* was the *Coefficient of Relative Effectiveness* (CRE), which was designed to evaluate the trade-offs between capital outlays and operating expenses. Such a measure was to be easily rationalized in terms of Marxian value theory since operating expenses ultimately reflect labor costs, and capital should be evaluated accord-

[85] For a detailed discussion of the various techniques used during this period, see Grossman, *op. cit.*, 315–343.
[86] "Recommendations of the All-Union Scientific-Technical Conference on Problems of Determining the Economic Effectiveness of Capital Investment and New Techniques in the USSR National Economy," *op. cit.*, 86–90.

ing to how well it economizes the use of labor. To illustrate how the CRE measure operates, we assume that a project-making organization must choose between two alternative projects both yielding the planned capacity increase. The two differ in terms of initial capital outlays (K) and resulting annual operating expenses (C), which, let us say, do not vary over time. Under normal circumstances, the higher the capital outlay, the lower the operating costs, and the CRE must evaluate this trade-off. It should be noted that a capital charge is *not* included in operating expenses—only a depreciation charge—an omission that may bias the CRE measure in favor of capital intensive projects. In our example, the CRE is given by the following formula, where the a and b subscripts refer to the two projects:

$$\text{CRE} = \frac{C_b - C_a}{K_a - K_b}$$

Thus, if project b costs 1 million rubles and project a costs 2 million rubles of capital outlay,[87] and project b's operating expenses are .2 million and project a's operating expenses are .1 million, then the CRE of project a (relative, of course, to project b) would be 10 percent. This should be interpreted to mean that for every additional ruble of capital outlay on project a, .1 ruble of operating costs would be saved over project b.[88]

The *Typical Method* further suggested that a norm be established—the standard coefficient of efficiency—for *each* branch. If a project's CRE fell below the norm, it should be rejected unless there are special reasons for not doing so. In this manner, a minimum profitability, or capital effectiveness, rate would be established for each branch. Because these norms varied by branch (with the higher the priority the lower the profitability norm for a given

[87] Capital outlay includes the cost of buildings, equipment, and installation, but excludes the cost of the site. Zauberman, *op. cit.*, p. 142.

[88] An equivalent test would be: Let E be the "standard coefficient of efficiency." Then the two projects could be compared by comparing their full costs—including an imputed interest cost:

$$C_b + EK_b \gtrless C_a + EK_a$$

The project with the lowest *full* cost would be chosen. See Bergson, *The Economics of Soviet Planning, op. cit.*, p. 254.

branch), capital profitability rates would not equalize among branches, as had been advocated by several prominent Soviet economists and many Western economists.[89] This result, however, was to be expected in view of the state's desire to promote priority industrial and military sectors independently of restrictive economic criteria. Although there is no definite evidence, the CRE norms actually established were most likely not high enough to equate the supply and demand for capital, and administrative capital rationing remained the primary mechanism for investment allocation, despite the CRE.[90]

Although the CRE was just one of many rules suggested between 1960 and 1969 it became the most important and most widely used. It is important to note how crude a measure it actually was, for it failed to come to grips with varying patterns of capital expenditures, different service lives of projects, risk differences, the different time spacing of operating cost economies, as well as a host of other problems.

An important question raised by the CRE criterion was whether a single uniform standard coefficient should be established for the entire economy, promoting eventual equalization of marginal rates of returns on investment projects in all branches.[91] The *Typical Method* was clearly in favor of differentiated standard branch norms. For the state to surrender its control over investment allocation and to replace it by a uniform mechanical rule was judged as contrary to the long-range vision of the Soviet leadership. The 1958 all-union conference on capital effectiveness leading up to the publication of the *Typical Method* was quite clear on this point: "Some projects with smaller effectiveness may be approved . . . because they accelerate the solution of the basic economic problem, and are necessary for defense, political and other reasons; . . ." and further: "capital investments are made on the basis of the economic laws of socialism which require the

---

[89] Bergson, *The Economics of Soviet Planning, op. cit.,* pp. 225–265; Judith Thornton, "Differential Capital Charges and Resource Allocation in Soviet Industry," *Journal of Political Economy,* vol. 79, no. 3 (May–June 1971), 545–561.

[90] Bergson, *The Economics of Soviet Planning, op. cit.,* pp. 262–263.

[91] See *ibid.,* p. 258 for a demonstration that a uniform norm will result in the equalization of the marginal productivities.

preferential development of the means of production. . . ."[92] An important point often overlooked in these discussions of the CRE is that the suggested rules generally pertain to the internal allocation of fixed sums of investment within a branch, and that only those investment alternatives would be evaluated that yield the planned increases in capacity. Also, the norms were generally not set to equate supply and demand, thus requiring a continuation of administrative rationing independently of the suggested rules. Thus, the leadership's acceptance of interest-like calculations in 1960 really represented no significant deviation from the centrally planned nature of the Soviet economy. Instead, the objective throughout was to make the allotted investment more effective and efficient within the context of planned choice.

Another common current running through official pronouncements during this period was the reluctance of planning authorities to rely too heavily upon a single criterion. For example, the 1958 conference report made it quite clear that, while the conference favored the CRE measure, it was to be used in combination with a number of other indicators where the situation required. If industrial prices failed to reflect relative scarcities, physical indicators were to be used along with the CRE criterion. The possibilities of substantial delays in project completion were also to be considered, as well as the interrelation of the project with other branches. Social factors such as the workers' safety were to enter into the calculation as well.[93]

New Investment Rules, 1969

In September of 1969 a new methodology for evaluating the relative effectiveness of investment projects was approved. The new *Standard Methodology for Determining the Economic Effectiveness of Capital Investments*[94] (referred to here as *Standard Methodology*) is quite similar to the CRE method, the major difference

[92] "Recommendations of the All-Union Scientific-Technical Conference on Problems of Determining the Economic Effectiveness of Capital-Investments adn New Techniques in the USSR National Economy," *op. cit.,* 88.
[93] *Ibid.,* 88–89.
[94] "Standard Methodology for Determining the Economic Effectiveness of Capital Investments," translated in *The ASTE Bulletin,* vol. 13, no. 3 (Fall 1971), 25–36. It originally appeared in *Ekonomicheskaia gazeta* [The economic gazette], no. 39 (1969), 11–12.

being the acceptance of a *uniform* standard norm to apply to all branches of the economy. The measurement suggested to compare alternative investment projects is the *Comparative Economic Effectiveness of Capital Investments,* referred to here as the CEE. The CEE measure requires that investment projects be selected so that:

$$C_i + E_n K_i = \text{minimum}$$

where: C_1 represents the current expenditures of the ith investment variant, K_i represents the cost of the investment project and E_n is the uniform *normative coefficient of effectiveness* of capital investments, which is the same for all branches. The *Standard Methodology* suggests that this normative coefficient be set at 12 percent. Thus, the *Standard Methodology* calls for evaluating investment projects on the basis of their *full* costs (operating costs plus imputed capital costs) with imputed capital costs calculated using a uniform coefficient for all branches.

An example of how the CEE method works would perhaps be helpful at this point: assume three alternative investment projects (Exhibit 4). As one might expect, there is a trade-off between operating costs and investment outlays in our example (the higher the K, the lower the C):

Exhibit 4 **Computation of the "Comparative Economic Effectiveness" (CEE) of Three Investment Projects**

Project	(1) Operating Costs (C)	(2) Investment Outlay (K)	(3) Uniform Normative Coefficient	Full Costs $(1 + [3 \times 2])$
1	300	510	12%	361.2
2	290	525	12%	353.0
3	285	590	12%	355.8

In our example, the projects could refer to investment projects within a branch or in different branches. Because the normative coefficient is uniform for the entire economy, this should make no difference in the evaluation process. The CEE investment criterion calls for the selection of the project having the lowest costs, e.g., the lowest *full* cost (the sum of operating expenses plus a capital charge). In Exhibit 4, the project with the lowest full cost, Project 2, should be selected for it yields the optimal trade-off between greater investment outlays and lower operating costs.[95]

In addition to establishing the CEE concept, the *Standard Methodology* provides detailed discounting procedures for evaluating in present value terms projects whose operating expenditures and capital outlays change over time. The *Standard Methodology* suggests using a discount rate of 8 percent, which it claims is in line with current depreciation procedures.

On the surface, the use of a uniform normative coefficient for the entire economy would seem to violate the branch priority principle and call for the allocation of investment strictly on the basis of rates of return. This conclusion seems to be further supported by the fact that the *Standard Methodology* calls upon the investment plan to allocate investment among branches according to a uniform coefficient of effectiveness. In fact, this may not prove to be so. First, the suggested normative coefficient (12 percent) will probably not be high enough to equate the supply and demand for capital—a point already noted by Soviet critics.[96] As long as this remains true, much capital allocation will be handled by administrative procedures. Second, the *Standard Methodology* states that deviations from the normative coefficient may be approved by *Gosplan* in order to stimulate technological progress, to allow for differences in wage and price levels, and to promote regional development. For example, a lower (8 percent) normative coefficient has already been established for the Far North, and there is talk of establishing an 8 percent norm for electrical power generation. The generally liberal allowance for exceptions to the uniform coefficient rule has become a matter of concern to reform-minded Soviet economists, one of whom writes that they "open the door to the broadest

---

[95] The importance of differential normative coefficients in preserving the branch priority system can be illustrated using Exhibit 4. Suppose that Project 2 is in light industry; whereas Projects 1 and 3 are in heavy industry. Instead of using 12 percent as a norm for light industry, a higher 30 percent rate is set. The CEE of Project 2 now becomes 447.5, which eliminates it from selection.

[96] V. Cherniavski, "The Measure of Effectiveness," *Problems of Economics: A Journal of Translations,* vol. 15, no. 8 (December 1972); and Kantorovich, *op. cit.,* pp. 152–162.

degree of arbitrariness" in investment decisions.[97] Third, the *Standard Methodology* suggests that the CEE index be supplemented by further indexes—productivity of labor, capital-output ratios, capital investment per unit of output, and selected physical indexes—to "take account of the influences of the most important factors on the economic effectiveness of capital investments and to take account of the interaction of this effectiveness with other divisions of the plan."[98] Fourth, the *Standard Methodology* states that the investment plan should follow the output plan of the national economy; for example, the allocation of investment among branches is still to be predetermined by the industrial supply and output plan. This statement seems to contradict one of the key provisions of the new investment rules—namely, that capital should be allocated among branches according to a uniform normative coefficient of effectiveness.[99]

Thus, we tend to view the new *Standard Methodology* as a step in the direction of investment allocation on the basis of rates of return irrespective of branch of production, but as avoiding a clear break with investment allocation according to the priority principle.

Proposals of Soviet
Mathematical Economists

An influential group of Soviet mathematical economists that includes such prominent Soviet academicians as L. V. Kantorovich, V. V. Novozhilov, and V. S. Nemchinov argues that the CEE criteria can be effectively used only if based upon a rational system of underlying prices.[100] "Objectively determined prices," they argue, should be generated by using linear programming techniques. Although the methods proposed by the mathematical school differ

[97] Quoted in V. Vainshtein, "On Methods of Determining the Economic Effectiveness of Capital Investment," *Problems of Economics: A Journal of Translations,* vol. 15, no. 3 (July 1972), 12.

[98] *Standard Methodology, op. cit.,* p. 31.

[99] Abouchar, *op. cit.,* 407.

[100] V. S. Nemchinov, ed., *The Uses of Mathematics in Economics* (Cambridge, Mass.: MIT Press, 1964); and L. V. Kantorovich, *The Best Use of Economic Resources* (Cambridge, Mass.: Harvard University Press, 1965).

among themselves, there is a unifying thread: The basic resource allocation problem is seen as choosing among the large number of alternative activities, whose usage levels are limited by resource availabilities, in such a manner as to optimize the economy's objective function. For example, the objective function may be the total cost of producing a planned bill of final output targets with the goal being to minimize this total cost. In the course of finding the optimal combination of economic activities, a set of "objectively determined prices" would emerge as the solution to the dual linear programming problem, which could then be used as rational resource prices. Importantly, an "objectively determined" price of capital would also be generated which would be rational in the sense that this price would equate the supply and demand for capital, which the Soviet mathematical economists propose to use as the normative coefficient of effectiveness.

An Evaluation of
Investment Choice

Investment choice in the Soviet Union has been far from perfect throughout the plan period. The gigantomania[101] of the early 1930s and the large percentage of uncompleted construction projects even today may be cited as the most visible wastes of the current system. There is much to criticize about investment choice throughout the plan period: the lack of a capital charge until recently, the reluctance of planners to rely exclusively on profitability criteria, and the overtaut investment planning. In the past, Western criticism of investment planning has centered on the use of differentiated branch norms that resulted in differentiated rates of return among sectors. All of these have been cited as major sources of inefficiency in the Soviet economy.[102]

However, when one considers the *relative* inefficiency of investment choice in the Soviet Union, the issue becomes much more complex, especially in the context of rapid economic development.

[101] Leon Smolinski, "The Scale of Soviet Industrial Establishments," *American Economic Review*, supplement, vol. 52 (1962), 138–148.
[102] Bergson, *The Economics of Soviet Planning, op. cit.*, p. 334; Judith Thornton, "Differential Capital Charges and Resource Allocation in Soviet Industry," *Journal of Political Economy*, vol. 79, no. 3 (May/June 1971), 545–561.

Some Western development economists stress that investment choice based upon capitalist marginal rules in developing economies is inefficient, owing to the existence of externalities and interdependencies.[103] For example, marginal efficiency calculations might necessitate the rejection of a vital road, canal, or factory that planners working with an integrated plan and a long time horizon might accept.[104] Thus, the issue of the relative efficiency of Soviet investment choice under conditions of rapid industrialization is very cloudy, and we are unable to provide a clear answer. The ultimate answer depends upon the compatibility of static and dynamic efficiency. What we suggest here is that the reader avoid drawing hasty conclusions until we take up this matter again in Part Four.

SUMMARY: RESOURCE ALLOCATION IN THE SOVIET UNION

We have surveyed how resources are allocated in the Soviet economy in the last two chapters. With several significant exceptions, resources are allocated administratively by the central plan. Material balance planning is used to allocate industrial supplies almost without reference to their prices, which are designed to equal average branch costs of production. Throughout the planning process, financial authorities and party officials monitor plan fulfillment, the former through the use of "ruble control." The Soviet manager is supposed to direct his enterprise in accordance with the *techpromfinplan,* which has been formulated by superior planning agencies. In fact, the manager does exercise some discretion in the operation of the enterprise, and in this area he is motivated by the managerial reward system, which has tended to be output oriented. The enterprise's investments are determined external to the enterprise with

[103] For example, see P. N. Rosenstein-Rodan, "Problems of Industrialization of Eastern and South Eastern Europe," *Economic Journal,* vol. 53, no. 210 (June–September 1943), 202–211.

[104] In the new *Standard Methodology,* it is clearly pointed out that a broad view of costs and benefits must be taken that should extend far beyond the project itself. Questions should be asked such as: how will the proposed project affect transportation facilities, related industries, labor supplies, etc.?

the basic allocation of investment funds being determined administratively in the investment plan.

The major exceptions to administrative allocation are the labor and the consumer goods market. In the Soviet Union, labor has been allocated primarily by differential wages, supplemented by other controls such as organized recruitment, placement of selectively educated graduates, and other administrative arrangements. Consumer goods, once produced in planned quantities, have primarily been allocated to consumers through the market. Thus retail prices have tended to approach market clearing prices just as wage rates have tended towards market clearing rates.

Selected Bibliography

SOVIET ENTERPRISE MANAGEMENT

Joseph Berliner, "Managerial Incentives and Decisionmaking: A Comparison of the United States and the Soviet Union," in M. Bornstein and D. Fusfeld, eds., *The Soviet Economy,* 3rd ed. (Homewood, Ill.: Irwin, 1970), pp. 165–195.

Joseph Berliner, *Factory and Manager in the USSR* (Cambridge, Mass.: Harvard University Press, 1957).

David Granick, *Managerial Comparisons of Four Developed Countries: France, Britain, United States, and Russia* (Cambridge, Mass.: MIT Press, 1972).

David Granick, *Soviet Metal Fabricating and Economic Development* (Madison: University of Wisconsin Press, 1967), chap. 7.

David Granick, *The Red Executive* (Garden City, N.Y.: Doubleday, 1960).

David Granick, *Management of the Industrial Firm in the USSR* (New York: Columbia University Press, 1954).

Alec Nove, *Economic Rationality and Soviet Politics* (New York: Praeger, 1964), chap. 5.

Barry M. Richman, *Management Development and Education in the Soviet Union* (East Lansing: Michigan State University, 1967).

Barry M. Richman, *Soviet Management* (Englewood Cliffs, N.J.: Prentice-Hall, 1965).

LABOR ALLOCATION IN THE SOVIET UNION

Abram Bergson, *The Economics of Soviet Planning* (New Haven, Conn.: Yale University Press, 1964), chap. 6.

Abram Bergson, *The Structure of Soviet Wages* (Cambridge, Mass.: Harvard University Press, 1944).

Emily Clark Brown, *Soviet Trade Unions and Labor Relations* (Cambridge, Mass.: Harvard University Press, 1966).

Janet Chapman, "Labor Mobility and Labor Allocation in the USSR," paper presented at the joint meeting of The Association for the Study of Soviet-Type Economics and The Association for Comparative Economics (Detroit, Mich.: December 1970.)

Janet Chapman, *Real Wages in Soviet Russia Since 1928* (Cambridge, Mass.: Harvard University Press, 1963).

Warren W. Eason, "Labor Force," in Abram Bergson and Simon Kuznets, eds., *Economic Trends in the Soviet Union* (Cambridge, Mass.: Harvard University Press, 1963).

M. Feshbach and S. Rapawy, "Labor Constraints in the Five-Year Plan," in Joint Economic Committee, *Soviet Economic Prospects for the Seventies* (Washington, D.C.: U.S. Government Printing Office, 1973).

Leonard J. Kirsch, *Soviet Wages: Changes in Administration and Structure Since 1956* (Cambridge, Mass.: MIT Press, 1972).

Mary McAuley, *Labor Disputes in Soviet Russia 1957–1965* (Oxford: Oxford University Press, 1969).

THE INVESTMENT DECISION

Alan Abouchar, "The New Soviet Standard Methodology for Investment Allocation," *Soviet Studies,* vol. 24, no. 3 (January 1973).

Abram Bergson, *The Economics of Soviet Planning* (New Haven, Conn.: Yale University Press, 1964), chap. 11.

P. Gregory, B. Fielitz, and T. Curtis, "The New Soviet Investment Rules: A Guide to Rational Investment Planning?" *Southern Economic Journal,* vol. 41, no. 3 (January 1974).

Gregory Grossman, "Scarce Capital and Soviet Doctrine," *Quarterly Journal of Economics,* vol. 67, no. 3 (August 1953).

Gert Leptin, *Methode und Effizienz der Investitionsfinanzierung durch Abschreibungen in der Sowjetwirtschaft* [Methods and efficiency of investment financing through depreciation in the Soviet economy] (Berlin: Osteuropa-Institut, 1961).

Alfred Zauberman, *Aspects of Planometrics* (New Haven, Conn.: Yale University Press, 1967), chaps. 13 and 14.

CHAPTER SEVEN

Soviet Agriculture

The history of Soviet agriculture forms a very important part of the overall story of Soviet economic development. This importance stems in part from the traditionally significant role played by the peasant in Russian and more recently in Soviet society; it also stems, however, from the Soviet experience as a most interesting case of the role of agriculture in a developing economy, and in particular, the unique Soviet solutions to development problems.

We have already examined important facets of Soviet agricultural development in the period prior to the introduction of planning in 1928, and in addition, have discussed the drive to collectivization and the immediate impact of that historic event upon the institutions and performance of Soviet agriculture. In this chapter, we turn first to a consideration of the organization and operation of Soviet agriculture in the postcollectivization period, and in particular, focus upon the collective farm (*kolkhoz*) and its role in the agricultural sector.

Second, from the point of view of the Soviet experience with economic development, it is important to consider the extent to which agriculture in fact "contributed" to this development—we can then formulate more accurately the role of agriculture in the Soviet development model. Finally, although the immediate impact of collectivization upon agricultural output was negative, it remains necessary to examine agricultural output and productivity performance in a long-run framework, which is done in the concluding section of this chapter.

THE ORGANIZATION OF SOVIET AGRICULTURAL PRODUCTION

Although various forms of collective production organizations had existed earlier in the Soviet Union, the predominant form—comprising 91.7 percent of all collectivized land by 1931—became the agricultural *artel*, or *kolkhoz*.[1] In addition, but initially playing a subservient role was the state farm, or *sovkhoz*. The state farm might well be described as a factory in the countryside insofar as important features of its organization and operation are very similar to the industrial enterprise. The *kolkhoz*, however, was, and in large measure remains, a form of organization unique to the Soviet bloc countries. Organizational aspects of Soviet agriculture are summarized in Table 14.

The *kolkhoz* is, in theory, a cooperative organization in which the peasants voluntarily join to till the soil, using means of production contributed initially by those who join, but now owned jointly by all in the *kolkhoz*. Under the *kolkhoz* charter of 1935 (since 1969 there has been a new charter), the means of production are said to be *"kolkhoz-cooperative"* property belonging to the *kolkhoz* in perpetuity.[2] In addition to the socialized sector of the *kolkhoz*

---

[1] The reader interested in the discussion of the different organizational forms might consult D. J. Male, *Russian Peasant Organization Before Collectivization* (Cambridge: Cambridge University Press, 1971); Robert G. Wesson, *Soviet Communes* (New Brunswick, N. J.: Rutgers University Press, 1963).

[2] As we shall see, the organizational and operational features of the typical *kolkhoz* have changed quite significantly over time. The new *kolkhoz* charter, finally published in 1969, in large measure served only to formally codify changes already made and authorized during the intervening years. Thus with the increased size of the *kolkhoz*, an expanded managerial structure was authorized, limited new autonomy for management was enacted—confirming earlier trends—and the labor day (*trudoden'*) as a method of calculating payments to labor was abandoned in favor of a wage system. Also, the designation "*kolkhoz*-cooperative" was dropped in the new charter. For a discussion of these changes, see Robert C. Stuart, *The Collective Farm in Soviet Agriculture* (Lexington, Mass.: Heath, 1972).

Table 14 **The Organization of Soviet Agriculture (selected indicators)**

	1928	1932	1940	1953	1957	1960	1965	1968	1970
Number of collective farms (in thousands)	33.3	211.7	236.9	97.0	78.2	44.9	36.9	36.2	33.6
Sown area of collective farms as a portion of total sown area (%)	1.2	70.5[a]	78.3	83.9	68.4	60.6	50.2	49.4	47.9
Number of state farms	1,407	4,337	4,159	4,857	5,905	7,375	11,681	13,398	14,994
Sown area of state farms as a portion of total sown area (%)	1.5[b]	n.a.	7.7	9.6	25.7	33.1	42.6	43.0	44.4
Sown area of the private sector as a portion of total sown area (%)[c]	97.3	n.a.	13.0	4.4	3.8	3.3	3.2	3.3	3.2

[a] Based upon aggregate sown area for 1933.
[b] Includes state farms and other state agricultural enterprises.
[c] The private sector consists of three parts: (a) private plots of collective farm members; (b) private plots of workers in industry and other state organizations; (c) the private peasant economy. The last was of minimal importance after the 1930s.

SOURCES: Selected volumes of *Narodnoe khoziastvo SSSR* [National economy of the USSR]; *Sel'skoe khoziastvo SSSR* [Agriculture of the USSR].

(land, equipment, buildings, etc.), the use of which is governed by the chairman and management board, each peasant is entitled to own a limited number of animals and to cultivate a private plot. These plots and private holdings have been very important in terms of their contribution to Soviet agricultural output, although they have been subjected to a considerable degree of restriction over the years.[3]

In reality, the voluntary aspects of *kolkhoz* membership have been absent. *Kolkhoz* members who depart for the city do not in fact receive the equity that they have contributed to the farm. In addition, the internal passport system has limited peasant labor mobility both within the rural sector and between the rural and urban sectors.

The highest organ of administration in the *kolkhoz* is the general meeting, or in some instances since 1958, meetings convened in the basic production units within the *kolkhoz*—the brigades. In theory, the general meeting elects the chairman of the *kolkhoz,* although in reality this position is generally filled by a party appointee through the *nomenklatura* procedure, and the vote is perfunctory. In addition to the chairman, the general meeting selects a management board that normally consists of the chairman and other leading personnel (specialists, brigadiers, etc.).[4] Again, although theoretically elected in practice the board is generally chosen by the chairman and secretary of the party committee.

---

[3] Although the presence of the private sector has been ideologically unpalatable to the regime, the importance of its product contribution relative to its input usage has been sufficiently great to insure its preservation. Over time, however, the official attitude towards the private sector has tended to fluctuate. The major work on this sector is Karl-Eugen Wädekin, *The Private Sector in Soviet Agriculture,* George Karcz, ed., Keith Bush, translator (Berkeley: University of California Press, 1973).

[4] The management board is relatively small (7–15 persons), thus making it suitable for operational management. In practice, there may be division of labor within this body—the chairman may be responsible for the field crop sector, the vice-chairman for the cattle sector, etc. Normally, this body may convene once a week or more frequently; meetings may last several hours. As we shall see later, the substantially increased size of the *kolkhoz* since the early 1950s has measurably increased the role of the brigade—especially the brigadier—and brigade meetings as a focus of decision-making activity. In addition, there has been a tendency to expand the presence of advisory bodies capable of supplying technical information to the decision-making centers. See Stuart, *op. cit.,* chap. 2.

Finally, the revision commission, an auditing body, is similarly selected.[5] In addition to such personnel matters, the general meeting also is supposed to exercise powers relating to membership matters, discipline, general approval of plan documents, and other administrative matters.

No discussion of the administrative structure of the *kolkhoz* would be complete without reference to the roles of the Communist Party and, prior to 1958, the Machine Tractor Stations (MTS). Within the *kolkhoz* there may exist one or more party organizations (a Primary Party Organization and possibly a candidate group or Party-Komsomol group).

It is difficult to know with any precision the impact of the party apparatus on the decision-making of the *kolkhoz*. However, the party organizations and their members are, as "leaders of the masses," responsible for the appropriate direction of state and party policy. More than this, however, the party is concerned with the immediate operation of the farm insofar as managerial personnel are typically party members and in addition will work closely with the secretary of the party organization.

In addition to a general leadership role, the party is directly concerned with what we would call personnel matters—selection and dismissal, work conditions, general morale, and so on. The party also organizes and runs campaigns to promote better farm performance. In short, the party is an all-pervasive force in the agricultural, just as it is in the industrial, enterprise.

We have already noted in Chapter Four that the Machine Tractor Stations (MTS) were established in 1933, basically to act as mechanisms of state control in the countryside and also to serve as a device to allocate the usage of machinery and equipment among the collective farms. From their beginnings, the MTS were powerful instruments of state control in the Soviet countryside in that they had a monopoly over agricultural specialists (until the early 1950s), and over most major farm equipment—both of which were absolutely essential to the success of the individual *kolkhoz*. But

---

[5] *Ibid.* The auditing commission has proven to be a very ineffective body, partly due to the nature of its tasks and possible conflicts with party personnel, and also the lack of personnel adequately trained in auditing matters. A knowledge of economic matters has never been a prerequisite for any position in a *kolkhoz*.

more than this, the director of the MTS, along with the chairman of the *kolkhoz,* was responsible for the execution of economic activity within the *kolkhoz*—thus the MTS played a decisive and continuing role in the day-to-day operations of the *kolkhoz,* and bore responsibility for its results. Under these circumstances, one can readily understand the close tutelage under which the *kolkhoz* fell. In fact, it was described by Khrushchev in the 1950s as the presence of "two bosses" in the countryside—an intolerable situation that ultimately led to the dissolution of these stations in 1958 and to the sale of their equipment directly to the *kolkhoz.*

AGRICULTURAL PLANNING: THE KOLKHOZ

The *kolkhoz* is not, in substance, an independent cooperative, for its most important decisions are planned from above. Like other economic entities in the Soviet system, the *kolkhoz* has an annual plan drawn up by planning organs and integrated with the overall national economic plan. Within the *kolkhoz,* this plan is broken down into short-run targets, although like the industrial enterprise, priority has been primarily placed on the *gross output* target. The distribution of this planned output is also predetermined by the plan insofar as the *kolkhoz* is required to meet certain compulsory deliveries at fixed prices set by the state. The remainder of the output could either be sold to the state at higher "above-quota" prices (the famous "two-level" pricing system, which was largely abandoned in 1958), sold in collective farm markets, or delivered to the collective farm members as partial in-kind payment for their labor services.[6] At the same time, input configurations are estab-

[6] The two-level price system was formally abolished in 1958, although thereafter farms were actively encouraged to deliver more than the state quotas. The two-level system was partially restored for grain in 1965. The whole matter of agricultural procurement has been the subject of ongoing discussion. For a survey of various positions, see Morris Bornstein, "The Soviet Debate on Agricultural Price and Procurement Reforms," *Soviet Studies,* vol. 21, no. 1 (July 1969), 1–20. In large measure the two-level pricing system could be abandoned as the Soviet Union grew richer and the agricultural sector declined in relative importance. For many years, however, this price system tended to institutionalize the Scissors Crisis of the 1920s.

lished within the plan, leaving little room for flexibility: land and equipment utilization (prior to 1958) was determined by the MTS and labor distributed by a system of norms specifying compulsory minimum participation rates for collective farm members in the socialized sector of the farm.[7] Capital funds might be obtained from retained earnings, in which case the portion of gross income to be set aside and the utilization of such funds are both spelled out in the plan with only limited room for the manager to shift funds from one to another.[8]

Although long-term planning has always existed in Soviet agriculture, it has had little operational meaning. Crop patterns, land usage, labor distribution, and other important microeconomic decisions have largely been made on a short-run basis by administrative planning organs external to the *kolkhoz*. These organs, though establishing plan targets in conjunction with the *kolkhoz* management board, have been concerned primarily with satisfying immediate superiors. Under this system, the familiar industrial problem of success indicators—the problems of defining capacity, achievement, and so on—has also plagued *kolkhoz* operations, worsened by the normal unpredictability of the natural environment in which agricultural production takes place.[9]

Distribution of Kolkhoz Output

The most crucial aspect of the *kolkhoz* has been its system of output distribution and labor payment, for this system has, over the

[7] Following the demise of the MTS in 1958, machinery and equipment were sold to the *kolkhozy* and the managerial functions of the MTS eliminated.
[8] *Kolkhoz* investment, unlike other agricultural and industrial investment in the Soviet system, is not budget financed. Capital investment must, therefore, be met from funds generated within the *kolkhoz* or by the use of loans from *Gosbank*. For a discussion of *kolkhoz* financing, see James R. Millar, "Financing the Modernization of *Kolkhozy*," in James R. Millar, ed., *The Soviet Rural Community* (Urbana: University of Illinois Press, 1971), pp. 276–303.
[9] The problem of setting appropriate targets based upon a realistic assessment of capacity has been peculiarly difficult in agriculture. Planners have tended to use various measurement techniques such as on-site inspection, past performance, and so on. In general, the "ratchet" effect has been prevalent, thus inducing *kolkhoz* management to hide production capability as inspectors search for a basis upon which to increase targets. The absence of significant long-term planning in agriculture has had a negative impact upon this process. For an extended discussion, see Stuart, *op. cit.*, chap. 6.

years, insured the steady flow of agricultural products to the state, in spite of spotty overall agricultural performance. As we shall see, this was the Soviet way of forcing agriculture to perform the necessary support role to industry that is required in the course of economic development.

Until 1958, as noted, the *kolkhoz* operated under a two-level price system. The state paid a fixed price for compulsory deliveries of important crops (grains, technical crops, etc.), which until the early 1960s was not adjusted to even cover gradually rising costs of production in the *kolkhoz*. These deliveries were not based upon output performance, but rather upon *sown* area—thus shifting the burden of unpredictability of agricultural returns onto the agricultural sector and away from the state.[10] Produce left over after the compulsory sales, and after in-kind payment had been made for MTS services, could be either sold to the state at higher above-quota prices or in the collective farm markets at retail prices. The latter have been the primary outlet for the produce of the private plots and a major source of money income for the peasant family.[11] Such a system might have worked more smoothly were it not for the dismal state of agricultural planning throughout much of the plan era, plus the normal problems of variability in this sector. In fact, farm capacity was frequently not known by planners, and targets were constantly ratcheted upwards in the expectation of improved performance. Thus achieving success was often limited to a one-time opportunity, for the level of state exactions increased accordingly, so that the collective farmers had no better standing than they had had initially.

Finally, an essential feature of the *kolkhoz* has been the

[10] The state farm was not well-suited to carry the burden of agricultural output fluctuations. In the case of crop failures, the state would cover losses in that it would have to meet the wage bill by subsidizing the state farm from the state budget. Therefore, resources would flow back into, not out of, agriculture. This explains why primary reliance was placed on the *kolkhoz* and not on the *sovkhoz* during the 1930s.

[11] The private sector has been and remains an important source of peasant family income. In 1953, for example, 45.7 percent of aggregate family income was derived from the private subsidiary economy. By 1963, this proportion had declined relatively little to 42.9 percent. See V. P. Ostrovskii, *Kolkhoz'noe krest'ianstvo SSSR* [*Kolkhoz* peasants of the USSR] (Saratov: Saratov University, 1967), p. 93.

method of labor payment—the labor day or *trudoden,* which was formally abandoned in 1966 in favor of a wage payment system as used in state farms and industrial enterprises. The labor day was not a measure of labor time and bore no necessary relation to the work day—rather it was an arbitrary unit in which all farm tasks were rated. A given task, for example ploughing a field, might yield the collective farmer a certain number of labor days, the value of which was uncertain because only at the end of the year could the *value* of the labor day—in money and in kind—be determined by dividing any remaining product and income (after compulsory state exactions) by the number of labor days earned by the *kolkhoz* as a whole. Then and only then could each person's labor day earnings be established.

To insure the state of a first and guaranteed claim upon output, this system was unique in that the collective farmer bore the burden of crop fluctuations by having the value of his labor days shrink. Indeed with labor earning a residual, there could be little incentive for managers to use labor effectively, let alone for the laborers to devote significant effort to production in the socialized sector of the *kolkhoz.* From other standpoints, however, the system was even less appropriate. First, the labor day was itself a largely arbitrary measure of work input. From farm to farm, region to region, and over time, the number of labor days granted for a given task could vary widely and with little relation to the actual or perceived effort required to complete a given task. In addition, income distributions to the peasants were small and very infrequent since the value of the labor day was not calculated until the termination of the year (advances were introduced in the 1950s, a matter to be discussed later) and thus the peasant was expected to expend effort for an unknown reward in the distant future. In this light, the relative promise of labor devoted to the private plot, and the lack of incentive to exert oneself in the socialized sector can be appreciated. Throughout the plan era, these private plots have occupied a small portion of peasants' work time but have produced roughly one-half of their aggregate family income, plus a significant contribution to agricultural output.[12]

[12] For a discussion of the contribution of the private sector see, for example, Karl-Eugen Wädekin, "Kolkhoz, Sovkhoz, and Private Production in Soviet

Finally, the labor day system of distribution prevented the use of cost accounting. It is little wonder that cost accounting did not exist on collective farms until the mid-1950s, at which point state farm wage rates were frequently utilized to value the labor component of *kolkhoz* production costs. Such a system must have made the cost information that went into decision-making virtually worthless and thus hindered the efficient utilization of farm inputs.

CHANGING PATTERNS IN SOVIET AGRICULTURE: THE KHRUSHCHEV ERA AND AFTER

Collectivization was a social transformation of the first magnitude. Not only did it produce a great social upheaval in its initial stages, but also it served to create a unique institutional structure that has lasted to the present day as a cornerstone of Soviet agrarian policy, despite its apparently negative impact upon incentives and efficiency. In the postwar period, however, there have been important changes in the agricultural sector. Although the impact of World War II upon agricultural production was severe, prewar agricultural gross production had generally recovered by the late 1940s.[13] As we shall discuss shortly, however, agricultural per-

---

Agriculture," in W. A. Douglas Jackson, ed., *Agrarian Policies and Problems in Communist and Non-Communist Countries* (Seattle: University of Washington Press, 1971), pp. 106–137.

[13] The reader interested in the details of the war period might read Erich Strauss, *Soviet Agriculture in Perspective* (London: Allen & Unwin, 1969), chap. 7; Lazar Volin, *A Century of Russian Agriculture* (Cambridge, Mass.: Harvard University Press, 1970), chap. 12. Useful sources in Russian would be the multivolume official history, P. N. Pospelov, ed., *Istoriia velikoi otechestvennoi voiny sovetskogo soiuza* [History of the great patriotic war of the Soviet Union, 1941–1945] (Moscow: Voenizdat, 1945); I. A. Gladkov, ed., *Sovetskaia ekonomika v periode Velikoi Otechestvennoi Voiny 1941–1945* [The Soviet economy in the period of the great patriotic war] (Moscow: Nauka, 1970), chaps. 5–6; Iu. V. Arutiunian, *Sovetskoe krestianstvo v gody Velikoi Otechestvennoi Voiny* [Soviet peasants in the years of the great patriotic war], 2nd ed., (Moscow: Nauka, 1970); I. E. Zelenin, *Sovkhozy SSSR (1941–1950)* [Sovkhozy of the USSR, 1941–1950] (Moscow: Nauka, 1969).

formance was not promising in terms of yields, costs, seasonality of production, and so on. Although Stalin did devote attention to agriculture during the postwar period, he did so primarily in terms of two rather grandiose schemes—first, the effort to achieve productivity gains through massive amalgamation of collective farms into gigantic complexes, and second, the so-called Stalin Plan for Transforming Nature, the essence of which was a vast irrigation network for the country.[14] Both were subsequently the subject of severe criticism by Khrushchev, and indeed, the path to higher productivity in Soviet agriculture was rather different in the Khrushchev era.

The Twentieth Congress of the Communist Party in 1953 devoted extensive time to a discussion of agricultural problems in the Soviet Union. In fact, Khrushchev was to stake—and perhaps ultimately end—his career on his many attempts to revitalize the agricultural sector on a long-run basis.[15] The changes of the Khrushchev era were by most any judgment extensive and important, though not all successful. We shall classify the policies of this period into three broad groups: (1) agricultural campaigns, (2) organizational changes, and (3) economic adjustments. Although these classifications are somewhat arbitrary, they will assist in developing an understanding of the period, and its importance for the future.

[14] The postwar developments in Soviet agriculture and the role of V. R. Williams and T. D. Lysenko, both interesting figures in the history of Soviet agriculture (and science), are discussed in Volin, *op. cit.,* chap. 13.

[15] For a useful survey of this period, see Jerzy F. Karcz, "Khrushchev's Agricultural Policies," in M. Bornstein and D. Fusfeld, eds. *The Soviet Economy,* 3rd ed. (Homewood, Ill.: Irwin, 1970), pp. 223–259; for a discussion of agricultural policy-making under Khrushchev, see Sidney I. Ploss, *Conflict and Decision-Making in Soviet Russia: A Case Study of Agricultural Policy, 1953–1963* (Princeton, N.J.: Princeton University Press, 1965); Werner G. Hahn, *The Politics of Soviet Agriculture, 1960–1970* (Baltimore, Md.: Johns Hopkins University Press, 1973); for a survey of the post-Khrushchev years, see Roger A. Clarke, "Soviet Agricultural Reforms Since Khrushchev," *Soviet Studies,* vol. 20, no. 2 (October 1968), 159–178; see also the discussion by Alec Nove, W. A. Douglas Jackson, and Jerzy F. Karcz in *Slavic Review,* vol. 29, no. 3 (September 1970), 379–428.

Agricultural Campaigns
Under Khrushchev[16]

Khrushchev associated himself with three main agricultural campaigns: the virgin lands program, the corn program, and the "plowup" campaign.[17] Let us consider each campaign briefly.

The virgin lands campaign was an effort to cultivate (using state farms) a large tract of land in Siberia and Kazakhstan, the purpose of which would be the expansion of grain output. Begun in 1954, the goal was initially quite modest—namely, the reclamation of 13 million hectares (one hectare is 2.47 acres) of land by 1955. In fact, the scheme proved to be more grandiose and by 1960, 42 million hectares had been seeded, representing roughly 20 percent of all sowings by all farms in that year. However, if the vision was grandiose, the results were less so. Although substantial (yet inadequate) amounts of funds were invested in this program, the marginal nature of the virgin lands soils, the highly variable climate (with a short growing season), and scarcity of other production inputs—notably irrigation—meant that for the most part yields remained low, and total output, although never very high, fluctuated significantly from year to year.[18] In retrospect, it would seem that the continuation of the program was primarily a result of the buoyancy created by the few good crop years. Finally, while the virgin lands territory might be highly questionable as a long-run scheme especially, with given technology and funding, one might consider the scheme a short-run expedient to avoid the immediate import of large supplies of grain. In this sense, the program was successful in that the average annual output of grain gained from the expansion of sown area was roughly 15 million tons for the period 1958–

[16] For a survey of these campaigns, see Joseph W. Willett, "The Recent Record in Agricultural Production," in *Dimensions of Soviet Economic Power* (Washington, D.C.: U.S. Government Printing Office, 1962), pp. 91–113.

[17] In addition, Khrushchev fostered a program in the late 1950s encouraging increased agricultural production in an effort to overtake the United States in the per capita production of selected products.

[18] It should be noted that this type of performance is not especially unusual for dryland farming. For a discussion, see Carl Zoerb, "The Virgin Land Territory: Plans, Performance, Prospects," in Roy D. Laird and Edward L. Crowley, eds., *Soviet Agriculture: The Permanent Crisis* (New York: Praeger, 1965), pp. 29–44; Frank Durkin, "The Virgin Lands Programme, 1954–60," *Soviet Studies,* vol. 12 (1961–1962), 255–280.

1963, thus allowing Khrushchev to gain political ascendancy and allowing the regime to buy time.[19]

A second major program initiated by Khrushchev was the corn program. Started in 1955 and based primarily upon adulation of corn production in the United States (under radically different conditions, it might be noted) and the fact that corn gives more fodder per acre than other types of feeds, this program increased the sown area of corn from 4.3 million hectares in 1954 to 37.0 million hectares by 1962. The purpose of the corn program was to solve the continuing fodder problem and thus enhance production of meat and related products.

The corn program, much like the virgin lands program was ill-conceived insofar as it was modeled on American success with corn yields, yet neglected important differentials between the Soviet Union and the United States. In particular, corn production requires a warm and humid climate—the Corn Belt of the United States—a type of climate basically absent from most of the Soviet countryside. In addition to planting the corn in clearly marginal areas without associated inputs—fertilizer, for example—Soviet leaders neglected to consider the many years of scientific effort devoted to the development of special hybrids suitable for the conditions of American agriculture, but not readily transferable to Soviet conditions. Corn has, however, become an important component of the Soviet fodder supplies.

Finally, Khrushchev's "plow-up" campaign begun in 1961 was designed to eliminate the grassland system of crop rotation prominent under Stalin, and thus drastically cut the area of land devoted to fallow. The purpose of fallow is, of course, to give the land a "rest" between crops and to allow a rebuilding of its nutrients. Undoubtedly such a scheme would be expected to yield short-run results, but its long-run effects would be uncertain, depending upon whether rational programs were instituted to replace the fallow program.

These schemes all reflected certain basic tenets of Khrush-

[19] This suggestion was made by Strauss, op. cit., p. 172. The production of the virgin lands area was not unimportant. The average annual contribution of roughly 15 million tons represents approximately 13 percent of the official average annual output of grains in the Soviet Union (1956–1965). For details, see Douglas B. Diamond, "Trends in Output, Inputs, and Factor Productivity in Soviet Agriculture," in New Directions in the Soviet Economy,

chev's agricultural policy. First, they "bought time" in the sense that they were, to a great extent, directed toward the achievement of short-run gains at the expense of the long-run health and productivity of the agricultural sector. Second, they were, without exception, unrealistic. All were carried out without sufficient planning, and accordingly, there was insufficient recognition of the demands that success in each campaign would place upon the available resources—manpower, fertilizers, capital investment, and so on. Third, Khrushchev was, for the most part, willing to ignore the weight of scientific evidence on fundamental questions such as crop selection and rotation. Fourth, these campaigns, which perhaps had their respective merits had they been applied selectively on a moderate scale, were discontinuously applied on a universal nationwide scale, thereby proving disruptive rather than beneficial to the farm sector.

Organizational Changes

While the flamboyancy of the above programs tended to hold the spotlight during the 1950s and early 1960s, there were at the same time some important and far-reaching organizational changes in progress. Most important, the nature of the *kolkhoz* and the administrative organs external to the *kolkhoz* underwent substantial readjustment.

While the *kolkhoz* and its related administrative organs had been relatively untouched by organizational change during the Stalin era, the late 1940s and early 1950s witnessed the beginning of a long-term campaign of amalgamation and conversion—collective farms were brought together to increase their size, and at the same time, many were converted into state farms. Between 1940 and 1969 the number of collective farms (*kolkhozy*) declined from 236,900 to 34,700, while socialized sown area in such collective farms increased from approximately 500 hectares to 2,800 hectares per *kolkhoz*.[20] The pace of amalgamation varied as did

part II–B (Washington, D.C.: U.S. Government Printing Office, 1966), p. 369.
[20] *Strana Sovetov za 50 let* [Country of the Soviets during 50 years] (Moscow: Statistika, 1967), p. 121; *Narodnoe khoziastvo SSSR v 1969 g.* [The national economy of the USSR in 1969], pp. 404–405. Further discussion of the amalgamation campaign can be found in Stuart, *op. cit.*, chap. 4.

its regional impact. However, the general trends were similar throughout the country. First, the amalgamation reflected a persistent trend in Soviet economic thinking—namely the belief that large-scale operations (known in industry as "gigantomania") were most efficient. If one examines closely the process of amalgamation, it is apparent that the number of *kolkhozy* and the number of brigades have tended to decline at roughly the same rate over time. Thus *kolkhozy* were simply being brought together under a single administrative structure, and what was formerly a single small *kolkhoz* became a brigade, and as such a subunit of a large *kolkhoz*. On balance, this pattern has probably been one of centralization of decision-making, although generalizations are inadvisable in view of the changing nature of the brigade as a basic production unit.

The Enhanced Role of the Brigade

In the past, the brigade was in many cases simply a short-term amalgamation created to complete a specific task such as harvesting. The current trend is towards a brigade of the "complex" type —that is, a long-term production unit to which land and labor are permanently attached (and since 1958, machinery and equipment as well). Thus the role of the brigadier (brigade manager) has assumed new importance since the brigade has become a permanent production unit with its own plan as a component part of the overall *kolkhoz* plan, its own land and equipment and labor supplies. In addition, the trend has been towards the introduction of *khozraschet* or economic accounting at the brigade level. In many of the larger and well-established *kolkhozy,* the tendency has been to create "departments" in which crop and animal sections will be subsumed, most probably using the *link* as a method for the organization of labor.[21] This pattern closely resembles that utilized in the state farms. Although the amalgamation campaign had all but ceased by the mid-1960s, the ultimate patterns, especially the future of the *kolkhoz* as an organizational form, remain unclear. The chang-

---

[21] The *link* is the smallest organized work unit in the collective farm and exists within a brigade. The concept of the link and its relevance in Soviet agriculture has been the subject of long-standing discussion in the Soviet Union. For details, see Dimitry Pospielovsky, "The 'Link System' In Soviet Agriculture," *Soviet Studies,* vol. 21, no. 4 (April 1970), 411–435.

ing characteristics of the typical *kolkhoz* have made it increasingly similar to the *sovkhoz* and thus less reminiscent of the unique organizational form introduced during the collectivization era.

Changing Decision-Making Patterns

Within the *kolkhoz,* decision-making patterns have changed in recent years and in addition, the quality of managerial personnel has been improved. During the past twenty years, there has been a continuing attempt to maintain a delicate balance between decision-making by the individual farm management—the upper-level managers and the production brigades—and by the regional agricultural authorities. While the annual production targets formulated by external economic planners remain the fundamental directing force of economic activity within the *kolkhoz,* certain important changes have taken place tending to increase decision-making freedom *within* the *kolkhoz.*

Since the mid 1950s, for example, there has been a tendency toward targeting output and letting the individual farm decide how best to produce it, rather than basing the expected yield on the land area to be planted. In addition, in the late 1960s there has been a renewed effort to introduce serious long-term planning and thus remove one of the major complaints of farm managers—the year to year manipulation of targets by state authorities that forces managers to engage in a guessing game with the state.

On the matter of input determination, there has also been some relaxation of controls. Prior to the mid 1950s, the proportion of farm income to be devoted to capital investment was determined centrally with only minimal regional variation; now this is basically a matter to be decided within the farm, although naturally there is pressure to increase investment. Nevertheless, the proportion of farm income reinvested now varies quite widely from farm to farm.

The abolition of the Machine Tractor Stations in 1958 meant the dissolution of a powerful external managerial force, though doubtless some of this power remains in the hands of the state and party through regional agricultural and party authorities. Nevertheless, in the early 1950s the agricultural specialists were removed from the MTS and placed in the collective farms themselves—an important move to improve the quality of collective farms' decisions —and finally in 1958, the machinery and equipment were shifted to the farms and especially to the brigade level in the form of complex mechanized brigades.

Insofar as decision-making *levels* are important, the impact of changes in the postwar period is less than clear. As we have noted, the amalgamation process has substantially increased the average size of the collective, and yet along with changing decision rules for managers, there have been important changes in the organization of the farm itself.

As of 1956 election procedures (to the extent these are meaningful) were frequently decentralized to the brigade meeting. In addition, the charter or basic operating document of the farm was to be formulated by the farm itself, and while there were external controls on this matter, it seems nevertheless to represent a measure of relaxation. The abolition of the MTS did, of course, help to remove the second of the famous "two bosses" referred to by Khrushchev.

If the brigade increased in importance during the 1950s and 1960s, it also grew in size to closely resemble the *kolkhoz* of earlier years. At the same time, there was a continuing effort to infuse the party apparatus deeper into the farm, not only by changing the organizational structure of the party within the farm, but also by enhancing the party status of managerial personnel.[22] Thus in 1952, 79.4 percent of collective farm chairmen were party members while by 1960, the proportion had increased to 95.3 percent.[23]

The Changing Quality
of Farm Management

If one can measure managerial quality in terms of formal educational achievement, then the quality of *kolkhoz* managers has increased quite significantly in the past twenty years.[24] The same can be said for assistant chairmen, although the proportion of brigade leaders with higher and/or secondary specialized education has *not* increased notably.

[22] For a discussion of the party in the *kolkhoz* during the 1950s and 1960s, see Stuart, *op. cit.,* chap. 2.

[23] *Narodnoe khoziaistvo SSSR v 1959 g.* [The National Economy of the USSR in 1959], p. 452.

[24] For a discussion of collective farm managerial personnel, see Stuart, *op. cit.,* chap. 8.

Apart from the *level* of education, the *type* of training received by managerial personnel is important. We have noted that in the industrial sector of the Soviet economy, there is a tendency to favor managers trained in technical skills (especially engineering) as opposed to those trained in economics and administrative skills. The pattern in collective agriculture has been markedly similar. Although data on the type of training is scarce, we can generally conclude that training in an agricultural discipline—agronomy, for example—along with party reliability are both most important for the potentially successful manager.

It is instructive to note that in 1955, Khrushchev conducted a campaign to divert from industry sufficient managerial personnel to replace approximately 25 percent of existing collective farm chairmen. This program reflected the importance attached to farm management by Khrushchev and, in addition, served to significantly improve the educational levels of the top management group.[25] At the same time, the educational level of collective farm specialists has been and remains high, in fact substantially higher than that of managerial personnel. In 1966, 91 percent of all zoo technicians and 94.6 percent of all agronomists in collective farms had completed higher or secondary specialized education. At the same time, however, only 10.9 percent of leaders of animal breeding sections and 10.4 percent of brigade leaders had received a similar level of education.[26]

From the standpoint of managerial decision-making in the *kolkhoz,* it is important to note that there has been a virtual absence of training in economics, accounting, and related subjects. For accounting personnel themselves, the picture has been bleak; in January of 1960, 47.4 percent of all *kolkhoz* accounting workers had no bookkeeping training whatsoever.[27] With this record, it is little wonder that the auditing commission discussed earlier was such an ineffective body in the *kolkhoz.*

[25] For a discussion of this campaign, see Jerry F. Hough, "The Changing Nature of the Kolkhoz Chairman," in Millar, *op. cit.,* pp. 103–120; Stuart, "Structural Change and the Quality of Soviet Collective Farm Management, 1952–1966," *op. cit.,* 121–138.
[26] Stuart, *The Collective Farm in Soviet Agriculture, op. cit.,* p. 182.
[27] *Ibid.,* p. 185.

Economic Adjustments

If Soviet agricultural development of the past can be described as "extensive" in character, Soviet authorities have recognized the need to increase output not only by expansion of inputs, but also by better use of those inputs. In Soviet parlance, the drive for greater efficiency in agricultural production falls under the rubric of "intensification."

Since the early 1950s, considerable emphasis has been placed upon monetary incentives, and in general, upon the introduction of *khozraschet* into collective farms.[28] The initial cost data on collective farms after cost accounting was introduced in the mid-1950s indicated that costs were very high and prices (average state purchase price, for example) did not cover costs for most agricultural products. Although such cost calculations were suspect, given the nature of the labor day and the absence of charges for land and capital, the general conclusion was that prices must be raised if farms could be expected to support increasing money distributions to peasants, and at the same time, set aside funds for capital investment.

The matter of agricultural price reform has been one of continuing debate throughout the postwar period. The debate has been concerned with much broader problems than simply the magnitude of prices. Questions such as regional price differentiation, price flexibility in the face of harvest fluctuations, methodology of price formation, and so on have been discussed. In spite of considerable indecision on these issues, one important pricing trend has prevailed—namely, increasing the level of prices vis-à-vis costs.[29]

---

[28] For a discussion of these trends, see Frank A. Durgin, Jr., "Monetization and Policy in Soviet Agriculture Since 1952," *Soviet Studies,* vol. 15, no. 4 (April 1964), 381–407.

[29] The importance of price increases in Soviet agriculture cannot be underestimated. After the introduction of cost accounting in 1956, studies revealed that for many products, not even the above-quota prices covered average costs of production. This pattern was reversed by price increases that for some products were very large. On the question of pricing reform, see Bornstein, *op. cit.;* on the question of cost-price comparisons, see Nancy Nimitz, "Soviet Agricultural Prices and Costs," in United States Congress, Joint Economic Committee, *Comparisons of United States and Soviet Economies* (Washington, D.C.: U.S. Government Printing Office, 1959), pp. 239–284; Stuart, *The Collective Farm in Soviet Agriculture, op. cit.,* chap. 7.

By the mid-1960s agricultural prices in general covered production costs (with the exception of animal products on state farms), though with markedly differing levels of profitability. In addition to price increases, other financial concessions were made to the farm sector: Tax payments were lessened, the two-level pricing system was abandoned in 1958 (though partially reconstituted in 1965), and payments on debts to the MTS for machinery and equipment were at first delayed, and finally partially written off. In sum, these measures significantly improved the financial health of the *kolkhozy*.

In addition to measures designed to improve the financial position of farms, further steps were taken to improve peasant incentives. Both the *form* and the *frequency* of payment of peasant earnings changed, thus partially offsetting the more negative aspects of the labor day system prior to abandonment of it in 1966. First, in the mid-1950s a decree recommended the introduction of monthly cash payments to stimulate greater productivity. Of the total annual payment received by a peasant, the cash portion increased and, in addition, it came to be paid throughout rather than at the end of each year. In 1957, only 22.4 percent of *kolkhozy* made money advances ten or more times per year, while in 1963, the corresponding figure was 52.5 percent.[30]

One of the most dramatic aspects of the pecuniarization process has been the very sharp upturn of the level of rural incomes in the post-Stalin era. As the authors of one recent study point out: "From 1953, the year of Stalin's death, through 1967, the total income of the agricultural population from farm wages and private plot activity more than doubled, while the number of farm workers declined by approximately 10 percent. . . ."[31] This pattern must have had a substantial impact upon rural-urban wage differentials being designed in part to stem the outflow of productive labor from the rural sector and, within the rural sector, to improve standards of living and thus motivate peasants toward greater participation and effort in the socialized sector of Soviet agriculture.[32]

[30] G. Ia. Kuznetsov, *Material'noe stimulirovanie truda v kolkhozakh* [Material stimulation of labor in collective farms] (Moscow: Mysl', 1966), p. 29.
[31] For a discussion of rural income levels in the post-1953 period, see David W. Bronson and Constance B. Krueger, "The Revolution in Soviet Farm Household Income, 1953–1967," in Millar, *op. cit.,* pp. 214–258.
[32] In terms of average annual wage from the socialized sector, the urban–

The ultimate culmination of the monetization trend came in 1966 when the *kolkhozy* were directed to abandon the labor day as an accounting device. *Kolkhozy* were instructed to pay wages in accordance with rates prevailing on nearby *sovkhozy* and where financial conditions did not allow the *kolkhozy* to meet these levels, the state bank was to provide appropriate loans. This did not mean, however, that payment would subsequently be entirely in monetary form, for peasants would still have to rely upon forage from the socialized sector to feed animals in the private sector.[33]

In addition to an improved income position of the peasants, available evidence suggests a decisively improved income position for managerial personnel. For agricultural specialists, tractor drivers, and others who formerly worked outside the *kolkhoz* but who are now members of *kolkhozy,* earnings were maintained at or above the level previous to the transfer. In 1961, a tractor driver earned 2.57 times more, per work day, than a collective farmer in the fields. In recent years, agricultural specialists (agronomists, zootechnicians, etc.) would earn 70 to 100 rubles per month depending upon level of education, experience, and so on. Despite relatively small bonus earnings, these personnel come close to earning the average monthly wage of the industrial sector.

The collective farm chairman has traditionally earned little more than the average peasant and, at the same time, turnover has been high.[34] In recent years, the basis of calculating managerial income

rural differential has been reduced; thus for 1952, the average annual wage in industry was 917 current rubles, in state farms and subsidiary state agricultural enterprises 494 current rubles, and in collective farms, 164 current rubles. For 1967, the corresponding figures were 1,344, 1,007, and 647 current rubles for industry, state agriculture, and collective farms, respectively. See Bronson and Krueger, *op. cit.,* p. 247. Preliminary evidence for the 1950s and early 1960s suggests that peasant participation in the socialized sector was not enhanced by this effort, and the importance of the private sector (as a portion of peasant family income) remained great. See Stuart, *The Collective Farm in Soviet Agriculture, op. cit.,* chap. 6.

[33] Although the private sector in the collective farm represents a very small portion of farm land, it represents an important portion of livestock. Since the private plots are not suitable for the growing of forage crops in any quantity, forage has normally been a part of the peasant's income in-kind received for working in the socialized sector of the farm.

[34] For a discussion of managerial incentives, see Alec Nove, "Incentives for Peasants and Administrators," in *Economic Rationality and Soviet Politics*

has changed. Rather than a myriad of performance indicators such as sown area, size of herds, and so forth, the prevailing pattern now emphasizes production performance per se—more output at lower cost. Available evidence suggests that collective farm chairmen now earn two, three, or more times the level of average peasant earnings. Unlike the industrial managers, however, farm managers have traditionally received only minimal bonuses, and even these have varied regionally and over time to quite a degree.

On balance, one would expect that the improved income position of managerial personnel in combination with higher peasant income would enhance the participation and effort of both groups in the socialized agricultural sector. While we do not have a measure for effort as such, we have noted that participation has not in fact increased. In 1953, for example, men devoted 75 percent of their work time to the socialized sector of the collective farm, 9 percent to the private plot, and 16 percent to external work. The figures for women during the same year were 59 percent, 10 percent, and 31 percent for the three sectors, respectively. By 1963, a year for which similar data are available, there had been virtually no change, with the exception of a slight expansion of the proportion of time spent by women in the private sector of the *kolkhoz*.[35]

SOVIET AGRICULTURE AND ECONOMIC DEVELOPMENT

The focus of this chapter thus far has been the organization and operation of Soviet agriculture. In this section, we turn to a consideration of Soviet agriculture in terms of its contribution to the process of economic development. Since we are concerned with the role of agriculture in the development process, the potential

---

(New York: Praeger, 1964), pp. 186–205; Robert C. Stuart, "Managerial Incentives in Soviet Collective Agriculture During the Khrushchev Era," *Soviet Studies,* vol. 22, no. 4 (April 1972), 540–555.

[35] I. F. Suslov, *Ekonomicheskoe problemy razvitiia kolkhozov* [Economic problems of the development of collective farms] (Moscow: Ekonomika, 1967), p. 193.

supportive functions of the agricultural sector in the course of economic development bear repetition at this juncture:[36]

1. Provision of manpower for industry
2. Expansion of output and marketings to supply foodstuffs for the expanding nonagricultural sector and raw materials for industry
3. Provision of agricultural products for export to earn foreign exchange to pay for importation of machinery and equipment
4. Assistance to capital accumulation in the industrial sector by the transfer of savings from the rural to the industrial sector

As far as the *first* supportive role is concerned, Soviet agriculture did without doubt provide a vast amount of manpower to industry within a relatively brief amount of time. Between 1926 and 1939 alone, the urban population increased from 26.3 million to 56.1 million—a net gain of some 30 million, and by 1959, this figure had increased to 100 million—a net overall increase of 73 million, of which 43.4 million (well over one-half) can be accounted for by migration from rural to urban areas.[37] This internal migration along with increasing participation rates of the urban population sustained an average annual rate of growth of the nonagricultural labor force of 8.7 percent between 1928 and 1937 while the agricultural labor force declined at an annual rate of −2.5 percent, during the same period. This vast transformation was effected by both market and nonmarket forces: first, a substantial gap between urban and rural incomes was created thereby promoting movement out of agriculture; second, massive recruitment campaigns were carried on in the countryside to facilitate the transfer.

How well Soviet agriculture performed the *second* supportive function during the crucial early years of industrialization is the subject of some controversy. Although statistics on marketings of *all* agricultural products external to the village are not readily available, the figures on *grain marketings* (Table 15) provide valuable insights.

[36] For a detailed discussion of the role of agriculture in economic development, the reader is referred to J. W. Mellor, *The Economics of Agricultural Production* (Ithaca, N.Y.: Cornell University Press, 1966).

[37] Warren W. Eason, "Labor Force," in Abram Bergson and Simon Kuznets, eds., *Economic Trends in the Soviet Union* (Cambridge, Mass.: Harvard University Press, 1963), pp. 72–73.

Table 15 **Average Annual Grain Output and Marketings**
(millions of tons; 1927–1928 = 100)

Period	Grain Output	Index	Grain Marketing, Gross[a]	Net[b]	Index Gross	Net
1927–1928	72.8	100	16.1	8.3	100	100
1928–1929	72.5	100	15.7	8.3	98	100
1929–1930	77.6	107	19.5	10.2	121	123
1930–1931	76.5	105	22.6	17.9	140	216
1931–1932	69.7	96	23.7	18.8	147	226
1932–1933	79.8	110	19.4	13.7	120	165
1933–1937	72.9	100	27.5		171	
1938–1940	77.9	107	32.1		199	
1954–1958	110.3	152	43.5		270	
1960–1963	126.0	173	50.0		311	
1964–1967	148.0	203	59.2		368	
1968–1969	166.0	228	62.3		387	
1969–1970	174.6	240	64.4		400	

[a] Gross marketings are all off-farm sales other than those within agriculture as such. They are defined as state purchases for the period 1960–1970.
[b] Net marketings are obtained from gross marketings by subtracting grain that is repurchased by the agricultural population or by farms through retail trade or government allocations.

SOURCES: Output data through 1958 from Strauss, *op. cit.,* pp. 304–305; grain marketing data from 1927–1928 through 1932–1933 from Karcz, *op. cit.,* p. 44; grain marketing data from 1933–1937 through 1954–1958 from Charles K. Wilber, "The Role of Agriculture in Soviet Economic Development," *Land Economics,* vol. 45, no. 1 (February 1969), 87–96; data for the 1960s from selected volumes of *Narodnoe khoziastvo SSSR* [The national economy of the USSR].

The evidence presented here suggests that the rate of increase of both gross and net grain marketings during the early collectivization years was substantially faster than the increase in grain production. Possibly more important, although gross marketings increased at a respectable pace over the precollectivization levels, *net* marketings (defined as gross marketings less repurchases by the rural sector) more than doubled between the years 1927–1928 and 1930–1931 from 8.3 to 17.9 million tons respectively. However, Jerzy Karcz has attempted to show that the *entire* increase in gross grain marketings between 1928 and 1933 can be accounted for not by the ability of the state to gather surpluses from *kolkhozy,* but by the reduction in animal herds—that would otherwise consume grains—that took place during collectivization.[38] However, one may question this conclusion in the light of the large state exactions during poor harvest years that exacerbated the famine of 1932–1934. Also the drastic decline in peasant living standards during the 1930s might be cited as counterevidence to Karcz's conclusions. Thus in the absence of a broader analysis of all agricultural products over a longer period of time, it is difficult to make an overall evaluation of the product contribution of the agricultural sector to economic development.

As far as the *third* function is concerned, Soviet agriculture did contribute to overall economic development during the First Five Year Plan by earning crucial foreign exchange to pay for machinery imports from the West. Betwen 1929 and 1931, Soviet imports increased by over 60 percent (in volume terms) despite the worsening terms of trade resulting from the collapse of agricultural prices in the world market during this period. In fact, Soviet imports were severely limited by balance of payments constraints—given the Western countries' unwillingness to grant long-term credits to the fledgling Communist regime. The Soviet government's sole recourse therefore was to continue to market abroad the traditional Soviet export commodities—grain and wheat, timber, and petroleum. Between 1929 and 1931, Soviet exports expanded somewhat less than 50 percent, and this expansion was spearheaded by an increase in the proportion of the total domestic output of agricultural products exported. In 1928, for example, less than one percent of the domestic output of grain, wheat, and corn was exported; yet by 1931, 14 percent of the domestic output of grain, 18 percent of wheat, and 2 percent of corn was exported. In this manner, agricultural exports were used to finance machinery and ferrous metals imports, which rose from one-third in 1928 to almost three-quarters of total Soviet imports by the end of the First Five Year Plan.[39] The costs of maintaining agricultural exports were considerable, for they worsened the famine of 1932–1934. As one student of this famine writes:

[38] Jerzy F. Karcz, "From Stalin to Brezhnev: Soviet Agricultural Policy in Historical Perspective," in Millar, *op. cit.,* p. 42.
[39] Franklyn D. Holzman, "Foreign Trade," Bergson and Kuznets, *op. cit.,* pp. 294–295.

The immediate cause was not poor harvests but the requisitioning of grain from moderate harvests in such quantities that not enough was left for the peasants themselves. The main reasons for this drastic policy appear to have been, first the attempt to maintain exports of agricultural produce and hence imports of machinery; . . .[40]

Perhaps the most notable "contribution" of Soviet agriculture to economic development relates to the *fourth* function—namely, its contribution of forced savings in the form of reductions in the rural population's standard of living, although this conclusion has also been subject to challenge. While estimates of the extent of this decline must be quite crude, Naum Jasny has estimated that per capita income of the farm population had fallen to 53 percent of the 1928 level by 1932–1933, which perhaps is not too unrealistic in view of the fact that the peasant's standard of living during the best prewar year for the Russian peasantry (1937) was still only 81 percent of 1928.[41] Jasny further estimates per capita agricultural income in 1927–1928 at 113 rubles (1926–1927 prices). Using Jasny's index one can estimate that the 1932–1933 per capita income for peasants was *about 60 rubles* (1926–1927 prices)—a decline of 53 rubles per capita. Although it would appear from such figures that Soviet agrarian policies succeeded in marshaling forced savings from the rural sector, such a judgment may, at this juncture, be premature for reasons discussed below. The burden of industrialization was also in part borne by the urban sector. Mindful of the significant decline in urban living standards during the 1930s, Abram Bergson notes the following:

Contrary to a common supposition, the industrial worker fared no better than the peasants under Stalin's five year plans. Indeed, he seemingly fared worse, although I believe he was able to maintain in some degree the margin he enjoyed initially in respect to consumption per capita.[42]

[40] Philip Hanson, *The Consumer Sector in the Soviet Economy* (Evanston, Ill.: Northwestern University Press, 1968), p. 36.
[41] Naum Jasny, *The Soviet Economy During the Plan Era* (Stanford, Calif.: Food Research Institute, 1951), p. 107.
[42] Abram Bergson, *The Real National Income of Soviet Russia Since 1928* (Cambridge, Mass.: Harvard University Press, 1961), p. 257. This question,

Furthermore, the concept of an agricultural *product* surplus "contributed" by agriculture to industry (as a concommitant of falling rural living standards) is not easy to define and appropriately measure. In particular, recent research seems to suggest that the net product contribution of the agricultural sector (that is, gross product contributed by the agricultural sector less input flows from industry to agriculture) may in fact have been substantially less than has commonly been supposed—thus our hesitation to conclude that significant forced savings did flow from agriculture to industry during the 1930s.[43]

It may also be that the process of collectivization as implemented in the Soviet Union, in addition to the immediate negative impact discussed earlier, may have been a negative factor in the long-run. For example, Jerzy Karcz has argued that one must consider as a cost of the Stalin era the long-standing persistence of the undesirable consequences of "command farming"—poor incentives, inadequate specialization, and distortion of decision-making patterns.[44] Indeed, he suggests that these must be considered a part of Soviet development strategy.

---

and recent evidence put forth by the Russian economist A. A. Barsov, has been discussed by Karcz, "From Stalin to Brezhnev: Soviet Agricultural Policy in Historical Perspective," in Millar, *The Soviet Rural Community, op. cit.,* pp. 48 ff. For a more detailed presentation of Barsov's views on this question, see the sources cited in footnote 44, and in addition, A. A. Barsov, *Balans stoimostnykh obmenov mezhdu gorodom i derevnei* [Balance of the value of the exchange between the city and the country] (Moscow: Nauka, 1969).

[43] The question of the agricultural product surplus as a contribution to the Soviet industrialization process has been raised by James Millar. For details, see James R. Millar, "Soviet Rapid Development and the Agricultural Surplus Hypothesis," *Soviet Studies,* vol. 22, no. 1 (July 1970), 77–93; Alec Nove, "The Agricultural Surplus Hypothesis: A Comment on James R. Millar's Article," *Soviet Studies,* vol. 22, no. 3 (January 1971), 394–401; James R. Millar, "The Agricultural Surplus Hypothesis: A Reply to Alec Nove," *Soviet Studies,* vol. 23, no. 2 (October 1971), 302–306; Alec Nove, "A Reply to the Reply," *Soviet Studies,* vol. 23, no. 2 (October 1971), 307–308. For a more positive view of the surplus, see Charles K. Wilber, *The Soviet Model and Underdeveloped Countries* (Chapel Hill: University of North Carolina Press, 1969), pp. 32–34.

[44] Karcz, *op. cit.,* p. 68. For a development of the command model, see Jerzy F. Karcz, "An Organizational Model of Command Farming," in Morris Bornstein, ed., *Comparative Economic Systems,* rev. ed. (Homewood, Ill.: Irwin, 1970), pp. 278–299.

Finally, as we shall see later, David Granick has argued that the Soviet view of an urgent need for capital investment expansion during these early years may have been overstated; in fact, the rapid collectivization policies, pursued presumably to achieve such an end, may have resulted in a sharp deterioration in the Soviet Union's stock of intangible capital, and especially *organization* when viewed as a major component of that stock.[45]

It is apparent that Soviet agriculture must be judged on a long-run basis and in terms of all facets of its potential contributions and associated costs, including those peculiar to the collectivization process as implemented in the Soviet case. Let us now turn to an appraisal of Soviet agriculture in terms of output and productivity performance to determine just how well, or poorly, it has performed in the long-run.

PERFORMANCE OF THE AGRICULTURAL SECTOR

In Table 16 we present official Soviet and Western calculated indexes of Soviet agricultural performance for the period 1913 through 1972. It is apparent that for the early years of collectivization, Soviet agriculture performed rather poorly, gross output growing at an average annual rate of one percent or slightly less between 1928 and 1937 (the latter a good crop year). Also, the production of livestock products declined during these years primarily due to destruction of animal herds by peasants resisting the collectivization of agriculture.

In view of our discussion of change in the Khrushchev years, it is notable that Soviet agriculture grew most rapidly between 1952 and 1958, the early years of experimentation with the virgin lands, abolition of the MTS, increased farm prices, and limited decentralization of decision-making. During this period, Soviet agriculture (as measured by the official index of gross agricultural output) grew at an average annual rate of around 9 percent, but decelerated considerably thereafter to an average annual rate of slightly above 3 percent between 1959 and 1970. According to the calculated

[45] David Granick, *Soviet Metal Fabricating and Economic Development* (Madison: University of Wisconsin Press, 1967), chap. 4 and pp. 365–366.

Table 16 **USSR Indexes of Gross Agricultural Output, 1913–1972 (official and calculated)**

	Total		Crops		Livestock	
	Official	Calculated	Official	Calculated	Oficial	Calculated
Territory of 1939 (1913 = 100)						
1913	100	100	100	100	100	100
1928	124	116	117	117	137	120
1933	101	—	121	—	65	—
1937	134	127	150	161	109	108
1940	156	122	172	145	116	99
Present Territory (1940 = 100)						
1940	100	100	100	100	100	100
1950	99	99	95	92	109	109
1952	101	101	95	96	113	109
1954	109	110	99	98	134	125
1956	137	142	130	136	155	151
1958	156	161	147	144	180	184
1959	157	155	140	131	191	198
1962	167	168	149	—	207	—
1965	180	179	161	—	223	—
1968	206	207	195	—	244	—
1969	201	197	182	—	244	—
1970	221	226	204	—	265	—
1971	—	226	—	—	—	—
1972	—	208	—	—	—	—
1975 plan	269	—	241	—	307	—

SOURCES: D. Gale Johnson, "Agricultural Production," in Abram Bergson and Simon Kuznets, eds., *Economic Trends in the Soviet Union* (Cambridge, Mass.: Harvard University Press, 1963), p. 208; Abraham S. Becker, *Soviet National Income, 1953–1964* (Berkeley and Los Angeles: University of California Press, 1969), p. 241; *Narodnoe khoziaistvo SSSR v. 1969 g.* [National economy of the USSR in 1969] p. 289; Douglas Diamond and Constance Krueger, "Recent Developments in Output and Productivity in Soviet Agriculture," Joint Economic Committee, *Soviet Economic Prospects for the Seventies* (Washington, D.C.: U.S. Government Printing Office, 1973), p. 336.

index, agricultural output failed to increase in 1971 and declined by almost 9 percent in 1972. Long-run individual crop figures are given in Table 17 and they tell essentially the same story, although as five year averages, annual fluctuations are removed. Annual fluctuations can be seen, however, for the years 1969 to 1972. They indicate that through 1970 output performance was rela-

Table 17 **Output of Selected Agricultural Products—USSR
(millions of tons)**

Period[a]	Grain	Cotton	Sugar Beets	Potatoes	Meat (slaughter weight)	Milk	Eggs (billion units)
1909–1913	65.2	.68	9.7	22.4	3.9	42.1	9.5
1924–1928	69.3	.58	7.9	41.1	4.2	29.3	9.2
1936–1940	77.4	2.50	17.1	49.4	4.0	26.5	9.6
1946–1950	64.8	2.32	13.5	80.7	3.5	32.3	7.5
1951–1955	88.5	3.89	24.0	69.5	5.7	37.9	15.9
1956–1960	121.5	4.36	45.6	88.3	7.9	57.2	23.6
1961–1965	130.3	4.99	59.2	81.6	9.3	64.7	28.7
1966–1968	162.8	5.96	85.1	95.2	11.2	79.3	33.7
1969	162.4	5.71	71.2	91.8	11.8	81.5	37.2
1970	186.8	6.9	78.3	96.8	12.3	83.0	40.7
1971	181.2	7.1	72.2	92.7	13.3	83.0	45.1
1972	168.0	7.3	74.6	77.7	13.6	83.2	48.2

[a] Data up to and including the series for 1936–1940 is based upon borders of the Soviet Union prior to September 17, 1939.

SOURCES: Data up to, and including, 1968 from *Narodnoe khoziaistvo SSSR v 1968 g.* [The national economy of the USSR in 1968], pp. 314–315; data for 1969 from *Narodnoe khoziaistvo SSSR v 1969 g.* [The national economy of the USSR in 1969] pp. 286–287; data for 1970–1972 (excluding grain) from Diamond and Krueger, *op. cit.,* p. 326. Grain output data (official Soviet gross output) for 1970 from *Narodnoe khoziaistvo v 1970 g.* [The national economy of the USSR in 1970], p. 309; for 1971 and 1972 computed from *Ekonomicheskaia gazeta* [The economic gazette], no. 5 (January 1973), p. 6.

tively good. In 1971 and 1972, however (due in large part to unfavorable weather), output performance has been poor. Thus it would seem that the growth of agricultural output in the Soviet Union has, over the long-run, been quite uneven, although one can argue that in comparison with other developing economies, the Soviet performance has been respectable.[46]

Certainly any evaluation of Soviet agricultural performance must consider factor productivity performance, that is, trends in output per unit of input, for it is important to determine whether the above growth was brought about largely by expansion of inputs (such as

[46] Wilber, *op. cit.,* pp. 39 ff. argues that when compared with other countries over various historical periods, the *growth rate* of Soviet agricultural output has been good.

sown acreage) or by increased output per unit of input. In Table 18, we present estimates of factor productivity for two important and possibly representative periods; the first, from 1928 to 1938, should shed light upon agricultural productivity performance during the crucial initial years of the industrialization drive, the second, from 1950 to 1959, should reflect the performance of the agricultural sector under more "normal" conditions.

Between 1928 and 1938, output per man-day actually declined (col. 8); whereas output per man (number engaged) rose (col. 9). The reason for this divergence is that while the number engaged in agriculture declined markedly, the number of man-days of those remaining in agriculture increased as the shift was made from part-time to full-time agricultural employment. Trends in output per man-day probably are more reflective of the labor productivity performance of Soviet agriculture in that they better reflect the true labor input, and output per man-day did decline.[47] As far as output per unit of total inputs (land, labor, capital, etc.) is concerned, it declined between 1928 and 1938 irrespective of how labor inputs are measured (cols. 11, 12). It is interesting to note that capital inputs to agriculture actually declined between 1928 and 1938 (col. 1), contrary to the vision of the Soviet leadership that foresaw a vast mechanization of Soviet agriculture through the auspices of the MTS. On the whole, one would have to conclude

---

[47] The reader should note that the measurement of factor productivity is complex and especially so in the Soviet case. The results are particularly sensitive to the indicators chosen and the weights used in aggregating those indicators. For a discussion of problems relating to Soviet agricultural statistics, the reader is referred to D. Gale Johnson, "Agricultural Production," in Abram Bergson and Simon Kuznets, eds., *Economic Trends in the Soviet Union* (Cambridge, Mass.: Harvard University Press, 1963); Arcadius Kahan, "Soviet Statistics of Agricultural Output," in Roy D. Laird, ed., *Soviet Agricultural and Peasant Affairs* (Lawrence: University of Kansas Press, 1963), pp. 134–160; Roger E. Neetz, "Inside the Agricultural Index of the USSR," in *New Directions in the Soviet Economy* (Washington, D.C.: U.S. Government Printing Office, 1966), pp. 483–493; Vladimir G. Treml and John P. Hardt, eds., *Soviet Economic Statistics* (Durham, N.C.: Duke University Press, 1972), part IV. For a discussion of recent trends and prospects through 1975, see Diamond and Krueger, *op. cit.,* pp. 316–339; and F. Douglas Whitehouse and Joseph Havelka, "Comparisons of Farm Output in the US and USSR, 1950–1971," in *Soviet Economic Prospects for the Seventies, op. cit.,* pp. 340–374.

Table 18 **Growth Indexes of Inputs and Factor Productivity in Soviet Agriculture, 1928–1959**

	(1)	(2)	(3a)	(3b)	(4)	(5)	(6)	(7)	(8)	(9)	(10)	(11)	(12)
	Capital	Land	Labor (man-days) A[a]	Labor (numbers engaged) B[b]	Current Purchases	Total Inputs A (weighted average of cols. 1, 2, 3a, 4)	Total Inputs B (weighted average of cols. 1, 2, 3b, 4)	Agricultural Output	Output per Man-Day A (col. 7 ÷ col. 3a)	Output per Numbers Engaged B (col. 7 ÷ col. 3b)	Output per Land Input (col. 7 ÷ col. 2)	Total Input Output per A (col. 7 ÷ col. 5)	Total Input Output per B (col. 7 ÷ col. 6)
						(1928 = 100)							
1928	100	100	100	100	100	100	100	100	100	100	100	100	100
1938	97	125	112	85	590	141	126	104	93	122	83	74	83
						(1950 = 100)							
1950	100	100	100	100	100	100	100	100	100	100	100	100	100
1959	194	129	93	99	193	115	118	154	146	156	119	134	130

[a] Labor measured in man-days.
[b] Labor measured in numbers principally engaged in agriculture.

SOURCE: D. Gale Johnson, "Agricultural Production," in Abram Bergson and Simon Kuznets, eds., *Economic Trends in the Soviet Union* (Cambridge, Mass.: Harvard University Press, 1963), pp. 216–218.

that the productivity performance of Soviet agriculture during the early period of collectivized agriculture was disappointing.

In contrast, the productivity performance of Soviet agriculture was much better during the second period (1950 to 1959). Output per man-day and per unit of total factor input grew at a respectable pace (at greater than 3 per cent annually). The capital stock of agriculture grew at a much more rapid rate than labor inputs indicating substitutions of capital for labor and the increased mechanization of Soviet agriculture.

The productivity performance of Soviet agriculture during the early 1960s was less impressive, and for the entire 1951 to 1964 period, agricultural output per unit of total factor inputs grew at an average annual rate of approximately one-and-one-half percent, as compared to the much higher rate during the 1950 to 1959 period which indicates a slowdown of productivity growth after 1959. Throughout the 1960s, productivity growth has been quite uneven. From 1961 to 1965, factor productivity declined at an annual rate of .04 percent. This was followed by a period of relatively good productivity growth from 1966 to 1970 at an annual rate of 2.1 percent. However, these gains were almost wiped out between 1970 and 1972 when factor productivity declined at an annual rate of 4.3 percent.[48]

Recently, an attempt to compare the productivity of Soviet agriculture on a relative basis with Western European agriculture has produced some rather surprising results—for the measures seem to point towards rather higher Soviet productivity levels than one might have anticipated. Thus, Soviet farm output per man-hour has been estimated to be above that of Italy and, depending upon the price weights chosen, at or only slightly below the level of France and Germany.[49] Such results are quite contrary to the traditional picture of Soviet agriculture as being inefficient relative to the agriculture sector in advanced Western countries.

Such views rest in large part upon comparisons of crop yields in the USSR and United States (Table 20), which show USSR crop

[48] Douglas B. Diamond, "Trends in Output, Inputs, and Factor Productivity in Soviet Agriculture," *New Directions in the Soviet Economy, op. cit.,* pp. 352–373; and Diamond and Krueger, *op. cit.,* p. 317.
[49] Earl R. Brubaker, "A Sectoral Analysis of Efficiency under Market and Plan," *Soviet Studies,* vol. 23, no. 3 (January 1972), 440.

yields to be generally much lower than corresponding yields in the United States. Of course, it is difficult to make cross-country productivity comparisons because of the variability of local conditions such as climate, soil quality, and so forth. For example, the poor Soviet yield performance could simply be the result of more unfavorable natural conditions. It is noteworthy, however, that USSR yields declined substantially relative to American yields after 1929—a relative change that cannot be attributed to natural conditions (Table 19). In other words, the rate of increase in output per unit of land input in the USSR did not keep pace with the rate of expansion in the United States, although for some crops this trend has been partially reversed in the 1960s. This general conclusion should be approached with caution because American farm policy has been to limit acreage; whereas the Soviet policy has been to expand acreage.

SOVIET AGRICULTURE: AN OVERVIEW

There is probably no sector in the Soviet economy that has been the subject of more discussion both within the Soviet Union and in other countries than agriculture. Western economists have typically been very critical of Soviet agriculture; they point to such persistent problems as output fluctuations, poor yields, high costs, and inadequate investment. One can, however, rationalize much of Soviet behavior in the agricultural sector in terms of a particular type of development strategy—albeit a strategy that concentrated largely on short-run gains. However, to develop at a rate such as the Soviet Union has in the past fifty years, and to the level it now enjoys, is an achievement of major significance. If the rural sector paid disproportionately for this pace of development, we must, when appraising the Soviet model as a development alternative, consider this price as opposed to other means of promoting development.

The role of agriculture in the Soviet strategy of economic development remains a matter of some controversy. On the one hand, we have noted that agriculture seems to have made a contribution to the development process—possibly smaller than originally thought—and yet for much of the plan era agricultural per-

Table 19 Crop Yelds: USSR—USA (all figures in centners per hectare)

Period	Grain			Cotton			Sugar Beets			Potatoes		
	USSR	USA	USA/USSR	USSR	USA	USA/USSR	USSR	USA	USA/USSR	USSR	USA	USA/USSR
1925–1929	7.9	13.0	1.65	8.8	5.8	.66	132.0	244	1.85	79.3	76.4	.96
1950–1954	7.8	17.0	2.18	16.5	10.1	.61	159.8	347	2.30	86.2	169.2	1.96
1955–1959	9.7	21.0	2.17	20.2	14.6	.72	180.6	387	2.14	91.0	193.7	2.12
1960–1964	10.4	28.9	2.78	19.8	15.0	.76	165.2	385	2.33	92.2	218.0	2.38
1965–1968	12.3	33.2	2.70	24.0	15.6	.65	219.7	390	1.78	111.5	237.0	2.13

SOURCES: Johnson, in Bergson and Kuznets, *op. cit,* pp. 228–234; *Narodnoe khoziaistvo SSSR v 1965 g.* [National economy of the USSR in 1965], pp. 313, 326, 329, 333, 336; *Narodnoe khoziaistvo SSSR v 1968 g.* [National economy of the USSR in 1968], pp. 350, 359, 361, 365, 367; U.S. Department of Agriculture, *Agricultural Statistics* (selected volumes).

formance has not been good, requiring in recent years substantial injections of state funds to modernize the sector. In fact, however, the contradiction is more apparent than real.

First, the contribution of the agricultural sector is not easy to define, and while the concept of a *net product contribution* on the part of agriculture has been challenged, this does not, of course, necessarily challenge the concept of an aggregate contribution, in nonproduct forms—for example, release of labor to the urban sector.

Second, to the extent that the agricultural sector may have made an aggregate contribution in the early years of the development process, this is not necessarily contradictory with a long-run history of only mediocre agricultural performance. In fact, the mechanisms that facilitated such a contribution to the initial development may in fact have contributed to mediocre long-run performance.

But, what of the future? While this is not the place to speculate about possible future agricultural performance, a few general comments are in order. It must be noted that Soviet agriculture has been, and will continue to be, plagued by unfavorable natural conditions. The regional diversity of the Soviet countryside defies generalizations—yet 47 percent of the territory is under permafrost, the north and northwest have an overabundance of moisture, while the south has very little moisture. Climatic factors have led to great instability in year to year production.

At the same time, the Russian peasant has been drawn rapidly and reluctantly into a modern industrial society, as the rural sector continues to decline in relative importance. Such a transformation, and in a relatively short span of time, inevitably creates difficulties of organization and motivation.

The prevailing attitude of Soviet leaders toward the agricultural sector contains two important threads. First, Soviet reconstruction of rural life is dedicated in the long-run to a planned nonmarket type of solution to economic problems. To resolve organizational problems, the state farm is utilized; to resolve problems of labor force distribution and utilization, the state injects industrial processing into the countryside, and so on. There is no evidence to suggest that this pattern of thinking will change. Indeed it is worth noting that for many of these programs (the virgin lands, the development of specialized farms around cities, and so on) the *sovkhoz* has been the basic organizational mechanism. Although Soviet agriculture remains dominated by the *kolkhoz,* which still accounts for almost 65 percent of agricultural employment, the *sovkhoz* has gained substantially in importance throughout the postwar period (from 8 percent to 35 percent of agricultural employment between 1950 and 1970 [50]) and may continue to grow in relative importance as new state programs are implemented through the *sovkhoz.*

Second, the Soviet view of the apparently "successful" capitalist countries (for example, the United States and Canada) suggests that even in these cases, the state is destined to play an important (if different) role in agriculture—and yet it sees a fundamental similarity—the necessity of the industrial sector in one form or another eventually to subsidize the inherently less profitable agricultural sector. In fact, since 1965, the state has been forced to pay rather large subsidies to agriculture—largely for meat and milk subsidies—as procurement prices have risen above retail prices.[51] One should, however, note an important distinction between Western and Soviet agricultural subsidies. Soviet farm subsidies are the result of the state's decision to hold retail food prices below clearing levels, which when combined with rising procurement prices, requires a farm subsidy. Agricultural subsidies in the West are, on the other hand, largely a result of state decisions to maintain agricultural prices above market clearing levels, thus requiring state purchases of excess food products.

How do these considerations translate into a program for the present day Soviet economy? To some degree the focus of attention has been on the future of the *kolkhoz* as an institution. Such attention may be misdirected, for while it is true that in large measure the *kolkhoz* has outlived its creators' original perception of its usefulness, it is also true that the *kolkhoz* has undergone fundamental change, so that its present image bears little resemblance to

---

[50] *Narodnoe khoziaistvo v 1970 g.* [National economy of the USSR in 1970], *op cit.,* p. 405.
[51] Keith Bush, "A Suggested Computation of the Soviet Agricultural Subsidy," *Radio Liberty Dispatch* (August 31, 1971).

the past.[52] In essence, the trend must be toward greater efficiency —the appropriate organization of production to extract maximum output from minimum inputs. In this respect, it is not apparent that the "good" *kolkhozy* are to be quickly abandoned, although many of the weak *kolkhozy* have been converted to *sovkhozy*. The Soviet strategy of agricultural development is broader, and tends to focus upon problems of the rural-urban balance and their resolutions through various organizational forms. The recent expansion of inter-*kolkhoz* organizations, the infusion of industrial production into the rural sector—these are rather conventional techniques to resolve specific problems of agricultural production. It remains to be seen, however, to what extent the Soviet system will be able to focus upon and successfully eradicate sources of inefficiency, and to switch from an "output at any cost" strategy to an efficiency posture so necessary for maturization.

Selected Bibliography

Roger A. Clarke, "Soviet Agricultural Reforms Since Khrushchev," *Soviet Studies,* vol. 20, no. 2 (October 1968), 159–178.

Douglas B. Diamond, "Trends in Output, Inputs, and Factor Productivity in Soviet Agriculture," *New Directions in the Soviet Economy* (Washington, D.C.: U.S. Government Printing Office, 1969), pp. 339–381.

Douglas Diamond and Constance Krueger, "Recent Developments in Output and Productivity in Soviet Agriculture," in Joint Economic Committee, *Soviet Economic Prospects for the Seventies* (Washington, D.C.: U.S. Government Printing Office, 1973), pp. 316–339.

[52] It is interesting to note that the declining importance of the *kolkhoz* over the years and its changing organizational structure rather closely fits Soviet ideological views on the development of the agricultural sector. Thus the *kolkhoz* has been viewed as an inferior form of landholding, and one that, after being strengthened economically and raised to the level of the *sovkhoz,* will be merged with the latter to form a new organizational form more appropriate for the future Soviet (Communist) society. At the same time, levels of living will be raised in the rural sector so that urban–rural differences will be minimized.

Maurice Dobb, *Soviet Economic Development Since 1917,* rev. ed. (New York: International Publishers, 1966).

Evsey D. Domar, "The Soviet Collective Farm as a Producer Cooperative," *American Economic Review,* vol. 56, no. 4, part I (September 1966), 734–757.

F. A. Durgin, Jr., "Monetization and Policy in Soviet Agriculture Since 1952," *Soviet Studies,* vol. 15, no. 4 (April 1964).

M. Fallenbuchl, "Collectivization and Economic Development," *The Canadian Journal of Economics and Political Science,* vol. 3, no. 1 (February 1967), 1–15.

W. A. Douglas Jackson, ed., *Agrarian Policies and Problems in Communist and Non-Communist Countries* (Seattle: University of Washington Press, 1971).

Naum Jasny, *The Socialized Agriculture of the USSR* (Stanford, Calif.: Stanford University Press, 1949).

Jerzy F. Karcz, "An Organizational Model of Command Farming," in Morris Bornstein, ed., *Comparative Economic Systems: Models and Cases,* rev. ed. (Homewood, Ill.: Irwin, 1969).

Jerzy F. Karcz, ed., *Soviet and East European Agriculture* (Berkeley and Los Angeles: University of California Press, 1967).

Jerzy F. Karcz and V. P. Timoshenko, "Soviet Agricultural Policy, 1953–1962," *Food Research Institute Studies,* vol. 4, no. 2 (May 1964).

Roy D. Laird and Edward L. Crowley, eds., *Soviet Agriculture: The Permanent Crisis* (New York: Praeger, 1965).

Roy D. Laird, ed., *Soviet Agricultural and Peasant Affairs* (Lawrence: University of Kansas Press, 1963).

James R. Millar, ed., *The Soviet Rural Community* (Urbana: University of Illinois Press, 1971).

Robert F. Miller, *One Hundred Thousand Tractors* (Cambridge, Mass.: Harvard University Press, 1970).

Walter Y. Oi and Elizabeth M. Clayton, "A Peasant's View of a Soviet Collective Farm," *American Economic Review,* vol. 58, no. 1 (March 1968), 37–59.

Erich Strauss, *Soviet Agriculture in Perspective* (London: Allen & Unwin, 1969).

Robert C. Stuart, *The Collective Farm in Soviet Agriculture* (Lexington, Mass.: Heath, 1972).

Lazar Volin, *A Century of Russian Agriculture* (Cambridge, Mass.: Harvard University Press, 1970).

F. Douglas Whitehouse and Joseph Havelka, "Comparison of Farm Output in the US and USSR, 1950–1971," in *Soviet Economic Prospects for the Seventies* (Washington, D.C.: U.S. Government Printing Office, 1973), pp. 340–374.

AGRICULTURAL PERFORMANCE AND ECONOMIC DEVELOPMENT

R. W. Davies, "A Note on Grain Statistics," *Soviet Studies,* vol. 21, no. 3 (January 1970).

Arcadius Kahan, "The Collective Farm System in Russia: Some Aspects of Its Contribution to Soviet Economic Development," in Carl Eicher and Lawrence Witt, eds., *Agriculture in Economic Development* (New York: McGraw-Hill, 1964), pp. 251–271.

Jerzy F. Karcz, "From Stalin to Brezhnev: Soviet Agricultural Policy in Historical Perspective," in James R. Millar, ed., *The Soviet Rural Community* (Urbana: University of Illinois Press, 1971), pp. 36–70.

Jerzy F. Karcz, "Back on the Grain Front," *Soviet Studies,* vol. 22, no. 2 (October 1970), 262–294.

Jerzy F. Karcz, "Thoughts on the Grain Problem," *Soviet Studies,* vol. 18, no. 4 (April 1967), 399–434.

James R. Millar, "Soviet Rapid Development and the Agricultural Surplus Hypothesis," *Soviet Studies,* vol. 22, no. 1 (July 1970), 77–93.

James R. Millar and Corinne A. Guntzel, "The Economics and Politics of Mass Collectivization Reconsidered: A Review Article," *Explorations in Economic History,* vol. 8, no. 1 (Fall 1970), 103–116.

Alec Nove, "The Agricultural Surplus Hypothesis: A Comment on James R. Millar's Article," *Soviet Studies,* vol. 22, no. 3 (January 1971), 394–401.

W. F. Owen, "The Double Developmental Squeeze on Agriculture," *American Economic Review,* vol. 56, no. 1 (March 1966), 43–70.

Charles K. Wilber, "The Role of Agriculture in Soviet Economic Development," *Land Economics,* vol. 45, no. 1 (February 1969).

CHAPTER EIGHT

Soviet Foreign Trade

In this chapter we examine the role of the foreign sector in the Soviet economy. We begin with a discussion of trade in the Soviet planned economy—in particular, the state trade monopoly and the nature of trade planning instruments utilized throughout the plan era. In addition to developing an understanding of how trade is planned, it is necessary to examine both the volume and structure of Soviet trade, and especially its distribution among various trading partners in the world—notably among socialist bloc member countries of the COMECON organization. These trends can give us a picture of Soviet trade policies.

Next we examine the role of foreign trade in economic development and especially its role in the Soviet development model. Finally, we turn to an examination of reform in Soviet trade planning and practice, and in the light of these developments, consider the prospects for trade in the future.

TRADE IN THE SOVIET PLANNED ECONOMY

The Planning of Foreign Trade

It will come as no surprise to the reader that the conduct of all Soviet foreign trade planning is centralized in various state organs.[1]

[1] For a brief, general survey of characteristics of Soviet bloc foreign trade,

272

In this important sense, the year-to-year conduct of foreign trade reflects, in the Soviet case, state policy as to the appropriate role for foreign trade in the planned economy. At the same time, however, relatively little is known in the West as to how decision-making patterns arise in the Soviet foreign trade sector, and accordingly we must limit our examination to the nature of prevailing organizational arrangements. We begin with an examination of the Soviet state trade monopoly and the foreign trade decisions *internal* to the Soviet economy; then we turn to *external* organizational arrangements and examine trade practices among the socialist bloc countries through the Council for Mutual Economic Assistance (COMECON).

The State Trade Monopoly

Soviet foreign trade is organized under the jurisdiction of the Ministry of Foreign Trade, *Gosplan,* and a number of foreign trade corporations (for example *Stankoimport, Raznoexport, Tractoro-export,* etc.). These trade corporations are the operative organizations and are dealt with by *Gosplan* through the Ministry of Foreign Trade. In the case of exports, for example, the trade corporation's task is to place appropriate orders with the relevant Soviet enterprises and to insure that delivery takes place. In the case of imports, the corporation must place orders abroad and supervise subsequent delivery of the goods to the particular Soviet user.

The foreign trade corporations work under the *khozraschet* system of management and hence are intended to be financially independent and responsible. This condition of financial responsibility has little practical meaning, however—a state of affairs resulting in large part from the impact of central planning upon Soviet foreign trade behavior.

Unlike a market economy, enterprise profitability is simply not important in the planning of Soviet foreign trade. The trade monopoly serves to separate those Soviet enterprises that produce

see Franklyn D. Holzman, "East–West Trade and Investment Policy Issues," in Commission on International Trade and Investment Policy, *United States International Economic Policy in An Interdependent World* (Washington, D.C.: U.S. Government Printing Office, 1971), pp. 363–395, and especially parts I–III; see also his "Foreign Trade Behavior of Centrally Planned Economies," in Henry Rosovsky, ed., *Essays in Honor of Alexander Gerschenkron* (Cambridge, Mass.: Harvard University Press, 1966).

goods for (or consume goods from) the foreign trade sector, from the organization that actually does the trading. Thus in the case of exports, the foreign trade corporation places the necessary orders with a Soviet enterprise, paying for the commodity at the prevailing internal price in rubles; the corporation then sells the commodity abroad at a price most likely based upon world market prices for the particular good. The proceeds of this sale enter the foreign exchange reserves of the Soviet state, and the producing enterprise has little knowledge or interest in this matter or the ultimate destination of these reserves. In the case of imports, the trade corporation buys abroad, utilizing state foreign exchange reserves and then sells the commodity to the internal consuming Soviet enterprise at the prevailing internal ruble price.

This system of trade planning and pricing serves to isolate the internal Soviet economy from the world economy. If there is a difference between the world price and the internal Soviet ruble price, this difference simply appears as a subsidy or excess profit, both of which are handled through the state budget with no implications for the internal Soviet enterprises. In fact, the Soviets have tended to sell and buy in the world market at prices well below internal prices.[2] This isolation of the internal Soviet enterprise—both as a producer and as a consumer—has important implications for Soviet foreign trade behavior, and in particular, sets it apart from the patterns usually found in the market economies.

First, the mechanisms of Soviet foreign trade planning lead to inconvertibility of the Soviet ruble. The Soviet ruble is not listed on world money exchanges and is not readily available to potential trade partners, thus insuring the Soviet trade monopoly control over all trade arrangements. With the Soviet system of centralized planning and price setting, Soviet and bloc country prices bear little or no necessary relation to scarcity prices or world market prices. There is, therefore, no common scale of value among bloc countries that might serve to measure trade volume in terms of value. The result is essentially bilateral trade both for trade with

[2] On this, see Franklyn Holzman, "The Ruble Exchange Rate and Soviet Foreign Trade Pricing Policies, 1929–1961," *American Economic Review,* vol. 57, no. 4 (September 1968), 807–812. Holzman also concludes that the ruble exchange rate has tended to be well overvalued, especially between 1950 and 1961 (pp. 815–818).

the West and the bloc countries, balanced in terms of world dollar prices. Such a result is inevitable given the nature of Soviet controls over trade arrangements, the nature of Soviet pricing, and the lack of meaning for the ruble or any other Socialist currency in foreign trade arrangements.

Thus inconvertibility and the state trade monopoly imply extensive use of bilateral trade agreements. Therefore, in the absence of a meaningful rate of exchange between the ruble and other currencies (as would be established through the foreign exchange market), Soviet trade is frequently carried on in terms of specific, individually negotiated arrangements with each individual country—with no multilateral clearing mechanism involved. There is no exchange of currency involved. In some cases (especially in trade with the West), credits are involved in such arrangements, and in rare cases payment is in gold.

Finally, in the sense that export earnings may be limited, balance of payments problems may exist. Yet, they will be repressed and trade will always "balance," since ultimately a single state organization is responsible for balancing imports and exports. Also, in the absence of a convertible currency, credits will not be available among Soviet bloc nations, at least not in the manner in which such credits arise among countries whose currencies are convertible. In the latter case, as an example, the United States purchases more goods and services from Canada than Canada does from the United States. However, since Canada is willing to hold United States dollars for use in other markets, this deficit is in a sense automatically financed. It is noteworthy that the recent expansion of Soviet-U.S. trade has been accompanied by expansion of U.S. bank financing of Soviet trade and an effort by U.S. banks to open offices in Moscow.[3]

The underlying reasons for such a trade mechanism will be discussed at greater length when we examine the general bases for

---

[3] While noting that long-run basic changes in trading patterns and clearing arrangements must occur if USSR trade with the West is to expand, for the short-run Gregory Grossman notes that large-scale credits will be required if Soviet purchases in the West are to increase. Thus the entry of U.S. banking facilities into the Soviet Union must be viewed as an important step toward facilitating an expansion of Soviet–U.S. trade. On this, see Gregory Grossman, "US–Soviet Trade and Economic Relations: Problems and Prospects," *The ACES Bulletin,* vol. 15, no. 1 (Spring 1973), 3–22 and especially 17.

Soviet foreign trade policies. It is important to note, however, that the conduct of foreign trade is an integral part of the overall Soviet planning mechanism and is in large measure based upon an expected advantage to be gained in part by the division of labor. At the same time, imports and exports may be manipulated to serve as balancing items in the national economic plan. Under these conditions, it is possible for planners to shield the Soviet economy from fluctuations in world market conditions and to lessen the influence of these fluctuations on Soviet trade patterns. Through the system of *material balances* discussed earlier, imports and exports may serve as *balancing items,* and as such would be planned in a manner similar to other commodities. That is, the foreign trade corporations draw up initial target figures, based largely upon past experience, that, after adjustment and coordination at the central level, flow back to them as plan directives. The end result of the planning process is an integrated trade plan (actually several plans) specifying trade volume, its geographic distribution, method of transport, payment arrangements, and so on.

Over time, efforts have been made to coordinate trade arrangements with the long-term national economic plan, a matter of some importance if trade is to be a useful factor for achieving long-run economic objectives.

The External Environment: COMECON

The Council for Mutual Economic Assistance (COMECON) was established in 1949 on the initiative of the Soviet Union, for the purpose of integrating the planned economies of the Soviet Union and Eastern Europe through the expansion of trade among member countries.[4] Although trade with the Eastern European members of COMECON has been and remains a significant component of Soviet trade volume, most Western economists would probably

---

[4] The members of COMECON are Albania (until 1962), Bulgaria, Cuba (since 1972), Czechoslovakia, the German Democratic Republic, Hungary, Poland, Romania, Mongolia, and the Soviet Union. For a more extensive discussion of trade integration in the bloc, see Michael Kaser, *COMECON, Integration Problems of the Planned Economies,* 2nd ed. (London: Oxford University Press, 1967); Frederic L. Pryor, *The Communist Foreign Trade System* (Cambridge, Mass.: MIT Press, 1963).

argue that only a minimal degree of economic integration has actually been achieved.[5] The economic integration of the bloc countries has been relatively slow for a number of important reasons. First, it is especially important to note that most East European countries have been focusing upon industrialization, and accordingly have stressed the establishment of their own heavy industry base rather than working for economic integration based upon diversified economic structures. Thus in spite of the Soviet initiative in starting COMECON, and Soviet economic and political pressure for integration on a continuing basis, trade arrangements within the bloc have almost always been on a bilateral basis and in large measure based upon rather immediate needs—in particular upon the availability of excess commodities and upon the need to balance the plan in a particular year.

Second, there has been only a most limited effort to integrate the planning mechanisms of the bloc countries, either in terms of the planning mechanisms themselves or even on such basic factors as the gathering and processing of necessary data.[6] Possibly most important, there have been only limited, though important, preliminary efforts to develop comparable yardsticks (prices, costs, and so on) to direct specialization and to achieve a more optimal trade structure. As with all Soviet trade, however, these sorts of efforts, to the extent that they attempt to make trade patterns relate directly to patterns of comparative advantage, may not be especially fruitful. Such a contradiction stems in large measure from the incompatibility of the conduct of foreign trade as we know it in market economies and the centralized and controlled planning apparatus presently operative in the Soviet Union.

Although the initial years of the COMECON arrangements saw little progress toward economic integration, efforts were made in the late 1950s and 1960s to achieve this end—for example, through the establishment of trade meetings, founding of the Bank for International Economic Cooperation, and so on.

---

[5] See, for example, Franklyn D. Holzman, "Foreign Trade," in Abram Bergson and Simon Kuznets, eds., *Economic Trends in the Soviet Union* (Cambridge, Mass.: Harvard University Press, 1963), pp. 308–309.
[6] For a discussion of decision-making in the bloc countries, see Pryor, *op. cit.*, chap. 7.

However, even to the extent that limited progress has been made in the development of appropriate bloc decision-making procedures and decision-making criteria, the impact of this sort of change upon planning techniques in the various COMECON countries has been minimal. It should also be noted that the forces hindering integration of the economic systems of the COMECON countries have been fundamental and important, a fact underscored by the depth of the Rumanian dispute with other COMECON members, and especially the Rumanian dispute with Czechoslovakia and the Soviet Union. This dispute brought to the surface issues which would be important in any integration effort. In particular, the problem arose of how to integrate the industrialized (USSR, East Germany and Czechoslovakia) and the less developed bloc countries (Rumania and Bulgaria) where the latter wish the political and economic independence brought about by the development of a strong domestic industrial base.[7] In the case of the COMECON countries, the dispute focused upon the unwillingness of the more developed members to supply the less developed members with the products of large-scale, less profitable heavy manufacturing, while yielding to the less developed members the more profitable sectors of manufacturing. In addition, problems of quality, pricing, and notably political pressure increased the level of hostilities until finally, in the late 1950s, Rumania began looking to the West for machinery imports, and credits with which to finance those imports. In practice, therefore, the apparent warmth shown by socialist countries to one another has proven to be illusory in the face of fundamentally different political and economic goals.

The External Environment:
Beyond COMECON

Soviet trade with socialist countries, although having risen quite significantly between 1946 and 1954 (see Table 20), declined from the postwar high of 83.2 percent in 1953 to 65.4 percent in 1971. This trend is in large measure accounted for by a dramatic decline

---

[7] The Rumanian dispute is an important example of the sorts of problems that have arisen in the COMECON efforts toward economic integration. For a discussion of the dispute and its background, see John Michael Montias, *Economic Development in Communist Rumania* (Cambridge, Mass.: MIT Press, 1967), chap. 4.

Table 20 **Soviet Foreign Trade—Geographic Distribution in Selected Postwar Years (percentages)**

	1946	1950	1953	1956	1959	1962	1965	1968	1969	1971
SOCIALIST COUNTRIES[a]	54.5	81.1	83.2	75.7	75.3	70.2	68.8	67.4	65.4	65.4
COMECON member countries	40.6	57.4	59.3	49.6	52.0	57.5	58.0	57.5	56.7	56.1
CAPITALIST COUNTRIES	45.5	18.9	16.8	24.3	24.7	29.8	31.2	32.6	34.6	34.5
Industrially developed	38.4	15.1	14.5	16.8	15.9	18.1	19.3	21.3	21.9	21.5
Developing	7.1	3.8	2.3	7.5	8.8	11.7	11.9	11.3	12.7	13.0
Total	100.0	100.0	100.0	100.0	100.0	100.0	100.0	100.0	100.0	100.0

[a] Includes Cuba and Yugoslavia.

SOURCE: Compiled from official Soviet foreign trade handbooks.

in Soviet trade with mainland China, counterbalanced only in part by the expansion of Soviet trade with Cuba and Yugoslavia. In 1960, for example, Soviet trade with China accounted for 14.9 percent of aggregate Soviet foreign trade volume; by 1969 it had dropped to a mere 0.3 percent.

The proportion of Soviet trade accounted for by capitalist countries has roughly doubled since the early 1950s. This pattern can be traced primarily to the expansion of Soviet trade with Western European nations, and in spite of significant Western restrictions.[8] The Soviet balance of trade with the West has typically been a deficit, resulting in large part from big grain purchases from Canada and other Western nations, and only partially met by shipments of gold.[9]

Soviet trade with less developed countries has fluctuated in the period since World War II, but has never been a substantial portion of Soviet trade volume, typically less than 10 percent. The volume of Soviet trade with less developed capitalist countries has, however, increased quite significantly in recent years. It must be emphasized that Soviet relations with the underdeveloped countries as opposed to dealings with the industrial powers of the West involve the question of foreign aid—where political and other mo-

[8] For a recent discussion of Western controls, especially the restrictions found in the Export Control Act of 1949 and the Mutual Defense Assistance Control Act of 1951, see Holzman, "East–West Trade and Investment Policy Issues," *op. cit.,* part III. In 1972, the U.S.-U.S.S.R. Commercial Commission was established to examine long-standing trade barriers in an attempt to expand commercial relations between the two countries. The impact of Western controls on Soviet–U.S. trade is a complex and controversial question. For a detailed analysis of the issue of granting MFN (most favored nation) status, see Anton Malish, Jr., *United States–East European Trade: Considerations Involved in Granting Most-Favored-Nation Treatment to the Countries of Eastern Europe,* United States Tariff Commission, Staff Research Studies, no. 4, Washington, D.C., 1972. For a briefer discussion, see Grossman, *op. cit.,* pp. 6 ff; Malish, "An Analysis of Tariff Discrimination on Soviet and East European Trade," *The ACES Bulletin,* vol. 15, no. 1 (Spring, 1973), 43–56; Thomas Wolf, "Effects of U.S. Granting of Most-Favored-Nation Treatment to Imports from Eastern Europe: The Polish Experience," *The ACES Bulletin,* vol. 15, no. 1 (Spring, 1973), 23–42.

[9] For a discussion of recent developments, see Robert S. Kovach and John T. Farrell, "Foreign Trade of The U.S.S.R.," in *Economic Performance and the Military Burden* (Washington, D.C.: U.S. Government Printing Office, 1970), p. 109.

tives, especially a desire to demonstrate the superiority of social-ism over capitalism may be substantially different.[10]

Soviet aid to less developed countries totaled $6.8 billion for the period 1954–1969, or roughly $450 million annually. As a compari-son, it is interesting to note that in recent years (1962–1970), the average annual volume of United States foreign aid to less devel-oped countries (in the form of loans and grants) has been $4.6 billion or about ten times larger, on an annual basis, than that of the Soviet Union.[11] In addition, there have been substantial differ-ences between United States and Soviet foreign aid disbursements, especially the extent to which the USSR has used such techniques as low interest rates, repayments on an in-kind basis, and so on to gain favor as a lending power. However, Soviet foreign aid dis-bursements have not increased significantly in recent years.

Soviet Trade Policy

Thus far we have examined the general role of foreign trade in the Soviet planning apparatus, and although it remains to examine the importance of foreign trade in the Soviet development experience, at this juncture we consider some of the basic factors underlying Soviet trade policy. Most Western observers would probably argue that both the volume and structure of Soviet foreign trade have been suboptimal, and that the volume of trade has been lower than it would have been for a market economy at similar levels of eco-nomic development. Recent empirical investigations of Soviet trade volume have focused upon what is described as a "trade gap," or levels of foreign trade turnover (exports plus imports) which has been typically less than that of market economies at similar his-torical stages.[12] This pattern is frequently said to represent a Soviet

[10] For an in-depth discussion of foreign aid, see, for example, Joseph S. Berliner, *Soviet Economic Aid* (New York: Praeger, 1958); Marshall I. Goldman, *Soviet Foreign Aid* (New York: Praeger, 1968).

[11] Orah Cooper, "Soviet Economic Assistance to the Less Developed Coun-tries of the Free World," in *Economic Performance and the Military Burden, op. cit.,* p. 121; United States Government, *Economic Report of the Presi-dent, 1972* (Washington, D.C.: U.S. Government Printing Office, 1972), table B-90.

[12] For discussion of this point, see, for example, Paul R. Gregory, *Socialist and Nonsocialist Industrialization Patterns* (New York: Praeger, 1970), pp. 119–120; Pryor, *op. cit.,* chap. 1.

bias against trade, or in the extreme, a drive towards "autarky." The apparent Soviet bias against trade arises from several inter-related factors. From the earliest days of the Soviet regime, the prevailing Marxist ideological framework has prescribed rejection of the traditional Western arguments concerning the benefits to be gained from engaging in foreign trade—the thesis of "comparative advantage"—just as it has called for rejection of all Western "economic laws." In addition, the Soviet perception (and in large measure, reality) of a "hostile capitalist encirclement" during the early years of Soviet development has mitigated against reliance upon foreign trade—and hence, dependence upon the West. This fear has prompted them to avoid significantly tying their planned economic system to the "anarchy" of the capitalist market systems.

Third, it might be noted that as a sector to be added to an already complicated planning system, foreign trade as a priority sector might significantly complicate the planning process—in particular, it might introduce forces largely outside of Soviet control into the plan deliberations, thereby increasing the degree of plan uncertainty. This sort of consideration might be sufficiently serious to offset any possible gains to be made from expanding trade operations.[13]

Fourth, it is necessary to realize that prevailing international monetary arrangements have limited the Soviet Union's participation in international trade, especially in the period since World War II when trade with the West has been expanding rapidly. Having declined to join the Inernational Monetary Fund, and lacking a convertible currency, the Soviets lack the means to finance balance of payments deficits except by the use of gold reserves. Thus their imports from the West are limited to the volume of their exports to the West, which, with the relatively small demand for Soviet goods in the Western market, results in an extremely small volume of trade.

For these reasons, the foreign trade sector has been of secondary importance in the process of resource allocation in the Soviet Union—in a real sense, a buffer sector operating within a general policy of avoiding too significant dependence upon trade.

[13] Holzman, in Bergson and Kuznets, *op. cit.,* pp. 301–302.

TRADE AND ECONOMIC
DEVELOPMENT

Traditional Western trade theory suggests that with varying resource availabilities in different countries, specialization of production and exchange with other countries can serve as an active
agent in promoting the development of less developed countries
(LDCs).[14] According to such theorizing, an LDC should, during
the early stages of modernization, seek to export those goods and
services in which it has a comparative advantage vis-à-vis potential
trading partners, and in turn, it should utilize the earnings from the
export sector for imports of goods and services needed for industrialization but not readily available within its own economy. In this
manner, the economy will begin to grow in terms of size and per
capita income. In the course of such growth, it should continue to
trade according to comparative advantage, and over a long period
of time as the economy grows more sophisticated it will be able to
substitute domestic production for imports and lessen its dependence upon trade.

If the developing nation expects a strong long-run external
demand for its exports and is not capable in the short-run of developing domestic industrial capacity to furnish those goods and services being imported, it may wish to pursue the trade policy outlined above. On the other hand, a lesser role for foreign trade may
be envisaged, where there is relatively limited export demand,
where reliance upon foreign trade is viewed as politically and/or
economically undesirable, or where the utilization of imports is
viewed as a short-run strategy that must be reversed as quickly as
possible. In the latter case, there may be an explicit policy on the
part of the LDC to import those goods and services required for
the early stages of industrialization (machinery and equipment, for
example), only on a short-term basis, but at the same time to force
the development of necessary domestic production capacity to provide the previously imported goods—the process of *import sub-*

[14] For a general discussion of the role of foreign trade in economic development, see, for example, James D. Theberge, ed., *Economics of Trade and
Development* (New York: Wiley, 1968).

stitution. Under the latter strategy, the developing country will emphasize the growth of industrial sectors (typically heavy industry) in which it possesses a comparative *disadvantage* vis-à-vis the developed world—a policy that may be justified on both political grounds (the need for self-sufficiency) and on economic grounds.[15]

Of course, such decisions rest not only upon commodity trade considerations, but also on the role of imported capital, the expected level of foreign aid, the desirability of foreign investment, and finally, desired regional development patterns.

Whether the LDC chooses to follow the traditional pattern of trading according to comparative advantage, or a policy of forced import substitution, the agricultural sector will be important, for one would expect LDC exports to be primarily agricultural products (for which an agricultural surplus would be desirable) or raw materials (such as minerals). These, after all, would be the only commodities of the LDC's economy demanded abroad. In such a situation, foreign trade could assist the development effort in the following manner. The foreign exchange earned from raw materials and agricultural commodity exports would be used to pay for capital, machinery, and equipment imports and, to the extent that it is not inherent in the equipment itself, international "know-how" of the broadest sort—managerial and administrative skills and especially technological knowledge. This equipment and knowledge would then be utilized to promote industrialization, and as economic development proceeds, domestic industrial capacity would then begin to replace imports, rendering the country more self-sufficient.[16] If the LDC continues to trade according to comparative advantage, the process of substituting domestic industrial capacity for imports will be a very slow and gradual one. On the other hand, the LDC may choose to *force* the pace of import substitution through trade monopolies, exchange controls, and rapid industrialization and begin to ignore comparative advantage after the process is underway.

---

[15] For an economic argument in favor of this sort of trade policy, see United Nations, *Towards a New Trade Policy for Development* (New York: United Nations, 1964).

[16] Hollis Chenery, "Patterns of Industrial Growth," *American Economic Review,* vol. 50, no. 4 (September 1960), 624–644.

Soviet Trade Patterns

As trade is a potentially important mechanism in the development process, it would be worthwhile to examine the extent and in what manner this mechanism was in fact utilized in the course of Soviet development. It will be recalled from our earlier discussion of the Soviet Industrialization Debate of the 1920s that the various development approaches put forth at that time included a wide range of possible alternative roles for the foreign trade sector, varying from heavy to minimal emphasis, and in the latter case emphasis upon economic self-sufficiency. The emphasis upon self-sufficiency as a desirable economic goal was in part grounded upon rejection of Western thinking on the appropriate role for foreign trade in the development process.[17]

Possibly more important than such theoretical considerations was the Soviet development strategy of using agriculture as a low priority sector with depressed rural living standards to finance high savings rates for the high priority sector—industry. Thus the very nature of Soviet development strategy prohibited extensive reliance upon foreign trade and sought to establish economic self-sufficiency. It should be noted also that the Soviet economy in 1928 had certain basic features that could support a minimal role for the foreign sector. Thus with a favorable and varied resource base, a political mechanism to enforce high internal savings rates, and a reasonable base for heavy industrial development from which to begin in 1928, substantial reliance upon foreign products and capital could be avoided. In particular, the existence of a state monopoly in foreign trade enabled the Soviet authorities to avoid noncritical imports (a pressing problem for many present LDCs) and to focus upon those imports most crucial for economic growth—in particular, machinery and equipment and associated technology. Strict controls over the flow of exports and imports allowed the promotion of industrialization goals with relatively low foreign trade volumes.

Our examination of the role of Soviet foreign trade in economic

---

[17] For elaboration of Soviet thinking during the days immediately following the Revolution, see, for example, Leon M. Herman, "The Promise of Self-Sufficiency Under Socialism," in M. Bornstein and D. Fusfeld, eds., *The Soviet Economy*, 3rd ed. (Homewood, Ill.: Irwin, 1970), pp. 260–288.

development will focus upon the magnitude of trade, that is, the aggregate trade volume (imports plus exports) and variations thereof over time. In addition, we shall examine the structure of Soviet trade, in particular, the relative importance of commodities, services, and capital flows, respectively.

Soviet trade patterns were, prior to 1917, as Franklyn Holzman has pointed out ". . . what one would have expected from such a nation."[18] Exports were primarily agricultural products or semifabricates, while imports were mostly producers' goods and raw materials. In 1913, for example, 60 percent of Russian exports were agricultural, 34.4 percent were raw materials and semifabricates, while 27 percent of imports were consumer goods, the remaining imports being raw materials and producer goods.[19]

Although trade was important in the period prior to 1900—for example, between 1886 and 1890, 46 percent of Russian wheat production was exported—this importance declined immediately prior to the Revolution, due in large part to the onset of World War I. In addition, what had previously been a favorable balance of payments position—commodity exports typically exceeding commodity imports offset by capital inflows—was sharply reversed by 1917. As Holzman points out, the portion of grain output exported in the immediate prerevolutionary period declined sharply, as did the foreign exchange earnings on this grain, largely due to growing competition in the world grain market.[20] In addition, while imports initially declined, by 1917 they had once again increased, thus leading to an unfavorable Russian trade position and the expansion of Russian debts abroad.

From the relatively low levels of the immediate prerevolutionary period, the volume of Soviet foreign trade increased quite significantly between 1917 and 1928. The prerevolutionary trade level was not, however, regained by 1928, and the instigation of the industrialization drive in that year significantly altered Soviet thinking on appropriate trade patterns and levels.

During the First Five Year Plan (1928–1933), the volume of both Soviet exports and imports increased rather significantly.

[18] See Holzman, in Bergson and Kuznets, *op. cit.*, p. 284.
[19] *Ibid.*
[20] *Ibid.*, p. 286.

Thus the volume of exports (1913 = 100) increased from 37.7 in 1928 to a high of 49.8 in 1933 while the volume of imports increased at a more rapid rate from 49.4 in 1928 to a high of 82.4 in 1931, thereafter declining (Table 21). In light of this significant and immediate expansion of foreign trade during the First Five Year Plan, it might well be that Soviet planners did not, in fact, initially plan to pursue a deliberate policy of autarky, rather that later economic events forced them into that course. Although the volume of Soviet foreign trade declined very sharply after the conclusion of the First Five Year Plan, this trend was in large part the result of a collapse in world markets (especially grain prices) brought on by the world depression of the 1930s.[21]

After the onset of the depression, the prices of Soviet exports and imports declined significantly, though the rate of decline of the former significantly outstripped that of the latter. An index of the prices of Soviet exports fell from 100 in 1929 to 48.7 in 1931, while the prices of Soviet imports declined from 100 in 1929 to 68 in 1931. The result of these price changes was a drastic decline in the Soviet commodity terms of trade.[22]

Although this significant increase in the volume of trade during the First Five Year Plan must be considered as very important to the initial industrialization effort, the decline in the terms of trade must have been an important factor in addition to the ideological and strategy considerations already noted leading the Soviet economy toward a different role for the foreign sector. After the First Five Year Plan, the volume of Soviet foreign trade declined sharply (see Table 21) thereafter until it began to increase again after World War II. For example, the share of exports in national income declined from 10.4 percent in 1913 to 0.5 percent in 1937, increasing thereafter to a high of 3 percent in 1969.[23]

---

[21] For a discussion of the role of foreign trade in the preplan and early planning years, see Michael R. Dohan, *Soviet Foreign Trade in the NEP Economy and Soviet Industrialization Strategy*. Unpublished doctoral dissertation, Massachusetts Institute of Technology, 1969.

[22] Holzman, in Bergson and Kuznets, *op. cit.* pp. 287–288.

[23] Holzman, in Bergson and Kuznets, *op. cit.*, pp. 289–290; Gregory, *op. cit.*, p. 112; Stanley Cohn, "General Growth Performance of the Soviet Economy," *Economic Performance and the Military Burden in the Soviet Union, op. cit.*, p. 17, table 20.

Table 21 **Imports and Exports of the USSR (1913 = 100)**

Year	Exports Composite Index	Imports Composite Index	Year	Exports Composite Index	Imports Composite Index
1917	6.9	176.3	1943	4.3	15.5
1918	0.5	7.7	1944	6.6	16.5
1919	0.0	0.2	1945	15.5	20.0
1920	0.1	2.1	1946	27.2	49.4
1921	1.3	15.3	1947	30.0	43.9
1922	5.4	19.6	1948	51.1	64.3
1923	14.3	10.4	1949	58.2	72.4
1924	22.2	18.9	1950	80.7	82.0
1925	25.1	37.8	1951	94.6	101.4
1926	32.2	33.8	1952	114.2	123.4
1927	34.7	38.9	1953	120.0	133.1
1928	37.7	49.4	1954	132.6	154.4
1929	44.4	48.3	1955	142.3	149.2
1930	57.0	72.1	1956	150.7	173.8
1931	61.4	82.4	1957	179.2	186.7
1932	53.7	59.1	1958	184.2	223.8
1933	49.8	31.9	1959	242.9	264.7
1934	43.2	24.0	1960	242.6	290.1
1935	38.0	26.3	1961	265.7	299.4
1936	28.6	30.3	1962	311.8	334.6
1937	30.0	27.8	1963	321.7	364.3
1938	26.2	32.3	1964	333.9	378.9
1939	10.6	20.4	1965	371.5	401.5
1940	21.8	27.7	1966	422.9	396.3
1941	14.4	29.1	1967	458.0	432.0
1942	4.8	17.6			

SOURCE: Michael Kaser, "A Volume Index of Soviet Foreign Trade," *Soviet Studies* vol. 20, no. 4 (April 1969), 523–526.

In sum, we note that trends in Soviet foreign trade during the industrialization drive suggest a substantial attempt at import substitution and, in addition, a decline in the importance of foreign trade—largely at this stage as a result of world market conditions, but subsequently as a result of the ideological considerations and of difficulties associated with planning foreign trade in a centralized and controlled economy noted above.

During the period since World War II, changes in the pattern of

Soviet trade have been distinctive on several counts. First, although beginning from a very low base, the increase in trade volume has been impressive: Soviet foreign trade turnover more than tripled during the 1950s and continued to increase rapidly in the 1960s. Second, and of equal importance, the geographical direction of Soviet foreign trade, as we have already noted, has changed quite significantly in favor of capitalist countries.

THE STRUCTURE
OF SOVIET
COMMODITY TRADE

We have already noted that the volume of Soviet foreign trade increased sharply during the First Five Year Plan (1928–1933), but declined thereafter. Equally important, however, was the changing composition of Soviet foreign trade during these early years, and especially the extent to which the changing pattern of foreign trade was directed toward immediate support of the rapid industrialization program.

On the import side, for example, there was a distinct movement away from the importation of consumer goods and towards producer goods. Producer goods and consumption goods accounted for 27 percent and 73 percent of aggregate Soviet imports in 1918; by 1931, the figures were 95 percent and 5 percent for production and consumption goods, respectively.[24] Also notable during the early years of Soviet industrialization was the increasing importance of imports of machinery and equipment. From a level of 15.9 percent of imports in 1913, machinery and equipment imports grew to account for 55.2 percent of imports in 1932.[25] This pattern changed significantly after the First Five Year Plan, basically through the development of domestic capacity in key industrial sectors (import substitution). Nevertheless, if we look at the portion of Soviet utilization of key industrial commodities (those of crucial importance to the industrialization effort) accounted for by imports, the result is striking and suggests that foreign technology

[24] Holzman, in Bergson and Kuznets, *op. cit.*, p. 297.
[25] *Ibid.*, p. 296.

may have been a very important element in the industrialization process.[26] In 1930, for example, 89 percent of aggregate Soviet consumption of turbines, boilers, and generators came from imports. In 1932, 66 percent of machine tools consumed in the Soviet Union were imported, and so on.[27]

Export patterns did not change radically during the early years of industrialization. Fuels, raw materials, and consumer goods remained important as a portion of aggregate export volume. Exports of grain increased during the First Five Year Plan, but fluctuated significantly thereafter.

For the period since World War II, there have been some important shifts on both the import and export sides. As a portion of aggregate imports, for example, consumer goods increased in importance from 18.3 percent in 1946 to 32.8 percent in 1970. Machinery and equipment imports also increased from 28.5 percent of all imports in 1946 to 35.1 percent of all imports in 1970. Imports of ores, raw materials, and fuels have been, and remain, relatively unimportant. Trends in Soviet imports and exports can be traced for the postwar years in Tables 22 and 23.

Since 1940, Soviet exports of consumer goods have declined quite sharply (from 33.3 to 11.8 percent of exports between 1946 and 1970), while exports of fuels and metals, and notably machinery and equipment, have expanded significantly.

We have already noted that the commodity composition of Soviet foreign trade varies quite significantly as between socialist and capitalist trading partners. Thus, in trade with the West, Soviet exports of raw materials are important, exports of machinery and equipment very small; in Soviet trade with Eastern European countries, however, exports of machinery and equipment form a very important portion of total Soviet exports.

---

[26] It is important to recognize that the shift in trade patterns during the First Five Year Plan not only provided producer goods so necessary for the immediate expansion of output, but also—and this may be the more crucial factor—provided prototypes of the best Western technology that could then be duplicated. For a discussion of the role of Western technology see Antony C. Sutton, *Western Technology and Soviet Economic Development, 1917 to 1930* (Stanford, Calif.: The Hoover Institution, 1968); *Western Technology and Soviet Economic Development, 1930 to 1945* (Stanford, Calif.: The Hoover Institution, 1971).

[27] Holzman, in Bergson and Kuznets, *op. cit.,* pp. 297–298.

Table 22 **The Structure of Soviet Imports (percentages)**

	1946	1950	1955	1959	1962	1966	1968	1970
Ores and concentrates	2.0	5.8	8.2	6.5	4.6	3.8	2.0	3.4
Base metals and manufactures	11.4	8.0	6.7	8.6	8.7	3.9	4.8	5.9
Fuels, lubricants and related materials	11.8	11.5	8.2	4.6	3.1	2.3	1.9	1.5
Machinery and equipment	28.5	21.5	30.2	26.6	34.8	32.4	36.9	35.1
Chemicals	1.1	2.2	1.7	2.2	3.3	5.0	5.7	3.9
Rubber and rubber products	0.3	3.6	1.4	3.9	3.9	2.4	1.8	1.6
Wood and wood products	3.9	3.8	3.0	1.9	1.8	1.9	2.1	2.2
Textile raw materials and semimanufactures	6.6	7.7	5.4	6.5	4.4	4.7	3.9	4.8
Consumer goods	18.3	23.5	21.6	28.3	28.3	34.3	31.9	32.8
Food[a]	13.9	16.9	16.9	10.7	11.0	18.1	12.4	13.6
Other consumer goods	4.3	6.6	4.7	17.6	17.3	16.2	19.5	19.2
Merchandise—other	8.6	5.1	10.1	8.9	5.5	5.2	5.0	4.5
Unspecified	7.6	6.9	3.4	2.1	1.6	4.0	3.9	4.3
Total[b]	100.0	100.0	100.0	100.0	100.0	100.0	100.0	100.0

[a] Includes raw materials for food processing industries.
[b] Components may not sum to totals due to rounding.

SOURCE: Compiled from official Soviet foreign trade handbooks.

Table 23 **The Structure of Soviet Exports (percentages)**

	1946	1950	1955	1959	1962	1966	1968	1970
Ores and concentrates	3.2	2.2	3.4	4.0	3.9	3.4	3.3	3.8
Base metals and manufactures	3.8	8.8	12.6	13.7	14.4	15.2	13.6	15.3
Fuels, lubricant and related materials	5.1	3.8	9.6	14.7	16.4	16.2	15.8	15.1
Machinery and equipment	5.8	11.8	17.5	21.5	16.6	20.8	21.6	21.5
Chemicals	4.0	3.1	2.1	2.2	2.5	3.1	3.5	3.3
Wood and wood products	4.3	3.1	5.1	4.8	6.0	7.0	6.4	6.5
Textile raw materials and semimanufactures	15.0	11.2	10.1	5.7	4.9	5.2	4.5	3.4
Consumer goods	33.3	22.4	14.5	17.5	16.1	11.7	12.5	11.8
Food[a]	27.6	18.4	11.2	14.6	13.0	8.8	9.7	9.4
Other consumer goods	5.7	4.0	3.3	2.9	3.1	2.9	2.9	2.4
Merchandise—other	17.6	7.0	4.8	4.1	3.2	2.8	3.6	2.0
Unspecified	7.9	26.6	20.3	11.9	16.0	14.6	15.2	14.3
Total[b]	100.0	100.0	100.0	100.0	100.0	100.0	100.0	100.0

[a] Includes raw materials for food processing industries.
[b] Components may not sum to totals due to rounding.

SOURCE: Compiled from official Soviet foreign trade handbooks.

Problems and Prospects

It could be argued that at an early stage of economic development, bilateral planning of foreign trade such as one finds in the Soviet Union can be quite effective, since priorities tend to be few in number and relatively visible, thus facilitating the planning of import-led growth.[28] As economic development proceeds, however, the increasing complexity and diversity of the economy may dictate changes in the planning of foreign trade, just as it may dictate changes in the planning of other sectors.

In practical terms, there seems to have been modification of the earlier Soviet drive towards autarky, for as we have seen, the period since World War II has witnessed significant growth in the volume of Soviet foreign trade. Granted that a large portion of this growth in Soviet foreign trade can be accounted for by the sovietization of Eastern Europe in the postwar years, nevertheless, the expansion of Soviet trade with the LDCs and an apparent willingness to expand trade with Western nations, especially the United States, cannot be overlooked.

If these patterns represent a reappraisal of the appropriate role of foreign trade in the Soviet political system, new thinking on the economic aspects of foreign trade can also be observed. Thus, in recent years (especially in the 1960s), in addition to a preliminary re-evaluation of the role of foreign trade in the Soviet economy, there has been new theorizing on the general role of foreign trade in planned economic systems. In addition to a renewed Soviet interest in the doctrine of comparative advantage, there has been a search for new criteria to apply to foreign trade planning and decision-making in the planned economies.[29] This search has focused upon profitability indicators, efficiency indicators, and to some degree, upon basic improvements to the Soviet price system.

[28] See, for example, Andrea Boltho, *Foreign Trade Criteria in Socialist Economies* (Cambridge: Cambridge University Press, 1971), pp. 128 ff. It should be noted that in the Soviet case, any possible advantages from bilateral trade agreements must have been minimal given the basic pattern of multilateral trading during the early plan years.

[29] For a discussion of the evolution of Soviet theoretical views of foreign trade, see Carl McMillan, "Some Recent Developments in Soviet Foreign Trade Theory," *Canadian Slavonic Papers,* vol. 12, no. 3 (Fall 1970), 243–272.

Finally, as with other sectors of the Soviet economy, there has been in the foreign trade sector a new measure of attention devoted to mathematical techniques, especially programming models. In these respects, the foreign trade sector of the Soviet economy has not been isolated from the more general pattern of economic reform in the Soviet Union, and yet, as with the general economic reform, practical achievements have been substantially more modest than the extent of discussion by Soviet economists and planners might imply.

To the extent that the above sorts of trends continue, we might expect Soviet foreign trade patterns of the future to be based upon new and different planning indicators, although the substantially unknown political component of the decision-making process will most likely make trade expansion a cautious venture. The pace of this type of expansion will depend upon several factors. First, it will depend upon the extent to which Soviet leaders are willing to open up the Soviet economy to the impact of (and instability associated with) the world community of nations. Developments in this direction are likely to be modest at best, since they would imply substantial modifications to the present planning system and, most notably, abandonment of direct controls and the introduction of new pricing arrangements. Nevertheless, some observers of the Soviet scene perceive changes in the Soviet leadership's attitude toward trade with the West as a means of bolstering a lagging economy through Western technology. Even the traditional concept of the advantages of self-sufficiency are now subject to challenge.[30] Such tendencies are, however, of recent origin and seem to be tied to recent economic difficulties. Whether this trend will continue in the long-run is not apparent. Second, the development of alternatives to bilateral trading mechanisms and a real commitment to integration in the case of the COMECON countries would be of major importance. Finally, in terms of trade with the West, recent willingness on the part of Western nations to abandon the Cold War stance and seriously consider reduction of trade barriers— such as the long-standing embargoes—will doubtless be important. It should be noted, however, that despite the optimism surrounding

[30] Edward Wilson et al., "U.S.–Soviet Commercial Relations," in Joint Economic Committee, *Soviet Economic Prospects for the Seventies* (Washington, D.C.: U.S. Government Printing Office, 1973), p. 643.

the relaxation of tensions between the Soviet Union and the West, there remain important factors besides Western controls that have in the past and may well in the future restrict Western purchases from the USSR—quality problems, lack of Soviet merchandizing ability, spare parts and servicing problems, and so on.[31] Important preliminary moves to expand trade between the Soviet Union and the United States have already taken place—notably the establishment of the Joint U.S.-USSR Commercial Commission in May of 1972 and the U.S.A.-USSR Trade Agreement signed by President Nixon in October 1972. This agreement, in addition to providing for a substantial increase in Soviet-American trade, also allows for the removal of two long-standing barriers—the granting of "most favored nation" status to the USSR by the United States, and settlement of Soviet lend-lease debts.[32] In recent months, a number of important commercial agreements have been announced in the areas of grain, textiles, technology, natural gas, and so on.

Selected Bibliography

Gunnar Adler-Karlsson, *Western Economic Warfare: 1947–1967* (New York: Humanities, 1968).

Andrea Boltho, *Foreign Trade Criteria in Socialist Economies,* (Cambridge: Cambridge University Press, 1971).

Alan A. Brown and Egon Neuberger, eds., *International Trade and Central Planning* (Berkeley and Los Angeles: University of California Press, 1968).

Michael R. Dohan, *Soviet Foreign Trade in the NEP Economy and Soviet Industrialization Strategy.* Unpublished doctoral dissertation, Massachusetts Institute of Technology, 1969.

---

[31] Gregory Grossman, *op. cit.,* 3–22.

[32] U.S. exports to the Soviet Union increased from $161.7 million in 1971 to $546.7 million in 1972. A major Soviet grain purchase in 1972 contributed to this significant increase. See Moscow Narodny Bank Limited, *Press Bulletin,* no. 592 (February 14, 1973), p. 10. Between July 1972 and November 1973, Soviet grain purchases abroad totaled almost 31 million tons (worth more than $2 billion). Such large grain purchases are scheduled to continue for at least three years. On this, see Douglas Diamond and Constance Krueger, "Recent Developments in Output and Productivity in Soviet Agriculture," in *Soviet Economic Prospects for the Seventies, op. cit.,* p. 327.

Marshall I. Goldman, *Soviet Foreign Aid* (New York: Praeger, 1967).

Gregory Grossman, "U.S.-Soviet Trade and Economic Relations: Problems and Prospects," *The ACES Bulletin,* vol. 15, no. 1 (Spring 1973), 3–22.

Franklyn D. Holzman, "East-West Trade and Investment Policy Issues," in *United States International Economic Policy in An Interdependent World* (Washington, D.C.: U.S. Government Printing Office, 1971), pp. 363–395.

Franklyn D. Holzman, "Foreign Trade Behavior of Centrally Planned Economies," in Henry Rosovsky, ed., *Industrialization in Two Systems: Essays in Honor of Alexander Gerschenkron* (New York: Wiley, 1966).

Franklyn D. Holzman, "Foreign Trade," in Abram Bergson and Simon Kuznets, eds., *Economic Trends in the Soviet Union* (Cambridge, Mass.: Harvard University Press, 1963), pp. 283–332.

Michael Kaser, *COMECON: Integration Problems of Planned Economies,* 2nd ed. (London: Oxford University Press, 1967).

Carl H. McMillan, "Aspects of Soviet Participation in International Trade." Unpublished doctoral dissertation, Johns Hopkins University, 1972.

Anton Malish, Jr., *United States-East European Trade: Considerations Involved in Granting Most-Favored-Nation Treatment to the Countries of Eastern Europe,* United States Tariff Commission, Staff Research Studies, no. 4, Washington, D.C., 1972.

Paul Marer, *Soviet and East-European Trade (1946–1969): Statistical Compendium and Guide* (Bloomington: Indiana University Press, 1972).

John Michael Montias, *Economic Development in Communist Rumania* (Cambridge, Mass.: MIT Press, 1967), chap. 4.

Frederic L. Pryor, *The Communist Foreign Trade System* (Cambridge, Mass.: MIT Press, 1963).

Glen Alden Smith, *Soviet Foreign Trade: Organization, Operations, and Policy, 1918–1971* (New York: Praeger, 1973).

Antony C. Sutton, *Western Technology and Soviet Economic Development 1930 to 1945* (Stanford, Calif.: The Hoover Institution, 1971).

Antony C. Sutton, *Western Technology and Soviet Economic Development 1917 to 1930* (Stanford, Calif.: The Hoover Institution, 1968).

Jozef Wilczynski, *The Economics and Politics of East-West Trade* (New York: Praeger, 1969).

Edward Wilson et al., "U.S.-Soviet Commercial Relations," in Joint Economic Committee, *Soviet Economic Prospects for the Seventies* (Washington, D.C.: U.S. Government Printing Office, 1973), pp. 638–659.

PART THREE

Economic Theory and Economic Reform

CHAPTER NINE

The Theory of Socialism:
The Socialist Controversy

In Part Two we considered how the Soviet economy "works," that is, how resources are allocated in the Soviet Union. In this connection, Soviet planning, namely material balance planning, financial planning and foreign trade planning and pricing were discussed along with Soviet labor policy and managerial practices. Nowhere was the *theory* of resource allocation in a centrally planned socialist economy discussed. Instead, the emphasis was on what was actually being done. This pragmatic approach to Soviet resource allocation is not accidental, for, as Alec Nove suggests, the Soviets have had "virtually no theory to guide them; and no theory of planning emerged from their activities."[1] In fact, Soviet texts on planning and resource allocation notably ignore the underlying theory,[2] other than some obligatory references to Marxian theory (largely as interpreted by Lenin) and the fact that the so-called planning principle rather than the chaos of the market should govern resource allocation. The emphasis of such works is largely on describing what is practiced, not on the underlying theoretical principles.

---

[1] V. S. Nemchinov, ed., *The Use of Mathematics in Economics* (Cambridge, Mass.: MIT Press, 1964), p. ix. Nove is the editor of this English translation.

[2] For example, *Ekonomicheskoe planirovanie v SSSR* [Economic planning in the USSR] (Moscow: 1967), and *Political Economy, A Textbook,* (East Germany: Deitz Verlag, 1964).

THE PROBLEM OF RESOURCE ALLOCATION UNDER SOCIALISM

In this chapter, we turn to the theory of socialism, that is, to the question of how a socialist economy is to solve the resource allocation problem. First, however, we should define what we mean under "socialism" insofar as there exists a wide variety of possible meanings for this term. In the usage here, a socialist economy is defined as one in which the factors of production other than labor, namely land and capital, are owned by society as a whole (as represented either by the state or by collective organizations). Of course, this definition does not directly define the necessary degree of social ownership of the means of production (is 70 percent enough?), but it is to be understood that we are talking about a society in which the overwhelming share of the nonlabor factors of production is owned by society as a whole.

Within this broad definition can be subsumed different types of socialism, an important distinction being the degree of resource allocation through economic planning versus the degree of allocation through the market. In this regard, two convenient categorizations would be *centrally planned socialism,* on the one hand, and *market socialism,* on the other hand; the Soviet economic system being a prime example of the former with Yugoslavia being, to a great extent, an example of the latter. A second important distinction has to do with the type of social ownership. Here one can distinguish between property owned directly by the state (the Soviet industrial enterprise) and property owned (at least in theory) by collective groups (the collective farm of the USSR).

The theory of socialism is considered at this juncture for two reasons. First, by providing a list of the theoretical socialist alternatives, it prepares the way for the discussion of economic reform of the Soviet command system in the next chapter. Second, by raising the issue of the viability and efficiency of socialism as a form of economic organization, it prepares the way for evaluating the performance of one type of socialist economic organization in Part Four—the economic performance of the Soviet economy.

EARLY SOVIET
THEORIES OF
SOCIALISM

The 1920s was a fairly productive period for economic theorizing in the Soviet Union, spawning the Soviet Industrialization Debate and the Planning Debate, both discussed in earlier chapters. During this period, some rough outlines emerged that probably would have eventually led to full-fledged theories of socialist resource allocation under conditions of central planning. On the one hand, talented economists were busy estimating national balances for the economy, an example being the well-known 1923–1924 balance of the national economy prepared by the Central Statistics Board under the direction of P. I. Popov.[3] Such efforts, the intellectual predecessors of input-output techniques later sophisticated by Professor Wassily Leontief in the United States, pointed the way for the future development of mathematical planning techniques involving both balancing and optimization of resource allocation—an approach that was blocked by the harsh reaction against mathematical economics during the Stalin years. Nevertheless, such efforts (premature, perhaps, given the state of knowledge at the time) were based on the premise that the socialist economy can be directed by mathematical planning models expressing input-output relationships among branches. It was not until the post-Stalin years that Soviet economists were allowed to return to this topic and to develop the relatively sophisticated theories of mathematical planning in a centrally directed socialist economy (although such theories are still not very widely used within the Soviet Union).

On the other hand, the Soviet Industrialization Debate forced the participants to deal with issues concerning the operation of a

---

[3] On this, see V. S. Nemchinov's comments on the 1923–1924 balance in *The Use of Mathematics in Economics, op. cit.,* pp. 2–10. Popov's original presentation of the 1923–1924 balance is translated in Spulber, *Foundations of Soviet Strategy for Economic Growth* (Bloomington: Indiana University Press, 1964), pp. 5–19. For a discussion of the early Soviet mathematical economics school, see Leon Smolinski, "The Origins of Soviet Mathematical Economics," *Yearbook of East-European Economics,* Band 2 (Munich: Günther Olzog Verlag, 1971), pp. 137–154.

mixed socialist economy comprised of peasant agriculture and socialist industry (at least large-scale industry). In particular, the participants in the debate were concerned with the formulation of working arrangements that would best link together the private and socialist sectors. In this regard, the right wing of the Bolshevik Party, as represented by Bukharin, Shanin, and others, favored the retention of market forces and economic incentives as far as possible. The essential link between socialized industry and peasant agriculture was to be private trade, which would provide peasants with incentives to market their surpluses. Preobrazhensky's method of linking private agriculture and socialized industry was quite different, calling for a more active role of the state in influencing economic decisions. He advocated a state monopoly of trade that would enable the state to create profits for industrial investment by manipulating the margins between purchase and sales prices.

By focusing attention on the linkages between the socialist sector and the private sector, the participants in the Soviet Industrialization Debate omitted perhaps the most crucial element in the operation of a socialist economy: what arrangements are to govern resource allocation that falls entirely within the socialist sector? Their neglect of this issue is an important point in view of their general consensus that the state should allocate investment goods (to be produced by state industry). In fact, the basic issue of the debate was how this investment should be allocated. Thus the state, not the forces of supply and demand, would determine the allocation of capital goods and—it follows from this—that there would be no automatic mechanism for determining their relative scarcities. This was the basic issue of the Socialist Controversy to which we shall turn shortly: How can producer goods be rationally allocated in the absence of scarcity prices?

A partial explanation of the failure to deal more fully with the economic theory of socialism is the widely held view of the time, advocated by Bukharin and Preobrazhensky in the early 1920s (before they parted company) in their joint work, *The ABC of Communism,*[4] and later by Stalin: that the "law of value"—supply and demand—was not operative in a socialist economy. In-

[4] N. I. Bukharin and E. A. Preobrazhensky, *The ABC of Communism*, Eien and Cedar Paul, trs. (London: The Communist Party of Great Britain, 1922); Spulber, *Soviet Strategy for Economic Growth, op cit.,* chap. 2.

stead, a new economic regulator, the planning principle, was to re-place the capitalist laws of supply and demand, and the tools de-veloped by bourgeois economists to analyze capitalist economies were seen as unnecessary constraints no longer relevant to a so-cialist society. Such a socialist economy could be scientifically di-rected by technicians and engineers without observing "economic laws." This view came to be more firmly entrenched and is reflected in the growing disregard for market forces displayed by economic planners in the late 1920s.[5]

By the beginning of the plan era, it had become dangerous to argue for either a positive role of market forces or for the exist-ence of economic laws (of supply and demand, for example) in a planned socialist economy. Increasingly planners shied away from concepts like "equilibrium" and "balanced growth" as unnecessary constraints on their freedom of action, and most economic theor-izing ground to a halt, to re-emerge only after the death of Stalin.[6]

To find meaningful analyses of the economic theory of social-ism, one must turn to Western discussions on the topic—namely, to the *Socialist Controversy,* a long-lasting and ongoing debate, largely among Western economists, over the viability of socialism as an economic organization. After reviewing this Western discus-sion, we shall return to Soviet theorists to consider the re-emergence of Soviet mathematical economics during the postwar period.

THE THEORY OF SOCIALISM IN THE WEST: THE SOCIALIST CONTROVERSY

The Socialist Controversy: Marx

Socialist administrators would have been indebted to Karl Marx had he devoted more of his energy to explaining how a socialist

[5] E. H. Carr and R. W. Davies, *Foundations of a Planned Economy,* vol. I, part 2 (New York: Macmillan, 1969), pp. 787–801.
[6] Spulber, *Soviet Strategy for Economic Growth, op. cit.,* chap. 2; Gregory Grossman, "Scarce Capital and Soviet Doctrine," *Quarterly Journal of Economics,* vol. 67, no. 3 (August 1953), 311–315; R. Dunayevskaya, "A New Revision of Marxian Economics," *American Economic Review,* vol. 34, no. 3 (September 1944), 531–537; Smolinski, *op. cit.,* pp. 150–151.

economy would operate. Instead he concentrated on the internal contradictions of capitalism that would eventually lead to its demise and replacement by socialism—a "superior" form of economic organization. Marx presented no systematic demonstration of the superiority of socialism and was quite cryptic about the functioning of such an economy,[7] so much so that it was long debated in the Soviet Union whether Marx's labor theory of value was meant to apply to socialism.[8]

If one follows the approach suggested by the Polish economist, Oskar Lange, that, insofar as commodities continue to be exchanged under socialism, and therefore continue to bear the chief characteristics of commodities in the Marxian sense, then it could be concluded that the law of value continues to operate under socialism. If so, Lange argues that the allocation of resources under socialism would proceed along the following lines. A "social plan" would apportion labor among occupations in accordance with the wants and needs of society. In turn, each worker would be credited with a receipt for the quantity of "socially necessary" labor that he has contributed (after deductions for social goods), which would give him command over consumer goods (of his choice) produced by the same quantity of labor. The problem of allocating resources in a socialist economy would then involve only the allocation of labor by the social plan, and labor would be the only true factor of production.[9]

That Marx's labor theory of value represents an imperfect operational solution to the problem of resource allocation need not detain us at this point. The important point is that Marx had very little to say about the actual operation of a socialist economy other than his labor theory of value, which itself contained many problems that limited its use in real-world situations. Instead, Marx made a simple claim that socialism would prove superior to the capitalist system that it was to replace.

[7] Abram Bergson, "Socialist Economics," in *Essays in Normative Economics* (Cambridge, Mass.: Harvard University Press, 1966), pp. 193–236.

[8] Dunayevskaya, *op. cit.,* 531–537.

[9] Oskar Lange, "On the Economic Theory of Socialism," in Benjamin Lippincott, ed., *On the Economic Theory of Socialism* (Minneapolis: University of Minnesota Press, 1938), pp. 131–133.

The Socialist Controversy:
von Mises

In an article entitled "Economic Calculation in the Socialist Commonwealth," which first appeared in German in 1922,[10] Professor Ludwig von Mises of the University of Vienna, mounted a formidable challenge to Marx's assertion of the superiority of socialism. Von Mises believed not only that socialism was an inferior alternative to capitalism but also that it was an unworkable economic system. The basis for von Mises' belief was quite simple: the state will own the factors of production other than labor (capital, land, intermediate products) and must therefore be responsible for their allocation among competing uses. Under such a system, von Mises argued, consumer goods and labor could probably be rationally allocated because there would still be a recognizable demand and supply for both. But what about producers' goods that re-enter the production process and are not purchased directly by consumers? They must somehow be allocated among socialist enterprises by a superior agency. Without a market to reveal to planners and to managers of state industry the relative values (prices) of the millions of intermediate producers' goods, "the command of a supreme authority would govern the business of supply. Instead of the economy of 'anarchical' production, the senseless order of an irrational machine would be supreme."[11] Thus, von Mises argued that producers' goods cannot be allocated rationally by the socialist state without knowledge of their true values (prices); yet their prices cannot be known without the existence of markets. Such would be the case even if the state could specify exactly what the *final* outputs of the economy should be, that is, even if the state knows exactly what the ends of the society are. The real problem remains, as

[10] Ludwig von Mises, "Die Wirtschaftsrechnung im socialistischem Gemeinwesen," *Archiv für Sozialwissenschaften* (April 1920). Translated as "Economic Calculation in the Socialist Commonwealth," in F. A. Hayek, ed., *Collectivist Economic Planning,* 6th ed. (London: Routledge & Kegan Paul, 1963), pp. 87–130. Von Mises' article entitled "Die Gemeinwirtschaft," first published in 1922, is also available in translation as "Economic Calculation in Socialism," in Morris Bornstein, ed., *Comparative Economic Systems,* rev. ed. (Homewood, Ill.: Irwin, 1969), pp. 61–68.
[11] Quoted in Bornstein, *op. cit.,* p. 62.

von Mises put it, "to place the means [the socially owned factors of production] at the service of the end."[12]

Von Mises' emphasis on placing *means* at the service of the ends suggests the following goal for the socialist economy: to produce a maximum quantity of final outputs in conformity with the ends of the society at a minimum cost of society's resources. According to von Mises, the state could not perform this task well. Not knowing the prices, it will not know the costs of production. Thus, it will neither be able to combine resources in a least cost fashion nor to choose optimal output combinations.

Why then, asked von Mises, not use artificial markets that simulate market behavior to provide planners with scarcity prices? Von Mises strongly discounts the feasibility of this approach, for it is impossible "to divorce the market and its functions in regard to the formation of prices from the working of a society which is based on private property in the means of production. . . . For the motive force of the whole process which gives rise to the factors of production is the ceaseless search on the part of the capitalist and the entrepreneur to maximize their profits by serving the consumers' wishes."[13] In other words, it is the profit motive that induces entrepreneurs to appropriately limit their demand for factors of production to cost minimizing proportions. Without this ultimate guiding force, factor demand under socialism would represent an artificial construct quite different from that in a market economy. The same is true of factor supply—capital allocation being a noteworthy example: the capitalist will disburse his capital among competing ends by balancing expected yields and risks. Under socialism, capital will be disbursed differently: insofar as the allocation of capital among competing uses determines the direction of expansion of the economy, the decision will be too important to be left to the "anarchy" of the market. Instead, capital must be allocated directly by the state to promote its long-run interests, which means an elimination of the capital market.[14]

Von Mises also relates the absence of rational economic calculation under socialism to the lack of individual responsibility and

[12] Quoted in Hayek, *op. cit.,* p. 103.
[13] Quoted in Bornstein, *op. cit.,* p. 64.
[14] *Ibid.,* p. 67.

initiative of socialist managers, which he sees as the "most serious menace to socialist economic organization."[15] This lack of managerial initiative can be explained by a breakdown of the link between managerial performance and managerial reward. No longer is the enterprise manager materially interested in the outcome of his operation. Further, one must continue to assume that human nature will not change radically; therefore while the well-being of any particular individual is dependent upon the diligence of others, one's own welfare is independent of one's own diligence. Even if the socialist manager is willing to take initiative and "exert himself with the same zeal as he does today . . . there still remains the problem of measuring the result of economic activity."[16] That is, how can managerial performance be evaluated without scarcity values?

The Socialist Controversy: Barone

If von Mises actually did believe that rational economic calculation was theoretically impossible in a socialist state even under ideal conditions, his position is easily refuted.[17] As early as 1907, an Italian economist, Enrico Barone, in an article entitled, "The Ministry of Production in the Collectivist State,"[18] demonstrated that a Central Planning Board (CPB) armed with perfect knowledge and perfect computation techniques could allocate resources efficiently without the market, by solving vast simultaneous equation systems.

Barone started from the proposition that under socialism some

[15] Quoted in Hayek, *op. cit.*, p. 116.
[16] *Ibid.*, p. 120.
[17] Von Mises' actual position on rational calculation under socialism has been subject to two different interpretations. One is that he argued that rational economic calculation would be impossible even if supermen staffed the Central Planning Board. Even though they would have perfect knowledge of all relevant variables—the utility functions of millions of consumers and the production functions of thousands of enterprises—rational economic calculation would still be impossible.

The second interpretation of von Mises suggests that rational economic calculation under the above conditions would be entirely possible in theory, yet impossible in practice owing to the enormous complexities confronting planners, who in practice are anything but supermen. For a discussion of these two interpretations, see Bergson, *op. cit.*, pp. 233–234.
[18] Translated in Hayek, *op. cit.*, pp. 245–290.

resources would remain in the hands of individuals, whereas the remainder would belong to the state. The CPB would establish *ratios of equivalences* between commodities and present and future consumption (the latter being called a "premium for deferred consumption"). Individuals would supply their resources in return for commodities produced by socialist enterprises and for resources owned by the state. Their terms of exchange, the ratios of equivalences, would be determined by the CPB. Socialist enterprises would maximize profits subject to their production functions accepting the established ratios of equivalences as parameters.

Individual demands, and consequently market demands, for consumer goods and services and for deferred consumption would be functions of the CPB's ratios of equivalences. The exact functional form would depend upon individual tastes (that need not be known by the CPB, which needs to know only the demand schedules themselves). Enterprise supply schedules would also depend on the ratios of equivalences, the functional form of such schedules depending upon the enterprise production functions, which the CPB must know to perform the necessary calculations. In addition, a supply and demand schedule for savings would also be present in the system of equations, based upon the established ratios of equivalences. The CPB could manipulate the supply of savings by controlling the distribution of returns on the state-owned assets.

Barone envisioned directing the socialist economy through a vast system of supply and demand equations on the basis of the ratios of equivalences rather than prices per se. The CPB would have to solve the system of equations to determine the equilibrium equivalence ratios. The data required for a solution would be: (1) individual demand schedules; (2) enterprise production functions; and (3) initial stocks of consumer goods and producer goods held by individuals, enterprises, and the state. Once the equilibrium equivalence ratios were determined, the CPB could solve for the equilibrium quantities of goods and services. On the similarity of this solution to the perfectly competitive solution, Barone writes:

> From what we have seen and demonstrated hitherto, it is obvious how fantastic those doctrines are which imagine that production in the collectivist regime would be ordered in a

> manner substantially different from that of "anarchist"
> production . . . all the economic categories of the old
> regime must reappear, though maybe with other names:
> prices, salaries, interest, rent, profit, saving, etc.[19]

Barone was quite skeptical about actually finding a solution in the manner described above. He argued that unless all enterprise production functions were of the fixed coefficient variety, the equations would be far too complex to solve.[20]

The Socialist Controversy: Lange

Advocates of socialism could find little comfort in Barone's theoretical proof of the possibility of rational economic calculation under socialism. Although it undermined the stricter interpretation of von Mises' position, it did little to solve the practical problem owing to the tremendous administrative burden envisioned in such a system.[21]

In response to such criticism, Oskar Lange, the noted Polish economist and professor at the University of Chicago during the 1930s, formulated a decentralized model of socialism, generally referred to as the "Competitive Solution," or as "market socialism," to bridge the gap between theoretical and practical feasibility.[22] The objective of the Competitive Solution was to reduce

---

[19] *Ibid.*, p. 289.

[20] *Ibid.*, p. 287.

[21] On this point, Lionel Robbins writes: "On paper, we can conceive this problem to be solved by a series of mathematical calculations. . . . But in practice this solution is quite unworkable. It would necessitate the drawing up of millions of equations on the basis of millions of statistical data based on many more millions of individual computations. By the time the equations were solved, the information upon which they were based would have become obsolete." L. C. Robbins, *The Great Depression* (London: Macmillan, 1934), p. 151.

[22] While parallel models of market socialism were developed by Fred M. Taylor, H. D. Dickinson, and Abba Lerner, it is Lange's model that has attracted most attention. We concentrate solely on Lange's formulation in this section. Those interested in the Taylor, Lerner, and Dickinson models should consult the following sources: F. M. Taylor, "The Guidance of Production in a Socialist State," *American Economic Review,* vol. 19, no. 1 (March 1929), reprinted in Lippincott, *op. cit.,* pp. 39–54; H. D. Dickinson, *Economics of Socialism* (London: Oxford University Press, 1939); Abba P.

the administrative burden of the CPB to manageable proportions by distributing decision-making authority between the CPB and lower economic units (households and enterprises). To accomplish this goal, Lange proposes the subdivision of the economy into distinct decision-making units. At the lowest decision levels would be individual households and socialist enterprises. At the intermediate level, would be the industrial authorities, and the CPB would make top-level decisions. Each level would have distinct responsibilities: (a) Households would allocate their limited income among the available consumer goods and services, and between present and future consumption. In addition, the households would decide upon the allocation of the productive resources at their command (mainly labor services). (b) Socialist enterprises would decide what quantities of outputs to produce subject to their production functions (technology) and the appropriate mix of factor inputs. (c) The industrial authorities would decide upon the rate of expansion or contraction of the industry as a whole. (d) The CPB would set prices and allocate the "social dividend," earned from the land, capital, and natural resources owned collectively by society.

Thus, Lange envisions an economy in which economic decisions are to be made both centrally and locally. Let us first consider the decentralized behavior of households under the Competitive Solution. Lange assumes that households will continue to behave as they would in a capitalist society. That is, they will attempt to maximize utility subject to their income constraints and in doing so, they will treat the prices set by the CPB as parameters. In addition, they will continue to sell or reserve their labor services by weighing the disutility of work against the utility of income. By behaving in this manner, the individual household will generate demand schedules for consumer goods and for savings, and supply schedules of labor services which, when aggregated, yield market supply and demand schedules.

Socialist enterprise managers, on the other hand, are instructed by the CPB to observe two rules in choosing output levels

---

Lerner, *The Economics of Control* (New York: Macmillan, 1944). We base our discussion of Lange's model largely on his article, "On the Economic Theory of Socialism," in Lippincott, *op. cit.*, pp. 55–142.

and input mixes: First, factors of production are to be combined so as to minimize the average cost of production.[23] The second rule is that the enterprise must choose to produce that level of output at which the price of the product (set by the CPB) equals its marginal cost. By following these two rules, socialist enterprises would generate supply schedules of outputs and derived demand schedules for factor inputs, all of which would be functions of the prices set by the CPB.

The industrial authority would also be given a rule whereby it would determine the total output of the industry. The rule would be that "each industry has to produce exactly as much of a commodity as can be sold or 'accounted for' to other industries at a price which equals the marginal cost incurred *by the industry* in producing that amount."[24]

Let us now turn to the crucial CPB function of setting prices. There would be freedom of choice of occupation and consumption, therefore the prices of consumer goods and wage rates would be determined by the market. On the other hand, the CPB would set producer goods prices at equilibrium levels by a trial and error method—that is, producer goods prices should be set to equate supply and demand. To do this, the CPB need not solve the system of supply and demand equations as in the Barone model. Instead, the CPB should start with an arbitrary set of prices (perhaps the presocialism prices). If a shortage exists at the established price, the CPB would raise the price, and if a surplus exists the price would be lowered. This trial and error search for equilibrium would continue until shortages and surpluses disappear. A market system determines equilibrium prices in much the same fashion, the difference being that the CPB replaces the market in the process of price adjustment. By following this trial and error approach, the CPB would gradually approach a complete set of equilibrium prices of producer goods that would form the basis for rational calculation. The innovative feature of this approach is that the CPB would not be required to know detailed microeconomic data. The CPB instead would make appropriate adjustments simply by ob-

[23] That is, the rate of technical substitution of one input for another must be equated with the factor price ratio.
[24] Lippincott, *op. cit.*, pp. 76–77.

serving actual market surpluses and shortages.[25] Lange concludes that such a ". . . substitution of planning for the functions of the market is quite possible and workable."[26]

What happens then, when the trial and error process yields an output mix that is not compatible with the objectives of the state? Lange's answer is that planners' preferences can be substituted for individual preferences within the framework of the Competitive Solution by driving a wedge between the consumer and the producer. The CPB would accomplish this through a double price system. The retail price would be set according to the trial and error process; the second price would be an accounting price established by the CPB that the manager would use to make his output decisions. The difference between the two prices would be a tax (or subsidy) collected (or paid) by the state. By manipulating the enterprise accounting price, the CPB could control supply and thus control the output of the economy.[27]

[25] In the graph below, the market demand (D) and market supply (S) schedules illustrate Lange's trial and error process. Assume that the CPB accepts the presocialism price P_o as the effective price. At P_o, D_o is demanded and S_o is supplied. Thus demand exceeds supply, which is revealed to the CPB as a shortage, after which the CPB will raise the price. By trial and error, the CPB raises and lowers the price in response to excess demand and excess supply until the equilibrium price P_e is attained at which point demand (D_e) equals supply (S_e).

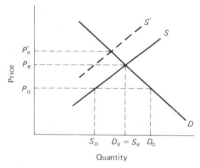

[26] Lippincott, *op. cit.*, p. 83.

[27] The graph above indicates how the double price system operates. By lowering the accounting price received by producers, the CPB can shift the market supply schedule to the left (from S to S') because producers equate price and marginal cost. As a result, the retail price is driven up and less will be produced at the new equilibrium position. This procedure would be followed if the CPB desired to discourage the production of a particular product. On the other hand, the enterprise price could be raised to encourage

Lange himself stressed the close similarity of his Competitive Solution to market economies, with the CPB acting largely as a substitute for competitive markets. Lange's model has been criticized as being nonsocialist for this reason—namely, that it results in the vindication of market principles "that it was the purpose of socialism to abolish."[28] If this is so, why not let the competitive market do the job in the first place? Lange builds the following case for the superiority of his model over the competitive capitalist solution.

First, his Competitive Solution breaks the link between the ownership of productive resources and the distribution of income, for society owns the nonhuman productive resources and the returns therefrom will accrue directly to the state as a social dividend. The state will allocate this dividend among the members of society in an equitable manner. On the other hand, in a society in which productive resources are owned privately, the distribution of nonwage income is determined on the basis of ownership of productive resource. Under socialism, all members of society will therefore share the returns from the socially owned resources and the principal income differences that do persist under socialism will result from wage differentials that will reflect primarily differences in disutility—the amount of discomfort involved in the job and training. The choice of occupation would be freer under socialism because educational and skill barriers would be eliminated almost entirely by the provision of universal free education.

A second advantage of the Competitive Solution noted by Lange is that it would better solve environmental problems caused by external economies. Under capitalism, the acts of production (factory pollution of water and air) or consumption (automobile exhaust fumes) often create social costs that do not enter into the choice

---

greater production of a desirable product. Lange makes an interesting comment on this system (which is actually used to some extent in the Soviet Union, see Chapter Five): "However, it does not seem probable that such a system would be tolerated by the citizens of a socialist community. The dual system of prices of consumers' goods would reveal to the people that bureaucrats in the Central Planning Board allocate the community's productive resources according to a preference scale different from that of the citizens." *Ibid.,* p. 96.

[28] Paul C. Roberts, "Oskar Lange's Theory of Socialist Planning," *Journal of Political Economy,* vol. 79, no. 3 (May/June 1971), 575.

equations of producers and consumers, who act on the basis of private costs. The resulting price system will therefore inadequately reflect true opportunity costs, mirroring instead only internal costs. External social costs will be ignored and society ends up with a misallocation of resources. Lange argues that the CPB would naturally place the interests of society above those of special consumer and producer groups, and the CPB would include both external and internal costs in setting prices, which means that the allocation of society's resources will be improved.

Third, Lange argues that the socialist society would be freed from the fluctuations of the business cycle. "The cumulative shrinkage of demand and output caused by a cumulative reduction of purchasing power could be stopped in a socialist economy. . . ." [29] By taking a broad overview of the economy, CPB would localize mistakes and prevent partial overproduction from turning into general overproduction.

Fourth, the economic wastes of imperfect competition that plague market economies would be avoided under market socialism. Socialist managers would not engage in such destructive behavior, but would instead observe Lange's two operational rules (cost minimization, equating price and marginal cost), and thus would act to benefit society rather than themselves or stockholders. In other words, Lange was arguing that the benefits of perfect competition can, paradoxically, only be derived under market socialism where managers are not driven by the lust for private profits but act as obedient civil servants.

Fifth, the rate of capital accumulation will be controlled "corporately" in a socialist society to ensure adequate provision of an economic base for future generations. Under capitalism, the level of aggregate savings, which is determined by individual and corporate time preferences, is dependent upon the often irrational distribution of income and, further, is often frustrated by an inadequate rate of investment. Total saving under socialism would equal aggregate personal saving plus state saving (the portion of the social dividend retained by the socialist state). If personal saving were to prove insufficient, the CPB would then increase the retained share of the social dividend, thus providing for future generations.

[29] Lippincott, *op. cit.,* p. 106.

Critics of the
Competitive Solution:
Hayek and Bergson

The main contribution of Lange's Competitive Solution is that it suggests a means of reducing the CPB's administrative burden by allowing considerable decision-making at the local level. Further, the amount of information required by the CPB would be much less than either von Mises or Barone imagined possible.

According to Lange, the only real drawback of the Competitive Solution is the potential danger of the "bureaucratization of economic life."[30] But insofar as the same danger is inherent in monopolistic capitalism, Lange concludes that "officials subject to democratic control seem preferable to private corporation executives who practically are responsible to nobody."[31]

Critics of Lange's Competitive Solution do not share his optimism. Instead, they raise serious questions about the operation of the Competitive Solution—namely, about the feasibility of trial and error pricing, managerial motivation, and political consequences.

The first issue, which has been stressed particularly by F. A. Hayek, is the workability of the trial and error method.[32] Modern economies, Hayek argues, produce millions of individual products. To regulate all of them would present an impossible task for the CPB. The CPB, finding it necessary to deal with a manageable number of commodities, would confine price setting to "establishing uniform prices for *classes* [italics added] of goods and that therefore distinctions based on special circumstances of time, place, and quality will find no expression in the price."[33] Thus the CPB would face the difficult, if not impossible, task of disaggregating prices within product groups in order to establish the millions of prices of individual products that differ according to quality, time, and style.

Pursuing this argument a step further, Hayek argues that even

[30] *Ibid.,* p. 109.
[31] *Ibid.,* p. 110.
[32] F. A. Hayek, "Socialist Calculation: The Competitive 'Solution,' " *Economica,* new series, vol. 7 (May 1940), reprinted in Bornstein, *op. cit.,* pp. 77–97.
[33] Quoted in Bornstein, *op. cit.,* p. 86.

after this simplification, price changes will be slower in coming about than under capitalism. To change a price, the CPB must first be made aware of the necessity of change, then must notify the numerous parties involved of the proposed changes, and must periodically publish complete lists of prices—activities that will be extremely time consuming and administratively costly. In a dynamic economy experiencing structural change, the task of the CPB would become even more exasperating because prices must be changed continuously to keep pace with changing tastes and technologies. Unless the CPB is able to keep up with such changes, the pace of economic progress will be retarded.[34]

To what extent are Hayek's objections answered by the advent of high-speed electronic computers? On this point, Abram Bergson argues that contemporary mathematical and computational procedures are not as yet sufficiently advanced to provide practical solutions when applied on an economywide basis. Also, comprehensive price fixing by computer would place an inordinate burden on managers and on the CPB as far as the gathering and processing of data are concerned.[35]

Managerial behavior under the Competitive Solution represents a second major point of contention. The question, stressed in particular by Abram Bergson, is how to insure that socialist managers will automatically observe the two rules suggested by Lange without detailed supervision by the CPB, which would impose a tremendous administrative burden.[36]

One possible alternative, investigated by Bergson, would be to encourage managers to maximize enterprise profits by tying

[34] There is another issue to the price setting function of the CPB under Lange's model, one which is well beyond the scope of this book. Would such a system actually tend to approach a general equilibrium by employing the trial and error method—that is, what are the convergence properties of the Lange model? It has been demonstrated in theoretical terms that some general equilibrium systems converge under certain sets of circumstances whereas others exhibit deconvergence patterns. Existence and convergence problems are also created by the presence of increasing returns to scale. If Lange's model fails to converge, scarcity prices could not be found and the system would not function properly. On this point, see Benjamin Ward, *The Socialist Economy* (New York: Random House, 1967), p. 32.
[35] Abram Bergson, "Market Socialism Revisited," *The Journal of Political Economy,* vol. 75, no. 5 (October 1967), 663–665.
[36] *Ibid.,* 657–661.

bonuses to profits. Bergson argues that in unconcentrated industries, the profit maximization rule may indeed induce enterprise managers to observe both of Lange's rules. On the other hand, socialist managers in concentrated industries would be induced by the profit maximizing rule to engage in monopolistic behavior. They would restrict output and force the CPB to raise prices, which the CPB would have to do to clear the markets in accordance with Lange's trial and error process. Society would lose as a result of the reduction of output, and the consumer would lose by paying higher prices. Yet the manager would gain by receiving a large bonus for his monopolistic behavior.

Bergson further argues that whereas profit maximization might lead to monopolistic behavior at the enterprise level, it would surely promote such behavior at the industry level, where industry managers would restrict industry output to gain a profit maximizing price from the CPB. Thus to reward socialist managers on the basis of profits would eliminate one of the most highly touted advantages of Lange's Competitive Solution—namely, the absence of monopoly behavior.

A final criticism of Lange's model concerns its political consequences—an issue raised by Hayek, who doubts its compatibility with democratic political institutions and political freedom. Such a system, he argues, will come to be run more and more on the basis of "conscious and arbitrary decisions" of the CPB. The CPB must decide how investment is to be allocated, the allocation of resources between communal consumption and individual consumption, etc. A "very large part of the resources of the society is put outside the control of the price mechanism and subject to purely arbitrary decision." Therefore, "in a planned system all economic questions become political questions, because it is no longer a question of reconciling as far as possible individual views and desires, but one of imposing a single scale of values, the 'social goal'. . . ."[37]

The Centralist Solution: Dobb

Another participant in the Socialist Controversy, noted British socialist Maurice Dobb, takes the position that a centrally planned socialist economy, which he calls the *Centralist Solution,* will prove

[37] Quoted in Bornstein, *op. cit.,* p. 96.

superior to competitive capitalism.[38] In direct opposition to von Mises and Hayek, Dobb maintains that resource allocation in such a system could proceed efficiently even though the CPB does not know the relative values of producer goods.

The advantages of competitive capitalism are much overrated according to Dobb. That a system of flexible prices under conditions of perfect competition will yield an efficient allocation of resources means very little from a practical point of view because it is obvious (even to the casual observer) that certain departures from the perfectly competitive "optimum," such as luxury excises, home construction subsidies, and food subsidies, render society as a whole "better off" than it was at the "optimum."[39] In fact, perfect competition is entirely compatible with a grossly inequitable distribution of income; therefore, it is a serious mistake to judge the optimality of resource allocation without first considering the optimality of the accompanying income distribution.

Second, Dobb argues that the ultimate goal of capitalist economies—the maximization of consumer satisfaction—is misplaced because the consumer is not necessarily "rational" in the true sense of the word. In a commercialized society, consumers are gullible, "unreflective, and easily moved by immediate or superficial stimuli." Worst of all, they "exhibit a tendency to myopic underestimation of the future, [they do not save enough] due to [a] 'deficiency of the telescopic faculty' in individuals. . . ."[40] Further, the collective wants of society (for museums, public health, parks, etc.) are not expressed in individual demand schedules and are therefore not reflected in the capitalist price system. The same is true of the external effects of consumption itself—automobile exhausts, excessive noise, etc.—which under capitalism remain external to the price system. A socially minded CPB could impose its scale of values upon society wherever necessary in cases of conflicts between social welfare and individual welfare. The substitution of such planners' preferences for consumer preferences would

---

[38] Maurice Dobb, *On Economic Theory and Socialism, Collected Papers* (New York: International, 1955), pp. 16–92.
[39] For a concise definition of this optimum, see Abram Bergson, "A Reformulation of Certain Aspects of Welfare Economics," in *Essays in Normative Economics, op. cit.,* pp. 3–26.
[40] Dobb, *op. cit.,* p. 73.

not necessarily mean the total elimination of the latter. Instead the CPB could make itself aware of consumer wants and would negate only those which are deemed socially harmful.

Dobb's third general criticism of competitive capitalism is that it is not capable of dealing with economic change and development. In a growing economy, certain kinds of development will occur only if planned by a central coordinating agency. If left to the vagaries of the market, essential investment projects that are individually unprofitable but collectively profitable will not be undertaken, and economic development will be slowed down. Price changes will be slow in coming about, knowledge will be imperfect, and uncertainty will be great, all of which will impede economic progress. For economic development to proceed smoothly, central planning must replace the market. The "function of such planning is that it is a means of substituting *ex ante* coordination of the constituent elements in the scheme of development . . . for the coordinating *ex post* which a decentralized price system provides."[41] Such *ex ante* coordination might generate a short-run loss in output owing to administrative allocation difficulties, but would pay off in a dynamic sense in that long-run gains in output would well outweigh the loss of short-term static efficiency.

Having stressed the deficiencies of competitive capitalism, Dobb then attacks the crucial question of how resources are actually to be administratively allocated by the CPB without the use of scarcity prices. It might be noted that the centralized method of resource allocation that Dobb suggests is patterned after Dobb's own observations of Soviet planning. Resource allocation under such a centralized system, according to Dobb, would not be as difficult as von Mises and Hayek claim. In the first place, it would not prove unduly difficult for the CPB to allocate the planned supplies of consumer goods and to plan the expansion of consumer goods branches. Necessities, whose use does not vary greatly among households—food, minimal clothing, public health facilities, education, and shelter—could be planned and allocated according to scientific norms established by dieticians, public health experts, and the like. The demand for such items would be highly inelastic, which means that relative prices have little impact on the quantity

[41] *Ibid.,* p. 76.

demanded anyway, and they should be supplied either free of charge or at the lowest price possible that would not encourage waste. The available quantities of non-necessities, on the other hand, could be allocated among consumers by a market. The CPB would, of course, determine the physical quantities of non-necessities to be produced and would decide on their rates of expansion.[42]

Allocation of producers' goods can also take place fairly independently of scarcity prices according to Dobb. He argues that the common assumption that inputs can be flexibly substituted for each other to produce given amounts of output does not hold up well as a true picture of enterprise technology. As a closer approximation to reality, it is more reasonable to assume that inputs must either be combined in rigid fixed proportions or combined according to a small number of possible input combinations. Given this limited choice of input mixes, scarcity prices play a negligible role in the allocation of inputs. Instead, inputs must be combined in fairly rigid proportions in recipe-like fashion, which must be observed irrespective of factor prices. The CPB, having gathered information on the various production processes, would then be able to allocate factor inputs to the various enterprises according to the

---

[42] The criterion that Dobb suggests to govern investment allocation in this sphere is best illustrated with an example. In the current period, assume the CPB has ordered x_0 and y_0 of commodities x and y produced. These quantities are then sold to consumers at market clearing prices. Assume that both products are produced at the same average cost (AC). The ratio P_{y0}/AC_{y0} is greater than P_{x0}/AC_{x0} indicating that y is in shorter supply than x. The CPB then examines the capital cost of increasing y_0 to y_1, which it can estimate by looking at the incremental capital-output ratio. If in the CPB's opinion, the increase in y is justified, then y receives the additional capital. It should be stressed that the decision will be made by the CPB on a discretionary basis, rather than as a blind response to such indicators.

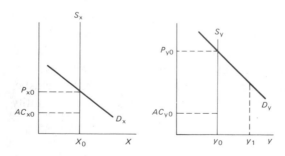

given technological requirements, and would not be required to compute scarcity prices of inputs.[43]

The Socialist Controversy
in the West: Summary

We have reviewed the Socialist Controversy over the viability of socialism as an economic system.[44] Beginning with Marx's unsupported assertion of the superiority of socialism, we noted fairly convincing arguments on both sides: von Mises claimed that socialism would fail to generate scarcity prices and would therefore be unable to make rational economic calculations. Barone demonstrated the theoretical possibility of rational economic calculation under conditions of perfect computation, information and foresight; yet he failed to demonstrate its practicality under more realistic conditions (a point stressed by Hayek). Lange's Competitive Solution, which allowed for both centralized and local decision-making and trial and error pricing, was suggested as a practical solution to the resource allocation problem but was criticized by Hayek and Bergson on the grounds that it was still too complex and failed to solve the problem of managerial behavior. Dobb's

[43] As an example, take the limiting case of fixed coefficients of production in which inputs must be combined in rigid fixed proportions in order to produce a certain amount of output. The isoquant has the familiar L shape:

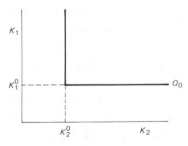

This particular production process requires the use of two inputs, which we designate as K_1 and K_2. A capitalist producer given the assignment to produce Q_0 would strive to do so at minimum cost, e.g., he would attempt to find the tangency between his Q_0 isoquant and the lowest isocost line. One can see that he will choose to combine K_2^0 and K_1^0 to produce Q_0 at all possible factor prices. Relative factor prices do not matter in this case. The CPB will know the shape of the isoquant and will simply order the producer to produce Q_0 and will give him K_1^0 and K_2^0. Prices are not needed.

[44] Cooperative socialism is discussed in Appendix 9.

Centralist Solution suggested that rigid central planning could be used to allocate resources in a fairly rational manner—if not in the short-run, then at least in the long-run—because of fixed coefficients of production and the general superiority of planners' preferences over consumer sovereignty.

THEORIES OF SOVIET PLANNING AND SOVIET MATHEMATICAL ECONOMICS

After years of repression during the Stalin period, mathematical economics reemerged as a discipline during the postwar period and in it there are important contributions to the theory of central planning in a socialist economy. It is surprising to note that one of the most original and important Soviet contributions in the area of mathematical economics was made in 1939—L. V. Kantorovich's paper on resource-utilization programming—during the Stalin purges.

The issue addressed by the Soviet mathematical economists is the central issue of the Socialist Controversy—namely, how are resources to be efficiently allocated in a socialist economy without markets to indicate scarcity values? The two prominent Soviet pioneers in this area are L. V. Kantorovich (optimal programming) and V. V. Novozhilov (criteria for investment choice),[45] both of whom were publishing papers on mathematical planning techniques in the late 1930s. After Stalin's death, the potential importance of mathematical economics came to be officially recognized and research was encouraged. In 1959, *The Use of Mathematics in Economics* was published under the editorship of V. S. Nemchinov, which contained the original papers of Kantorovich and Novozhilov. Since then, subsequent volumes in this series have appeared, the Central Economics-Mathematics Institute of the

[45] For a review of Kantorovich's and Novozhilov's contributions, see Robert W. Campbell, "Marx, Kantorovich and Novozhilov: Stoimost' Versus Reality," *Slavic Review*, vol. 20, no. 3 (October 1961), 402–418. For a general survey, see Michael Ellman, *Soviet Planning Today* (Cambridge: Cambridge University Press, 1971).

Academy of Science has been established, mathematical economics journals such as *Mathematics and Economic Methods* are being published, and the three most prominent Soviet mathematical economists—Nemchinov, Kantorovich, and Novozhilov—have been awarded the coveted Lenin Prize.

To synthesize the views of the mathematical economists on the theory of resource allocation under central planning, one should note that their central thesis is that resources can be allocated in a rational manner in such an economy through the use of mathematical planning techniques. Because the basic resources available to the economy at one point in time—land, labor, capital, raw materials—are limited, the resource allocation problem becomes one of allocating these limited resources among competing uses in an optimal manner.

At the enterprise level, the enterprise has output targets and limited resources with which to produce these outputs. The allocation of enterprise resources, therefore, can be carried out in terms of an output program that falls within resource constraints and minimizes the use of scarce resource inputs while fulfilling the output target. Thus the manager would operate his enterprise by solving linear programming problems consisting of an objective function (the output targets), resource constraints, and a system of equations expressing technological processes available to the enterprise. The optimal solution of such a model would not only instruct the manager as to which processes and which process intensities to use, but would also indirectly supply him with resource valuations in the form of *shadow prices* that would relate to him the *opportunity costs* (scarcity values) of the resources at his disposal. In this manner, both the resource allocation problem and the valuation problem would be solved simultaneously, thus enabling the enterprise to rationally allocate the resources at its disposal.[46]

Planning authorities could also avail themselves of the same mathematical techniques in developing regional and national plans. The main difference between such planning and enterprise operation would be the greater amount of detail required at the enter-

[46] For a discussion of possible uses of programming in the operation of the Soviet enterprise, see L. V. Kantorovich, "Further Developments of Mathematical Methods and the Prospects of Their Application in Economic Planning," in Nemchinov, *op. cit.,* pp. 317–319.

prise level. At the regional and national planning levels, the mathematical planning models constructed would encompass fewer commodity designations and would be at higher levels of aggregation. In all cases, the planning authorities would have specified objectives to meet (their objective functions), limited resources that could be employed to meet these objectives, and a number of technological production processes from which to choose. Thus a fixed target of outputs could be produced at a minimum cost of resources, or outputs could be maximized subject to resource constraints. As in the case of the enterprise, the scarcity values of the resources used could be indirectly computed as shadow prices from the optimal production program, and these scarcity values could then be used as a guide for planners.

The original criticisms of socialist planning (von Mises, Hayek) remain even if one accepts the logical consistency of such techniques as well as the assumptions upon which they are based. Insofar as the economy produces millions of commodities, such mathematical planning techniques would drastically overtax the computational and data gathering ability of the economy. Well recognizing this problem, the Soviet mathematical economists suggest the construction of a series of interrelated plans. The higher the planning agency, the higher the level of aggregation of products dealt with. Thus a national plan consisting of a relatively small number of highly aggregated and important commodities would be constructed, which would then be subdivided into a series of regional plans also dealing with a manageable number of commodities, and so on down to the individual enterprise.[47]

Proponents of mathematical planning techniques well recognize the limitations inherent in their approach given the stage to which their knowledge has advanced. Yet they stress that realizable optimum plans can be developed that will result in a better utilization of society's resources. Areas where further advances are required are "better and more complete technical data, statistical indicators and methods of economic analysis as such."[48]

[47] Kantorovich, in Nemchinov, op. cit., pp. 319–321; and Benjamin Ward, "Linear Programming and Soviet Planning," in John P. Hardt et al., Mathematics and Computers in Soviet Economic Planning (New Haven, Conn.: Yale University Press, 1967), pp. 189–193.
[48] Kantorovich, in Nemchinov, op. cit., p. 320.

While the use of mathematical planning techniques remains limited in the Soviet Union in actual planning,[49] the contributions of the Soviet mathematical economists should not be under-rated, for they have taken the first steps toward defining the underlying theoretical model of resource allocation and valuation under central planning.

[49] On this, see Vladimir Treml, "Input-Output Analysis and Soviet Planning," in Hardt et al., *op. cit.,* pp. 101–104; and Ward, in Hardt et al., *op. cit.,* pp. 193–195.

Appendix 9

Cooperative Socialism

The General Model. The cooperative variant of socialism in which the workers themselves collectively manage socialist enterprises is a fairly recent entry into the Socialist Controversy. Introduced by Benjamin Ward[1] and loosely patterned after Yugoslav socialism, cooperative socialism represents a decentralized form of socialism that places heavy reliance on market forces to allocate scarce resources while preserving the basic feature of socialism: public ownership of the nonhuman factors of production. In considering the cooperative variant in this appendix, we continue to pursue the basic issue of the Socialist Controversy: the feasibility and efficiency of different forms of socialism. The cooperative variant of socialism would operate in the following manner:

The productive assets used by cooperative enterprises are owned by the state, which levies a fixed charge (a tax) on the enterprise for their use. The enterprise is administered by a group of workers—probably the senior workers—that hires, or elects, a manager to carry on the daily operation of the enterprise. He is subject to dismissal by the workers if he fails to perform satisfactorily. The manager determines the output and input mix of the enterprise for the ongoing production period and is free to vary the level of cooperative employment by hiring and firing junior employees. Prices of both consumer and producer goods are determined by the market and are free to fluctuate according to changing supply and demand conditions. The state administers the public sector and levies taxes on capital assets. Earnings in excess of operating expenses and taxes accrue to the cooperative.

To assess the workability of such a system, it is necessary to

---

[1] Benjamin Ward, "The Firm in Illyria: Market Syndicalism," *American Economic Review,* vol. 48 (September 1958), 566–589. A more recent and complete statement of Ward's model is found in Ward, *The Socialist Economy* (New York: Random House, 1967), chaps. 8–10. A sophisticated mathematical treatment of Ward's model is found in S. C. Maurice and C. E. Ferguson, "Factor Usage by a Labour-Managed Firm in a Socialist Economy," *Economica,* New Series, vol. 30, no. 153 (February 1972), 18–31.

determine how such cooperative enterprises will behave. First, their behavior is considered in the short-run with fixed capital assets and then in the long-run, in which both labor and capital are variable. The key assumption is that the cooperative management seeks to maximize the net earnings per worker, that is, if Q represents output (which in the short-run is solely a function of L), L represents labor input (which is assumed homogeneous), P represents the price of Q, and T represents the fixed tax on capital, then the cooperative seeks to maximize the expression:

$$PQ/L - T/L$$

This objective is achieved when L is chosen so that the value of the marginal product of the last worker hired $P \cdot MP_L$ is equated with net earnings per worker:[2]

$$\frac{(PQ - T)}{L}$$

Next, let us consider the long-run case in which both labor and capital can be varied. We use K to represent the variable capital input and r to represent the rental charge per unit of capital. The other symbols remain the same as in the short-run case. The firm's objective remains to maximize average net revenue, which is defined by the following expression:

$$\frac{PQ - rK - T}{L}$$

Average net revenue will be maximized by employing capital to the point where the value of its marginal product equals the capi-

---

[2] Maximize: $y = PQ/L - T/L$, where $Q = f(L)$ and $f'(L) = dQ/dL$ (the marginal productivity of labor MP_L.

$$\frac{dy}{dL} = \frac{L \cdot Pf'(L) - Pf(L) + T}{L^2}$$

which when set equal to zero equals: $P \cdot f'(L) = \frac{PQ - T}{L}$

In geometric terms, the optimum can be represented as in Figure 5. The cooperative will employ L^0 and each member receives OC as his full wage. The operational rule that the enterprise observes in hiring labor is: hire an additional worker if the value of his marginal product exceeds average net revenue because he will increase average net revenue. If the value of his marginal product is less than average net revenue, his hiring would cause average net earnings to fall.

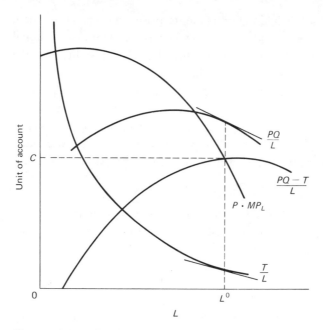

Figure 5. The Labor-Managed Enterprise—Maximization of Net Revenue Per Worker

tal rental rate $(P \cdot MP_K = r)$—the same as the competitive capitalist counterpart—and by continuing to observe the same short-run rule for choosing the optimal quantity of labor:

$$P \cdot MP_L = \frac{PQ - rK - T}{L}$$

except that the variable capital costs must now be deducted in addition to taxes to compute average net revenue.[3]

---

[3] Maximize: $y = \dfrac{PQ - rK - T}{L}$

        where $Q = F(K,L)$

            $= \dfrac{P \cdot F(K,L) - rK - T}{L}$

(1) $\dfrac{\partial y}{\partial K} = \dfrac{1}{L}(P \cdot F'_K - r) = 0$

        where $F'_K = \dfrac{\partial F}{\partial K}$, the marginal productivity of capital

and

Thus far the microeconomic behavior of the cooperative enterprise has been described in the short- and long-runs. It should be noted that we have dealt only with the simplest case of all—that of a perfectly competitive cooperative enterprise that cannot exert any influence over its product and factor prices insofar as it represents only a very small portion of both markets. To summarize to this point, we note that the cooperative chooses its capital and labor inputs and its output levels so as to maximize net revenue per worker. In doing so, the enterprise generates demand schedules for capital and labor inputs, and supply schedules of outputs. The worker-consumer continues to maximize utility subject to his budget constraint and thus generates demand schedules for consumer goods and services. These enterprises and consumers come together in the marketplace (without interference from the central government) where the scarcity values of consumer goods and services and producer goods are freely determined. Consumers and producers then make their decisions on the basis of these scarcity prices. The socialist state's role is kept to a minimum. It uses indirect aggregate monetary and fiscal controls and operates the public sector of the economy.

Evaluation of Cooperative Socialism

We now turn to the basic points of contention in the current controversy over worker-managed socialism. This controversy is of some importance given the increased attention being accorded the worker-management model in the socialist world, not only in Yugoslavia but also by the economic reformers of Eastern Europe.

The originator of the cooperative variant, Professor Benjamin Ward, emphasizes its negative features and is quite skeptical about its desirability in real-world situations.[4] In particular, Ward

---

(2) $$\frac{\partial y}{\partial L} = \frac{1}{L^2}[LPF'_L - PF(K,L) + rK + T] = 0$$

where $F'_L = \frac{\partial F}{\partial L}$, the marginal productivity of labor

which reduces to:

(1a) $$P \cdot F'_K = r$$

(2a) $$\frac{PQ - rK - T}{L} = P \cdot F'_L$$

[4] Ward, *The Socialist Economy, op. cit.,* chaps. 8 and 9.

stresses the peculiar nature of the cooperative enterprise's supply responses to price changes. In the short run, an increase in the output price—resulting from an increase in demand, for example—will induce the cooperative firm to produce a smaller quantity of output, hire a smaller quantity of labor.[5] Thus the short-run market supply schedule has a negative slope, which means that it would be difficult for the market to converge towards the equilibrium price. Under these circumstances, the scarcity values of such commodities would have little meaning. In the long-run, the danger of negatively sloped supply schedules is still present although less likely than the short-run case, especially if wage costs represent a relatively small portion of total costs.[6]

Ward's second criticism of the cooperative variant is that it would probably result in a misallocation of capital and labor resources. In the latter case, two enterprises producing the same product, paying the same taxes, and having the same endowment of capital would hire marginal workers producing different marginal value products unless enterprise production functions were identical.[7] This could not occur under perfectly competitive capitalism where all such firms would hire labor to the point where $w = P \cdot MP_L$. Insofar as they would all pay the same market wage (w), the value of marginal products would be equal. The existence of different marginal products as would exist under the cooperative variant indicates inefficiency, since overall output

---

[5] From the short-run equilibrium condition, it is evident that in equilibrium the following must hold:

$$\left| \frac{d(PQ/L)}{dL} \right| = \left| \frac{d(T/L)}{dL} \right|$$

but

$$\frac{d(PQ/L)}{dL} = \left[(LP)\frac{\partial Q}{\partial L} - \frac{Q}{L} \right]$$

and

$$\frac{d(PQ/L)}{dL} = \frac{T}{L^2}$$

therefore if P increases, the slope of PQ/L is steeper than the slope of T/L, and less L must be hired to regain the equilibrium.

[6] Ward, *The Socialist Economy, op. cit.,* pp. 206–207.

[7] Refer again to the equilibrium condition and consider two firms producing the same homogeneous product and receiving P, and both paying T. Unless the production functions of the two firms are identical, $P \cdot MP_L$ of the one firm would not equal $P \cdot MP_L$ of the second firm and thus labor is misallocated between the two firms.

could be increased by transferring workers from low into high marginal productivity occupations to equalize marginal value products.

A similar misallocation of capital could also occur because the cooperative enterprise would choose new technology not on the basis of the discounted value of net profit but on the basis of the present discounted value of average profits per worker. The enterprise might be induced by this criterion to adopt highly capital-intensive processes that generate negative overall net profits but that are so labor saving that they raise average net profits per worker for the remaining senior workers.

Ward's third criticism of the cooperative variant is that in its imperfectly competitive form, in particular in its monopolistic and oligopolistic forms, it would prove less efficient than either its competitive cooperative or its imperfectly competitive capitalist counterparts. The monopolistic cooperative, in observing the maximum average net revenue rule, would hire less labor (and produce less output) than its competitive cooperative counterpart[8] and would produce a lesser quantity (and sell at a higher price) than its monopolistic capitalist counterpart.[9] Furthermore, coopera-

---

[8] Ward, *The Socialist Economy, op. cit.*, p. 202.

[9] To show this, consider the cooperative monopolist as paying a contract wage (w) to the cooperative members. The difference between this contract wage and average net revenue represents average profits per worker. The cooperative will seek to maximize average profits:

$$y' = \frac{PQ - wL - T}{L}$$

$$= \frac{PQ - T}{L} - w$$

The constant w will play no role in the choice of L. To maximize y':

$$\frac{dy'}{dL} = f'(L)\left[\frac{\partial P}{\partial Q}Q + P\right] - \frac{PQ + T}{L}$$

The first order maximum condition is:

$$f'(L)\left[\frac{\partial P}{\partial Q}Q + P\right] = \frac{PQ - T}{L}$$

where $P = F(Q)$ and $Q = f(L)$

or

$$MR \cdot MP_L = \frac{PQ - T}{L}$$

where $\frac{\partial P}{\partial Q}Q + P = MR$

Assume that the capitalist monopolist pays the same w and T and faces the

tive oligopolists have an incentive to collude, the result of which is a lower output and a higher price than capitalist collusive oligopoly, which follows from the above monopoly conclusions. Nevertheless, Ward's analysis of imperfect cooperative competition remains incomplete and his results are tentative.

A final problem that Ward envisions for the cooperative socialist economy is the lack of entrepreneurial activity and promotion. Given the prohibition of individual equity holdings in such an economy, the particular individual or group of individuals that foresees and takes advantage of new and profitable business opportunities will not personally benefit because of joint profit sharing within the cooperative. Therefore the primary incentive to engage in entrepreneurial activity is missing and it is an open question whether an economy can progress under such conditions.

Contrary to Ward, Jaroslav Vanek argues that the cooperative variant of socialism is superior to other economic systems. Vanek's views are outlined extensively elsewhere, and we shall limit ourselves here to a cursory summary of his main points:[10]

According to Vanek, the perfectly competitive cooperative variant is just as efficient as its perfectly competitive capitalist counterpart because, assuming identical technologies within industries and freedom of entry, it will make the same input and output decisions as its perfectly competitive counterpart. Productive efficiency is only half of the story, however. The most important feature of the competitive cooperative variant is that it results in a dual optimization of collective welfare. Not only is it efficient in the

---

same demand schedule as the cooperative monopolist. His profits are maximized by observing the following rule:

$$MR \cdot MP_L = w$$

In order for the two monopolists to hire the same quantity of L, the following must hold:

$$wL = PQ - T$$

i.e., both firms must be making zero profits. If profits are positive, the cooperative monopolist will hire less L (produce less Q) and sell at higher price than his capitalist counterpart.

[10] Jaroslav Vanek. "Decentralization Under Worker Management: A Theoretical Appraisal," *American Economic Review*, vol. 49, no. 5 (December 1969), 1006–1014, and *The General Theory of Labor-Managed Market Economies* (Ithaca, N.Y., and London: Cornell University Press, 1970).

production sphere, but distribution is determined by the cooperative workers collectively, and such collective social justice will prove more equitable than capitalism, where hired workers are rewarded according to their marginal revenue products.

Second, Vanek doubts that the short-run supply schedules of competitive cooperative enterprises will actually have negative slopes as Ward theorizes. First, if the firm produces more than one product, or is faced with an external labor supply constraint, the firm's supply schedule will be upward sloping.[11] Second, it is doubtful that a collective will mercilessly expel members from the cooperative simply to increase profits per remaining worker by a marginal amount, which means that the cooperative will be relatively unresponsive to product price changes.

Third, Vanek argues that in the real world where oligopoly and monopolistic competition predominate, the imperfectly competitive variant of cooperative socialism will prove superior to its imperfectly competitive capitalist counterpart. Under such conditions, the cooperative firm will produce less than a profit maximizing capitalist firm and, as a result, there will be more room in the market for competitors. The desire to maximize net revenue per worker provides a natural limitation on the size of cooperative enterprises, a limit that does not exist under capitalism. Further, much of the social waste of capitalism that goes for demand creation and product differentiation will be avoided, in that the cooperative does not have a great incentive to engage in such activities.

Fourth, the cooperative enterprise will generate a greater demand for capital than its capitalist counterpart for reasons already pointed out by Ward[12]—the cooperative will willingly engage in investment projects that increase net revenue per remaining worker even if overall profits are reduced as a result. Looking at the supply side as well, the cooperative economy is also able to generate a large volume of net savings to support this demand for capital. In paying the value of capital's marginal product for the use of

[11] This view is shared by E. Domar for different reasons. Domar demonstrates that when labor supply limitations are considered in terms of a positively sloped cooperative labor supply schedule, the negative supply schedule result disappears. E. Domar, "The Soviet Collective Farm as a Producer Cooperative," *American Economic Review,* vol. 56, no. 4, part I (September 1966), 734–757.

[12] Ward, *The Socialist Economy, op. cit.,* pp. 208–214.

capital, the economy can generate a high rate of net savings just by retaining capital income for reinvestment, and these funds can be supplemented by private and public saving as well.

Finally, Vanek argues that the greatest strength of cooperative socialism lies in its "special dimensions," which are absent from other economic systems.[13] The absence of conflict between labor and management serves as an example of this special dimension. The cooperative environment allows things to happen—social community action, technology changes that reduce money income, and collective consumption—all of which would be unheard of in a capitalist context.

Selected Bibliography

Abram Bergson, "Market Socialism Revisited," *Journal of Political Economy,* vol. 75, no. 5 (October 1967).

Abram Bergson, "Socialist Economics," *Essays in Normative Economics* (Cambridge, Mass.: Harvard University, Belknap Press, 1966), pp. 193–236.

Maurice Dobb, *On the Economic Theory of Socialism, Collected Papers* (New York: International, 1955), chap. 3.

F. A. Hayek, ed., *Collectivist Economic Planning* (London: Routledge & Kegan Paul, 1963), chaps. 1, 3, 5, and appendix A.

Branko Horvat, *Towards a Theory of Planned Economy* (Belgrade: Yugoslav Institute of Economic Research, 1964).

Abba P. Lerner, *The Economics of Control* (New York: Macmillan, 1944).

Benjamin E. Lippicott, ed., *On the Economic Theory of Socialism* (Minneapolis: University of Minnesota Press, 1938), reprinted by McGraw-Hill, 1964.

Paul C. Roberts, "Oskar Lange's Theory of Socialist Planning," *Journal of Political Economy,* vol. 79, no. 3 (May-June 1971).

Howard Sherman, "The Theory of Socialist Planning: Comment," *Journal of Political Economy,* vol. 81, no. 2, part 1 (March-April 1973).

[13] Vanek, "Decentralization Under Worker Management," *op. cit.,* 1011.

Jaroslav Vanek, *The General Theory of Labor-Managed Market Economies* (Ithaca, N.Y., and London: Cornell University Press, 1970).

Benjamin Ward, "Marxism-Horvatism: A Yugoslav Theory of Socialism," *American Economic Review,* vol. 57, no. 3 (June 1967), 509–523.

Benjamin Ward, *The Socialist Economy* (New York: Random House, 1967), chaps. 8, 9, 10.

Benjamin Ward, "The Firm in Illyria," *American Economic Review,* vol. 48, no. 4 (September 1958), 566–589.

CHAPTER TEN

Soviet Economic Reform

The discussion and implementation of economic reform in the Soviet Union has, especially in the post-Stalin era, attracted widespread attention in the West. This interest stems in large measure from the fundamental meaning of reform—which is to improve or perfect—and the implication, therefore, that the Soviets are having problems by their own admission with their centrally planned economy. This interest also stems from the actual and proposed utilization of the techniques of market economies to improve (or remove) the planned economic order, which raises the inevitable question: Is the Soviet economy becoming more "capitalistic"? Examination of Soviet economic reform is, therefore, very basic to our appraisal of *how well* planned economies function (Chapter Eleven) and, especially, the extent to which their effectiveness of operation may be related to different levels of economic development.[1] Why is economic reform thought to be necessary by important elements of Soviet society, and what are the problems faced by Soviet economic reformers?

If economic systems are classified along a continuum, two polar extremes can be recognized: a centralized administrative model on the one hand, and a decentralized market model on the

[1] It is not surprising that the reform movement in the Soviet Union has helped create considerable controversy over whether the USSR and American economies are "converging." For more on this, see our discussion of convergence in Chapter Thirteen.

other. In both extreme models—and indeed, in the real world mixed models—there tend to be fundamental structural and operational factors that can, at varying stages in the process of economic development, inhibit the best performance of the economic system. In the Soviet case, these inhibitive factors, which derive directly from the centralized nature of decision-making, have already been elaborated at some length in this study: the matter of "success indicators," imbalances and shortages in the material-technical supply system, overcommitment of investment funds and the resultant noncompletion of capital investment projects, the absence of spare parts resulting in a low level of equipment utilization, low levels of process and product innovation, a relatively low level of consumer satisfaction, and so on. Most of these problems are not new; they were as much a part of the Soviet economic system of the 1930s as of the 1970s, for they stem in large measure from the fundamental problems of organization—in short, the problem of insuring that where a measure of local decision-making power exists (even on an informal basis), local decisions conform to the wishes of central planners, and that they do so in the absence of useful decentralized information mechanisms, such as market clearing prices.

If the problems noted above are not new to the Soviet economy, why then the apparent recent emphasis upon economic reform? The Soviet reform movement is in fact not recent; change has been ongoing—though severely circumscribed under Stalin—for many years, and yet the direction of emphasis has changed. During the Khrushchev years (1954–1964), considerable emphasis was placed upon *organizational* change, much of which could be labeled as administrative shuffling, with little or no impact upon the fundamental operation of the system. More recently, though, the emphasis has been on the desirability of changing both the microbehavior of the system and the relationship of the planner to the enterprise by introducing tools of decision-making and economics normally associated with market economies, some of which are being "rediscovered" in the Soviet Union.

WHY ECONOMIC REFORM?

The search for change has been intensified by lagging economic performance. Our analysis of Soviet economic performance (Chapter Eleven), especially in terms of the rate of growth of output, and our comparisons with other developed countries indicate that the Soviet record has, on balance, been impressive, and yet with troubling signs.

First, and possibly most important to Soviet leaders, the rate of Soviet economic growth has been declining in recent years. Although still very respectable by international standards, the downward trend in the average annual rate of growth of output, most notable in the official Soviet data (see Table 25) is unmistakable.[2] For a country whose economic prestige around the world (by its own perception) rests largely upon a rapid rate of economic growth, such a pattern is clearly undesirable.[3] Further it is recognized that the period of "easy" Soviet growth is past, that is, growth based upon the shift of labor from agriculture to industry, the importation of more advanced technology, the education of a largely illiterate population, and raising the labor participation rate. It may be, of course, that for the 1970s, prevailing economic reality may necessitate acceptance of a growth rate slower than that of the past, an alternative to be examined in Chapter Eleven.

Second, the Soviet capital-output ratio (k/o) has generally been rising since 1958.[4] Although k/o ratios have generally risen in other industrialized countries during the postwar period, the rise

[2] It should be noted that the slowdown in Soviet growth rates is difficult to measure with precision due to the serious impact of the index number problem (discussed in Chapter Eleven) during the initial spurt of industrialization in the 1930s. Thus the *severity* of the slowdown will depend in large measure upon the analyst's choice of various growth estimates for the early 1930s.

[3] For example, the most prominent comparison of Soviet and American economic performance found in the *National Economy of the USSR* [*Narodnoe khoziastvo SSSR*] shows the Soviet economy expanding about four times as fast as the American economy during the postwar period.

[4] Stanley H. Cohn, "General Growth Performance of the Soviet Economy," in *Economic Performance and the Military Burden in the Soviet Union* (Washington, D.C.: U.S. Government Printing Office, 1970), p. 12.

has been more rapid in the Soviet Union. This trend is especially disturbing to the Soviets since they were able to hold down the k/o ratio during much of the 1930s and early 1950s (Chapter Twelve), and because, with a declining growth rate, now even greater capital infusions would be required to return Soviet growth to its previous rate.

Third, there has been undoubtedly a rise of consumer pressure in the Soviet Union, as is evidenced by the increase in unsold inventories coupled with excess purchasing power.[5] This pressure is unlikely to subside, rather it is more likely to increase as Soviet planners continue to emphasize monetary incentives for workers, but at the same time neglect the production or importation of sufficient quantities of high quality consumer goods. Such trends take on added importance in combination with the declining growth rate and rising k/o ratio, for the consumer can no longer be neglected for the purpose of raising the investment rate. In this sense, it is important that the Soviets have given specific attention to economic reform in the light industry sector.

A fourth reason for interest in reform is the growing complexity of the Soviet economy—that is, the expanding numbers of interconnections among producers, consumers, suppliers, and so on, all of which significantly enhance the difficulty of planning. Recent censuses of Soviet industry reveal over 50,000 distinct industrial enterprises in the USSR. In a sense, as the economy grows and the number of sectors and their product range broaden, the priority principle becomes less and less useful. Soviet planners are no longer able to put on "steel blinkers."[6] Instead, they must now choose between steel, aluminum and plastics, all of which in certain instances may do the same job to a significant degree. In addition, to the extent that the system grows more complex, mistakes that are made in the planning process will be more serious—they will reverberate throughout the system with less likelihood of being quickly arrested. Further, it will not be possible to continue to utilize buffer sectors indefinitely, as in the case of consumer goods

[5] D. Bronson and B. Severin, "Consumer Welfare," in *Economic Performance and the Military Burden in the Soviet Union, op. cit.,* pp. 93, 99.

[6] This was Khrushchev's often quoted criticism of planning during the Stalin years. See Marshall Goldman, "Economic Growth and Institutional Change in the Soviet Union," reprinted in M. Bornstein and D. Fusfeld, eds., *The Soviet Economy,* 3rd ed. (Homewood, Ill.: Irwin, 1970), p. 350.

—long used as a buffer to insure the priority of heavy industry, for consumer pressure will increasingly deny this outlet to Soviet planners.

Finally, though probably least important, is the potential influence of Western market economies. This influence is partly transmitted through the resurgence of economic theory in the Soviet Union, with its emphasis on optimization and the "rediscovery" of Western economic theory.[7] In addition, the relative abundance of consumer goods in the market economies, a condition that is supposed to be attained under socialism following the establishment of the industrial base, must be of interest, especially with the growing awareness among Soviet citizens of higher living standards in the West. Also, it might be noted that in recent years, market economies, for example West Germany and Japan, have performed—in terms of annual rates of growth of output—noticeably better than the Soviet Union.

In sum, the Soviets' interest in economic reform can be traced to lagging growth, declining capital productivity, growing consumer expectations, and the feeling that the current system fails to optimally utilize available resources. The old growth pattern based on the rapid expansion of the quantity of inputs can no longer be followed, which means that future growth will be dependent upon productivity increases (better utilization of inputs) generated through improvements in the economic system.

THE NATURE OF REFORM— ORGANIZATIONAL CHANGE

To the extent that the term *reform* is used to categorize change in the structure and operation of the Soviet economy, the phenomenon is not new. Most observers, however, would probably wish to isolate two sorts of changes: first, those of a purely organizational

---

[7] For example, well-known Western textbooks are now available in translation in the Soviet Union. Examples are: Paul Samuelson, *Economics;* R.G.D. Allen, *Mathematical Economics;* W. Baumol, *Economic Theory and Operations Research;* and many others.

nature, not having much direct impact upon the fundamental nature of the economic system; second, those sorts of changes vitally affecting the operational and structural features of the resource allocation system. In a sense, this categorization is artificial, and yet it allows us to consider the myriad organizational adjustments so prevalent during the Khrushchev era. These changes were surely aimed at solving basic economic problems, and yet they were probably misdirected away from the more fundamental resource allocation problem of decentralization of decision-making.

Although economic reform in the Soviet system has not been unidirectional, there is one crucial level at which reform must be examined—namely the question of centralization and decentralization of decision-making. If, for example, the growing complexity of the system complicates the planning procedures at the center, one possible solution is the decentralization of more decisions to lower levels so that central planners need not be concerned with those decisions. The important question, however, is which decisions will be handled in this manner, and at what level will they be resolved? This is the most basic issue of economic reform in the Soviet Union.

Unfortunately, the concept of decentralization of decision-making is difficult to characterize with accuracy.[8] If one thinks, however, simply in terms of the administrative *levels* at which decision-making choices are exercised, the changes of the 1950s, which we describe as *organizational changes,* must be viewed as having had little or no impact upon the system.

The minutiae of this period need not detain us here. The concept of regional versus hierarchical planning is of importance, however, and was emphasized in a major reform instituted by Khrushchev in 1957. As the reader will recall (Chapter Four), the minis-

[8] See, for example, Leonid Hurwicz, "Centralization and Decentralization in Economic Process," in Alexander Eckstein, ed., *Comparison of Economic Systems* (Berkeley and Los Angeles: University of California Press, 1971), pp. 79–102; Leonid Hurwicz, "Conditions for Economic Efficiency of Centralized and Decentralized Structures," in Gregory Grossman, ed., *Value and Plan* (Berkeley and Los Angeles: University of California Press, 1960), pp. 162–183; Leonid Hurwicz, "On the Concept and Possibility of Informational Decentralization," *American Economic Review, Papers and Proceedings,* vol. 59, no. 2 (May 1969), 513–524; Thomas Marschak, "The Comparison of Centralized and Decentralized Economies," *American Economic Review, Papers and Proceedings,* vol. 59, no. 2 (May 1969), 525–532.

terial system was instituted in the 1930s and involved the planning
of the economy through industrial ministries—thus steel output was
planned by a ferrous metals ministry quite apart from the location
of the steel producer, raw materials, and so on. The criticisms of
this system are familiar, but most of all, Khrushchev focused upon
the tendency of the ministry to become autarkic and to place their
own interests above the interests of the economy as a whole. Given
supply shortages, for example, ministries would attempt to develop
their own supplies and hoard where necessary.

The solution proposed was the creation, in 1957, of regional
economic councils (*sovnarkhozy*) to unify the chain of command
from top to bottom and to focus upon regional aspects of economic
development—in Soviet parlance, the so-called territorial principle.[9] Thus the economy was reorganized on a regional basis
with regional enterprises (steel, textiles, cement, etc.) being subordinated to the appropriate *sovnarkhoz*.

The *sovnarkhoz* system was abandoned by Khrushchev's suc-
cessors in 1965 because, in a fundamental sense, it suffered from
the same problems as the ministerial system (only now occurring
on a regional basis) but lacked other redeeming features. As we
noted above, this sort of reform had little fundamental impact upon
the system insofar as the *level* of decision-making was virtually
unchanged, and the myriad problems associated with centralization (success indicators, supply, and so on) remained unsolved.
Against this background of organizational change so common in
the 1950s, the reforms of the 1960s do seem of greater potential
importance.

ECONOMIC REFORM IN
THE 1960s AND 1970s

Soviet economic reform in the 1960s and 1970s has been the subject of a great deal of debate, both in the Soviet Union itself and
in the West. Our attention to this discussion is essential, for the
period since Stalin's demise in 1952 is synonymous with the rebirth

[9] For details, see Oleg Hoeffding, "The Soviet Industrial Reorganization of
1957," *American Economic Review, Papers and Proceedings,* vol. 49, no. 2
(May 1959), 65–77.

of discussion about economic matters. Although circumscribed in certain respects by dogma, not since the Industrialization Debate of the 1920s could one hear, for example, a discussion on price formation under socialism with views ranging from the most orthodox Marxian positions to those of the mathematical school advocating the use of scarcity prices derived from linear programming models.

Western views on Soviet economic discussion and the various reform proposals vary widely. This divergence of views among Western observers results in large part from the very limited nature of the actual reforms and the resultant emphasis on what they portend—an inevitably speculative venture. There are those who view (or viewed) such reforms as tantamount to establishing a market mechanism in the Soviet Union,[10] and confirming the once popular view that strict, centrally planned socialism simply cannot operate in reality. On the other hand, others (and this is probably the majority view) view these reforms as demonstrating the administrative flexibility of the socialist economic order, and as serving in large measure to improve and *preserve* the current system of economic planning.[11]

What has been the nature of Soviet economic reform and what has it achieved? During our examination of reform measures, it is well to bear in mind that the whole reform process, as we have noted, is multidimensional, and in greater or lesser degree, one that has been ongoing for a number of years. To simplify the discussion, we shall focus upon the major changes, and in particular, attempt to appraise changes in the level of decision-making: Who has the power to make what decisions, and on what basis?

This section concentrates primarily upon *actual* rather than proposed economic reform in the Soviet Union. The major exception to this rule is our discussion of the Liberman proposals, which

[10] A partial exponent of this view is Marshall I. Goldman, "Economic Revolution in the Soviet Union," *Foreign Affairs* (January 1967), 319–331.

[11] Examples of this view are: Abram Bergson, "Planning and the Market in the USSR: The Current Soviet Planning Reforms," in Alexander Balinky et al., *Planning and the Market in the USSR: The 1960s* (New Brunswick, N.J.: Rutgers University Press, 1967), pp. 43–64; Gertrude Schroeder, "The 'Reform' of the Supply System in Soviet Industry," *Soviet Studies*, vol. 24, no. 1 (July 1972).

remain largely unimplemented and superceded by the two major reforms that are covered—the Light Industry Experiments and the Kosygin Reforms. It is important to distinguish between proposed reforms and actual reforms in the Soviet context—a distinction often missed in popular writings. In our view, *actual economic reform in the USSR has been quite modest;* whereas some proposed economic reforms are quite radical and far-reaching.

The Liberman Proposals

The proposals of Evsei Liberman, a professor of engineering economics at Kharkov University, much discussed in the West largely due to their emphasis on profits, are a convenient focus for the beginning of our reform discussion. Although Liberman had been writing about enterprise performance and arguing for a reduction in tutelage over managers since the 1920s, his ongoing research was first brought to the level of public discussion in 1962 with the publication of his article: "The Plan, Profits and Bonuses" in *Pravda.*[12] Most importantly, its publication in the official party newspaper signaled an official sanctioning by the Soviet leadership of reform discussion.

Several facets of this early reform era deserve comment. First, Liberman has gained prominence well out of proportion to the importance of his proposals.[13] To this day, they remain largely unimplemented, and his renewed emphasis on profits—the aspect of his proposals that has attracted most attention in the West—was most limited. Liberman is quite clear in pointing out that the central planning of output would be maintained in full vigor and that profits would serve as a basis for managerial rewards only after the output targets for quantity and assortment had been met. If enterprises failed to meet their output targets, they would be "deprived of the right to bonuses."[14] Thus Liberman did not propose that profits act as the fundamental guide for economic activity, but rather profits were to have a slightly more important role *along*

---

[12] Translated in Bornstein and Fusfeld, 3rd ed., *op. cit.,* pp. 360–366.

[13] For a discussion of Liberman's career, see Robert C. Stuart, "Evsei Grigorevich Liberman," in George W. Simmons, ed., *Soviet Leaders* (New York: T. Y. Crowell, 1967), pp. 193–200.

[14] Liberman, in Bornstein and Fusfeld, 3rd ed., *op. cit.,* p. 361. Also see E. G. Liberman, *Economic Methods and Effectiveness of Production* (White Plains, N.Y.: International Arts and Sciences Press, 1971).

with other success criteria and would be the source of bonus payments (if any were forthcoming).

To turn to the details of Liberman's proposals,[15] we note that Liberman suggests that bonus payments (after fulfillment of the planned output target) should be a decreasing logarithmic function of the profit/capital ratio, thus encouraging the expansion of profits but the reduction of capital usage (an implicit capital charge). Profitability norms would be established for each industry, which would serve as the basis for evaluating managerial profit performance. To encourage enterprise managers to set ambitious targets for themselves, rewards would be higher for successful fulfillment —or perhaps even underfulfillment—of an ambitious profitability plan than for the overfulfillment of an "easy" target.

The number of centrally planned enterprise directives would be limited to the quantity and assortment of output and its delivery. The enterprise itself would plan its own material and labor inputs and new technology. This would prove possible under the new system, according to Liberman, because the new emphasis on profits would encourage managers to seek out cost economies and new reserves rather than building up excess stocks.

On the crucial issue of centralization versus decentralization of decision-making, Liberman remains ambiguous. All the basic instruments of central planning—price setting, the state budget, ruble control, state control of large investments—would be maintained along with the centralized planning of material supply.[16] How this system could be made compatible with enterprises planning their own inputs is not spelled out in detail by Liberman other than his assertion ("with reasonable confidence") that the two will prove compatible.[17] On the crucial issue of the price system, Liberman also equivocates, although he does suggest that the current Soviet price system would act as a serious impediment to the actual implementation of his proposals by giving unfair profitability advantages to some producers while discriminating against others.

---

[15] For a succinct statement of the Liberman proposal and its relation to a cost-profit calculus, see Alfred Zauberman, "Liberman's Rules of the Game for Soviet Industry," *Slavic Review,* vol. 22, no. 4 (December 1963), 734–744.
[16] Liberman, in Bornstein and Fusfeld, 3rd ed., *op. cit.,* pp. 362–363.
[17] *Ibid.,* p. 363.

Nevertheless, he believes that his system would force managers to press for more rational prices.[18]

The publication of the original Liberman proposals in 1962 sparked considerable controversy and a period of open discussion in the Soviet press and academic journals between 1962 and 1965.[19] During this period, the various factions—ranging from the conservative antireformers, to the Liberman supporters and the more radical reformers, especially the mathematical school—were given the opportunity to state their positions. Delayed by a politically conservative leadership, considerable criticism over the issue of profit and its meaning in a socialist economy, and in particular, a total lack of willingness to let important decisions to be made by the "anarchy" of the market, nothing was done until 1964 when a new administrative reform (experiment) began.

The Light Industry Experiments

One of the major criticisms of the Soviet planning system, especially relevant in recent years, has been the lack of a feedback mechanism between the consumer and producer—a phenomenon especially prominent in the clothing industry, where an accumulation of unsaleable inventories has resulted. In a step to resolve this problem, an experimental program was begun in 1964.[20] In Moscow the Bolshevichka factory and in Gorky the Maiak factory were to receive their production orders directly from a selected group of retail outlets rather than being assigned quantitative output targets. Unsold stocks or returned output would detract from plan fulfillment. In particular, attention was to be paid to consumer demand as a determinant of production, with bonuses (set between

[18] Michael Kaser, "Kosygin, Liberman, and the Pace of Soviet Industrial Reform," reprinted in George Feiwel, ed., *New Currents in Soviet-Type Economies: A Reader* (Scranton, Pa.: International Textbook, 1968), p. 334.
[19] For English translations of the major contributions to the debate, see M. E. Sharpe, ed., *The Liberman Discussion: A New Phase in Soviet Economic Thought* (White Plains, N.Y.: International Arts and Sciences Press, 1965). For a comprehensive discussion, see George Feiwel, *The Soviet Quest for Economic Efficiency* (New York: Praeger, 1967). For a chronological account of the 1962 to 1965 debate, see Kaser in Feiwel, *New Currents in Soviet-Type Economies, op. cit.,* pp. 330–343.
[20] For a discussion of this experiment, see Goldman, *op. cit.,* 322; Kaser in Feiwel, *New Currents in Soviet-Type Economics, op. cit.,* pp. 337–338; E. Zaleski, *Planning Reforms in the Soviet Union, 1962–1966* (Chapel Hill: University of North Carolina Press, 1967), pp. 122–140.

40 and 50 percent of basic pay) dependent upon fulfillment of delivery and profit plans, not output plans.

Although these experimental enterprises remained under a considerable degree of tutelage from above, in particular, the centralized control of material supplies, their performance in this program was considered a success, and in subsequent years the program was expanded, even to heavy industry. By 1965, this reform was to extend to 25 percent of garment factories, 28 percent of footwear factories, 18 percent of textile mills, and 30 percent of leather factories.[21]

The extent to which this reform, typically dubbed the "direct links" reform, was implemented after 1965 is not known. In fact, these changes were subsumed by the official general (and more conservative) reform of September 1965 and thus this direction of change seems to have been blunted. Apparently there remained a general lack of willingness to free these experimental enterprises from administrative controls, and hence many of the supply, incentive, and other problems of Soviet industry continued to plague these enterprises.

THE KOSYGIN
REFORMS OF 1965

The most important—though possibly most modest—economic reform in the Soviet Union was announced by Premier Kosygin in September of 1965 as a general reform to be gradually implemented in total by 1970.[22] First, we consider the substance of the 1965 reform proposal, after which we evaluate its implementation in the period 1965 through 1971 and its modification thereafter.

Enterprise Planning and Management Under the 1965 Reform. The basic thrust of the Kosygin plan was a reduction in the number of enterprise targets to be set from above, and most important, replacement of gross output by "realized output" (sales) as the

[21] Marshall Goldman, "Economic Growth and Institutional Change in the Soviet Union," in P. Juviler and H. Morton, eds., *Soviet Policy-Making: Studies of Communism in Transition* (New York: Praeger, 1967), pp. 63–80, reprinted in Bornstein and Fusfeld, 3rd ed., *op. cit.,* p. 357.

[22] See, for example, Alexei Kosygin, "On Improving Management of Industry," in Bornstein and Fusfeld, 3rd ed., *op. cit.,* pp. 387–396.

primary indicator of success for the enterprise. In addition, the number of indicators for labor planning—previously four—was to be reduced to a single indicator: the magnitude of the wage fund. Thus the enterprise manager was now to face the following eight targets established within the central plan, compared to the earlier system of twenty to thirty targets:

1. Value of goods to be sold
2. Main assortment
3. The wage fund
4. Amount of profit and the level of profitability
5. Payments to and allocations from the state budget
6. The volume of investment and the exploitation of fixed assets
7. Main assignments for the introduction of new technology
8. Material and technical supplies

Turning to financial aspects of planning, several important changes were decreed. Possibly most important, an interest charge on capital (fixed and working capital) was proposed, to be implemented at a 6 percent rate effective in 1966.[23] In addition to this new capital charge, provisions were made for a new role to be played by *Gosbank*. This new role centered upon a reduction in the importance of the state budget, and in its place the utilization of *Gosbank* facilities for the financing of enterprise investment.

Thus a new expanded role was envisaged for *Gosbank,* especially in the provision of investment funds at differentiated charges depending upon usage. Also, *Gosbank* was to play a role in facilitating the clearance of debts among enterprises and also between enterprises and their customers in the trade network.

The Kosygin schema also placed new emphasis upon the importance of accounting. Ties to the budget as a source of investment finance and subsidies were to be reduced and a production development fund was to be established. This fund was to be fed from three main sources: profits, amortization of equipment, and sales of unneeded equipment.

Profits and Incentives Under the 1965 Reform. The changing role of profits envisioned in the September 1965 reforms was relatively modest. Prices were to be reformed to allow enterprises to

---

[23] This rate could be lower for unprofitable enterprises. See Zaleski, *op. cit.,* p. 143.

be profitable under normal conditions of operation, in order to end one of the long-standing results of average branch cost pricing— a good many enterprises continually suffering losses. In addition, the role of profit was to change in two respects. First, although profit was always a part of the Soviet managerial (*khozraschet*) system in the Soviet Union, it was now to have a position of greater importance along with the now more limited number (eight) of indicators of managerial success.

Second, profits were to be an important source of funds for decentralized investment by enterprise managers (a 20 percent share for decentralized investment was projected[24]) and were to be used as a source of funds for bonus payments to workers. The former would be channeled through two funds—the production development fund and the fund for social welfare and housing (to build factory-owned apartments)—while the latter would be channeled through a new material incentive fund. These three funds were to replace the old *enterprise fund* and were designed to enhance the importance of profits for enterprise activity in addition to giving enterprise managers greater freedom of decision-making.

Prior to the 1965 reform, worker bonus schemes had been subject to criticism not only because of the meager amounts involved, but also because the funding was typically from the wages fund rather than from profits. The 1965 rules for the utilization of the new material incentive fund are complex.[25] Briefly, however, this fund was to be placed largely under the control of the enterprise itself to provide material incentive payments above and beyond those normally provided by the wages fund.

How successful has the reform been with respect to a changing role for profits? Although it is rather early to see definitive trends, two observations might be made. First, it is apparent that in terms of increasing the importance of profits as a success indicator for management, little progress has been made. As we shall see, output (now in the form of sales) remains an all-powerful indicator, and profits remain a secondary indicator of enterprise success along with seven other targets. In addition, where managers

[24] Keith Bush, "The Implementation of the Soviet Economic Reform," *Osteuropa Wirtschaft,* no. 2 and no. 3 (1970), 67–90, 190–198.
[25] Leonard J. Kirsch, *Soviet Wages: Changes in Structure and Administration Since 1956* (Cambridge, Mass.: MIT Press, 1972), chap. 7.

might enjoy a measure of freedom in the utilization of profits, for example in the case of decentralized investment or worker bonuses, in many instances other constraints have been raised, such as the inability of management to contract for material supplies or the tightening of centralized regulations over bonuses.

Second, in terms of the magnitude of profits, there has been some progress. For the first three years of the reform, profits in converted enterprises grew at a more rapid pace (about 50 percent faster between 1965 and 1968) than those in the nonconverted enterprises. Decentralized investment has also increased, though at a rate substantially less than that envisaged in the original reform blueprint.[26] Nevertheless, these figures seem to suggest increased managerial interest in profitability in the years immediately following the 1965 reform—an interest that was to lead to "undesirable" behavior and a resurgence of centralized controls after 1971.

IMPLEMENTATION AND MODIFICATION OF THE 1965 ECONOMIC REFORM

As noted at the outset, the very notion of economic reform in the socialist countries is a complex matter. Even the terminology means different things to different observers. In this sense, reform is a subject of continuing controversy, since relatively few Western observers agree upon the scope and importance of these reforms in the various countries, and most important of all, few agree upon the importance of their impact upon the respective economic systems.

Our appraisal of Soviet economic reform will rest upon four questions. First, to what extent has the general reform of 1965 been implemented—that is, in a formal sense, what proportion of enterprises in the system is today operating in some sense (degree) under the new system? Second, and a more substantive issue, what changes have come about in *financial planning* within the enter-

[26] Keith Bush, "The Soviet Economic Reform After Six Years," *Radio Liberty Report,* CRD 258/71, August 1971, p. 6; and Bush, "The Implementation of the Soviet Economic Reform," *op. cit.,* 67–90, 190–198.

prise, and most important, to what extent has managerial control over enterprise finances been enhanced? Third, to what extent has managerial control over labor allocation been enhanced? Fourth, to what extent do enterprise managers enjoy new freedom in the matter of output determination and technological change, and to what extent are they appropriately motivated to achieve enterprise goals?

The Reform—Formal Implementation

Initially, two phases of implementation of the reform were anticipated. The first, or "extensive," phase was to be the phased conversion of nonagricultural enterprises to the new system. The second, or "intensive," phase, scheduled to begin in 1970, would be the one in which the true potential of the reform would be realized.[27] In terms of the original format (September 1965), all industrial enterprises were to be converted to the new system by the end of 1968, and the remainder of the economy by the end of 1970. The exception was agriculture, where the introduction of full *khozraschet* into *sovkhozy* was to take place at a somewhat slower pace. The progress of the reform is summarized in Table 24. Two general comments are in order.

Table 24 **Conversion of Industrial Enterprises to New Economic System, 1966–1970 (as percentages of all industry)**

At End of:	Number of Enterprises Converted	Percentage of All Enterprises Converted	Percentage of Total Output	Percentage by Number of Staff	Percentage of Total Profit
1966	704	1.5	8	8	16
1967	7,248	15	37	32	50
1968	26,850	54	72	71	81
1969	36,049	72	84	81	91
1970	41,014	83	93	92	95

SOURCE: Keith Bush, "The Soviet Reform After Five Years," Radio Liberty Research Dispatch, CRD 258/71, August 1971, p. 2.

[27] Gertrude Schroeder, "Recent Developments in Soviet Planning and Incentives," in Joint Economic Committee, *Soviet Economic Prospects for the Seventies* (Washington, D.C.: U.S. Government Printing Office, 1973), p. 12.

First, although the original timetable has not been met, in a formal sense, the major proportion of industrial enterprises have in fact been converted to the new system.

Second, and most important, the reform has not been implemented in some very important sectors of the economy, notably the construction industry and also in the material-technical supply system. As of 1971, only 10 percent of both construction and repair organizations and material-technical supply organizations were operating under the new system.[28] These patterns indicate a significant degree of resistance against the general reform movement. Finally, it is well to remember that these figures on reform implementation are formal, and above all, they do not mean that where "implemented" the reform system looks like and actually operates according to the original conception outlined above. In fact, as we shall note below, the original conception of the reform itself has been significantly altered since 1971, casting more doubt on the importance of such conversion figures.

The Reform—Financial Aspects

One of the most significant aspects of the September 1965 reform blueprint was the emphasis upon decentralized investment (at the enterprise level) through the newly formed production development fund and the utilization of bank credits, which have normally accounted for only a very small portion of investment in fixed capital.

As previously indicated, the volume of decentralized investment derived from the production development fund has expanded in the converted enterprises, but still remains very small, and tends to be concentrated in the most profitable enterprises where, presumably, need is least important.[29] In addition, the problem of appropriately marrying a centralized system with decentralized elements of resource allocation—especially in the crucial area of

---

[28] *Planovoe khoziastvo* [The planned economy], no. 5 (1971), as summarized by *ABSEES: Soviet and East European Abstract Series,* vol. 2, no. 2 (October 1971), p. 99.

[29] According to the original reform proposal, decentralized investment was to amount to 20 percent of industrial investment. In 1968, however, the production development fund was only 2–3 percent of fixed production capital in converted enterprises thus being mainly a source for replacement. See Bush, "The Implementation of Soviet Economic Reform," *op. cit.,* 13.

investment—is especially acute in the case of the Soviet economic reform. On the one hand, managers are encouraged to invest on a decentralized basis, while on the other hand, they continue to be unable to negotiate the purchase of investment goods through the material supply network. These supply problems are familiar to any student of the Soviet system, and exist in spite of a system of fines for nondelivery and various attempts to develop the concept of "free sales";[30] the supply system remains largely centralized and out of reach of the typical enterprise manager. Thus far, decentralized investment has barely accounted for replacement expenditures in most instances.[31] A further factor limiting the manager's control over decentralized investment has been the growing centralized regulation of the size and distribution of the production development fund, especially since 1972—a matter discussed below.

The attempt to expand the role of the banking system as a supplier of credit has been unfulfilled. Credits, though available, have been utilized less in the converted than in the nonconverted enterprises basically because it is the profitable enterprises that invest, and they have sufficient internal reserves. It should also be noted that those enterprises converted have had surplus working capital resulting from an inability to spend production development and social-cultural and housing funds simply due to the absence of a mechanism for decentralized investment.

The Reform—Labor Allocation

Clearly any economic reform that attempts to decentralize decision-making must focus upon the extent to which enterprise management is able to manipulate its labor inputs. The question of labor allocation is a crucial issue of economic reform, for if a cost-profit calculus is to have real meaning, substitution of inputs becomes a prime sphere of managerial decision-making and may well imply the dismissal of labor by enterprises.

[30] Goldman, *op. cit.,* 323; Schroeder, *op. cit.,* pp. 107–111. On the lack of material supplies as a brake upon decentralized enterprise investment, see for example, D. Allakhverdian, "O finansovykh problemakh khoziaistvennoi reformy" [About the financial problems of economic reform], *Voprosy ekonomiki* [Problems of economics], no. 11 (1970), pp. 63–74.
[31] Bush, "The Implementation of the Soviet Economic Reform," *op. cit.,* 72–80.

Nominally, the 1965 reform enhanced the manager's freedom to allocate labor by retaining only one central constraint—the wage bill—over labor staffing, as opposed to the earlier system of detailed specifications. Of course, the wage tariff is still centrally determined. Because the original statement by Kosygin in 1965 placed considerable emphasis upon the reduction of the number of indicators governing the enterprise labor force, this was originally seen by some Western observers as the main decentralizing factor of the entire reform.[32] In fact, the significance of such changes has been reduced for two reasons. For those enterprises not covered, obviously the change is of little importance, and this applies for all changes of course, not just labor allocation. Second and more crucial, the *substance* rather than the *number* of indicators is the important matter to the enterprise manager. Indeed in the Soviet case, the post-1965 system seems to have retained central control over both the wages fund and the utilization of this fund, although new freedom was supposed to exist in the latter area.[33] This result, along with trade union pressure against the right of enterprises to dismiss unnecessary workers, has left enterprise managers' decision-making power virtually unchanged from the prereform era. The continued reluctance of Soviet managers to fire excess labor is seen in the *Shchekino* experiments. Introduced on a trial basis in October 1967 in the *Shchekino* chemical combine, this innovation encouraged management to eliminate redundant labor by allowing the enterprise to retain wage bill savings to increase wages of remaining workers.[34]

[32] For example, Abram Bergson argued in a 1967 article that the Soviets chose to decentralize decision-making in the area of labor staffing because wage rates happen to be the most rational—in the sense of equating supply and demand—of all Soviet prices. Thus managers could be trusted to make correct decisions. See Bergson, "Planning and the Market in the USSR," in Feiwel, *New Currents in Soviet-Type Economics, op. cit.,* p. 345.

[33] According to the reform plan, the wage fund was to remain centrally planned, while enterprises were to have freedom in distributing the fund to various classes of personnel. This freedom has in reality been very limited, and thus in essence, Soviet wage determination procedures remain substantially unaffected by the 1965 reform. See Kirsch, *op. cit.,* chap. 7.

[34] Janet Chapman, "Labor Mobility and Labor Allocation in the USSR," paper presented at the joint meeting of ASTE and ACE (Detroit, Mich.: December 1970), p. 5; Emily Clark Brown, "Continuity and Change in the Soviet Labor Market," *Industrial and Labor Relations Review,* vol. 23, no. 2 (January 1970), 171–190.

Modification of the 1965 Reform

As we have emphasized, the basic thrust of the 1965 reform program was a reduction of the tutelage of the enterprise manager by higher planning organs. Has this goal been achieved in any degree? Initially, the idea was to create a system whereby managers would be encouraged to respond spontaneously to various economic "levers"—profits, bonuses, increased authority over investment, and so on—so as to make the Soviet enterprise more efficient. For this reason, the number of plan targets were to be reduced, reliance was to be placed upon more rational success indicators such as sales and profitability, managers and workers were to become materially interested in the outcome of enterprise performance by tying bonus funds to enterprise activity, and so on. In other words, more decision-making authority was to pass to the manager.

Between 1965 and 1971, there is evidence of greater managerial spontaneity in response to those economic levers, especially as regards the disposition of bonus funds. As managers began to exercise their new-found authority, planners and bureaucrats began to react against "undesirable" spontaneous enterprise actions and to press for amendments to the 1965 rules. During the very period when the reform was scheduled to move into its "intensive" phase, amendments and modifications were introduced that significantly altered the content of the original reform.[35] The particular shortcomings that these amendments sought to correct were the unduly large shares of new bonus funds received by managerial personnel, the lack of attention to labor productivity and quality improvement, the unwillingness of managers to request taut production targets or to economize costs, and so on—many of the very shortcomings that the 1965 reform sought to eliminate in the first place.

Between June 1971 and April 1973, a number of changes were introduced that significantly modified the original reform proposal. First, rigid regulations governing the size of enterprise incentive funds replaced the original more flexible system. Now the ministry, based upon limits determined by *Gosplan,* is to determine the size

---

[35] This and the following discussion is largely based on Gertrude Schroeder, "Recent Developments in Soviet Planning and Incentives," *op. cit.,* pp. 11–38.

of enterprise incentive funds by fixing planned incentive fund targets. The size of the various incentive funds is thus to depend upon enterprise performance vis-à-vis planned indicators, basically upon the fulfillment of output, profitability, and labor productivity targets. Incentive funds are also to depend upon three additional targets: the plan for key products in physical units, the plan for consumer goods, and plans for changes in product quality and new products. Furthermore, the size of the incentive fund is to be tied to the tautness of the enterprise plan: The higher the output, profitability, and labor productivity targets, the larger the potential incentive funds. Rewards for overfulfillment of low targets would be reduced by 30 percent.

Second, strict controls over the distribution of enterprise incentive funds were introduced. In the new regulations, limits are placed upon the rate of growth of managerial bonuses, average wages are not allowed to increase faster than labor productivity, and regulations are established to reduce bonus differentials among branches. Significantly, managerial bonuses are tied to fulfillment of sales and profitability plans *plus* the fulfillment of the physical assortment plan, and the ministries are allowed to add additional conditions if they so desire.

Third, the manager's control over the size of the production development fund (for investment) was circumscribed. Under the modified rules, the proportion of enterprise profits to be allocated to this fund is to be set by the ministry in accordance with bank credits planned for decentralized investments.

Finally, and perhaps most importantly, the number of centrally determined enterprise targets has again been expanded. Six new targets have been reinstated since 1970: labor productivity, gross output, consumer goods assignments in heavy industry, quality targets, material and fuel economy targets, and the size of basic incentive funds.

In general, the period since 1971 has witnessed a reversal of official attitudes toward the solution of basic economic problems (perhaps as a result of lagging economic performance during the early phases of the reform). Rather than relying on economic "levers" at the enterprise level, attention is being increasingly directed toward improving planning methods and increasing tutelage over enterprises to improve economic performance. Thus rather than reducing the number of plan indicators as was envisioned in 1965, they are again being increased and incentives are being tied to the fulfillment of all of them, that is, a return to the earlier system. Emphasis is now on new planning methods—increased attention to perspective planning, automated plan calculations, the formulation of new scientific norms, automated supply systems, automated information-retrieval systems, and so on—and upon new organizational methods; in particular, on the formation of "production associations" (trusts) to take over many of the responsibilities of the ministries.[36]

This change in focus away from economic levers and toward improving planning techniques and organizational shuffling has caused one Western authority on Soviet economic reform writing in 1973 to conclude that ". . . after seven years of the reform, economic methods, or 'levers,' have been effectively converted into administrative 'levers' . . . As a consequence, centralized planning and administration are even more entrenched. . . ."[37]

It is also worth noting that the continuing problem of plant managers understating capacity and hence insuring success and bonuses remains firmly intact, in spite of attempts to change the bonus system. The lack of success in this area stems in large part from the distribution of profits (the level of which has grown steadily in the converted enterprises) in old ways—largely to the state budget—with only minimal emphasis upon bonuses and decentralized investment. In a very real sense, the old ways remain at all levels and tend to reinforce one another, thus in practice making the reforms very limited in terms of increasing managerial freedom.

THE INDUSTRIAL
PRICE REFORM,
1966–1967

An implicit factor in the Soviet reform discussion is the issue of industrial prices. As was pointed out in Chapter Five, industrial prices

[36] Paul Cook, "The Political Setting," in *Soviet Economic Prospects for the Seventies, op. cit.,* pp. 10–11.
[37] Schroeder, "Recent Developments in Soviet Planning and Incentives, *op. cit.,* p. 36.

have been set to equal average branch cost of production (capital and rental charges omitted) plus a planned profit margin *without* reference to demand. Such prices are not scarcity prices, in the sense that they do not equate supply and demand, nor do they reflect full marginal cost even when performing a clearing function. In fact, more often than not, industrial prices have been allowed to diverge from costs owing to the administrative complexity of price reform, thus necessitating state subsidies for enterprises making losses.

Against this background, one can understand the complexities of the decentralization issue, that is, the extent to which crucial economic decisions can be left up to enterprise managers without first having the primary information mechanism upon which such decisions are to be based—a "rational" price system. In this context, one can perhaps understand the relative willingness of Soviet authorities to give managers more discretion in the area of labor staffing where prices tend to be based more on scarcity.

Such considerations culminated in the general reform of industrial prices during 1966–1967. Did this reform transform the Soviet price system into a useful information mechanism for decentralization? Our answer is quite simple: it did not.

It is interesting to note that the 1966–1967 price reform was conducted separately from the Kosygin Reform of 1965, and, as we already noted, was not a major consideration in the earlier Liberman discussions. The goals of the 1966–1967 industrial price reform were quite modest. In view of the enhanced role of profits and monetary incentives envisioned in the Kosygin Reform, it was deemed essential to set industrial prices at average cost plus a profit margin sufficient to eliminate the pattern of subsidization of unprofitable enterprises. Thus price revision did become an important vehicle for implementation of the reform. No attempt was made to set prices so as to equate supply and demand—if this is possible at all in a planned economy where costs are not minimized and demand may not be known. The more radical views, especially those of the mathematical school, advocating the generation of scarcity prices through linear programming models or through an auctioning process instead, were rejected. Prices were raised, in 1966 and 1967 though still on the basis of average costs, thus notably reducing the number of planned loss enterprises and to some degree reducing profitability differentials as among branches of industry.[38] In addition, a new centralized organ, the State Committee for Prices (under *Gosplan*) was established, apparently with rather broad powers, to administer the operation of the price system.

The most critical appraisal of this reform would be to evaluate Soviet prices as mechanisms for resource allocation in the fullest sense. Cast in this light, the price reform seems to have left things pretty much as they were, in the sense that familiar complaints of the past can still be heard. It should be noted, however, that prices formed in markets do not always meet desired goals, and the centralized determination of these sorts of prices is a formidable task. The recent Soviet price reform has broken ground, especially in the ideological sphere. In the case of price setting in the extractive industries, mining for example, a variant of marginal cost pricing has been used with a recognition of rental charges for natural resources. Further, the recent emphasis upon capital charges is a notable departure for Soviet thinking about price setting. In some measure, therefore, the recent price reforms may have gotten away from simply changing the *level* of prices and toward changing the *bases* upon which prices are established.

ECONOMIC REFORM AND TECHNOLOGICAL CHANGE

In recent years, and especially in connection with the discussion on economic reform, economists and planners in the Soviet Union have devoted increasing attention to the question of technological change and its impact upon Soviet economic performance.[39] This attention focuses in large measure upon an apparently

[38] Gertrude E. Schroeder, "The 1966–67 Soviet Industrial Price Reform: A Study in Complications," *Soviet Studies,* vol. 20, no. 4 (April 1969), 464 ff.
[39] By technological progress we mean technological change in a broad sense —invention and innovation in both product and process. For detailed examination of this area by Western economists, see, for example, R. Amann, M. J. Berry, and R. W. Davies, *Science and Industry in the USSR,* part V, (Birmingham, England: University of Birmingham, Centre for Russian and East European Studies); Joseph S. Berliner, "Innovation and Economic

rather limited overall Soviet achievement in the development and application of new technology. Thus, in spite of a high political priority and a substantial amount of resources devoted to technological improvement, there seems to be a reasonable measure of agreement among Western observers that Soviet achievements in this area, though highly variable as between priority and nonpriority sectors, are nevertheless substantially behind the level of achievement in the West.[40] Why is this so, and what efforts in terms of economic reform are being made to improve the Soviet technological achievement?

The measurement of technological achievement and especially relating these differing levels of achievement with various causal factors is most complex. In a recent study of product and process innovation in Soviet industry, Joseph Berliner has identified four crucial aspects of the Soviet system and outlined their impact upon the process of technological change: organizational structure, prices, decision rules, and incentives.[41]

Organizational structure of Soviet industry appears to inhibit innovative activity. Any change in routine patterns of behavior, for example those involving new or revised forms of interorganizational contact, are likely under Soviet conditions (see Chapter Six)

Structure in Soviet Industry," paper presented at a meeting of The Association for Comparative Economics, New York, 1969; Gregory Grossman, "Innovation and Information in the Soviet Economy," *American Economic Review,* vol. 56, no. 2 (May 1966), 117–130; Gertrude E. Schroeder, "Soviet Technology: System vs. Progress," *Problems of Communism,* vol. 19, no. 5 (September–October 1970), 19–30; Gertrude E. Schroeder, "The Economic Reform as a Spur to Technological Progress in the USSR," *Jahrbuch der Wirtschaft Osteuropas* [Yearbook of East-European Economies], Band 2 (Munich, 1971), pp. 343–374. For a study of product quality viewed within the framework of technological change, see Martin C. Spechler, "The Economics of Product Quality in Soviet Industry," unpublished doctoral dissertation, Harvard University, 1971.

[40] The Soviet effort in research and development is substantial with research and development investments of over 3 percent of GNP in both the Soviet Union and in the United States. Also, for the year 1965, the level of manpower devoted to research and development in the Soviet Union was greater than that in the United States, in spite of a slowdown in the Soviet effort during the early 1960s. Although Soviet technological achievement is generally viewed as being less than that of the United States, it is, in the Soviet Union, based largely upon priority sectors and tends, therefore, to be spotty. See R. Amann et al., *op. cit.,* pp. 385, 487, 576.

[41] Joseph S. Berliner, *op. cit.,* p. 1.

to make plan fulfillment by managers more difficult, and thus will be avoided. For the enterprise manager, the price of underfulfillment of the plan is high in terms of lost bonuses, no promotion, and so on. Moreover, the pricing structure inhibits the development of new products because new products are typically less profitable than old products, and indeed may be difficult to characterize in such a fashion that a new product classification and accordingly a higher price can be obtained.[42]

Prices, of course, have meaning only insofar as they are utilized by those who actually make decisions. As Berliner points out,[43] if the decision rules are such that managerial response to prices is of little importance, as has been the case in the Soviet Union, then the establishment of prices at "correct" levels will be of minimal importance to the whole process of technological change. At the same time, it would seem to be inherently difficult to centralize the planning of innovation.

The bonus system for Soviet managers is also biased against innovational activity insofar as it reflects the decision rules established within the planning system, not to mention the relatively very small magnitude of possible rewards associated with innovative activity as compared with the high level of risk.

If the framework for innovative activity is less than adequate, what steps have been taken to alter the structure? In recent years, Soviet leaders have placed great emphasis at the highest levels upon the significance of technological progress for the future development of the Soviet economy. Indeed, in all of the areas noted by Berliner, Soviet commentary and action can be seen. Some of these changes have already been mentioned in other contexts, most are discussed in the cited literature: special funds for innovative activity, revised decision rules—especially after the September 1965 reforms—to make new products and processes more attractive to the enterprise (price supplements to serve as incentives to product improvement), reorganization of research and development facilities, techniques to encourage diffusion of innova-

---

[42] *Ibid.,* pp. 6–9. Prices are supposed to reflect quality. The 1965 reform, in theory, provided for price increases for improved quality and substantial bonuses for personnel associated with this effort. In practice, however, the reform seems to have had little impact upon product quality. See Spechler, *op. cit.,* pp. 116–160.

[43] Berliner, *op. cit.,* pp. 9 ff.

tive activity, and the adoption of new investment criteria in 1969 (Chapter Six). In fact, one of the major factors behind the modification of the 1965 reform rules in 1971 and thereafter was the continuing reluctance of managers to introduce new technology and raise product quality. Thus the size and distribution of enterprise bonus funds were more closely tied to the introduction of new technology and raising quality standards. In general, however, Soviet authorities have increasingly sought to attack the problem through centralized administrative means: establishing revised quality norms, press campaigns, computerizing the system of planning material input norms, and so on.[44]

It is, of course, too early to consider the impact of the recent Soviet effort in the technological sphere upon the productivity of the Soviet economy. There seems to be considerable agreement among Western observers, however, that improvement will be very slow, and this in large measure due to Soviet efforts to seek solutions primarily through administrative channels where more basic change is missing. As one observer of Soviet technological policy notes: "Thus, the current reforms retain all the features of the Soviet milieu that deterred innovation in the past, and they even add some new deterrents of their own."[45] In a fundamental sense, therefore, Soviet economic reform in the crucial area of technological progress seems to have been as conservative as it has been in all other areas. Major advances in Soviet technology in the near future are likely to be more dependent upon the introduction of Western technology than upon innovation at home. At what pace the Soviets will be able to acquire Western technology will depend upon the rate of expansion of economic relations with the capitalist world.[46]

---

[44] Gertrude E. Schroeder, "Recent Developments in Soviet Planning and Incentives, *op. cit.,* pp. 18–35.

[45] Gertrude E. Schroeder, "Soviet Technology: System vs. Progress," *op. cit.,* 29.

[46] Raymond Hutchings, "Soviet Technology Policy," in *Soviet Economic Prospects for the Seventies, op. cit.,* pp. 82–83.

THE REFORM
IN PERSPECTIVE

Economic reform is neither a recent nor a new phenomenon to the countries of the socialist bloc. In fact, most of the Eastern European countries have adopted reforms since the mid-1950s.[47] In reviewing these reforms, one can note that they all attempt to respond to the problems of excessive centralization, of restrictive managerial behavior, of an irrational price system—which are exactly the same problems with which Soviet reformers are grappling. This suggests that the deficiencies of the Soviet economic system are not unique, but are general concomitants of centrally planned socialism.

The most striking feature of economic reform in the Soviet Union is its conservative nature. Its goal throughout has been to retain the most basic features of the original economic system— centralized planning of outputs and inputs, centralized administration of prices, centralized allocation of investment—but to make it a more workable system by using "realized output" as a success indicator, reducing the number of planned targets, introducing capital charges and so on. None of these changes, however, alter the basic system. Not only have the Soviet reforms been very conservative, especially compared to some of the more far-reaching reforms in Eastern Europe—notably in Hungary, Czechoslovakia, and Poland—but also these Soviet reforms have been largely unimplemented in fact—for example, in the continued centralized allocation of investment, and, in some cases, have even been reversed, for example, the reintroduction of six centralized plan targets and the tightening of administrative controls over bonuses.

The conservative nature of economic reform in the Soviet Union is not necessarily an indictment of such efforts, for there is no reason to believe that systemic improvements are more easily attained in planned than in market economies. In fact, it is an open

[47] For accounts of economic reform in Eastern Europe, see the selection of articles in George R. Feiwel, *New Currents in Soviet-Type Economies,* (Scranton, Pa.: International, 1968), part II; Bela Belassa, "The Economic Reform in Hungary," *Economica,* vol. 37, no. 145 (February 1970), 1–22; J. Wilczynski, *Socialist Economic Development and Reforms* (New York: Macmillan, 1971).

question to what extent marginal improvements in the Soviet system, introduced in isolation, can be effective and to what extent they will be counterproductive.[48] Also the question of timing of reform is a difficult one; what is the proper sequence of reform? Should a general price reform precede limited decentralization of decision-making, or vice versa, and so on? Such crucial questions remain largely unanswered even in theoretical terms. Many of the "solutions" may appear straightforward in theory, though certainly much less so in practice. In this sense, the niceties of the competitive market model can readily lead to overstatement of the potential of economic reform and inevitably to criticism for lack of practical achievement in the light of these overly optimistic expectations. In this context, one can perhaps understand the natural reluctance of Soviet authorities to depart on a program of radical reform.

A second argument against substantive reform of the Soviet economy stems from a Soviet view of the superiority of the "planning principle," that is, the system by which crucial economic decisions are made by rational experts—planners—rather than by the anarchy of the market. To place more decision-making power in the hands of individual managers and consumers will subject the economy to anarchistic forces and will thus destroy the basic strength of the current system.[49]

A third explanation of the conservatism of Soviet economic reform is the role of vested interests. The people most directly affected by the reform—the ministries, the banking system, the planning organs, party officials—have tended to resist significant decentralization of decision-making authority, which is tantamont to a reduction in their own decision-making power. The fact that the letter of the economic reform has not always been observed can also be explained by vested interest, for there have often been

---

[48] An example of this is the "rejection or transplants" phenomenon noted by A. Zielinski in the Polish case. Thus the system tended to reject transplants from market systems—in particular the use of a capital charge. A. Zielinski, "Economic Reform in Poland," CESES Seminar, Sorrento, Italy, Summer 1968.

[49] Goldman, "Economic Growth and Institutional Change in the Soviet Union," and Kosiachenko, "Important Conditions for Improvement of Planning," in Bornstein and Fusfeld, 3rd ed., *op. cit.*, pp. 345–359, and 381–386, respectively.

differences between those generating and those implementing economic reform.

ECONOMIC REFORM—
ALTERNATIVES

Soviet leaders have never been enamoured with the market model, so they should not be expected in the future to adopt even the rudiments of its underpinnings, except where absolutely essential to achieve effective local decision-making—that is, local decision-making that accords with central wishes but in the absence of direct contact and influence. Even then, such elements of the market will most likely be developed within the context of the central planning system. In this respect, the utilization of mathematical methods does hold promise for the future.[50]

Although there are ideological and practical limitations to the application of mathematical methods in Soviet planning, they can, it would seem, be applied and effectively utilized at several levels within the system. In the matter of price formation, linear programming models might well improve the quality of the prices—in terms of relative prices actually representing relative scarcities—and in addition, the computation speed of such models might well add a badly needed measure of price flexibility. It is ironic that such prices, in theory at least, can more accurately represent the niceties of the market model than those formed in actual markets. Yet the ideological resistance remains great, and the computational difficulties are perhaps for the present insurmountable.

On the macroeconomic level, the planning of inputs and outputs might well be incorporated into a general model that would have the advantage of greater accuracy, greater speed in terms of information flows, and the ability to compute several variants—thus improving the chances of reaching an optimal plan. Although such a model for the entire system would be beyond existing com-

[50] For a discussion of mathematical methods in the context of Soviet planning, see John P. Hardt et al., *Mathematics and Computers in Soviet Economic Planning* (New Haven, Conn.: Yale University Press, 1967); and Michael Ellman, *Soviet Planning Today—Proposals for an Optimally Functioning Economic System* (Cambridge: Cambridge University Press, 1971).

puter capacity, ongoing research suggests that models can be sub-divided (by region or on other grounds) to facilitate computation.

Whether it be an individual firm or an entire economic system, a fundamental problem of the bureaucratic organization that must be considered is the need to develop a structure in which desired central control can be executed, but where local decision makers have authority and responsibility (either formal or informal), and managers and others can be induced to achieve central goals. In the Soviet case, the adjustment of the system is complicated by ideological barriers, routinization of frequently imperfect aspects of the system, and possibly most of all, the generally uncharted waters of mixing elements of a market system with a fundamentally planned economic system.

In the latter respect, there is of course a significant set of practical alternatives as represented by the various reform pro-grams of the Eastern European socialist economies.[51] These var-iants, from the more extreme case of Yugoslavia to the notably conservative case of Albania represent a wide range of variants of the industrialization process under socialism. The East European systems, though presently at varying stages of economic develop-ment, all began during the early 1950s to implement the Stalinist model of industrialization under pressure from the Soviet Union. Although that pressure has not ceased, as the events in Hungary (1956) and Czechoslovakia (1968) attest, these economies have, nevertheless, found it necessary and, with quite significant varia-tions, possible to implement changes in their economic arrangements. These reforms have focused on the organization of agricultural production, and most important, the relaxation of centralized control and the implementation of planning with economic tools: prices, costs, profits, and decentralized managerial control. They should, at least in some measure and with reservation, be a learn-ing mechanism for the reform of Soviet planning arrangements. Outside of Yugoslavia, the most radical reform (the Hungarian "New Economic Mechanism" of 1966) envisions significant decen-

---

[51] There is a large body of literature on the reforms in Eastern European countries. A useful and recent compendium of papers can be found in *Economic Developments in Countries of Eastern Europe* (Washington, D.C.: U.S. Government Printing Office, 1970); see especially the survey of de-velopments in Eastern Europe by John P. Hardt, pp. 5–40.

tralization through the abolition of output targets and the enhancement of the role of profits.[52] Nevertheless, even in this case, bureaucratic opposition and vested interests remain intact and make it difficult, if not impossible, to implement the reform as intended. In light of this experience, one may wonder whether truly meaningful reform is possible in the Communist economies.

Selected Bibliography

Alexander Balinky et al., *Planning and the Market in the USSR: The 1960s* (New Brunswick, N.J.: Rutgers University Press, 1967).

Joseph S. Berliner, "Innovation and Economic Structure in Soviet Industry," in Association for Comparative Economics, *Proceedings,* New York, December 1967, pp. 1–16.

Keith Bush, "The Implementation of the Soviet Economic Reform," *Osteuropa-Wirtschaft,* nos. 2 and 3, 1970.

George Feiwel, *The Soviet Quest for Economic Efficiency* (New York: Praeger, 1967).

Jere L. Felker, *Soviet Economic Controversies* (Cambridge, Mass.: MIT Press, 1966).

Willem Keizer, *The Soviet Quest for Economic Rationality* (Rotterdam: Rotterdam University Press, 1971).

Alexei Kosygin, "On Improving Management of Industry, Perfecting Planning, and Enhancing Economic Incentives in Industrial Production," as reprinted in M. Bornstein and D. Fusfeld, eds., *The Soviet Economy* 3rd ed. (Homewood, Ill.: Irwin, 1970), pp. 387–396.

E. G. Liberman, *Economic Methods and the Effectiveness of Production* (White Plains, N. Y.: International Arts and Sciences Press, 1971).

Karl W. Ryavec, "Soviet Industrial Management: Challenge and Response, 1965–1970," *Canadian Slavic Studies,* vol. 2 (Summer 1972), 151–177.

Karl W. Ryavec, "Soviet Industrial Managers, Their Superiors and

---

[52] Belassa, *op. cit.,* 20–22.

the Economic Reform: A Study of an Attempt at Planned Behavioral Change," *Soviet Studies,* vol. 21, no. 2 (October 1969), 208–229.

Gertrude E. Schroeder, "Recent Developments in Soviet Planning and Incentives," in Joint Economic Committee, *Soviet Economic Prospects for the Seventies* (Washington, D.C.: U.S. Government Printing Office, 1973), pp. 11–38.

Gertrude E. Schroeder, "The 'Reform' of The Supply System in Soviet Industry," *Soviet Studies,* vol. 24, no. 1 (July 1972), 97–119.

Gertrude E. Schroeder, "The 1966–67 Soviet Industrial Price Reform: A Study in Complications," *Soviet Studies,* vol. 20, no. 4 (April 1969), 462–477.

Eugene Zaleski, *Planning Reforms in the Soviet Union, 1962–1966* (Chapel Hill: University of North Carolina Press, 1967).

Alfred Zauberman, "Liberman's Rules of the Game for Soviet Industry," *Slavic Review,* vol. 22, no. 4 (December 1963), 734–744.

PART FOUR

Soviet Economic Growth and Performance

CHAPTER ELEVEN

Soviet Economic Growth and Performance

Our survey of the Soviet economy is virtually complete at this point; yet to fail to consider how well the Soviet economy has performed relative to other economies would be a significant omission. In fact, this ultimately is what the study of differing economic systems is all about: Which economic organization seems to function the "best"? Although we recognize that it is risky to generalize from the performance of one economy to the performance of the system,[1] that is, to treat Soviet economic performance as representative of the command socialist system as a whole, we compare the performance of the Soviet command economy with that of industrialized market economies in this chapter. Of special interest are the comparisons between the USSR and the United States, despite the different levels of development of the two countries. This is not to deny that other comparisons, such as the USSR with West Germany or Japan, are just as relevant.[2] The United States and the Soviet Union are nonetheless the world's two largest economic powers, with fairly equal population sizes. Considerable research has already gone into Soviet-American comparisons and the Soviets themselves tend to judge their economic performance relative to the United States. In this chapter we emphasize long-run

[1] Philip Hanson, "East-West Comparisons and Comparative Economic Systems," *Soviet Studies,* vol. 22, no. 3 (January 1971), 327–343.
[2] Angus Maddison, *Economic Growth in Japan and the USSR* (New York: Norton, 1969).

performance and concentrate on secular trends. The often considerable variation around the secular trend is not considered in detail.[3]

In comparing the economic performance of countries, there are two major definitional problems. First, it is often difficult to measure the various economic performance criteria in an unambiguous manner. For example, measures of economic growth—a frequently used performance criterion—are often dramatically affected by the choice of constant price weights—the index number problem. Thus direct comparisons of growth rates tend to be difficult to interpret. If it is difficult to evaluate the relative growth performance of countries, although one can narrowly define economic growth in rather specific terms, it is even more difficult to measure less easily quantifiable performance criteria, such as environmental quality or dynamic efficiency.

The second major definitional problem is even more difficult to come to grips with. In view of the multitude of possible performance criteria—economic growth, environmental quality, efficiency of resource utilization, relative standards of living, equity of income distribution, and so on—how can one rank the performance of one economy relative to another unless one outperforms the other in all performance categories? As an example, let us assume that the Soviet economy has outperformed the American economy in terms of growth and equity of income distribution, but that the United States economy has outperformed the USSR in all other categories. Which country deserves the higher overall rating? This depends, of course, upon the relative importance of the various performance criteria, which is a matter of individual judgment, not of objective economics.[4]

In sum, there seems to be no unambiguous way to objectively evaluate the performance of one economy relative to another ex-

[3] The reader interested in pursuing the question of cyclical instability in socialist economic systems should consult G. J. Staller, "Fluctuations in Planned and Free Market Economies," *American Economic Review,* vol. 54, no. 4, part I (June 1964), 385–395.
[4] For a discussion of the success criteria problem, see Bela Belassa, *The Hungarian Experience in Economic Planning* (New Haven, Conn.: Yale University Press, 1959), pp. 5–24. Also Alexander Eckstein, ed., *Comparison of Economic Systems* (Berkeley and Los Angeles: University of California Press, 1972), parts I and II.

cept in obvious (and rare) cases where one outperforms the other in all categories. Given, however, the widespread interest in performance evaluation, what can be done? Our answer is to examine the performance of the Soviet economy and selected market economies in terms of what we consider the six most important performance criteria: (1) economic growth, (2) dynamic efficiency, (3) static efficiency, (4) equity of income distribution, (5) consumer welfare, and (6) environmental quality. We realize that we are necessarily omitting criteria that others might consider important—military power, price stability, and economic fluctuations, for example—a subjective decision on our part.

SOVIET ECONOMIC
GROWTH

Although it is not widely recognized, measures of the long-term growth of real GNP are often quite sensitive to the choice of constant price weights. If one measures the growth rate of an economy that has successfully transformed itself into an advanced industrial country, the computed real growth rate will often be much higher if constant preindustrialization prices are used as weights. This phenomenon is called *index number relativity,* or the "Gerschenkron Effect," after Professor Alexander Gerschenkron, who analyzed it in his study of Soviet industrial production.[5]

Although the explanation of index number relativity might seem a digression to the reader, we attempt to provide an intuitive explanation of this phenomenon because of its importance in evaluating USSR growth, especially during the 1930s: In the course of industrialization, a negative correlation exists between the rates of growth of sector outputs and the rates of growth of sector prices. The fastest growing sectors in the course of industrialization— machinery, electricity, transportation equipment—all tend to experience *relative* declines in prices (relative to the prices of the slowly growing sectors, such as food products and textiles) as advanced technology is introduced and economies of scale are

---

[5] Alexander Gerschenkron, "The Soviet Indices of Industrial Production," *Review of Economics and Statistics* vol. 29, no. 4 (November 1947), 217–226.

achieved. Thus, if constant preindustrialization prices are used, the most rapidly expanding sectors will receive relatively large weights, whereas the other sectors will receive relatively small weights. Conversely, if postindustrialization prices are used, the rapidly expanding sectors will receive relatively small price weights (which reflect the reductions in their relative prices), and the other sectors will receive relatively large price weights.[6]

This may seem quite academic to the reader, but the annual Soviet growth rate of real GNP between 1928 and 1937, as calculated by Abram Bergson of Harvard University, is 11.9 percent using the preindustrialization prices of 1928, and 5.5 percent when calculated in postindustrialization prices of 1937.[7] The complexity of the question is increased when one realizes that *comparable* estimates of American growth in preindustrialization prices, say of the 1810s, are not available.[8] What then is the "true" growth rate of the Soviet Union or of the United States? There is, in fact, no single "true" growth rate. Instead, there are a whole series of growth rates, one for each set of price weights, which yield a *range* of growth rates. Fortunately, for purposes of cross-country comparisons, truly significant differences arise only when comparing growth rates computed using pre- versus postindustrialization prices, owing to the large structural changes that occur during industrialization. Differences between growth rates in constant post-

[6] For example, consider a hypothetical case in which the USSR in 1928 produced 100 "units" of textiles and 50 "units" of machinery, and that is all. The 1928 per unit prices of textiles and machinery were *1 R* and *2 R*, respectively. Assume further that in 1970, the USSR produced 200 "units" of textiles and 1000 "units" of machinery, and the prices of textiles and machinery had risen to *10 R* and *10 R*, respectively. If one values both 1928 and 1970 outputs in 1928 prices, 1970 output is *11 times* 1928 output. If one values both 1928 and 1970 output in 1970 prices, 1970 output is *8 times* 1928 output. A formal analysis of the index number problem is found in Richard Moorsteen, "On Measuring Productive Potential and Relative Efficiency," *Quarterly Journal of Economics,* vol. 75, no. 3 (August 1961), 451–467.

[7] Abram Bergson, *The Real National Income of Soviet Russia Since 1928* (Cambridge, Mass.: Harvard University Press, 1961), p. 261.

[8] Growth in the United States between 1834 and 1908 has been estimated in 1860 prices. See Robert Gallman, "Gross National Product in the United States, 1834–1909," in *Output, Employment and Productivity in the United States after 1800* (New York and London: National Bureau of Economic Research, 1966), pp. 3–75. These estimates are not comparable with the Kuznets figures in 1929 prices cited in Table 25 because the two differ on current price estimates.

industrialization or constant preindustrialization prices tend to be smaller. Nevertheless, index number relativity continues to operate in industrialized countries, only to a smaller degree.

With these reservations in mind, we shall contrast "comparable" Soviet and American growth rates; in other words, we shall concentrate on growth rates that employ "late" year (postindustrialization) price weights. This method, however, does not eliminate all biases resulting from index number problems but acts instead only as a crude adjustment. The cited Soviet growth rates have been estimated by American economists, who have recalculated Soviet GNP using Western GNP definitions[9] to ensure the comparability of Soviet and American rates.[10] For reference purposes, we include the official estimates of growth rates of Soviet *net material product,* which differs from the standard Western concept by its exclusion of services not directly connected with physical production.

In Table 25, we supply annual growth rates of Soviet real GNP during the plan era (1928–1972) and of the United States between 1869 and 1972. The Soviet figures are based largely on the estimates by Abram Bergson, which are the most widely accepted Western estimates of Soviet growth. They have been extrapolated forward to 1972 using Stanley Cohn's and the Department of Commerce's estimates of Soviet GNP between 1955 and 1972.[11]

What conclusions can be drawn from Table 25 concerning Soviet growth performance relative to that of the United States?

[9] Of course, there is the problem of valuation of Soviet GNP, because established prices often fail to reflect costs of production owing to substantial subsidies and indirect taxes. The figures cited employ the factor cost concept, which eliminates subsidies and indirect taxes. There is still a problem in that such factor costs fail to adequately reflect capital costs, but various adjustments show that overall growth rates are not substantially altered by the inclusion of capital costs. See Bergson, *op. cit.,* p. 219.

[10] For studies of the availability and reliability of Soviet statistics, see Vladimir G. Treml and John P. Hardt, eds., *Soviet Economic Statistics* (Durham, N.C.: Duke University Press, 1972). Also see Abram Bergson, "Reliability and Usability of Soviet Statistics," *The American Statistician,* vol. 7, no. 3 (June–July, 1953), 19–23.

[11] The Bergson figures are in 1950 prices and the Cohn figures employ 1959 weights; thus this is a mixed index. Differences that arise as a result of the mixed weighting scheme are most likely very minimal. Differences between this index and one based on the Bergson 1937 price weighted figures are negligible.

Table 25 **Long-term Growth of GNP in the USSR and USA**
(annual rates of growth)

USSR	Bergson– Cohn Estimates	Official Soviet Estimates (net material product)
1860–1913	2.25–2.75[g]	—
1928–1940	5.4[a]	15.0[d]
1950–1960	7.0[b]	10.0[e]
1960–1972	4.7[c]	6.7[e]
1928–1972	5.1[b]	9.3[f]
1928–1972, effective years	5.5[b]	—
1950–1972	5.8[b]	8.3[f]

United States	1860 Prices	1929 Prices	1958 Prices
1834–1943 to 1879–1888	4.4	—	—
1879–1888 to 1899–1908	3.7	3.8	—
1899–1908 to 1929	—	3.4	—
1929–1950	—	—	2.8
1950–1960	—	—	3.2
1960–1972	—	—	4.1
1929–1972	—	—	3.2
1950–1972	—	—	3.7

[a] 1950 prices.
[b] Combined index, 1950 prices 1928–1955, 1959 prices 1955–1969, 1968 weights 1970–1972.
[c] 1959 and 1968 weights.
[d] 1926–1927 prices.
[e] 1955 prices.
[f] Combined index, 1926–1927 prices for the 1928–1940 period, and 1955 prices for the 1950–1970 period.
[g] Moving weights. The official Soviet estimates for 1972 are based upon the "planned" growth of national income.

SOURCES: Abram Bergson, *The Real National Income of Soviet Russia Since 1928* (Cambridge, Mass.: Harvard University Press, 1961), pp. 180, 210, 261; Stanley Cohn, "General Growth Performance of the Soviet Economy," in United States Congress, Joint Economic Committee, *Economic Performance and the Military Burden in the Soviet Union* (Washington, D.C.: U.S. Government Printing Office, 1970), p. 17; *The Economic Report of the President* (selected years); *Dostizheniia sovetskoi vlasti za 40 let v tsifrakh*

First, it is obvious that Soviet growth since 1928 has been more rapid than American growth during the same period. The average annual growth rate of the Soviet economy between 1928 and 1972 was 5.1 percent, whereas the rate for the United States between 1929 and 1972 was 3.2 percent. If one measures Soviet growth only during "effective years";[12] that is, if one eliminates the war years, Soviet growth rises to 5.5 percent, almost 2.5 percent above the American annual growth rate.

Second, the Soviet growth rate during the postwar period (1950–1972) of 5.8 percent far exceeded the comparable American rate of 3.7 percent (1950–1972)—a difference of 2.1 percent annually.

Third, Soviet growth in the postwar period has been declining, from a high of 7.0 percent between 1950 and 1960 to 4.7 percent between 1960 and 1972. During this latter period, the worst growth years were 1962 (3.3 percent), 1963 (2.2 percent), 1969 (2.3 percent), and 1972 (2.0 percent).[13]

Fourth, the official Soviet estimates of the growth of *net ma-*

[12] The practice of computing Soviet growth for "effective years" was originated by Gregory Grossman of the University of California, Berkeley, as a suggested measure of what long-term Soviet growth might have been in the absence of the war. Gregory Grossman, "Thirty Years of Soviet Industrialization," *Soviet Survey* (October 1958). One could perhaps argue that the Great Depression should be omitted from computing the long-term United States growth rate, except that it could be argued that the business cycle is inherent to the capitalist system and should be included.

[13] Stanley Cohn, "General Growth Performance of the Soviet Economy," in *Economic Performance and the Military Burden in the Soviet Union* (Washington, D.C.: U.S. Government Printing Office, 1970), p. 9; Hardt, *op. cit.,* p. ix.

[The accomplishments of the Soviet regime over 40 years in numbers] (Moscow: 1957), p. 327; *Narodnoe khoziastvo SSSR v 1970 g.* [The National Economy of the USSR in 1970], p. 56; Robert Gallman, "Gross National Product in the United States, 1834–1909," in *Output, Employment and Productivity in the United States after 1800* (New York and London: National Bureau of Economic Research, 1966), p. 26; Raymond Goldsmith, "The Economic Growth of Tsarist Russia, 1860–1913," *Economic Development and Cultural Change,* vol. 9, no. 3 (April 1961), 472; Peter G. Peterson, *U.S.-Soviet Commercial Relations in a New Era* (Washington, D.C.: Department of Commerce, 1972), p. 4; John P. Hardt, "Summary," in Joint Economic Committee, *Soviet Economic Prospects for the Seventies* (Washington, D.C.: U.S. Government Printing Office, 1973), p. ix.

terial product in constant prices are much larger than the American estimates of Soviet growth using Western GNP concepts and different price weights. Such differences are greatest when comparing the 1928–1940 period, part of which is explained by the Soviets' use of preindustrialization 1926–1927 prices until 1950.[14] From the Soviet viewpoint, this is more than a matter of academic interest; it is difficult to determine if Soviet growth has actually been declining in recent years, because the earlier rate (1928–1940) is not really known. Another cause of the differences between American and Soviet estimates is the Soviets' omission from net material product of selected services (such as passenger transportation, government employees, lawyers, housing) which have been among the slowest growing sectors in the Soviet Union.

Fifth, United States growth rates during early periods of industrial transformation are closer to the Soviet plan period rates than are the twentieth century American rates. Thus the American economy grew at 4.4 percent annually between 1834–1843 and 1879–1888, which is .5 percent less than the Soviet rate during the 1928 to 1940 period.[15] In fact, the United States rate of 6.6 percent during the 1869–1878 to 1879–1888 decades exceeded the Soviet 1928–1940 rate.

Sixth, whereas the Soviet growth rate of 7.0 percent between 1950 and 1960 was extremely rapid by international standards, it was by no means unprecedented among the major industrial powers during this period. The annual West German growth rate be-

---

[14] Bergson calculates Soviet growth between 1928 and 1937 as 11.9 percent annually in 1928 prices, compared with the official claim of 16.9 percent. Bergson, *The Real National Income of Soviet Russia Since 1928, op. cit.,* p. 216. In recent Soviet publications the official Soviet estimates of Soviet growth during the 1930s have been severely criticized as being unrealistic and inconsistent; on this, see A. L. Vainshtein, *Narodnii dokhod Rossi i SSSR* [The national income of Russia and the USSR] (Moscow: 1969) pp. 99–108. For a further discussion of the official Soviet figures, see Alec Nove, "1926/7 and All That," *Soviet Studies,* vol. 9, no. 2 (October 1957), 117–130.

[15] In these comparisons, we use early year price weights for the United States (1860 prices) and late year price weights for the USSR—a seeming violation of the principle stated above. For some reason index number relativity does not show up in these calculations for the United States, probably because of different calculating methods used by Gallman (the 1860 price estimates) and Kuznets (the 1929 price estimates). Note that for the same period (1879–1888 to 1899–1908), the 1929 price weights yield a higher growth rate (Table 25).

tween 1950 and 1960 was 7.5 percent and the Japanese rate for the same period was over 9 percent.[16] It may not be a coincidence that those major industrial powers that suffered the most extensive wartime destruction also experienced the most rapid growth rates in the immediate postwar period.

Seventh, Soviet growth rates during the plan era well exceeded the long-term growth rate during the tsarist period (1860–1913). In fact, the long-run Soviet growth rate during 1928–1972 is roughly double the 1860–1913 rate. Thus the Soviet period saw a secular acceleration of (Russian) economic growth.

Eighth, Soviet growth between 1928 and 1972 well exceeds the long-term growth rates of the other now industrialized economies, including the United States (Table 26). Only the long-term Japanese growth rate (4.1 percent) approaches the Soviet 1928–1972 rate. The above comparison does, however, assume that the 1928–1972 Soviet rate is indeed the long-term growth rate of the

Table 26 **Long-term Growth of GNP of Selected Countries (average annual growth rate)**

United Kingdom	1855–1864 to 1963–1967	2.1%
France	1831–1840 to 1963–1966	2.0
Belgium	1900–1904 to 1963–1967	1.9
Netherlands	1860–1870 to 1963–1967	2.4
Germany (West Germany after 1945)	1850–1859 to 1963–1967	2.8
Denmark	1865–1869 to 1963–1967	2.9
Sweden	1861–1869 to 1963–1967	3.2
Italy	1895–1899 to 1963–1967	2.8
Japan	1874–1879 to 1963–1967	4.0
United States	1834–1843 to 1963–1967	3.6
Canada	1870–1874 to 1963–1967	3.5
USSR	1928 to 1972	5.1

SOURCES: Simon Kuznets, *Economic Growth of Nations* (Cambridge, Mass.: Harvard University Press, 1971), pp. 11–14; and Table 25, above.

[16] Maurice Ernst, "Postwar Economic Growth in Eastern Europe," in *New Directions in the Soviet Economy, part IV* (Washington, D.C.: U.S. Government Printing Office, 1966), p. 880; *United Nations, Yearbook of National Accounts Statistics* (selected years).

Soviet economy, although it is computed using a much shorter time period than the other rates. This assumption may eventually not prove to be the case in view of the declining Soviet growth pattern. For the other countries, however, there seems to be no consistent difference between early period and late period rates;[17] so perhaps the shorter Soviet period does not distort our overall conclusion that the long-term Soviet growth rate is the highest recorded. We emphasize that we are dealing with long-term rates, which conceal the fact that growth rates as high or higher than the long-term Soviet rate have been attained by some of these countries (Japan, the United States, Germany) in the past during various subperiods.

Thus we conclude that Soviet economic growth during the plan era was more rapid than American growth throughout the twentieth century and was more rapid than the long-run growth of other industrialized countries. Soviet growth during the 1950s was especially rapid but was surpassed by the two other major industrial powers—Germany and Japan—which had also suffered extensive war damage. Only during the period of industrial transformation between the Civil War and 1900 did American growth approach the Soviet rate during the plan era. These conclusions are probably sufficiently general to not be notably affected by the index number problem and the other measurement problems mentioned above.

Let us now turn to a deeper question: To what extent was the more rapid Soviet growth a consequence of the Soviet economic system per se or of other special factors unrelated to the system? This is a fundamental issue in appraising alternative systems, for we are interested in the merits of the system independent of special circumstances.[18] In this regard, certain special factors probably affected long-run Soviet growth performance. First, the Soviets industrialized late and could therefore borrow more advanced technology from the West. Second, the large Soviet population, concentrated as it was in agriculture at the beginning of the plan era, provided, as we have seen, a plentiful supply of labor for industry.

---

[17] Simon Kuznets, *Economic Growth of Nations* (Cambridge, Mass.: Harvard University Press, 1971), pp. 37–43.
[18] On this point see Abram Bergson, "Comparative Productivity and Efficiency in the Soviet Union and The United States," in Eckstein, *op. cit.*, pp. 161–240.

Economies of scale could be therefore achieved without diminishing marginal productivity of capital in the course of Soviet industrialization. On the negative side, Soviet agricultural resources were limited relative to population with only a small proportion of land suitable for cultivation.[19] Although it is impossible to weigh the impact of each of these factors on Soviet growth, one can speculate that the Soviets' borrowing of more advanced technology was an important factor in explaining rapid growth especially during the 1930s and the immediate postwar period.

Special factors aside, to what extent was the more rapid Soviet growth a product of the Soviet system of central planning and political dictatorship? It would seem that much of the superior Soviet growth performance can be explained by the substitution of growth-oriented planners' preferences for consumer sovereignty. In this manner, the state was able to opt for a pattern of development conducive to rapid economic growth by planning high investment rates, high labor participation rates, and by expanding the education of the labor force. In the case of educational levels, for example, in 1926 only 6 percent of the over-fifteen-year-old population (89 million) had received education beyond the seventh grade. By 1959, this percentage had risen to 39 percent (of 148 million).[20] The high investment ratios (Chapter Three) and labor participation rates (Chapter Six) have already been discussed in earlier chapters.

The growth bias of Soviet planning can be illustrated by comparing the pattern of Soviet growth (the growth of household consumption vis-à-vis gross investment) with that of the United States (Table 27). The major difference between the two is the much more rapid growth of investment than consumption in the USSR as opposed to the more rapid growth of consumption—with the exception of the very early 1834–1888 period—in the United States. The most extreme case of this is the negligible growth of household consumption in the USSR between 1928 and 1937, a period when investment was expanding at over 14 percent annually. Although

[19] Bergson, *The Real National Income of Soviet Russia Since 1928, op. cit.,* p. 260.
[20] Nicholas DeWitt, "Education and Development of Human Resources: Soviet and American Effort," *Dimensions of Soviet Economic Power* (Washington, D.C.: U.S. Government Printing Office, 1962), p. 244.

Table 27 **Differential Growth Patterns, GNP by Final Use, USSR—United States (annual growth rates)**

USSR	(1) Household Con-sumption	(2) Gross Invest-ment	(3) GNP	(4) 1÷2
1928–1937[a]	.7	14.5	5.5	.05
1950–1955[a]	8.7	8.7	7.6	1.00
1958–1964[b]	4.8	7.4	5.9	.65
1965–1969[f]	6.2	6.8	4.9	.91
1928–1955[a]	2.8	7.9	4.8	.35
United States				
1834–1843 to 1879–1888[c]	4.0	6.5	4.4	.62
1879–1888 to 1899–1908[d]	3.8	3.8	3.8	1.00
1899–1908 to 1914–1923[d]	3.1	3.0	3.1	1.03
1929–1950[e]	2.7	2.6	2.6	1.04
1950–1970[e]	3.6	2.0	3.6	1.80
1929–1970[e]	3.2	2.3	3.1	1.39

[a] 1937 ruble factor cost.
[b] 1958 adjusted factor cost.
[c] 1860 prices.
[d] 1929 prices.
[e] 1958 prices.
[f] 1955 prices.

SOURCES: Bergson, *The Real National Income of Soviet Russia Since 1928, op. cit.*, p. 210; Abraham Becker, *Soviet National Income 1958–1964* (Berkeley: University of California Press, 1969), p. 256; Simon Kuznets, *National Product Since 1869* (New York: National Bureau of Economic Research, 1946), Table II–16; Gallman, *Output, Employment and Productivity in the United States After 1800, op. cit.*, pp. 26–34; *The Economic Report of the President*, 1971, p. 198; Stanley Cohn, "The Economic Burden of Defense Expenditures," in *Soviet Economic Prospects for the Seventies, op. cit.*, p. 151.

investment expanded more rapidly than consumption in the United States between 1834 and 1888, the extreme differences noted in the Soviet case were avoided.[21]

[21] This growth orientation is also reflected in the differential growth pattern of the various originating sectors of Soviet GNP (Table 28). The consumption-oriented sectors (trade, services, and agriculture) expanded more slowly than total output in the USSR: whereas in the United States they have expanded (during the period in question) at roughly the same rate as GNP, with the exception of agriculture.

DYNAMIC EFFICIENCY
AND THE GROWTH
OF PRODUCTIVITY

A second criterion for evaluating the performance of economies is *dynamic efficiency,* which "relates to the community's capacity to add to its technological knowledge and to exploit such knowledge with increasing effect."[22] We use this criterion in addition to economic growth because as we just noted, the Soviet Union deliberately adopted a rapid growth strategy of high investment rates, high labor participation rates, borrowing of more advanced technology, and rapid expansion of education and training. Thus one would be surprised if the Soviets had *not* attained relatively high rates of economic growth. This is not to detract from the Soviet growth achievement, just to place it in its proper perspective.

In such a case, dynamic efficiency might prove a useful second

Table 28 **Annual Rates of Growth: Major Economic Sectors**

	USSR, 1928–1969		United States, 1947–1969	
	(1) Sector Growth	(2) Sector Growth ÷ GNP Growth	(3) Sector Growth	(4) Sector Growth ÷ GNP Growth
Agriculture	2.0	.39	1.5	.39
Industry	7.5	1.47	4.2	1.08
Construction	7.3	1.43	2.8	.72
Transportation and communications	8.4	1.65	4.3	1.10
Trade	4.2	.82	4.0	1.03
Services	4.1	.80	4.0	1.03
GNP	5.1		3.9	

SOURCES: R. Moorsteen and R. Powell, *The Soviet Capital Stock, 1928–62* (Homewood, Ill.: Irwin, 1966), pp. 622–624; Cohn, "General Growth Performance," *op. cit.,* p. 17; *The Economic Report of the President,* 1969, p. 207.

[22] Abram Bergson, *Planning and Productivity Under Soviet Socialism* (New York: Columbia University Press, 1968), p. 52.

performance criterion, for it measures the rate at which a country is able to increase the efficiency of resource utilization over time; that is, the rate of increase of the amount of output derived from a given amount of factor inputs. Dynamic efficiency can be measured only imperfectly and indirectly. Its most common measure is the rate of growth of output per unit of *combined* factor inputs.[23] A less general measure would be the rate of growth of output per unit of labor (or capital) input. One measures the rate of growth of output per unit of input by subtracting the growth rate of the input from the growth rate of output. For example, if GNP grows at 5 percent annually and combined factor inputs grow at 3 percent annually, the annual rate of growth of output per unit of combined factor input would be 2 percent.

From this description of total factor productivity, one can see that it provides only an indirect link to dynamic efficiency because one can only imperfectly measure the rates of growth of factor inputs in both qualitative and quantitative terms. For example, it is extremely difficult to measure changes in the quality of Soviet capital and labor force relative to such changes in the United States or other countries. Further, how does one measure nonconventional inputs such as management? As a result, only conventional inputs such as land, labor, and capital can be measured and generally only in quantitative terms.[24] The danger, therefore, is that important

[23] To determine the rate of growth of combined inputs—labor and capital— the individual growth rates of labor and capital, respectively, must be combined in some manner. In similar studies for Western countries, the two growth rates are generally combined by computing a weighted average, the weights being the labor and capital shares of total income. In the Soviet case, capital does not generate income; therefore there is no real "capital share" of total income. For this reason, "synthetic" factor shares have been used for the Soviet case, based largely upon factor shares found in Western countries. For examples of the use of "synthetic" factor shares, see Bergson, *The Economics of Soviet Planning* (New Haven, Conn.: Yale University Press, 1964), pp. 341–343; R. Moorsteen and R. Powell, *The Soviet Capital Stock, 1928–1962* (Homewood, Ill.: Irwin, 1966), pp. 264–266.

[24] Attempts have been made to adjust for quality differences and to measure nonconventional inputs, but they rest very heavily upon rather tenuous assumptions made by the researchers themselves. See, for example, Edward Denison, *Why Growth Rates Differ* (Washington, D.C.: The Brookings Institution, 1967). For an attempt to adjust Soviet inputs for quality differences, see Earl R. Brubaker, "The Age of Capital and Growth in the Soviet Nonagricultural Nonresidential Sector," *Soviet Studies*, vol. 21, no. 3 (January

changes in nonconventional inputs and qualitative changes in conventional inputs will be ignored, thus distorting the estimation of the growth of output per unit of input.

In Table 29, we relate several measures of the rates of growth of factor productivity in the Soviet Union, United States, and selected other countries both over the long-run and for the 1950 to 1962 period. The table includes both the rate of growth of output per unit of combined (capital and labor) input (column 5) and also the growth of output per unit of specific factor input; namely, labor productivity (column 6) and capital productivity (column 7).

Looking at both the long-term trends (panel A), and the 1950 to 1962 trends (panel B), we see that the Soviet Union distinguishes itself from the United States and other countries by a more rapid growth of both labor and capital—2.2 percent and 7.4 percent, respectively between 1928 and 1966. This reinforces our earlier point that one would expect more rapid Soviet output growth because of the more rapid growth of inputs—thus our hesitancy to use growth as our sole performance criterion. In the USSR, about 65 percent of long-term growth (column 1 ÷ column 4, panel A) is accounted for by growth of inputs; whereas in the United States and other countries (the United Kingdom is somewhat of an exception) a much smaller portion of growth can be attributed to the growth of inputs. The significance of this pattern is that Soviet growth has tended to be quite dependent upon an expanding labor force and capital stock, rather than upon expanding output per unit of input. Thus Soviet growth has tended to be *extensive* (based upon expanding inputs) rather than *intensive* (based upon better utilization of inputs)—a rather expensive growth pattern in terms of economic costs, for capital is expanded at the expense of current consumption and labor is expanded at the cost of leisure.

Turning to the rate of growth of output per unit of combined input (column 5), we see that the long-term Soviet rate (1928 to 1966) is perhaps somewhat below, or roughly equivalent to, the long-term productivity growth rates in the United States, France, Canada, and Norway. It is difficult to generalize on the basis of such narrow differences because the impact of wartime destruction on

1970), 350–359, and "Embodied Technology, The Asymptotic Behavior of Capital's Age, and Soviet Growth," *Review of Economics and Statistics,* vol. 50, no. 3 (August 1968), 304–311.

Table 29 **Annual Rates of Growth of Inputs and Productivity: USSR, United States, and Selected Countries** (annual growth rates)
Panel A: Long-term Trends

	(1)	(2)	(3)	(4)	(5)	(6)	(7)
					Output Per Unit of Combined Input (1–4)	Labor Productivity (1–2)	Capital Productivity (1–3)
	Output	Labor, Manhours	Capital	Combined Inputs			
USSR (GNP) 1928 to 1966	5.5[a]	2.2	7.4[b]	3.5[a]	2.0	3.3	−1.9
United States (GNP) 1929 to 1957	3.0	.5	1.0[b]	.6	2.3	2.5	2.0
United Kingdom (GDP) 1925–1929 to 1963	1.9	.8	1.8[b]	1.1	.8	1.1	.1
France (GDP) 1913 to 1966	2.3	−.5	2.0[b]	.2	2.2	2.8	.3
Canada (GNP) 1926 to 1956	3.9	.8	2.9[b]	1.2	2.7	3.1	1.0
Norway (GDP) 1899 to 1956	2.8	.3	2.5[b]	.7	2.1	2.5	.3

Panel B: Postwar Period, 1950–1962, National Income

	(1) Output (National Income)	(2) Labor, Manhours	(3) Reproducible Capital	(4) Combined Inputs	(5) Output Per Unit of Combined Input (1–4)	(6) Labor Productivity (1–2)	(7) Capital Productivity (1–3)
USSR	6.2	1.4	10.1[b]	3.6[d]	2.6	4.7	-3.9
United States	3.4	.8	3.9[c]	1.5	1.9	2.6	-.5
Denmark	3.4	.6	3.9[c]	1.4	1.9	2.8	-.5
France	4.7	.2	3.4[c]	1.0	3.7	4.5	1.3
Germany	7.3	1.7	5.4[c]	2.7	4.5	5.6	1.9
United Kingdom	2.4	.4	2.3[c]	.8	1.6	2.0	.1
Italy	6.0	.8	2.5[c]	1.3	4.7	5.2	3.5
Norway	3.5	-.1	3.4[c]	.8	2.7	3.6	.1
Netherlands	4.6	.9	4.0[c]	1.7	2.8	3.7	.6

[a] 1937 prices.
[b] Total fixed capital (average of net and gross stock for the USSR).
[c] Reproducible capital, average of gross and net stock.
[d] Combined using weights of .75 and .25 for labor and capital respectively.

SOURCES: Panel A: Moorsteen and Powell, *op. cit.*, pp. 38, 166, 315, 361–362, 365, and A. Becker, R. Moorsteen and R. Powell, *Soviet Capital Stock: Revisions and Extension, 1961–1967* (New Haven, Conn.: The Economic Growth Center, 1968), p. 11, 25, 26. Simon Kuznets, *Economic Growth of Nations, op. cit.*, p. 74. Panel B: Kuznets, *op. cit.*, p. 74. Abram Bergson, *Planning and Productivity Under Soviet Socialism* (New York: Columbia University Press, 1968), pp. 53, 94.

Soviet productivity is difficult to gauge, because such estimates are quite sensitive to measurement errors, and because the use of synthetic factor weights for the USSR requires that a margin of error be included. As far as the 1950 to 1962 period is concerned, the annual rate of growth of output per unit of combined input in the Soviet Union—2.6 percent—while it exceeded the American rate of 1.9 percent, is only average as far as Western Europe is concerned, being well exceeded by France, Germany, and Italy.

The same conclusion holds for the relative rate of growth of labor productivity in the Soviet Union (column 6). The long-term growth of Soviet labor productivity (3.3 percent annually) is slightly above the average rates in the other countries examined (but well above the United Kingdom). Soviet labor productivity growth in the postwar period was extremely rapid (4.7 percent annually) and far exceeded the American rate, but only matched its growth in France, Germany, and Italy.

Trends in Soviet capital productivity relative to the other countries (the rate of growth of output per unit of capital input) are interesting to note. The long-term growth rate of Soviet capital productivity is minus 1.9 percent annually, which indicates a rising capital-output ratio over the long-run. Of the surveyed countries, none has a long-term negative rate of growth of capital productivity, although the United States and Denmark registered negative rates of small magnitude during the postwar period. The declining productivity of the Soviet capital stock can perhaps be partially explained by the law of diminishing returns (in view of the very rapid growth of Soviet capital relative to labor),[25] and it could also possibly be an indication of the inefficient capital utilization discussed in the section on investment choice (Chapter Six).

In sum, both the long-term and postwar (1950–1962) comparisons show Soviet dynamic efficiency, as measured indirectly by the rate of growth of output per unit of combined input, to be neither exceptionally large nor small when compared to trends in the United States and other industrialized Western countries. Instead, Soviet productivity performance could be described as average. What these figures do indicate quite clearly is the extent to

[25] M. L. Weitzman, "Soviet Postwar Growth and Capital–Labor Substitution," *American Economic Review,* vol. 60, no. 4 (September 1970), 676–692.

which the fast Soviet growth rate may be attributable to the policy
of rapidly expanding inputs.

SOVIET STATIC EFFICIENCY

Not only is the changing efficiency of an economy over time—dynamic efficiency—a possible performance criterion, but one might
also consider its efficiency at one point in time—*static efficiency*.
The two concepts are interrelated in that an economy's dynamic
efficiency in the long-run will determine its static efficiency at a distant point in time, and static efficiency, in turn, may have an important impact upon dynamic efficiency in the long-run. In any
case, the efficiency of the economy today is a matter of concern
and interest. In this section, the focus is upon the static efficiency
of the Soviet economy relative to that of the United States and selected other market economies.

Static efficiency is defined intuitively by Bergson as ". . . the
degree to which *equity apart* [our italics], the community is in
fact able to exploit the economic opportunities that are open."[26]
The degree of static efficiency therefore will depend on the available stock of technological knowledge and on the effectiveness of
its utilization, both of which serve to define the economic opportunities open to the community at a given point in time.[27]

[26] Bergson, *Planning and Productivity under Soviet Socialism, op. cit.,* p. 15.
See also Joseph Berliner, "The Static Efficiency of the Soviet Economy,"
American Economic Review, vol. 54, no. 2 (May 1964), 480–490.
[27] This static efficiency concept can be illustrated using the Production Possibilities Schedule (PPS). If the economy is operating on its PPS (Point *A*),
then it has attained maximum static efficiency. If it operates below the PPS
(Point *B* for example), it has failed to attain maximum static efficiency.
The available stock of technological knowledge will determine the location
of the schedule, and an increase in this stock will move the schedule out.
Thus, with an increase in the stock of technological knowledge, Point *A*
will now be below the new PPS, and if the economy is to remain statically
efficient, it must advance to a higher point on the new PPS.

How then, is the relative static efficiency of the Soviet economy to be measured? Again, as in the case of dynamic efficiency, static efficiency can only be measured indirectly by comparing the magnitude of the output that is derived from a unit of "combined" factor inputs at one point in time. It is immediately obvious from our discussion of dynamic efficiency that such "factor productivity" comparisons measure static efficiency indirectly because inputs differ in quality and some of them cannot be measured at all. In measuring output per unit of input at one point in time, differences in climate and soil fertility (an important factor in determining agricultural productivity), scale differences, cultural factors, and many other variables that may or may not affect productivity tend to be ignored for they cannot readily be included.[28] There is yet another problem: to compute the relative magnitudes—as opposed to rates of growth—of output per unit of combined factor inputs suitable for cross-country comparisons, both output and factor inputs must be measured in a common unit. Soviet output must either be valued in foreign prices (American prices, for example) or the output of the other country must be valued in ruble prices. The same is true of combined factor inputs (land, labor, and capital). Index number relativity will affect such measurements because output mixes and relative prices vary among economies, and what one country produces in abundance at relatively low prices will likely be produced in smaller quantities at relatively higher prices by another country. In this manner, the relative GNP of one country valued in its own prices will be smaller than when valued in the prices of another country.[29]

A further problem in the Soviet case is that combined factor inputs (capital, land, and labor), which are measured by the total cost of such inputs, cannot be measured directly because capital and land fail to generate rent and interest—under the labor theory of value—as they do under capitalism. Therefore "synthetic" capi-

---

[28] Philip Hanson, op. cit., 332–343.

[29] An illustration and explanation of this phenomenon in American–Soviet GNP comparisons is found in Robert Campbell, "Problems of United States-Soviet Economic Comparisons," in *Comparisons of the United States and Soviet Economies* (Washington, D.C.: U.S. Government Printing Office, 1959), part I, pp. 13–30.

tal charges must be computed by applying an "arbitrary" rate of return to the value of net capital stock and the choice of this rate of return can significantly affect the outcome of factor productivity comparisons.[30]

Despite all the shortcomings noted above, we relate Abram Bergson's estimates of national income per unit of combined factor (labor and reproducible capital) input in American prices for the Soviet Union, the United States, and several European countries in 1960 (Table 30). The United States price weighted index was chosen because Soviet factor productivity makes its best showing using this variant.

The calculations of national income per unit of factor input show that the Soviet economy derives slightly less than fifty percent as much output per unit of combined input as does the American economy, about three-quarters as much as France, Germany, and the United Kingdom, and about the same amount of output per unit of input as Italy. Although it is possible that these computed productivity differentials could be accounted for by input quality

Table 30 **National Income Per Unit of Combined Factor (Labor and Reproducible Capital) Inputs, 1960 U.S. Price Weights (United States = 100)**

United States	100
France	62
Germany	63
United Kingdom	63
Italy	45
USSR	45

SOURCE: Abram Bergson, *Planning and Productivity Under Soviet Socialism* (New York: Columbia University Press, 1968), p. 22.

[30] Hanson, *op. cit.*, 340, argues that perhaps Soviet labor is in "excess supply" because of labor hoarding in industry and seasonal unemployment in agriculture. A low weight should therefore be attached to labor and a high weight to capital. This would raise Soviet factor productivity considerably relative to the United States because the Soviet labor force is larger than the American labor force.

differences[31] and by omitted factor inputs, such as land or entrepreneurship, this seems unlikely.[32]

Thus one would have to conclude that insofar as the level of output per unit of combined capital and labor input in the Soviet Union is low relative to the other countries surveyed (except Italy), the static efficiency of the Soviet economy leaves much to be desired. The sources of this static inefficiency have been described in Chapters Five and Six—the managerial bonus system, irrational prices, deficient investment allocation criteria, lack of incentives to innovate and introduce new technology, etc.—and may be more severe than the sources of economic inefficiency in the industrialized West. It is interesting to note that Soviet estimates show Soviet industrial efficiency (output per production worker) to be less than one-half of American industry.[33]

Just what does the low Soviet output per unit of input tell us about static efficiency in the Soviet Union? On the one hand, it might be noted that low output per unit of input and low levels of economic development tend to go together, and the Soviet Union, like Italy—whose factor productivity is also low—is less developed (in terms of development indicators like per capita income and percentage of rural population) than the other countries in Table 30. Thus the Soviet productivity deficit should perhaps be regarded as a function of the low level of development of the Soviet Union and not as an indicator of its static inefficiency.[34] On the other

[31] Bergson has made adjustments for quality differences in the Soviet and American labor forces—as indicated by the larger Soviet female labor force and lower educational levels of Soviet workers. These adjustments, which are admittedly very crude, raise Soviet factor productivity relative to the United States by about 10 percentage points, but fail to alter the overall conclusion of the relatively low productivity of the Soviet economy. Bergson, *The Economics of Soviet Planning, op. cit.,* p. 342.

[32] The major source of the low factor productivity of the Soviet economy seems to be the low productivity of the commerce and service sectors. On this, see Earl R. Brubaker, "A Sectoral Analysis of Efficiency under Market and Plan," *Soviet Studies,* vol. 23, no. 3 (January 1972), 443.

[33] Gertrude Schroeder, "The Economic Reform as a Spur to Technological Progress in the USSR," *Janrbuch der Wirtschaft Osteuropas* [Yearbook of Eastern European Economics] Band 2 (Munich: Gunther Olzog Verlag, 1971), p. 346.

[34] The problem of comparing the productivity performance of two countries at different levels of development can be illustrated using the Production Possibilities Schedule (PPS). The country at the higher level of development

hand, the growth of Soviet factor productivity over time (Table 29) has been only average when compared with other industrialized countries; therefore the Soviet Union does not seem to be closing its productivity gap as it gradually closes its development gap—a result that one would expect if low productivity were solely the result of low economic development.

The low level of static efficiency in the Soviet Union has evoked considerable discussion among Western students of the Soviet economy. We summarize briefly two representative points of view: On the one side, Alec Nove and Peter Wiles,[35] both English economists, argue that the Soviets deliberately sacrificed static efficiency to achieve their long-run political objectives—the restructuring of the economy, the transformation of property relations, the expansion of military power, and rapid economic growth. Static efficiency, they argue, could have been achieved only at the expense of these goals, by adopting a more gradual marginalist approach and by eliminating political control over economic decisions. Thus the static inefficiency of the Soviet economy today can be viewed as a deliberate policy decision, just as the rapid Soviet growth rate can be considered a deliberate policy choice of the Soviet leadership—with static inefficiency as the price that the Soviet leadership willingly paid for rapid economic development.

In opposition to this line of reasoning, Abram Bergson[36] argues that rapid economic development and static efficiency are

---

would have a higher PPS (*aa*) than the country at a lower level of development (*bb*). Thus both countries may be operating at maximum static efficiency (at points *A* and *B*), yet the computed productivity at *A* will be greater than at *B*.

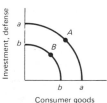

Consumer goods

[35] See Alec Nove, "The Politics of Economic Rationality," in *Economic Rationality and Soviet Politics* (New York: Praeger, 1964), p. 53; and P. J. D. Wiles, *The Political Economy of Communism* (London: Blackwell, 1963), chap. 11.

[36] See A. Bergson, *Planning and Productivity Under Soviet Socialism, op. cit.,* pp. 16–19, and *The Economics of Soviet Planning, op. cit.,* chap. 14.

not necessarily incompatible as Nove and Wiles maintain, for an economy with greater static efficiency will produce a larger output and, consequently, a larger volume of savings (with the same savings rate), which will promote economic growth. Bergson does grant, however, that in a centrally planned economy, the state may opt to promote growth by autonomously increasing the savings rate, through the introduction of forced savings, administrative economic controls, collectivization, and autarky—measures which may reduce static efficiency yet generate growth. If the state does so, however, it is at the expense of reduced living standards, which is in itself a significant cost to be considered in evaluating the performances of economies. According to Bergson, the basic question, therefore, should be: To what extent could similar rates of growth or slightly lower rates have been attained in the Soviet case through maximum utilization of resources (static efficiency) without sacrificing living standards?

One further aspect of the relative efficiency of the Soviet economy that fails to show up in output or input measures is that such figures often indicate output per unit of *employed* labor and capital inputs.[37] Although the Soviets do not publish aggregate unemployment figures, one can probably safely assume that aggregate unemployment in the Soviet Union is less than in the United States, where unemployment occasionally rises to 6 or 7 percent of the entire labor force, with 3 to 4 percent considered as normal. Thus unemployment is a major source of inefficient resource utilization in the United States that the Soviets have largely avoided, although the Soviets do seem to suffer from "under-employment" as discussed above. In addition, capital capacity in the United States also tends to stand idle during downturns in the business cycle. On the other hand, it is difficult to predict the magnitude of the waste of capital resources in the Soviet Union that results from the stockpiling of fixed and working capital by the Soviet manager for the sake of building a safety factor. In the American economy, such stockpiling adds to inventory costs and interest expenses, thereby reducing profits and is, therefore, avoided as much as possible.

[37] Hanson, *op. cit.,* 338.

An even thornier issue in estimating factor productivity concerns the relative quality of output. Factor productivity measures relate the volume of output per unit of input; whereas the output measures (especially in the case of Soviet consumer goods) inadequately reflect the relative quality of output that, according to numerous reports, in the Soviet Union is poor.[38] The production of a large quantity of defective goods using minimal inputs would show up well in factor productivity estimates, introducing a bias into such measures.

EQUITY OF INCOME DISTRIBUTION IN THE SOVIET UNION

A fourth performance criterion for evaluating economies is how "equitably" income is distributed among members of the population. Of all the suggested criteria, this is the most difficult to evaluate objectively because different individuals and different societies have different views on what constitutes an "equitable" or "inequitable" distribution of income. Some may argue that income is equitably distributed when divided equally; others may argue that equity requires large income differentials to reward risk, effort, and past frugality. Income derived from ownership of property is a very thorny question, for in the United States, for example, the largest income differences among spending units result from differences in property income as opposed to wage and salary income. Whether it is equitable to allow such disparities in property income is a subjective judgement, yet is crucial in contrasting equity in the Soviet Union and the United States. In view of these issues, we suggest that the definition of a "good" or "poor" income distribution must remain subjective over a fairly wide range.

The Soviets have not published much data on the distribution of income among families. The income distribution data that have been published omit collective farmers—roughly 18 percent of the

[38] Bergson, *The Economics of Soviet Planning, op. cit.,* pp. 293–297; and Philip Hanson, *The Consumer in the Soviet Economy* (Evanston, Ill.: Northwestern University Press, 1968), p. 63.

Soviet labor force[39]—the lowest paid workers in the Soviet Union.[40] Therefore the published income distribution data would probably *overstate* the equality of income distribution in the USSR.[41] From the scattered evidence that is available on industrial wage income, we note that Soviet wage differentials within industrial branches between high and low paid workers during the 1930s and early 1950s were probably greater than in the United States, but since the mid-1950s, Soviet differentials have been narrowed substantially until they are now probably smaller than American differentials. In general, the trend in recent years has been toward the concept of "equal pay for equal work" with wages to be determined by job content—working conditions, skill requirements, on-the-job incentives—rather than by some measure of productivity, which may be viewed as an attempt to introduce more equity into Soviet wage determination.[42] Such cross-country wage differential comparisons are quite crude and inexact, but the important point is that Soviet industrial wage differentials have at times been as large as in the United States. This result is in keeping with the Marxian theory of income distribution in the transitional stage of socialism, during which the worker's contribution to society should determine his share of society's output: inequality of income distribution would only be eliminated when society attains a higher stage of socialism—a state of absolute abundance—when distribution will proceed according to need.[43]

[39] Murray Feshbach and Stephen Rapawy, "Labor and Wages," in *Economic Performance and the Military Burden in the Soviet Union* (Washington, D.C.: U.S. Government Printing Office, 1970), p. 75.

[40] David Bronson and Constance Krueger, "The Revolution in Soviet Farm and Household Income, 1953–1967," in James R. Millar, ed., *The Soviet Rural Community* (Urbana: University of Illinois Press, 1971), p. 229.

[41] P. J. D. Wiles and Stefan Markowski, "Income Distribution Under Communism and Capitalism," *Soviet Studies,* vol. 22, nos. 3 and 4 (January, April 1971), 244–369, 487–511.

[42] Leonard J. Kirsch, *Soviet Wages: Changes in Structure and Administration Since 1956* (Cambridge, Mass.: MIT Press, 1972), chaps. 1 and 8; Murray Yanowitch, "The Soviet Income Revolution," *Slavic Review,* vol. 22, no. 4 (December 1963), reprinted in M. Bornstein and D. Fusfeld, eds., *The Soviet Economy,* 2nd ed. (Homewood, Ill.: Irwin, 1966), pp. 228–241; Abram Bergson, *The Economics of Soviet Planning, op. cit.,* pp. 106–120; Wiles and Markowski, *op. cit.,* 501–507.

[43] Abram Bergson, "Principles of Socialist Wages," in *Essays in Normative Economics* (Cambridge, Mass.: Harvard University, Belknap Press, 1966).

When one considers the overall distribution of income among families as opposed to industrial wage income alone, it is fairly clear that income is distributed much more equally in the Soviet Union than in the United States. The reason for this is the lack of property income in the Soviet Union, where all income-earning property (with some minor exceptions) is owned by the state. As we have noted, the existence of property income explains the wide disparities in the American income distribution. On the basis of very sketchy Soviet data on the distribution of wages and salaries (omitting collective farm families),[44] one can estimate that the share of per capita income received by the top 10 percent of spending units in the USSR (1966) was approximately 4.5 times that of the lowest 10 percent. This figure represents a dramatic decline from the 1946 Soviet figure of 14 times. On the other hand, the 1967 figure for the entire United States economy was about 28 to 1.[45] As far as the overall distribution of income in the Soviet Union—including collective farm incomes—is concerned, it is doubtful that it varies too dramatically from the above cited distribution, but it would probably be more unequal. There is, in fact, some evidence from an unidentified Soviet sample, which likely includes collective farm families, that the total Soviet income distribution is more unequal than the above published figures indicate.[46] Further factors complicating evaluation of the Soviet income distribution are the widespread use of official cars, dachas (summer homes), foreign vacations, and other fringe benefits by upper income groups that do not enter such estimates. On the other side, many medical, educational, and social services are provided free of charge to low income groups, which also do not enter into such estimates but would tend to equalize real incomes.

Our overall conclusion is that income is distributed more equally in the Soviet Union than in the United States, largely owing to the absence of property income in the USSR. Although there is some evidence to suggest that, in general, income tends to be distributed more equally in the socialist bloc countries than in Western market economies,[47] the underlying data are still sketchy at best.

[44] Wiles and Markowski, *op. cit.*, 503. We construct this estimate from their Table 27.
[45] *Statistical Abstract of the U.S., 1969,* p. 321.
[46] Wiles and Markowski, *op. cit.*, 507.
[47] *Ibid.*, 507.

CONSUMER WELFARE
IN THE SOVIET UNION

How well an economy meets the material wants and needs of its population with its *given productive capacity* is yet another way to evaluate economic performance. By "material wants and needs," we refer to those that can be satisfied through the consumption of material goods and services; items relating to mental and spiritual well-being are omitted, even though they are potentially important in determining overall welfare.

The level of consumer satisfaction in any given country must be evaluated in terms of existing productive capacity, for countries rich in terms of productive potential would naturally be expected to provide higher living standards than poor countries. This fact should be kept in mind throughout this section.

If one attempts to measure the level of consumer satisfaction in the Soviet Union relative to that of the United States or Western Europe, one encounters difficulties. First, the most frequently used measure of the relative level of consumer satisfaction is the per capita quantities of consumer goods and services made available to the consumer. According to this standard, either per capita quantities of selected consumer goods and services or aggregate per capita consumption may be compared. Both measures have their own deficiencies aside from the almost impossible task of measuring quality differences. If one compares per capita consumption of selected commodities, one must realize that consumption patterns vary according to the level of development and cultural differences. For example, the per capita consumption of wheat products in the Soviet Union exceeds that of the United States, but the per capita consumption of most personal services and consumer durables in the United States exceeds that of the USSR. In this example, these differences are explained, to a great extent, by differences in per capita income, which means that single consumption indicators can provide misleading impressions of consumer welfare. The aggregative measure—total per capita consumption—must be measured in value terms; therefore, in comparisons between two countries the prices of one country must be used to weigh the quantities of consumer goods and services made available in both countries. Yet relative consumer prices vary among countries: commodities that are important consumption items in one country (where the price is relatively cheap) tend to be unimportant in another country (where the price is relatively expensive). Thus the relative per capita consumption level of one country will be *higher* when valued in the prices of a second country and vice versa—another example of index number relativity.

A further problem in the measurement of consumer satisfaction is that *average* consumption figures veil the underlying distribution of goods and services among the population, and the nature of this distribution has a great deal to do with the level of consumer satisfaction. Prominent Western economists have argued that relative, not absolute, consumption levels are most important in determining consumer satisfaction, for individuals tend to judge their own economic well-being relative to the level of living of their neighbors.[48] If income is distributed fairly evenly, the chances of feeling deprived relative to someone else are smaller than if income is unevenly distributed. For example, in 1957, the average personal income of the poorest fifth of American families was about the same as *average* income in the Soviet Union.[49] Is then the proper conclusion that the American poor are as "well-off" as the average Soviet citizen? In terms of how well both are provisioned with physical quantities of goods and services (index number problems aside), the answer may be yes, yet in terms of perceived welfare levels, the answer is probably no, because the American poor would feel relatively deprived owing to the existence of much higher living standards around them.

Another problem in evaluating Soviet consumer welfare involves the relatively large share of communal consumption in the Soviet Union. Communal consumption—for example, communal services such as health care and education provided free of charge —accounts for a substantial share of total consumption in the So-

[48] James Duesenberry, *Income, Saving and the Theory of Consumer Behavior* (Cambridge, Mass.: Harvard University Press, 1949).
[49] Janet Chapman, "Consumption," in Abram Bergson and Simon Kuznets, eds., *Economic Trends in the Soviet Union* (Cambridge, Mass.: Harvard University Press, 1963).

viet Union.[50] Such services are, of course, provided free of charge and are not subject to a market test as to the value of the satisfaction they provide. In fact, their value is determined by the costs of supplying them. Thus it is difficult to compare consumption levels of countries having different shares of communal consumption.

The foregoing discussion points to the loose relationship between the consumption of commodities and the level of satisfaction derived therefrom; yet it is perceived satisfaction that is of most interest. Thus it is possible to argue (as the Soviets have done) that the underprovisioning of the Soviet consumer relative to American or Western European standards does not imply lower levels of satisfaction, because of the new social consciousness of the Soviet man, who will accept this as a necessary cost of building socialism, and whose recognition of his patriotism enhances his perceived level of welfare. The validity of such arguments is well outside the scope of this work.

With the above reservations in mind, we present estimates of total per capita consumption in the Soviet Union (including communal services) as a percent of total per capita consumption in the United States and several other countries (Table 31). All figures are calculated in United States prices to present the Soviet figures in the most favorable light (in view of index number relativity). While these figures are admittedly crude measures of the relative quantities of goods and services consumed per capita (see the notes to Table 31), they should impart rough orders of magnitude.

The striking feature of Soviet per capita consumption is that it is quite low relative to the United States, the United Kingdom, France, and West Germany, both in 1955 and 1968, being roughly one-third of the American level and roughly one-half of the British, French, and West German levels during this period. Soviet consumption per capita compares more favorably with Italy, being roughly three-quarters of the Italian level.

We suggested above that consumer welfare must be evaluated not in terms of absolute magnitudes but relative to productive

[50] Between 1937 and 1964, communal consumption accounted for between 8 and 9 percent of Soviet GNP. In the United States, it accounts for about 3 per cent (1956). See Bergson, *The Real National Income of Soviet Russia Since 1928, op. cit.,* p. 237. Abraham Becker, *Soviet National Income, 1958– 1964* (Berkeley: University of California Press, 1969), p. 220. Janet Chapman, "Consumption," in Bergson and Kuznets, *op. cit.,* p. 263.

Table 31 **Total Per Capita Consumption and Per Capita GNP of the Soviet Union as a Percent of the United States and Other Countries, 1955 and 1968 (valued in United States prices)**

USSR as a Percent of:	1955		1968	
	Total Per Capita Consumption	GNP Per Capita	Total Per Capita Consumption	GNP Per Capita
United States	27	36	33	47
United Kingdom	41	53	52	72
France	47	59	—	—
Germany	48	57	49	63
Italy	79	94	75	98

METHODOLOGY: Total Soviet per capita consumption as a percent of United States consumption (valued in United States prices) in 1955 and 1968 (reference 1) serves as the basis for further comparisons. Total consumption per capita in the Soviet Union relative to the other countries is computed from the relation of total consumption per capita in these countries relative to the United States. This is estimated by extrapolating the Gilbert and Kravis 1955 estimates (reference 3) using constant price consumption indexes (reference 2) adjusted for population changes. Per capita GNP figures were estimated in the same manner.

SOURCES: (1) *Economic Performance and the Military Burden in the Soviet Union, op. cit.*, p. 14, p. 97. (2) United Nations, *Yearbook of National Accounts Statistics* (1969). (3) M. Gilbert and Associates, *Comparative National Products and Price Levels* (Paris: Organization for European Economic Cooperation), p. 36.

capacity. Thus one should ask to what extent the relatively low Soviet per capita consumption is a consequence of relatively low per capita GNP. Table 31 indicates that the major portion of the low Soviet per capita consumption can be accounted for by low per capita GNP, which shows that, even if the Soviets had devoted the same proportion of their resources to consumption as the other countries shown, there would still be a substantial "gap" in Soviet per capita consumption.[51] In all cases, Soviet per capita consumption compares much less favorably than per capita GNP, which shows that the Soviets directed a relatively larger share of total

[51] For further evidence on the Soviet consumption "gap," see Paul Gregory, *Socialist and Nonsocialist Industrialization Patterns* (New York: Praeger, 1971), p. 152.

Table 32 **Total Investment Expenditures as a Percent of GNP,
USSR and Selected Countries, 1964**
(Soviet data in factor cost, other data in market prices)

USSR	35
United States	17
France	23
Germany	28
United Kingdom	19
Italy	22
Japan	39

SOURCE: Abraham Becker, *Soviet National Income, 1958–1964* (Berkeley: University of California Press, 1969), pp. 220, 271.

resources to nonconsumption items such as investment and defense, and this was, of course, an administrative decision. As Table 32 indicates, the Soviets devote a much larger share of GNP to investment than the major Western countries. The sole exception is Japan, which devotes only a negligible proportion of its resources to defense. Despite the virtual equality of per capita GNPs in the USSR and Italy, Soviet per capita consumption is still about three-quarters of the Italian level.

The reader should now well understand the importance of using multiple criteria to evaluate economies. The Soviet economy grew at such a rapid pace largely because it was decided to devote labor and capital resources to this pursuit. Per capita consumption remained below levels attainable from Soviet productive capacity as a consequence of these policies—thus a tradeoff between growth and consumption. In a long-run sense, the two are not incompatible, for economic growth will raise productive capacity, which can eventually be used to raise consumption levels.

The *structure* of Soviet consumption reflects both the relatively low per capita income of the Soviet Union and the efforts of the state to educate and keep the population healthy. Relative to the United States, Soviet per capita consumption compares more favorably in necessities such as basic food products and health care than in non-necessities such as durable goods. For example, Soviet per capita consumption of food products and health and education services are both 57 percent of the American level (1968); whereas, for durable goods, the figure is 9 percent. A few individual comparisons bring this point home: In 1968, the average caloric intake of grain products and potatoes in the USSR exceeded that of the United States; yet the caloric intake of meat and fish was less than 50 percent of the United States figure and this latter figure does not take quality differences into consideration—which may be substantial. In 1968, there were 412 automobiles per 1000 persons in the United States; the Soviet figure was 5 per 1000. On the other hand, in the Soviet Union the number of doctors per person, hospital beds per person, and teachers per person exceeds that of the United States. The Soviet consumer remains relatively deprived as far as housing is concerned. The 1969 per capita availability of 77 square feet of housing space, although it represents a 20 percent improvement since 1960, is still well below the 97 square-foot minimum standard required for health and decency as established by Soviet authorities.[52]

Let us now consider to what extent the Soviets have been able to reduce their per capita consumption "gap" between 1928 and the present. This is an important question because the current low Soviet consumption level would seem less significant if it were being steadily eliminated. We therefore compare the long-term growth rate of per capita consumption (including communal services) in the Soviet Union during the plan era with comparable United States rates (Table 33).

Table 33 indicates the very respectable performance of Soviet per capita consumption during the plan era as measured against long-term United States rates. The long-term Soviet rate of 2.8 percent (1928–1969) far exceeds the comparable rate for the United States during the same period. It should be noted, however, that the United States rate from the Civil War to the Great Depression (1869–1873 to 1927–1929) compares more favorably with the Soviet plan era rate. The rate of growth of Soviet consumption during the first two Five Year Plans (1928–1937) was very slow compared with the postwar rate. Thus the fairly high long-term Soviet growth rate of per capita consumption is an average

[52] All of the above figures are from David W. Bronson and Barbara S. Severin, "Consumer Welfare," in *Economic Performance and the Military Burden in the Soviet Union, op. cit.*, pp. 97–98.

Table 33 **Annual Rates of Growth of Per Capita Consumption: USSR, 1928–1969—United States, 1869–1969 (including communal services)**

USSR		United States	
1928–1969	2.8	1869–1873 to 1927–1929	2.4
1928–1937	1.1	1929–1969	1.7
1950–1969	4.5	1950–1969	2.3

SOURCES: Janet Chapman, "Consumption" in Abram Bergson and Simon Kuznets, eds., *Economic Trends in the Soviet Union* (Cambridge, Mass.: Harvard University Press, 1963), pp. 238, 245–246; David W. Bronson and Barbara S. Severin, "Consumer Welfare" in *Economic Performance and the Military Burden in the Soviet Union, op. cit.,* p. 97. The Soviet figures are in 1937 factor cost for the 1928 to 1958 period and in 1955 weights for 1958 to 1969. The United States figures are from *Historical Statistics of the United States, Colonial Times to 1957,* pp. 7, 144; *Statistical Abstract of the U.S., 1970,* p. xiii; *The Economic Report of the President, 1970,* p. 178. The 1869–1873 to 1927–1929 figures are in 1929 dollars. The 1929–1969 figures are in 1958 dollars.

of the slow growth of per capita consumption during the 1930s and of the rapid growth of the postwar period.

To sum up trends in Soviet per capita consumption, we note that per capita consumption in the Soviet Union is low compared to consumption levels in the U.S. and Western Europe. The major portion of the Soviet consumption gap can be accounted for by low per capita income but some of it is attributable to the administrative decision to devote a relatively larger proportion of total resources to investment. The pattern of Soviet consumption also reflects the decision of Soviet authorities to de-emphasize nonnecessities and to concentrate on essential goods and health and education, all of which are required to maintain and increase the productivity of the Soviet labor force. Looking at trends in Soviet consumption over time, one must conclude that the rate of growth of per capita consumption in the Soviet Union during the plan era has been quite respectable, far exceeding comparable United States rates. If this trend continues, the consumption gap will continue to be gradually reduced in the future, just as it has been since the end of World War II. In this sense, there may be some merit to the Soviet argument that living standards can be raised over the long-run by sacrificing current consumption.

SOVIET ENVIRONMENTAL QUALITY

Although market economies have made only limited practical progress towards the resolution of environmental problems, their existence has been the subject of considerable theoretical analysis. Pollution is said to arise as an *externality* of the system, since under certain circumstances, the price system in effect breaks down, and where decision-making is decentralized under a profit guidance system involving private ownership, private costs and benefits may well diverge from social costs and benefits.[53] But what about pollution under different resource allocation arrangements where the price system plays a much less important role, as in the Soviet case?

This is the question posed in this final section of our evaluation of Soviet economic performance: Has the Soviet economic system succeeded in providing a "better" environment than its market economy counterparts? We address ourselves to this question by first considering the theory of *environmental disruption* (ED) under Soviet command socialism. Then we turn to actual environmental disruption in the Soviet Union.

Advocates of socialism have long argued on theoretical grounds that ED will not arise in a socialist society. Although the specifics of various arguments have varied, the essential thread is the *level* of decision-making in such a system. Where decisions are centralized and the objective function—the outcome that planners are trying to achieve—for the economy includes environmental quality, there need never be externalities since there is literally nothing external to the decision-makers. A similar argument could be made for local decision-making if the planners develop an incentive structure that ensures the harmony of local decisions with central goals (assuming the necessary concomitant of perfect information flows at all levels). It is necessary, of course, that appropri-

---

[53] See, for example, Karl W. Kapp, "Social Costs of Business Enterprises," in Marshall Goldman, *Ecology and Economics, Controlling Pollution in the 1970s* (Englewood Cliffs, N.J.: Prentice-Hall, 1972), pp. 125–133.

ate resource valuations, which reflect central goals, be available to the central decision-makers.[54]

Oskar Lange, the classic advocate of the socialist cause, argues in his famous article *On the Economic Theory of Socialism,*[55] that under socialism, the price system will be more comprehensive, and, in effect, a high value will be placed by the CPB upon a clean environment. Maurice Dobb[56] makes a similar argument when he suggests that although information availability and digestion may be a problem in the real world, nevertheless socialist planners will tend to make decisions with maximum global vision and an eye to their environmental impact. Jan Tinbergen, the noted Dutch economist, has also endorsed the notion that, in general, decisions made at the highest possible levels will minimize the problem of externalities.[57]

Such theoretical arguments to the contrary, it is becoming a well-documented fact that environmental disruption is, in fact, a serious problem in the Soviet Union.[58] Thus the Soviet press and literature abound with cases of soil erosion, poisoning of rivers and lakes with industrial effluents and chemical fertilizers, industrial air pollution, and so on—problems that have become too common in the industrialized West. Growing concern in the Soviet Union is reflected in the formation of conservationist groups, in-

[54] Arthur Wright, "Environmental Disruption and Economic Systems: An Attempt at an Analytical Framework," *The ASTE Bulletin,* vol. 13, no. 1 (Spring 1971), 11–12.

[55] Benjamin E. Lippincott, ed., *On the Economic Theory of Socialism* (Minneapolis: University of Minnesota Press, 1938), pp. 103 ff., reprinted by McGraw-Hill, 1964.

[56] Maurice Dobb, *Welfare Economics and the Economics of Socialism* (Cambridge: Cambridge University Press, 1969), p. 133.

[57] For a discussion of this point, see Dobb, *op. cit.,* pp. 133–134; for a survey of theorizing on environmental quality, see Marshall I. Goldman, *The Spoils of Progress: Environmental Pollution in the Soviet Union* (Cambridge, Mass.: MIT Press, 1972), pp. 12–22.

[58] As Marshall Goldman has written, "Most conservationists and social writers are unaware that the USSR has environmental disruption that is as extensive and severe as ours." See Goldman, *op. cit.,* p. 2; also Marshall I. Goldman, "Externalities and the Race for Economic Growth in the Soviet Union: Will the Environment Ever Win?" *Journal of Political Economy,* vol. 80, no. 2 (March/April, 1972); Keith Bush, "Environmental Disruption: The Soviet Response," *L'Est,* no. 2 (June 1972).

creasing press attention, and the passage of a number of (generally ineffective) laws concerned with environmental quality.[59]

Pursuing our evaluation of Soviet economic performance a step further to include environmental disruption, it would be difficult to compare the *stock* of pollution in the Soviet Union vis-à-vis other countries in the absence of generally accepted measurement standards. In Soviet-American comparisons, however, there is some agreement that in terms of the total stock of pollution (as opposed to the annual flow of pollution) the Soviet Union has a less serious problem. This however should not be taken to mean that the Soviet economy or command socialist economies in general have coped better with environmental disruption; rather that one might expect a lower level of environmental disruption in countries at lower stages of development, be they capitalist or socialist. The Soviet Union being at a lower stage of development— in terms of per capita income—than the United States and the major industrialized Western European countries should therefore have a smaller stock of environmental pollution.

There is ample evidence of this. The Soviets have yet to reach the age of mass motoring, with the current stock of passenger automobiles roughly equivalent to American 1913 levels.[60] The flush toilet, with its tremendous demands on fresh water, is still not universal in Soviet urban housing.[61] The density of population is still relatively low. Packaging in light industries and food industries is still a rarity, thus reducing the solid waste disposal problem that has plagued industrialized Western countries.[62] The fact that there is concern about such problems suggests that the Soviet Union is passing rapidly from the stage so typical of less developed countries, where environmental problems are viewed as distinctly secondary to economic growth and as a phenomenon with which only rich countries can concern themselves.

[59] Although the power of the state and the Soviet view of the superiority of the public sector should be positive forces in the control of environmental disruption, the specific techniques used in the Soviet case, notably administrative penalties and criminal prosecution, seem to have been most ineffective. On this see Goldman, *The Spoils of Progress, op. cit.,* pp. 28–37.
[60] Bush, *op. cit.*
[61] *Ibid.*
[62] *Ibid.*

Because environmental disruption does seem to be a concomitant of the industrialization process itself, it is difficult to evaluate the performance of the Soviet system in this regard without some quantifiable notion of what constitutes a "normal" level of pollution for a given level of economic development. Only in this manner could one judge whether the Soviet economy has performed "better" or "worse" in providing a suitable environment. In some areas, the Soviet system may have natural advantages over market economies—for example, the unwillingness of Soviet planners to meet the pent-up demand for private automobiles and their stress upon cheap mass urban transit, the ability of urban and regional planners to develop master plans for areas independently of private developers, the stress on multifamily dwellings that make use of centrally supplied warm water for washing and heating, and so on.[63] However, it is almost impossible to draw an overall balance from such isolated examples.

Why then is there pollution in the Soviet economy?[64] Three possible reasons might be considered. First, it may be that planners have simply not been concerned with environmental quality until the level of development became such that, in combination with the international demonstration effect, its presence becomes pervasive. More important, however, is the possibility that environmental quality has been discarded as one of the costs of rapid economic growth. In effect, we might consider the Soviets as having purchased rapid growth in the short-run by simply not recognizing the real costs of that growth—in effect, postponing some of the costs by letting them accumulate in the form of a stock of pollution. Thus disinvestment in the environment would be considered as a rather typical aspect of Soviet economic development just as it has characterized economic growth generally in market economies. This could well be a very negative feature of rapid development models for the presently less developed countries, especially as the developed countries bring pressure to bear for the preservation of the environment.

[63] *Ibid.*

[64] It might be noted that recent Soviet discussion tends not to stress the absence of pollution on theoretical grounds mentioned here, but rather tends to admit the existence of pollution, arguing that socialism will more effectively eradicate the problem.

A second factor leading to environmental disruption in the Soviet Union may be the breakdown of *valuation*—a problem not unique to the Soviet Union. Planners are simply unaware of appropriate resource valuations, including the costs of environmental disruption, and hence may be unable to allocate them in a "rational" manner even if they so desired. This, in effect, is a breakdown of the information mechanism common to both market and planned economies. We suggest that this is a likely partial explanation in view of the Soviets' inability to compute scarcity prices in general either with or without social costs.[65] In the Soviet context, the valuation problem is further complicated by Marxian theory, which is prejudiced against charging for natural resources (the labor theory of value).

Third and possibly most important, perfectly centralized decision-making as visualized in the idealized versions of the socialist economic model has not proved to be practical in the real world. Yet the myth of fully centralized decision-making in the Soviet Union persists as gallantly as that of perfect competition. In fact, most crucial economic decisions are made not by a small group of planners at the apex of the planning hierarchy who take the broad overview of the economy, but by ministerial and regional authorities, and by plant managers, none of whom can see (or cares to see) the total impact of his actions. In effect, there has been no pressure group concerned with the environment. Instead, administrators and managers are concerned with performing well in line with directives given them by their superiors, and, as we noted above, success in the Soviet economy has been determined primarily on the basis of fulfilling output goals. Less easily quantifiable goals (especially in view of the price system) such as cost reductions, innovations, and environmental quality have not played a role in influencing decision-making. Thus, where environmental groups have existed in the Soviet Union, they find themselves in the awkward position of having to lobby against regional *Gosplan* organizations, national ministries, or even the party itself on projects

[65] Some Soviet economists have argued that each factory should be accountable for both direct *and* social costs. However, such has not been the case, primarily due to the absence of appropriate cost measurement and the potential conflict with Marxian ideology. On this see Goldman, *The Spoils of Progress, op. cit.*, pp. 46 ff.

that create environmental disruption,[66] in other words, against the very organizations that in theory are to prevent environmental disruption from taking place. In fact, there is no all-union agency for protecting the environment. Rather environmental protection has tended to be placed in the hands of various agencies, all with limited powers.

In a recent study of Soviet pollution, Marshall Goldman has argued that in the Soviet case, the centralization of power has, as we have noted, meant neglect of the environment. Goldman notes, however, that this position could be reversed, and in a number of important areas the Soviet political apparatus could be a very positive force in the prevention of environmental disruption.[67] Thus the provision of heat and hot water through centralized systems in large cities, zoning and plant location, de-emphasis of obsolescence of consumer goods, provision of parks and sewage recycling are all areas where a centralized political structure may be advantageous.[68] Thus it may be that Soviet leaders have consciously purchased rapid growth at the expense of the environment. Indeed, the Soviet government is increasingly stressing the need for preservation of the environment. It remains, however, to see how effectively verbal pressure will be translated into action.

[66] The Ministry of Power's handling of Lake Baikal is a case in point. Despite protests from residents concerning the environmental damage that such a project would cause, dam construction was pushed through, although other sources of electricity were already available at cheaper cost. Goldman, "Externalities," *op. cit.* Another case in point is the Central Committee's irrigation program that calls for the diversion of Siberian rivers to irrigate dry regions in Kazakhstan and Central Asia, which will have an important impact on the climate of the Far North. On this see Bush, *op. cit.*

[67] The discussion here is based on Goldman, *The Spoils of Progress, op. cit.,* pp. 272 ff.

[68] It is ironic to note that in most of these areas—with the possible exception of Soviet experiments with sewage treatment and central provision of heat— Soviet performance has been inferior to that of Western market economies. For example, the number and size of preserves (parkland) has declined in the Soviet Union in recent years, and as a portion of total land, preserves account for .28 percent in the Soviet Union (1966), 1.5 percent in the United States, 1.5 percent in Canada, 4 percent in Great Britain, and 6.9 percent in Japan. See *ibid.,* p. 274.

Selected Bibliography

OVERALL EVALUATION PROBLEMS

Bela Belassa, *The Hungarian Experience in Economic Planning* (New Haven, Conn.: Yale University Press, 1959), pp. 5–24.

Abram Bergson, "East–West Comparisons and Comparative Economic Systems: A Reply," *Soviet Studies,* vol. 23, no. 2 (October 1971), 282–295.

Abram Bergson, *The Economics of Soviet Planning* (New Haven, Conn.: Yale University Press, 1964), chap. 14.

Abram Bergson, "National Income," in Abram Bergson and Simon Kuznets, eds., *Economic Trends in the Soviet Union* (Cambridge, Mass.: Harvard University Press, 1963), pp. 1–37.

Robert Campbell et al., "Methodological Problems Comparing the US and USSR Economies," in Joint Economic Committee, *Soviet Economic Prospects for the Seventies* (Washington, D.C.: U.S. Government Printing Office, 1973), pp. 122–146.

Alexander Eckstein, ed., *Comparison of Economic Systems* (Berkeley and Los Angeles: University of California Press, 1971).

Philip Hanson, "East–West Comparisons and Comparative Economic Systems," *Soviet Studies,* vol. 22, no. 3 (January 1971).

Vladimir G. Treml and John P. Hardt, eds., *Soviet Economic Statistics* (Durham, N.C.: Duke University Press, 1972).

Charles K. Wilber, "Economic Development, Central Planning, and Allocative Efficiency," *Yearbook of East-European Economics* (Munich: Günther Olzog Verlag, 1971), pp. 221–246.

SOVIET ECONOMIC GROWTH

Abraham Becker, *Soviet National Income, 1958–1964* (Berkeley: University of California Press, 1969).

Abram Bergson, *The Real National Income of Soviet Russia Since 1928* (Cambridge, Mass.: Harvard University Press, 1961).

M. Bornstein, "A Comparison of Soviet and United States National Product," in M. Bornstein and D. Fusfeld, eds., *The Soviet Economy* (Homewood, Ill.: Irwin, 1962).

Stanley Cohn, "General Growth Performance of the Soviet Economy," in *Economic Performance and the Military Burden in the Soviet Union* (Washington, D.C.: U.S. Government Printing Office, 1970).

Stanley Cohn, *Economic Development in the Soviet Union* (Lexington, Mass.: Heath, 1969), chap. 7.

A. L. Vainshtein, *Narodnii dokhod Rossi i SSSR* [The national income of Russia and the USSR] (Moscow: 1969).

DYNAMIC EFFICIENCY AND THE GROWTH OF PRODUCTIVITY

Abram Bergson, "Development Under Two Systems: Comparative Productivity Growth Since 1950," *World Politics,* vol. 23, no. 4 (July 1971), 579–617.

Abram Bergson, *Planning and Productivity Under Soviet Socialism* (New York: Columbia University Press, 1968).

Earl Brubaker, "Embodied Technology, the Asymptotic Behavior of Capital's Age, and Soviet Growth," *Review of Economics and Statistics,* vol. 50, no. 3 (August 1968), 304–311.

R. Moorsteen and R. Powell, *The Soviet Capital Stock, 1928–1962* (Homewood, Ill.: Irwin, 1966).

SOVIET STATIC EFFICIENCY

Abram Bergson, "Comparative Productivity and Efficiency in the USA and USSR," in Alexander Eckstein, ed., *The Comparison of Economic Systems* (Berkeley: University of California Press, 1971), pp. 161–218.

Abram Bergson, *Planning and Productivity Under Soviet Socialism* (New York: Columbia University Press, 1968).

Abram Bergson, *The Economics of Soviet Planning* (New Haven, Conn.: Yale University Press, 1964), chap. 14.

Joseph Berliner, "The Static Efficiency of the Soviet Economy," *American Economic Review,* vol. 54, no. 2 (May 1964), 480–489.

Evsey Domar, "On the Measurement of Comparative Efficiency," in Alexander Eckstein, ed., *The Comparison of Economic Systems* (Berkeley: University of California Press, 1971), pp. 219–232.

EQUITY OF INCOME DISTRIBUTION IN THE SOVIET UNION

Abram Bergson, *The Structure of Soviet Wages* (Cambridge, Mass.: Harvard University Press, 1944).

P. J. D. Wiles and Stefan Markowski, "Income Distribution Under Communism and Capitalism: Some Facts About Poland, the U.K., the USA and the USSR," *Soviet Studies,* vol. 22, nos. 3 and 4 (January, April 1971), 344–369, 487–511.

Murray Yanowitch, "The Soviet Income Revolution," *Slavic Review,* vol. 22, no. 4 (December 1963).

CONSUMER WELFARE IN THE SOVIET UNION

David W. Bronson and Barbara S. Severin, "Soviet Consumer Welfare: The Brezhnev Era," in Joint Economic Committee, *Soviet Economic Prospects for the Seventies* (Washington, D.C.: U.S. Government Printing Office, 1973), pp. 376–403.

David W. Bronson and Barbara S. Severin, "Consumer Welfare," in *Economic Performance and the Military Burden in the Soviet Union* (Washington, D.C.: U.S. Government Printing Office, 1973), pp. 93–99.

Janet Chapman, "Consumption," in Abram Bergson and Simon Kuznets, eds., *Economic Trends in the Soviet Union* (Cambridge, Mass.: Harvard University Press, 1963), pp. 235–282.

Janet Chapman, *Real Wages in the Soviet Union* (Cambridge, Mass.: Harvard University Press, 1963).

Bernice Q. Madison, "Social Services: Families and Children in the Soviet Union Since 1967," *Slavic Review,* vol. 31, no. 4 (December 1972), 831–852.

Bernice Q. Madison, *Social Welfare in the Soviet Union* (Stanford, Calif.: Stanford University Press, 1968).

Robert J. Osborn, *Soviet Social Policies: Welfare, Equality, and Community* (Homewood, Ill.: The Dorsey Press, 1970).

SOVIET ENVIRONMENTAL QUALITY

Keith Bush, "Environmental Disruption: The Soviet Response," *L'Est,* no. 2 (1972).

"Environmental Disruption: The Comparative Effects of Externalities," The *ASTE Bulletin,* vol. 12, no. 1 (Spring 1971), papers delivered at a meeting of the Association for the Study of Soviet-Type Economies, Detroit, December 1970.

Irving K. Fox, ed., *Water Resources Law and Policy in the Soviet Union* (Madison: University of Wisconsin Press, 1971).

Marshall I. Goldman, ed., *Ecology and Economics: Controlling*

Pollution in the 1970s (Englewood Cliffs, N.J.: Prentice-Hall, 1972).

Marshall I. Goldman, "Externalities and the Race for Economic Growth in the USSR: Will the Environment Ever Win?" *Journal of Political Economy,* vol. 80, no. 2 (March/April 1972), 314–327.

Marshall I. Goldman, *The Spoils of Progress: Environmental Pollution in the Soviet Union* (Cambridge, Mass.: MIT Press, 1972).

CHAPTER TWELVE

The Soviet Experience: An Approach to Economic Development

Our examination of the Soviet economic system has emphasized two recurring themes: the first is the operational efficiency of resource allocation in the Soviet command economy. The second theme is the Soviet model of economic development. We touched upon this latter topic in earlier chapters—the economic development (or lack of it) of tsarist Russia (Chapter One), the Soviet Industrialization Debate (Chapter Three), the planning of industrial supply and labor for economic development (Chapters Five and Six), the role of agriculture in Soviet economic development (Chapter Seven), and the role of trade in Soviet economic development (Chapter Eight). In this chapter, we return to the central issue of the *Soviet Development Model*—what it is, how it works, and its relevance—both politically and economically—to the presently less developed countries (LDCs). In the process, we hope to bring together the material from earlier chapters and to formulate as precisely as possible a picture of the Soviet approach to economic development.

Our approach is to consider important components of the Soviet Development Model (SDM), and how these components and the model in total differ from the typical Western pattern of economic development. Second, we consider the unique institutional arrangements that served as a vehicle for the SDM, namely, the collective farm, the political dictatorship of the Communist Party,

417

and the central planning apparatus. Third, we consider the environment in which the SDM has operated, to determine whether certain preconditions were necessary for its implementation. Finally, we examine the relevance of the Soviet model to the development problems of the LDCs.

THE SOVIET DEVELOPMENT MODEL

The relatively small amount of attention that has been devoted to elaborating the SDM by Western economists is surprising in view of its importance as a major alternative development pattern— although the gaps in our knowledge on this subject have been narrowed in recent years.[1] On the basis of available research on the SDM, we delineate the following as its most essential components.[2]

(1) Planners' preferences, dictated by the Communist Party

[1] The most extensive and comprehensive work on this area is Charles K. Wilber, *The Soviet Model and Underdeveloped Countries* (Chapel Hill: University of North Carolina Press, 1969). Other authors making significant contributions are Oleg Hoeffding, "State Planning and Forced Industrialization," *Problems of Communism*, vol. 8, no. 6 (November–December 1959); Nicholas Spulber, *Soviet Strategy for Economic Growth,* (Bloomington: Indiana University Press, 1964); Alec Nove, "The Soviet Model and Underdeveloped Countries," *International Affairs,* vol. 36, no. 1 (January 1961); Norton Dodge and Charles Wilber, "The Relevance of Soviet Industrial Experience for Less Developed Economies," *Soviet Studies,* vol. 21, no. 3 (January 1970), 330–349.

[2] Our elaboration of the components of the SDM is drawn from the following studies: Wilber, *op. cit.,* part I; Gur Ofer, *The Service Sector in Soviet Economic Growth* (Cambridge, Mass.: Harvard University Press, 1973); Paul Gregory, *Socialist and Nonsocialist Industrialization Patterns* (New York: Praeger, 1970); Frederic Pryor, *Public Expenditures in Communist and Capitalist Nations* (Homewood, Ill.: Irwin, 1968); Franklyn Holzman, *Soviet Taxation* (Cambridge, Mass.: Harvard University Press, 1955); Franklyn Holzman, "Foreign Trade" in Abram Bergson and Simon Kuznets, *Economic Trends in the Soviet Union* (Cambridge, Mass.: Harvard University Press, 1963), pp. 283–332; Holland Hunter, *Soviet Transportation Policy* (Cambridge, Mass.: Harvard University Press, 1957); Ernest W. Williams, Jr., *Freight Transportation in the Soviet Union* (Princeton, N.J.: Princeton University Press, 1962); Simon Kuznets, "A Comparative Appraisal," in Bergson and Kuznets, *op. cit.* In this chapter, we do not footnote summary material drawn from earlier chapters.

through the planning hierarchy, replace consumer preferences. This changeover is made possible by the establishment of a political dictatorship that places the means of production in the hands of the state. As a response to the imposition of planners' preferences, the structure of final and intermediate demand is changed dramatically within a relatively brief period of time in favor of a few selected (priority) heavy industrial branches—in particular, metallurgy, machine building, and electricity. In turn, the allocation of resources, especially investment resources, to light industry and agriculture is severely restricted in relative terms. These two trends reflect themselves in prominent structural shifts in the end use of GNP: the aggregate investment rate rises markedly and rapidly while the share of GNP devoted to personal consumption falls. Investment is channeled selectively into the above mentioned heavy industrial branches; residential construction, transportation, light industry, and agriculture are, relatively speaking, neglected. The share of communal consumption (public health, education, etc.) of total consumption rises at the expense of private consumption. The rise in public consumption, however, is not sufficient to counter the relative decline in total consumption (as a percentage of GNP).

The service sector that generally increases in relative importance in the course of economic development—as the demand for final services tends to rise more rapidly than income and because services are needed to lubricate interactions among economic units —fails to grow rapidly despite the rise in health and education services; thereby, limiting the flow of resources into "nonproductive" sectors.[3] Development of the commerce sector is especially restricted because the limitations placed on the consumer goods sector retard the rate of growth of the retail trade network, the absence of property ownership limits the need for banking, legal, and other commercial services and the material balance system in large measure replaces the wholesale trade network.

(2) Sectorial relationships change. Agriculture is collectivized and private trade is virtually eliminated. In this manner, the state can ensure sufficient deliveries of agricultural products to the

---

[3] By "nonproductive" sectors we use the Marxian meaning of an economic sector that produces services not directly connected with the production of a physical commodity.

cities by making the deliveries mandatory. The prices at which farms must sell produce to the state are set at low levels for two purposes. The first is to force a transfer of savings from the countryside to industry to finance the rising industrial investment rate (via the turnover tax on food products). The second purpose is to reduce rural real incomes to facilitate the transfer of labor out of agriculture into higher priority industrial occupations, offering relatively higher real wages. The depression of rural living standards encourages the younger and more productive age groups to leave the collective farms for the city, and organized state recruitment campaigns in the countryside are used to promote this movement.

(3) In industry, especially in high priority branches and mainline activities, highly capital-intensive factor proportions are adopted. In this manner, the movement of population from the rural to urban areas, though quite rapid, is held below what it would have been had labor-intensive factor proportions been used in industry. The result of this policy is a below average ratio of urban population to total population, relative to the level of development, which further enables planners to restrict the flow of resources into "nonproductive" municipal services required to maintain the urban population.[4] Urbanization is also held down by encouraging high labor participation rates among the existing urban population, especially of women. The low absolute real income levels and (in later years) laws against parasitism and absenteeism are used to encourage such high labor participation rates.

The rapid expansion of priority industrial branches such as machinery, metallurgy, and electricity is made possible by generous allocations of scarce capital by planning authorities. In addition, in the priority areas, relatively high sector wages are set to attract the most highly skilled industrial workers into the priority branches. On the other hand, the relatively neglected light industrial sectors are those with high capital-output ratios, notably printing, paper, and food products.[5]

Not having developed sophisticated industrial planning techniques, the Soviets use "campaigns" to eliminate bottlenecks that arise as a result of taut planning. In addition, industrial planning is

---

[4] Ofer, *op. cit.,* chap. 1.
[5] Gregory, *op. cit.,* p. 144.

simplified by limiting product differentiation. This product strategy is expected to encourage standardization, limit the spare parts problem, and facilitate maintenance and repair. Scarce industrial capital is stretched by multiple-shift arrangements (often three per day) and by utilizing capital until it is totally worn out. Further capital saving techniques involve the combining of advanced capital-intensive Western technology in primary processes with old fashioned labor-intensive methods in auxiliary processes and the limiting of social overhead investment in transportation, roads, apartment buildings, schools, and hospitals.[6] Instead, social overhead capital carried over from earlier periods is simply utilized more intensively.

At the industrial enterprise level, large-scale and highly integrated plants are chosen. This *"gigantomania"* is sanctioned for reasons of international prestige (having the world's largest dam, for example) and because it is hoped that unit costs will eventually be lower owing to economies of scale.[7] Furthermore, a very long planning time horizon is adopted and interest rate calculations are not used, both of which condone the long gestation periods involved in such projects. Highly integrated plants are chosen because of the primitive state of the material supply system, a factor that would make less integrated plants quite vulnerable (and thus the plan) if material supplies and transportation services were not forthcoming as planned. Thus machinery producing plants, for example, produce their own steel and are in charge of shipping their finished products.[8] The integrated nature of industrial plants, in turn, enables planners to limit the size of the "nonproductive" service sector—in particular, wholesale trade.

(4) Inflation, monetary controls, and the "money illusion" play important roles in the Soviet industrialization process. The shift of resources away from consumer and toward producer goods means that the growth of disposable real income will be held below

[6] Dodge and Wilber, *op. cit.*, part II.
[7] For a statistical comparison of the scale of Soviet industrial establishments with American establishments, see Alexander Woroniak, "Industrial Concentration in Eastern Europe: The Search for Optimum Size and Efficiency," *Notwendigkeit und Gefahr der Wirtschaftlichen Konzentration* (Basel: Kyklos Verlag), pp. 265–284.
[8] David Granick, *Soviet Metal Fabricating and Economic Development: Practice Versus Policy* (Madison: University of Wisconsin Press, 1967).

the overall growth rate. In its extreme manifestations, real disposable income declines.[9] However, it is necessary to preserve an incentive for the industrial worker. To do so, wages are allowed to rise (more rapidly, of course, in priority sectors) out of pace with the supplies of consumer goods thereby creating an inflationary problem in the consumer sector. Prices of consumer goods are centrally set and are raised—as a consequence of the wage inflation—at a more rapid rate than wages, on the grounds that workers will be more concerned with what is happening to their *money* wages than with their *real* wages. To preserve equity during this period of rapid inflation, some rationing of necessities is implemented; however, sales at above-rationing prices are permitted—in fact, a complex multiple price system is used—to preserve the incentive effect of higher differential wages.

Personal income taxes are not used as a major source of state revenue because it is assumed that indirect taxes better preserve worker incentives. The form of indirect taxation adopted—the turnover tax—is ideally suited for this purpose as it is a hidden tax and the consumer is unaware of the tax's proportion of the retail price. He is therefore unaware of the extent to which he is bearing the burden of industrialization.[10] In addition, the multiple price system is a rich source of revenue, insofar as such price differentials are accounted for almost entirely by the turnover tax.

Tax revenues gathered in this fashion are then used directly to finance nonagricultural investment, the funds for which are allocated administratively by an investment plan. Very little, if any, investment is determined at the plant level. Throughout this process, the state bank monitors the amount of cash in the hands of the

---

[9] One can question whether the decline in real income is a fundamental aspect of the SDM rather than an unforeseen result of the world depression, collectivization problems, poor harvest of 1931, and so on. In fact (as indicated in Chapter Three), the First Five Year Plan projected a substantial increase in consumer goods as well as falling consumer prices. Also industrial wages were not supposed to rise as fast as they did. Our view is that the SDM does call for a *relative* shift in resources away from consumption and for holding the rate of growth of real incomes below attainable levels. Whether this policy will result in absolute declines, as was true in the Soviet case, will depend on the situation. It will, however, result in a relative decline.

[10] Franklyn Holzman, "Financing Soviet Development," in M. Abramovitz, ed., *Capital Formation and Economic Growth* (Princeton, N.J.: Princeton University Press, 1955), pp. 229–287.

public through its control of enterprise deposit accounts and—via its control over enterprise credit and interenterprise transactions —monitors plan performance and fulfillment at the enterprise level, thus providing a secondary source of information on enterprise operations for the planning apparatus.

(5) A significant portion of government expenditure is used to finance industrial investment. The remainder serves to finance defense, administration, and public consumption expenditures, which grow at a fairly rapid rate. Considerable public resources are channeled into growth-boosting expenditures such as public health and education, on the grounds that a healthy and well-trained labor force is required to man the economy. The focus of education is upon technical specialization, with little emphasis on liberal arts subjects. The state embarks on a mass campaign of vocational education that takes place, to a great extent, on the job in the factory. In this manner, the state saves scarce capital by not having to build additional schools, universities, and technical institutes. A further device to stretch educational resources is the emphasis on night school training, correspondence courses, and self-instruction. Throughout, the worker is encouraged to acquire additional training by a schedule of highly differentiated wages, which favors the skilled worker over the unskilled worker.

(6) The expansion of transport capacity is severely limited during the initial period of industrialization in order to restrict investment in social overhead capital. Instead, planners count on substantial improvements in the effective capacity of the transport sector by improved levels of *utilization,* coupled with a pattern of industrialization explicitly designed to minimize the need for transport services. To achieve this latter objective, strong emphasis is placed upon locating industrial establishments at the site of raw materials.[11] A further aspect of SDM transportation policies is the emphasis on railways as opposed to other forms of surface

[11] Soviet planners have long stressed the need for economic development in all regions of the country. The Ural-Kuznetsk Combine was designed to tap the mineral resources of the Ural mountains and the coal resources of the Kuznetsk area, and to be appropriately combined to form a large industrial center. For a detailed discussion of the program, see, for example, Franklyn Holzman, "The Soviet Ural-Kuznets Combine: A Study of Investment Criteria and Industrialization Policies," *Quarterly Journal of Economics,* vol. 71, no. 3 (August 1957), 367–405.

transportation thereby enabling authorities to avoid expensive and time consuming highway construction.[12]

(7) The economy's relationships with the outside world change as well. The state establishes a foreign trade monopoly to insure that dealings with the outside world are in accordance with the needs of industrialization, and the planning of international trade simply becomes an extension of the overall planning apparatus. Initially, agricultural products are exchanged for the machinery —in particular, machine tools that can be used to make other machinery—vital to the early stages of industrialization, and heavy reliance is placed on imports of foreign technology. However, the long-term emphasis is placed upon lessening dependence on the rest of the world, for such reliance is viewed as incompatible with the planned nature of the economy. This autarky approach dictates that the country must develop its own productive capacity to produce as complete a range of industrial and agricultural products as possible on the basis of its own domestic resource base. Domestic production is therefore substituted for imports and specialization of production in line with comparative advantage tends to be neglected.[13] This process of import substitution contributes to the structural changes noted above.

THE SOVIET DEVELOPMENT MODEL: A COMPARISON WITH WESTERN TRENDS

The above summary outlines some major features of the SDM. Upon closer examination, it could perhaps be argued that there is

[12] Hunter, *op. cit.*, chap. 3 and especially chart 4, p. 49; Williams, *op. cit.*, pp. 136–137.

[13] One could also perhaps argue that the Soviet autarky model is not a true component of the SDM, rather a historical accident of the world depression and hostility of capitalist trading partners. While these factors were of course important in forcing the USSR into a position of low reliance on trade, it is also true that there are noteworthy factors in the system itself (the inability of a planned economy to tie itself to outside economies) that have caused both the USSR and Eastern Europe to maintain low foreign trade proportions in spite of changing political climates.

nothing patently new about the Soviet model, for there are marked similarities between it, and the process of economic development in the West. For example, it has been widely noted that the product share of heavy industry increases during the process of development.[14] One would also expect the investment rate to rise during the course of development. In most Western countries, the agricultural terms of trade have declined over the long-run, and the process of import substitution has caused a lowering of foreign trade proportions as the economy grows in size, just as in the Soviet case.[15] A further common feature of development in both systems is the rapid expansion of universal education and specialized training during the development process.

Thus, many aspects of the SDM are not new. Others—for example, material balance planning, the substitution of planners' preferences, the collective farm, the de-emphasis of services, and many others—are innovative features of the SDM. One important fact, however, should not be neglected—that is that the SDM involves considerable differences in magnitude and timing when it comes to the implementation of these common elements. Recent research in this area is beginning to make this point quite clear.

Putting aside differences in institutional approaches—the collective farm, the political dictatorship, and material balance planning—which will be discussed in the next section, we note below the essential *quantitative* differences between the SDM and the Western development model.

(1) The relative increase in heavy industry, which generally occurs in the course of development, was greater both in *magnitude* and in *speed* in the Soviet Union than in Western countries. The increases in the combined metallurgy and engineering product share of manufacturing in the USSR of 26 percentage points (from 19 to 45 percent) between 1928 and 1937 required from fifty to seventy-five years in other countries, and many industrialized Western countries have yet to attain a heavy industry share as large as the USSR had achieved as early as 1937.[16]

[14] Walter Hoffman, *The Growth of Industrial Economies* (Manchester, England: Manchester University Press, 1958); and Gregory, *op. cit.,* p. 168.
[15] Simon Kuznets, *Modern Economic Growth* (New Haven, Conn.: Yale University Press, 1967), pp. 300–303.
[16] Gregory, *op. cit.,* pp. 28–29, Appendix B.

(2) The rapidity of the increase in the investment rate in the Soviet Union is another distinctive feature of the SDM. In 1928, gross investment as a percent of GNP (measured in 1937 factor costs) was 12.5 percent; by 1937 this figure was 25.9 percent, after peaking at 32 percent in 1935.[17] Such high investment rates have been matched and even surpassed by several Western countries. However, in Western countries, the rise in the investment rate was gradual and began several decades after industrialization was underway, not during its initial stages.[18]

(3) Another distinctive feature of the SDM has been its combination of a high investment rate with a relatively low marginal capital-output ratio during the initial stages of industrialization.[19] In Western countries, either investment rates and marginal capital-output ratios were both low, or high investment rates were combined with high marginal capital-output ratios. The Soviet marginal capital-output ratio did begin to rise substantially after 1958, but prior to that it had remained relatively stable throughout the entire 1928 to 1958 period—the war years excluded. The Soviets were able to maintain the stability of the marginal capital-output ratio largely by limiting investment in residential construction and transportation (with high capital-output ratios) and by intensive multishift utilization of existing industrial capital stock.[20]

(4) Extremely rapid shifts of resources out of agriculture into industry are also characteristic of the SDM. In the course of Western economic development, the labor force and product shares of agriculture generally declined, but in the Soviet Union the decline in the share of labor and product of agriculture which took place between 1928 and 1940 (Table 8, Chapter Three) required from 30 to 50 years to complete in other countries.[21]

(5) As far as sectoral productivity relationships are con-

[17] R. Moorsteen and R. Powell, *The Soviet Capital Stock, 1928–1962* (Homewood, Ill.: Irwin, 1966), pp. 358, 361. The 1935 figure is estimated by applying the Moorsteen and Powell investment rate index to the Bergson 1937 figure.

[18] Kuznets, "A Comparative Appraisal," in Bergson and Kuznets, *op. cit.,* pp. 353–354.

[19] The marginal (or incremental) capital-output ratio is the ratio of the change in capital stock to the change in output, ($\Delta K / \Delta Q$).

[20] Kuznets, "A Comparative Appraisal," in Bergson and Kuznets, *op. cit.,* pp. 354–357.

[21] *Ibid.,* pp. 345–347.

cerned, the Soviet experience is distinctive for the relatively low output per worker in agriculture compared to output per worker in industry. In fact, ratios of sectoral product per worker are, in the Soviet case, quite similar to those of the LDCs, where traditional and backward agricultural sectors prevail. There is evidence that labor productivity (in full-time equivalents) in Soviet agriculture actually declined between 1928 and 1940, quite in contrast to the industrialization experiences of other countries, where agricultural labor productivity generally kept pace with the overall productivity growth of the economy.[22]

(6) The SDM also differs from the Western experience as far as the decline in the share of private consumption is concerned. In the course of economic development in the West, the GNP share of private consumption normally declines. The distinctive feature of the trend in private consumption in the Soviet Union was the magnitude and rapidity of its relative decline—not to mention the *absolute* decline. In 1928, private consumption accounted for 80 percent of Soviet GNP. By 1940, this figure had dropped to 50 percent (Table 8, Chapter Three). In other countries, during the course of their economic development, the drop was from 80 percent to between 60 and 70 percent—a decline that required from 30 to 80 years to complete—as opposed to a mere 12 years in the Soviet case.[23]

(7) A further distinctive feature of the SDM is the rapid rise in the labor participation rate—the ratio of the labor force to the population. During the 1928 to 1940 period, the Soviet population grew at 1.2 percent annually; whereas the labor force grew at 3.7 percent annually. Thus there was a 2.5 percent annual rate of growth of the labor participation rate. As Simon Kuznets notes: "No such accelerated use of labor relative to population appears to have occurred in other countries."[24] As was noted above, most of this increase in the labor participation rate is to be explained by the rise in the female participation rate.

(8) The relatively low Soviet foreign trade proportions during industrialization are also a distinctive feature of the SDM. Commonly, a country's dependence on foreign trade is gradually re-

[22] *Ibid.,* pp. 350–352.
[23] *Ibid.,* pp. 358–361.
[24] *Ibid.,* p. 341.

duced in the course of development as the economy grows in scale —a consequence of gradual import substitution.[25] In the Soviet case, the ratio of exports to national income dropped dramatically from 3.5 percent in 1930 to 0.5 percent in 1937. Part of this drop can be explained by the collapse of world prices of primary products during the world depression (as noted above), but Soviet trade ratios prior to and after the depression remain quite low by international standards. As Kuznets notes: "[The low Soviet foreign trade proportions] reflect a forced isolation of a large population from contact with the rest of the world, not paralleled in any non-Communist country within modern times."[26]

(9) A final distinctive feature of the SDM is the extent to which the relative size of the service sector, especially commercial services such as trade, banking, and insurance have been depressed below "normal" levels in the Soviet Union. When compared with the development experience of Western countries, a Soviet service "gap" is evident in the sense that the labor force share of services is much below that expected of a market economy at a similar level of development. Thus the Soviet economy has developed without devoting as much resources to services as have "normally" been required in the course of Western economic development.[27]

MECHANISMS AND INSTITUTIONS OF THE SOVIET DEVELOPMENT MODEL

Our analysis of the SDM to this point has emphasized its characteristic features and the quantifiable differences between it and the Western development model. It was shown that the emphasis on heavy industry, the rapidity of the rise in the investment rate, the relative stability of the capital-output ratio, the relatively low productivity of agriculture, the rapidity of the rise in the labor participation rate, the relatively low foreign trade proportions, and the

[25] Kuznets, *Modern Economic Growth, op. cit.,* pp. 300–302.
[26] Kuznets, "A Comparative Appraisal," *op. cit.,* p. 367.
[27] Ofer, *op. cit.,* chap. 3.

relative neglect of services in the course of Soviet economic development tend to differentiate the Soviet from the Western model. The consequence of these quantitative differences have been dealt with in the preceding chapter, namely, the rapid rate of growth of output, the slow growth of consumption, the relatively poor performance of agriculture, and so on.

One cannot, however, evaluate the SDM strictly in terms of such indicators of performance. Instead, it is necessary to evaluate the *full* costs and benefits of the Soviet model *including* the costs and benefits incurred through the introduction of institutional changes into Soviet society. We grant that it is virtually impossible to objectively evaluate the costs and benefits of varying institutional arrangements, yet to omit them would be to omit a crucial element of the Soviet model. The impact of varying institutional arrangements upon economic development is a matter of great complexity and a subject on which there are relatively few insights;[28] yet the introduction of new institutions or changes in established institutions likely plays an important role in the development process.

In the Soviet case, crucial institutional changes accompanied (or perhaps, made possible) the above noted structural changes. In this section, we emphasize two critical institutional aspects of the SDM—the *kolkhoz* and the Soviet political-administrative model.

The Kolkhoz and Soviet
Economic Development

The picture presented in Chapter Seven suggested that Soviet agriculture, while not performing well according to traditional indicators was, nevertheless, able to make a "contribution" to the Soviet development effort. The *kolkhoz* was viewed as a crucial institu-

---

[28] Alexander Gerschenkron has emphasized the role of changing institutions in the course of industrialization in his theory of relative backwardness. In his view, for example, the development of the investment bank was crucial to the rapid development of Germany during the second half of the nineteenth century, and the acceptance of an entrepreneurial role by the tsarist bureaucracy made the spurt of industrial growth of the tsarist economy after 1880 possible. On this, see Alexander Gerschenkron, *Economic Backwardness in Historical Perspective* (Cambridge, Mass.: Harvard University Press, 1962), chap. 1.

tion responsible for this contribution through its unique system of distribution, by which the authorities attempted to extract an agricultural surplus from the countryside.

In a somewhat artificial and simplified framework, our evaluation of the *kolkhoz* from a development point of view is carried out in terms of (a) its immediate contribution to the development process, and (b) its longer term contribution to the changing structure of the agricultural sector. Let us initially consider the short-run implications of the *kolkhoz*.

Apart from introducing political control into the countryside (to be examined later), the unique developmental feature of the *kolkhoz* was its labor-day system of distribution, which along with obligatory deliveries, was purportedly used to extract a surplus from collective agriculture. The traditional view—expounded by the Soviets themselves and by some Western authors—suggests that this is how Soviet agriculture through the *kolkhoz* made an immediate contribution to development, and provided the rationale for the collectivization process.[29] This view of the positive contributions of the *kolkhoz* to Soviet economic development has been challenged recently. First, even at the existing (under collectivization) levels of grain marketings there is some question concerning the existence of an agricultural surplus. James Millar has argued that, in fact, there may have been *no net product* surplus generated by collective agriculture in the sense that input flows from the industrial to the agricultural sector may well have offset the flows of agricultural products in the opposite direction.[30] In addition, the onerous nature of the collectivization process per se, and of the *kolkhoz* in operation after collectivization, may have lowered—below what might have been possible under alternate arrangements—the total agricultural output, and thus potential marketings.[31]

It remains for further research to determine whether an agricultural product surplus did indeed exist during the 1930s. It does seem clear, however, that the *kolkhoz* as a development mech-

[29] See, for example, Maurice Dobb, *Soviet Economic Development Since 1917*, 5th ed. (London: Routledge & Kegan Paul, 1960), chaps. 7–10.
[30] For a discussion of this point, see Chapter Seven.
[31] See, for example, the argument in Jerzy F. Karcz, "From Stalin to Brezhnev: Soviet Agricultural Policy in Historical Perspective," in Millar, *op. cit.*, pp. 36–70.

anism did have an important long-run negative impact on agricultural output (Chapter Seven), which must be considered when evaluating its *net* impact upon Soviet economic development. But, apart from the immediate need for a product surplus, what of the other roles of collective agriculture in "contributing" to Soviet economic development?

Turning to the massive transfer of manpower out of the rural into the industrial sector during the 1930s, it is not apparent that the *kolkhoz* played an indispensable role in this process. As we have noted (Chapter Six), both market and nonmarket mechanisms were utilized to effect this transfer. In fact, the transfer was accomplished in many respects along the lines suggested by standard economic theorizing—the utilization of wage differentials, provision of housing in urban areas, increasing educational skills, and so forth—policies that are largely independent of the *kolkhoz* as an institution. Thus it is quite possible that the vast transfer of manpower from the countryside could have been accomplished as well or better without the *kolkhoz*.

One might argue that the *kolkhoz,* insofar as it was designed to extract a "surplus," in fact hindered the achievement of the long-run transformation of the rural sector. True, rural incomes were kept very low by the nature of the *kolkhoz,* but with a centrally planned system it should have been possible to achieve a balance of the various forces that induce appropriate levels of migration from the countryside, but without the artificially low levels of rural incomes that have had long-run negative effects.[32]

If it indeed turns out that there was no product surplus from collective agriculture as Millar maintains, it will be a major indictment of the *kolkhoz* as a developmental institution, for on other grounds, it does not appear to have been theoretically necessary. Although these are "iffy" questions, they are nevertheless sufficiently important to warrant our attention. So far, our discussion

[32] Two points are worth noting in this regard. First, the range of issues associated with rural–urban differences in levels of living, and hence, apportionment of the "burden" of industrialization between these sectors, remains in large measure to be researched. Second, it should be noted that the theoretical literature pertaining to rural–urban migration during economic development and the factors contributing to that process are couched almost entirely in the framework of a market economy. In short, the alternatives open to a nonmarket economy remain also to be investigated.

has been limited to economic considerations. A final argument in favor of the *kolkhoz* may be that it was a politically desirable institution in the countryside, despite its undesirable economic features. This issue will be taken up in the discussion of the political model.

Let us now consider the *kolkhoz* in a long-run context. It has proven very difficult, if not impossible, to transform the *kolkhoz* from a pattern of extensive to intensive cultivation, and thus many of the long-term problems discussed in Chapter Seven remain to the present day. Doubtless such difficulties stem in part from a general neglect of the agricultural sector—in terms of investment, equipment, fertilizers, and so on—yet recent trends toward total modification or abandonment of the *kolkhoz* seem to indicate that the *kolkhoz* itself shares some of the responsibility. Our examination of the changing organization of the agricultural sector, especially in the post-Stalin years, indicated that in many cases the *kolkhoz* has simply been converted into a *sovkhoz*. In other cases, the nature of the *kolkhoz* has been so fundamentally changed that it bears little resemblance to the original model of earlier years.[33] Thus the *kolkhoz,* as it was originally conceived, probably no longer exists today, and Soviet agriculture, quite unlike the original perception of its contributory role, is now the *recipient* of subsidies from the state, beginning in the mid-1960s.[34]

Although the organizational format of Soviet agriculture under conditions of intensive agricultural production remains to be fully elaborated, it may be that the *kolkhoz* was, at least on economic grounds, a mistake. The Soviets' perception of its potential product contribution during the initial stages of industrialization may have proved erroneous, which in the face of the poor long-term performance of collective agriculture leaves little to support the *kolkhoz*. Also its role in promoting structural change—for example, the transfer of labor to the industrial sector—might well have been

[33] See, for example, Robert C. Stuart, "Structural Change and the Quality of Soviet Collective Farm Management, 1952–1966," in Millar, *op. cit.,* pp. 121–138.

[34] In recent years (1965–1969), these subsidies may have been as high as nine billion rubles on an annual basis. These figures suggest a *negative* flow of resources from agriculture. On this see Keith Bush, "A Suggested Computation of the Soviet Agricultural Subsidy," *Radio Liberty Dispatch,* August 13, 1971.

performed more appropriately and with less expense by other methods. The reader should bear in mind, however, that there has been only limited research on agricultural organization and production during the early years of Soviet industrialization. In particular, it remains for future research to investigate the role of the *sovkhoz* during these early years.

The Soviet Political-Administrative Model

The reader must be aware that our attempt to categorize the institutional components of the SDM is artificial, and yet it allows us to identify in a preliminary fashion those features of the SDM that may be crucial to its duplication under varying circumstances. Certainly the Soviet political-administrative model, which encompasses the party and the state planning apparatus, must be deemed as one of its most important institutional components, without which other features of the SDM may have proven infeasible.

The Soviet political-administrative model has been described above (Chapter Five), at least in formal terms, so we shall not again elaborate its characteristics at this point. Instead we note that the Communist Party is responsible not only for dictating goals and objectives but also for directing the implementation of these goals. The planning apparatus, on the other hand, is responsible for directing the economy in accordance with the mandates of political authorities. Through this system of controls and directives, the market is replaced by a complex system of administrative controls in which both the party and state apparatus participate.

The overriding objective of the Soviet political-administrative model has been to provide a mechanism through which the efforts of the population could be harnessed—indeed, totally committed—to the task of economic growth as established by the political leadership. Thus the earlier system that combined market and plan (NEP) was replaced by an elaborate system of obligatory central planning monitored by the party and state apparatus. In this manner, economic decisions came to be made largely at higher administrative levels. The rationale for the pervasive political-administrative direction of economic activity was the assumption that an ideologically motivated administrative apparatus could more readily initiate economic development than market arrangements.

Like any system that attempts to generate the initial stages of economic growth, the Soviets' substitution of planners' choice for individual choice involved both costs and benefits, the evaluation of which will often rest upon subjective value judgements. On the one hand, one must be able to evaluate the purely *economic* costs and benefits of the Soviet political-administrative model. In this regard, the appropriate question is: Could Soviet development achievements have been attained or even exceeded under differing institutional arrangements? Or at a minimum, could one anticipate that the negative aspects of the political model might diminish over time after economic development has been initiated? On the other hand, one must be able to evaluate the *political* and *social* costs and benefits of the Soviet political-administrative model—an evaluation that can only proceed on a subjective basis. Finally, there is the problem of tradeoffs between political and economic objectives that makes an overall evaluation even more difficult.

Ultimately, the strictly economic contribution of the Soviet political-administrative model must be measured in terms of its impact on the course of Soviet economic development, for its rationale has been that it could initiate development "better" than alternative arrangements. In this regard, we note that the Soviet political-administrative model has "mattered" in the sense that the Soviet pattern of economic development has differed significantly in terms of speed and magnitude of structural change from the "normal" Western pattern. In the preceding section, we noted the crucial quantitative differences between Soviet and Western development patterns—differences that are to be attributed to different underlying institutional arrangements.[35] Thus the principal economic success of the Soviet political-administrative model has been the manner in which it was able to speed up the process of structural change and allocate resources to priority (growth) sectors.

A secondary aspect of the economic impact of the Soviet

[35] The reader is referred to the following studies of the impact of the economic system upon development patterns: Ofer, *op. cit.;* Gregory, *op. cit.;* Paul Gregory, "Cross Section Comparisons of the Structure of GNP by Sector of Origin: Socialist and Western Countries," *Kyklos,* vol. 24, no. 3 (1971), 444–454; Frederic Pryor, *Public Expenditures in Communist and Capitalist Nations* (Homewood, Ill.: Irwin, 1968).

political-administrative model involves the issue of decision-making efficiency under alternative institutional arrangements. Insofar as the Soviet political-administrative model resulted in economic decisions being made at relatively high levels by a relatively small number of individuals, this may have resulted in a more optimal usage of scarce decision-making talent in a relatively backward country. On the negative side, the practice of placing political appointees, known to be sensitized to the directives of the party, in responsible economic positions—as plant manager, collective farm chairman, and so on—may have had an adverse effect on decision-making efficiency; so it is difficult to draw an overall balance.

Again, as with our evaluation of the *kolkhoz,* a distinction must be made between the short- and long-run. The ability of the Soviet political-administrative model to focus resources upon growth sectors with reasonable accuracy was initially a substantial strength. At a higher level of economic development, however, these same mechanisms have become markedly less useful, and if the Soviet political-administrative model cannot be successfully modified to meet the requirements of a more sophisticated economy, this may be one of its most substantial long-run costs. If the alternative to the Soviet political-administrative model were a continued lack of economic development, then this opportunity cost (its inability to adapt to modern times) may be much less than commonly perceived. To make such an evaluation, however, would require knowledge of what Soviet economic development would have been under alternative arrangements—an unanswerable question.

Turning now to an evaluation of noneconomic consequences of the Soviet political-administrative model, we note that they are difficult to evaluate objectively. The imposition of a political dictatorship over individuals and the economy may be regarded as "good" or "bad" by different individuals, depending upon individual preferences. On this point, we would like to express one note of caution, that is, the danger of considering the excesses of the Stalin era as characteristic features of the Soviet political model. The Stalin purges, the forced collectivization, the harsh punishment of managerial failure, and the draconic labor legislation are more likely properly associated with specific political figures (Stalin) rather than with the Soviet political model per se.

The tradeoffs between economic and political goals can be

more objectively evaluated. For example, we noted that from an economic standpoint there may have been better alternatives to the *kolkhoz*.[36] However, if the Soviet leadership concluded that the degree of political control of the countryside made possible by the *kolkhoz* was necessary for political survival, the issue becomes more complex, for what is the "price tag" on political survival? It could perhaps also be argued that the largely political decision to hold trade levels below "normal" levels (autarky) may have been a costly one in economic terms. However, if independence from capitalist markets was a critical political and military requirement in the minds of the Soviet leadership, then the autarky decision may not have been as costly as supposed. Also the widespread use of political appointees—whose principal qualification was party loyalty rather than technical expertise—as plant managers, collective farm chairmen, and industrial planners probably had adverse economic consequences. Yet this practice can perhaps be justified in terms of the necessities of political power and control in such a system.

Institutional factors may play differing roles in the elaboration of a development strategy in the long- and the short-run, and in terms of the level of analysis—macroeconomic versus microeconomic variables. To the extent that the particular institutional arrangements chosen in the Soviet case are viewed as having negative characteristics, these may tend to be mitigated over time. Thus political modernization, like economic modernization, may in significant part be the product of historical necessity. On this score, the modification of the Soviet political structure and institutions over time has been the subject of much discussion in the West. Although the range of issues is beyond the present study, the

---

[36] It is worth considering the possibility that any evaluation of Soviet agriculture (and especially the *kolkhoz*) and Soviet development when couched in *economic* terms may be partially misdirected. Thus while the *kolkhoz* has long been presented in official Soviet viewpoint as an independent cooperative organization formed on the basis of local peasant initiative, Western observers have suggested that in fact it has borne little resemblance to a cooperative organization, and accordingly, its *potential for political control* may well have been paramount in the minds of Soviet leaders during the period of rapid industrialization. Thus the demise of the *kolkhoz* in both form and substance in recent years is not surprising, not to mention the abandonment of the Machine Tractor Stations in 1958.

reader is referred to the general literature on political convergence, for example, the arguments made by Huntington and Brzezinski.[37] At the same time, it may be that political modernization arises from the emergence of special interest groups, or from the professionalization of groups within the bureaucracy.[38]

A COMPARISON OF THE SOVIET UNION IN 1928 WITH THE LDCs

We have outlined the essential features of the SDM and have stressed how it differs—both in quantitative terms and in institutions—from the pattern of economic development in the non-communist world. The relevance of the SDM for use by the LDCs hinges upon two questions. First, *can* the LDCs use the Soviet model to attack their development problems with their existing total resource bases? Second, *should* the LDCs use the Soviet model if they are able to do so? To answer the first question, we must consider to what extent the implementation of the SDM in the Soviet Union was dependent upon existing conditions unique to the USSR and not found elsewhere. In this regard, the existing economic, social, political, and resource bases of the Soviet Union on the eve of the First Five Year Plan must be considered.

As we noted in Chapter One, the Bolsheviks inherited a relatively backward economy from their tsarist predecessors. The majority of the population was illiterate and unsuited for work in modern factory industry, which existed like an enclave alongside tradition-bound agriculture and handicraft. The peasant was quite poor, and there was limited mobility out of agriculture to the city. Further there was extensive dependence upon foreign capital to

[37] Zbigniew Brzezinski and Samuel P. Huntington, *Political Power: USA/ USSR* (New York: Viking Press, 1964).
[38] On the question of interest groups, see H. Gordon Skilling and Franklyn Griffiths, eds., *Interest Groups in Soviet Politics* (Princeton, N.J.: Princeton University Press, 1971). On the development of "Technocrats," see, for example, Jeremy R. Azrael, *Managerial Power and Soviet Politics* (Cambridge, Mass.: Harvard University Press, 1966). For an attempt at measurement, see Milton C. Lodge, *Soviet Elite Attitudes Since Stalin* (Columbus, Ohio: Merrill, 1969).

support industrialization. All of these are characteristics of under-development quite familiar to the LDCs today. Yet despite its relative backwardness, there is evidence to suggest that the Russian economy did have a fairly substantial headstart when compared to the starting points of today's LDCs.

First, the Soviet Union on the eve of the First Five Year Plan (1928) was a much richer country—on a per capita income basis—than most LDCs today. Although such figures are highly speculative, it has been estimated that Russian per capita income in 1913 was between $242 and $444 in 1969 prices.[39] Many of today's LDCs are not that fortunate, with average per capita income well below the 1913 Russian figure in most cases. On a regional basis, the majority of African and Asian countries fall well below the 1913 Russian figure, while the Latin American countries equal or surpass the Russian figure.[40] As far as the Russian initial per capita income compares with initial figures of the now industrialized countries at the beginning of their modern economic growth, we find that Russian per capita income in 1913 was not notoriously high or low compared with starting points in Europe and North America, but was quite high compared to Japan.[41]

A second advantage possessed by the Soviet Union vis-à-vis the LDCs relates to agricultural marketings. Despite all the inefficiencies noted in Chapter 1, Russian agriculture tended to market a fairly substantial portion of its output outside of villages. For example, during the 1909–1913 period, Russian agriculture marketed 19 million tons of grain (roughly 25 percent of total output) outside of villages.[42] Thus Russian agriculture was able to produce a fairly sizeable surplus, (surplus defined as product exceeding the requirements of the peasant population)—a crucial requirement for successful economic development. Whether this was a *net* surplus is, of course, another question, but this surplus was available for exports and for feeding the urban population. In many LDCs,

[39] Stanley Cohn, *Economic Development in the Soviet Union* (Lexington, Mass.: Heath, 1970), p. 111.

[40] United Nations, *Yearbook of National Accounts Statistics, 1969, International Tables,* vol. II (New York: 1970), Table 1A.

[41] Simon Kuznets, *Economic Growth of Nations* (Cambridge, Mass.: Harvard University Press, 1971), p. 24.

[42] R. W. Davies, "A Note on Grain Statistics," *Soviet Studies,* vol. 21, no. 3, 319, 326.

agriculture tends to operate closer to the peasant subsistence level and is unable to provide this margin so crucial to successful industrialization.

A third economic advantage inherited by the Soviet regime was the Russian experience with rapid industrial growth after 1880 which, although it failed to lead to *sustained* modern economic growth—owing to lagging agricultural performance—did provide some of the prerequisites for later economic development. This industrialization provided the nucleus of a factory labor force and trained managerial personnel as the factory enterprise rose in the place of handicraft manufacturing. We have already noted the burgeoning growth of the railroads during this same period—a valuable asset for an industrializing country. Such invaluable industrialization experience is a rarity in the LDCs today. Most lack a trained factory labor force; manufacturing is dominated by handicraft production. Potential managers and entrepreneurs are also lacking, along with a developed transportation network—the latter requiring extensive social overhead capital investment before industrialization can begin.

An essential feature of the SDM was its dictatorial political-administrative model, which established the unity of purpose and the means of imposing rapid industrialization upon the population in the Soviet Union. In this regard, we should note the peculiar applicability of such a model to the Soviet Union, for the Soviets came to power in a country accustomed to autocratic direction by a central government, with the majority of the population conscious of its national identity.[43] This is quite in contrast to many LDCs, in which regions or tribes command the loyalty of people rather than the central government, the latter often an artificial construct of the colonial past. This contrast between the Soviet Union and the LDCs is an essential one, perhaps more important than economic considerations, for the SDM requires the political cohesion, power, and purpose necessary to implement the hard, and often unpopular, resource allocation decisions. For a political leader in an LDC to try to do the same without the necessary political prerequisites would be devoid of success and would probably cost him his job.

[43] Cohn, *op. cit.*, p. 99.

A third contrast between the Soviet Union on the eve of in-dustrialization and the LDCs today involves relative resource bases. A varied and complete natural resource base is an essential requirement for the SDM to operate successfully. To pursue an autarky policy without a full complement of resources would be risky, especially given the Soviet emphasis on heavy industry and its vast natural resource requirements. A large-scale economy is also a necessity with a heavy industry bias. In the Soviet case, scale and resource endowments were particularly suited to the SDM industrialization pattern. The Soviet Union, with only very limited exceptions, has a very favorable natural resource base, and accordingly, with the prevailing pattern of population growth, a very favorable ratio of population to natural resources. Water resources, for example, are abundant although natural features have in some cases inhibited their best use. Reserves of fuels—coal, oil, and natural gas—are abundant, with coal serving initially as the primary fuel. The mineral base of the Soviet Union is also more than adequate, with roughly one-half of world reserves of iron ores within its borders. Lumber resources are immense, lo-cated largely in the northern regions. As far as agricultural re-sources are concerned, the picture is less favorable, with much of the Soviet Union's vast terrain inhospitable for agricultural pro-duction. In all, fully 70 percent of Soviet territory is unarable due to adverse natural conditions. The most fertile agricultural regions are found in central European Russia, and there the soils are rela-tively poor when compared with those of the United States or Canada. Although the Soviet Union is not particularly well endowed for agricultural production, it does have adequate land and water resources which could serve as a base to support the industriali-zation process.[44]

A final contrast between the Soviet Union and the LDCs has been the absence of population pressures in the USSR, which has made the task of Soviet economic development easier. Between 1913 and 1970, the annual rate of growth of population in the Soviet Union has been well under one percent, owing to loss of life

[44] For an assessment of the Soviet resource base, see Theodore Shabad, *Basic Industrial Resources of the USSR* (New York: Columbia University Press, 1969).

during the two world wars and to low birth rates.[45] This is quite a contrast to the population problems of the LDCs, which have been subject to rather severe population pressures with annual rates of growth of population often exceeding 2 percent.

Thus there are important differences between the Soviet Union on the eve of the First Five Year Plan and today's LDCs. Whether these differences obviate the use of the SDM by the LDCs is open to question. One argument is that the LDCs should not emulate the SDM because it was only the substantial headstart of the Soviets that enabled them to use their model of development as well as they did.[46] If the LDCs were to attempt the same policies while starting at a much lower level of development, the consequences could be disastrous. Channeling resources into heavy industry and away from agriculture and the consumer sector in an economy already close to subsistence would raise the specter of starvation, terrible deprivation, and political discontent. In this regard, it is noteworthy that most major LDCs have either turned fairly quickly away from the Soviet pro-heavy industry–antiagriculture emphasis, or have attempted to avoid the disastrous deprivation of the agriculture sector, probably for these very reasons.[47]

Others tend to look more optimistically upon the relevance of the SDM to the LDCs. Charles Wilber,[48] in particular, stresses that while the Soviet model could not realistically be applied in small, resource-poor LDCs, this is not to deny its applicability elsewhere where more favorable conditions prevail. The SDM would be relevant to LDCs with the necessary natural and human resources and the market potential to support the development of heavy industry.

[45] James W. Brackett, "Demographic Trends and Population Policy in the Soviet Union," in *Dimensions of Soviet Economic Power* (Washington, D.C.: U.S. Government Printing Office, 1962), pp. 487–590.
[46] Oleg Hoeffding, *op. cit.;* Nove, *The Soviet Economy,* 2nd ed. (New York: Praeger, 1969), pp. 342–345; Cohn, *op. cit.,* pp. 98–101; Angus Maddison, *Economic Growth in Japan and the USSR* (London: Allen & Unwin, 1969), pp. 134–135.
[47] Dwight Perkins, *Market Control and Planning in Communist China* (Cambridge, Mass.: Harvard University Press, 1964), chaps. 3–4; J. Bhagurati and S. Chakravaty, "Contributions to Indian Economic Analysis," *American Economic Review Supplement,* vol. 54, no. 4 (September 1969).
[48] Wilber, *op. cit.,* pp. 13–15.

In addition, Wilbur argues on the basis of nonmonetary development indicators—literacy, energy consumption, wheat yields, and
so on—that a number of LDCs probably rank higher on the development scale than Russia in 1913, contrary to the arguments
made above.[49] In all, Wilbur estimates that the combined popula-
tions of LDCs possessing the necessary prerequisites for the SDM
number more than 900 million—a substantial portion of the developing world's total population.[50]

THE SOVIET MODEL: AN EVALUATION

The most comprehensive treatment of the Soviet experience in a
development framework is the study by Charles K. Wilbur.[51] In
this study, Wilbur attempts to appraise the social costs of Soviet
development in terms of selected indicators—living standards, excess mortality, and human values. The conclusion is not surprising
—the costs of the SDM were indeed high, and yet a genuine dilemma exists: the persistence of underdevelopment in itself implies severe costs. Yet the capitalist development experience in the
United States, Germany, England, and even tsarist Russia, for example, also resulted in heavy costs. Thus economic development
by whatever path implies cost, and even the loss of personal freedom and the brutality experienced under Stalin (which may not be
a fundamental component of the SDM anyway) may be a relative
matter. One can certainly argue, as Wilbur does, that freedom as
we understand that concept has relatively little meaning in many
of the world's presently underdeveloped nations. However, most
of the Western analysis pertaining to the Soviet development ex-
prience has followed the pattern utilized in this chapter, namely
examination of the structure and logic of the Soviet model, the
conditions in which that model was developed in the Soviet Union,
and its potential applicability to the LDCs.
    Cast in this framework, there has been considerable criticism
of the Soviet approach as it relates to the LDCs, first in terms of the

---

[49] *Ibid.*, pp. 15, 147–155.
[50] *Ibid.*, p. 14.
[51] *Ibid.*

sorts of preconditions that may or may not be found in presently underdeveloped countries (as discussed above) and second in terms of the need for modification of the basic model.

In view of possible differences in preconditions, it is probably reasonable to predict that in the foreseeable future, few, if any, countries will adopt the Soviet model in any form even close to that utilized in the Soviet Union. The environment of application will be examined and adjustments made as necessary. More important, though, must first be a fundamental and in-depth examination of the Soviet model itself, and this especially in conjunction with a reappraisal of many of the traditional views about the process of economic development.

The lines along which such a reappraisal might be pursued have been touched upon in this chapter. In our discussion of agriculture, for example, we noted the new effort to reappraise Soviet agricultural policy, not only in terms of its short-run contributions to the initial stages of Soviet economic growth, but also in terms of its long-run health.

Indeed, even the long-respected Soviet policy of high investment ratios concentrated in "growth" sectors has been the subject of critical appraisal. In a study of Soviet metal fabricating—a crucial sector in the development process—David Granick has argued that Soviet growth rates could have been higher and investment levels lower under different policies.[52]

While the reader is referred to Granick's study for a full discussion, the essence of his argument can be outlined here, since it is one of the first in-depth sectoral studies for these crucial early years.

The author suggests that the so-called replacement crisis[53] was in large measure a myth—thus the Soviet emphasis upon investment for the expansion of physical capital, at least in this sector, was misdirected. First, much of the expanded capacity was

[52] David Granick, *op. cit.*
[53] This was a prominent issue in the Soviet Industrialization Debate. It was suggested that the average age of physical capital was increasing rapidly, thus necessitating a sharp upturn in investment levels even to maintain the capital stock at a given age level. See Alexander Erlich, "Development Strategy and Planning: The Soviet Experience," in Max F. Millikan, ed., *National Economic Planning* (New York: Columbia University Press, 1967), p. 33.

not usable, due primarily to lack of appropriate coordination—basically a function of the excesses of central planning. Second, intangibles were neglected, notably institutional and organizational factors in industry, and a significant   decline in morale resulting from the collectivization program in agriculture.

The study by Granick is directly relevant to any examination of Soviet development strategy, and especially to the desirability of a "big push" investment program. The conception, for example, that in certain stages of economic development high investment levels concentrated in "growth-oriented" sectors will tend to "bury mistakes" amid rapid growth, does not seem to have been borne out in the case of Soviet metal fabricating. In addition, where technology was borrowed from abroad, it was not always effectively utilized.

Finally, Granick's study sheds light on the concept of *gigantomania,* especially the argument that large-scale industrial establishments have peculiar advantages in a development context, in particular, high levels of efficiency, spillover effects into other sectors of the economy, and so on. Again, the Soviet experience in the metal fabricating sector casts serious doubts upon these conceptions.

Possibly most important, this study places deserved emphasis upon the organizational aspects of economic development, suggesting in part, that although our ability to specify appropriate organizational arrangements in a developmental model may be severely limited, we cannot simply overcome our shortcomings with high investment ratios—or indeed if we try, the resulting development will be at high cost.

The Soviet development model of the 1930s certainly did provide the necessary critical minimum effort to place the Soviet economy on a path of rapid economic growth within a fairly brief period of time. In evaluating the success of this effort, three questions must be raised: (1) Were the rather extreme measures of the 1930s, most notably collectivization and reductions in living standards, necessary? (2) Was the Soviet development model executed with maximum benefit and minimum cost? (3) Could the Soviet model be transplanted, possibly in part, to the presently less developed nations?

These three questions point out the fact that a full evaluation of the Soviet development model cannot be made on the basis of "what happened" but must include consideration of alternatives foregone and costs incurred. Our evaluation of Soviet economic growth indicated quite clearly that economic growth and development in the Soviet Union after 1928 was rapid and that the transformation from an agricultural to an industrial economy was made within a very brief period of time.

As we have stressed, however, the costs of the Soviet model have been difficult to estimate. Solid data on real consumption was not made available until the late 1950s. Little is known about peasant living standards during the 1930s. The loss of life as a direct or indirect result of rapid industrialization and forced collectivization can only be guessed at by interpolation because the necessary data have not been published. Thus the economic benefits of the Soviet model—rapid growth, military power, and so on—are highly visible; whereas the costs remain hidden.

Some costs such as the imposition of a political dictatorship of the Communist Party are difficult to establish because they represent personal value judgments that political democracy is "better."

A further difficulty is our limited historical experience with the Soviet development model. We are able to observe what went on in the Soviet Union after 1928, albeit with significant gaps in our knowledge, and what went on in socialist Eastern Europe and the communist Asian countries during the post-World War II period. On the other hand, we have the long historical experience of the capitalist countries with varying organizational and political formats. Further, it has been argued by some Western analysts that the inefficiencies of Soviet planning result in significant waste that will retard the long-run development of the economy. Thus it could be that the short-term strengths of the Soviet model may well turn into long-term weaknesses. Further, the Soviet economy seems to be experiencing some of the problems of the advanced capitalist market model. While the quest for intensive development and substantially increased efficiency are pursued, the Soviet economy has, nevertheless, experienced substantial reductions in growth rates during the past fifteen years. Further, while the levels of pollution in the Soviet and American systems are debatable (as well as their relations to levels of economic development), it seems that environmental decay in general—and pollution, in particular—are growing problems for the Soviet economy. The perceived theoretical superiority of the socialist model in the handling of externalities may facilitate a more expeditious solution of such problems. In the meantime, however, it seems as though the Russians, like the Americans, have achieved a measure of economic performance at the rather severe price of a significant measure of disinvestment in the environment.

The Soviet experience is not, therefore, a development panacea. It is, however, like the capitalist market model, one whose strengths and weaknesses must be examined, especially as they bear upon specific development problems.

Selected Bibliography

THE SOVIET DEVELOPMENT MODEL

Donald W. Bowles, "Soviet Russia as a Model for Underdeveloped Areas," *World Politics,* vol. 14, no. 3 (April 1962), 483–504.

Stanley H. Cohn, *Economic Development in the Soviet Union* (Lexington, Mass.: Heath, 1970).

Alexander Erlich, "Development Strategy and Planning: The Soviet Experience," in Max F. Millikan, ed., *National Economic Planning* (New York: Columbia University Press, 1967).

Alexander Gerschenkron, *Economic Backwardness in Historical Perspective* (Cambridge, Mass.: Harvard University Press, 1962).

David Granick, *Soviet Metal Fabricating and Economic Development: Practice Versus Policy* (Madison: University of Wisconsin Press, 1967).

Paul Gregory, *Socialist and Nonsocialist Industrialization Patterns* (New York: Praeger, 1970).

Oleg Hoeffding, *Soviet State Planning and Forced Industrialization as a Model for Asia* (Santa Monica, Calif.: The Rand Corporation, August 1958).

Alex Inkeles, "The Soviet Union: Model for Asia?—The Social System," *Problems of Communism,* vol. 8, no. 6 (November-December 1959), 30–38.

W. Klatt, "Soviet Agriculture as a Model for Asian Countries," *China Quarterly,* no. 5 (January-March 1961), 116–130.

John M. Montias, "The Soviet Economic Model and the Underdeveloped Countries," in Nicolas Spulber, ed., *Study of the Soviet Economy,* Russian and East European Series, vol. 25 (Bloomington: Indiana University Press, 1961), pp. 57–82.

Alec Nove, "The Soviet Model and Underdeveloped Countries," *International Affairs,* vol. 37, no. 1 (January 1961), 29–38.

Gur Ofer, *The Service Sector in Soviet Economic Growth* (Cambridge, Mass.: Harvard University Press, 1973).

Frederic L. Pryor, *Public Expenditures in Communist and Capitalist Nations* (Homewood, Ill.: Irwin, 1968).

Francis Seton, "Planning and Economic Growth: Asia, Africa and the Soviet Model," *Soviet Survey,* no. 31 (January-March 1960), 38–40.

Robert C. Stuart, *The Collective Farm in Soviet Agriculture* (Lexington, Mass.: Heath, 1972).

Charles K. Wilber, *The Soviet Model and Underdeveloped Countries* (Chapel Hill: University of North Carolina Press, 1969).

CHAPTER THIRTEEN

Conclusions and Prospects

Our study of the Soviet economy is now complete. It would be of little value to repeat here those conclusions and summary comments contained in each chapter. In this section, therefore, we limit ourselves to a few general comments and focus, in particular, upon possible future trends and patterns.

At the outset we argued that there was benefit to be gained from a study of Soviet economic development, hence our focus upon the Soviet experience as an alternative to development under a market system, and as a system whose strengths and weaknesses deserve close scrutiny. From the vantage point of the contemporary Soviet citizen, the standard of living in the Soviet Union has risen rapidly and today stands at a level never before known in that country. To this must be added the fact that the Soviet economy is now the world's second largest, sustaining a military establishment rivaling that of the United States. Of course, this considerable economic development has not been without cost, and certainly the costs associated with Soviet economic development might be deemed intolerable to those living in a different political environment, with differing value systems. Such considerations would certainly be of great importance at present to any less developed country considering the Soviet approach as a model for development. Even setting aside ideological considerations, we have noted that it would be difficult to construct an objective picture of the full costs and benefits associated with the Soviet model.

448

The pace of Soviet economic growth has been rapid throughout the plan era, even though not unmatched historically, and yet the devotion to rapid growth in a few sectors has made Soviet development at best very narrow. Consumer choice has been neglected, and yet such a criterion for evaluating the performance of an economic system may be systematically biased in favor of the relatively affluent West. For this reason, we have attempted to evaluate the Soviet model using a fairly comprehensive set of indicators. No summary evaluation of Soviet economic performance should rest on consumption indicators alone.

The economist, unlike the physical scientist, cannot normally conduct experiments under the series of controls associated with a laboratory environment. To a great extent, the study of economies with differing economic systems is exciting insofar as it provides the observer with a "lab" system, in which the goals and organizational arrangements to achieve those goals differ from what many in the West—nurtured by the introductory economics textbook—have come to accept as the basic norm.

Viewing the Soviet economy as a social and economic experiment, and with due regard for the important Soviet growth achievement, it must be noted that many of the negative features associated with Western market economies have not been avoided, despite differing organizational arrangements and a decisive effort to manipulate the pattern of social and economic development. Our discussion of environmental decay in the Soviet Union is a case in point. While its level is, in both capitalist and socialist countries, a matter of some uncertainty, its existence in major proportions in the two classic examples—the Soviet Union and the United States —seems to be uncontested. Even those problems long associated with capitalism, for example unemployment, may in the future be matters of more serious concern to Soviet planners.

The Soviet economic system may prove to be more viable than capitalism in the resolution of such problems, though only time will allow us to judge. Meanwhile, comparison and evaluation of differing economic systems are made more difficult, for the result will surely depend heavily upon the criteria chosen. At the same time, the sorts of issues raised above suggest a fundamental similarity of economic systems, and in terms of purely structural indictators—such as output structures, urbanization, etc.—differing economic systems do seem to follow a generally similar pattern of economic development at least in terms of direction of change. This must lead to further research on the nature of economic systems, the impact of differing organizational arrangements upon development patterns, and the relevance of these considerations for the notion of "convergence" of market and command Socialist economies. In our view, it cannot easily be established whether the Soviet command economy is becoming more like its market economy counterparts, because of the problems of contradictory indicators and measurement difficulties, unlike some observers who perceive converging USSR-USA patterns—on the basis of either ongoing reform of the Soviet system or the growing similarity of all mature industrialized economies.[1]

TRENDS FOR THE FUTURE

It would serve little useful purpose to speculate on possible very long-term trends in future Soviet economic development. We do, however, have the recently announced Soviet Ninth Five Year Plan (1971–1975), which in conjunction with ongoing changes in the

[1] For a discussion of the convergence hypothesis, see, for example, Jan Tinbergen, "Do Communist and Free Economies Show a Converging Pattern?" *Soviet Studies,* vol. 12, no. 4 (April 1961), 331–341; P. J. D. Wiles, "Will Capitalism and Communism Spontaneously Converge?" *Encounter,* vol. 20, no. 6 (June 1963), 84–90. For a good recent summary of general arguments, see H. Linnemann, J. P. Pronk, and J. Tinbergen, "Convergence of Economic Systems in East and West," in Emile Benoit, ed., *Disarmament and World Economic Interdependence* (New York: Columbia University Press, 1967), pp. 246–260. For more critical views, see L. Leontiev, "Myth About Rapprochement of the Two Systems," in Jan S. Prybyla, ed., *Comparative Economic Systems* (New York: Appleton-Century-Crofts, 1969), pp. 477–483; James R. Millar, "On the Merits of the Convergence Hypothesis," *Journal of Economic Issues,* vol. 2, no. 1 (March 1969), 60–68; Jan S. Prybyla, "The Convergence of Market-Oriented and Command-Oriented Systems: A Critical Estimate," in Prybyla, *Comparative Economic Systems, op. cit.,* pp. 467–476; Robert C. Stuart and Paul R. Gregory, "The Convergence of Economic Systems: An Analysis of Structural and Institutional Characteristics," in *Jahrbuch der Wirtschaft Osteuropas* [Yearbook of East-European Economies], Band 2 (Munich: Gunther Olzog Verlag, 1971), pp. 425–442.

Soviet economy can serve as a basis to examine trends over the next decade.

The Ninth Five Year Plan seems to be notable in two important respects.[2] First, it implies a very good rate of economic growth by Western standards (slightly under six percent) but relatively slow by Soviet standards and certainly slower than the rates of growth achieved in the past. On the sectoral breakdown of this growth, industry is scheduled to grow at an annual rate of slightly over 7 percent with agriculture growing at slightly under 4 percent. Second, it seems to place greater, though restrained, emphasis upon improving consumer welfare. For the first time since 1928, the growth rates planned for Group B of industry are higher than Group A,[3] so that by 1975, the ratio of A to B output is scheduled to decline from 2.76 to 2.71.[4] Thus the shift in priorities[5] toward the consumer seems to be quite limited.

The new plan suggests that Soviet economic growth will in the future become somewhat slower than it has been in the past.[6] In large part, this new position has been forced upon Soviet leaders as they seek to modify a model of economic development that

[2] For a discussion of this plan, see Norton T. Dodge, ed., *Analysis of the USSR's 24th Party Congress and 9th Five Year Plan* (Mechanicsville, Md.; Cremona Foundation, 1971); for the document itself, see Joint Publications Research Service, U.S. Department of Commerce, *State Five Year Plan for Development of the USSR National Economy for the Period 1971–1975* (Springfield, Va.: National Technical Information Service, 1972).

[3] According to Soviet statistical practices, Group A encompasses producer goods and Group B covers consumer goods. One cannot, however, directly relate Group B output to the output of consumer goods. Heavy industry (Group A) produces consumer durables, and some light industry products—textiles, for example—are included in Group A.

[4] Herbert Block, "Value and Burden of Soviet Defense," in Joint Economic Committee, *Soviet Economic Prospects for the Seventies* (Washington, D.C.: U.S. Government Printing Office, 1973), pp. 199–200.

[5] The much heralded shift in priorities is not dramatic, especially as far as the allocation of investment resources is concerned. Keith Bush, "Resource Allocation Policy: Capital Investment," in *Soviet Economic Prospects for the Seventies, op. cit.,* pp. 39–44. There is the further question of whether light industry (B) targets will be met, especially in light of their dependence upon lagging agricultural performance. Block, *op. cit.,* pp. 199–200.

[6] Our discussion here is based on M. Yves Laulan, ed., *Prospects for Soviet Growth in the 1970s* (Brussels: NATO Directorate of Economic Affairs, 1971), and the sources cited below.

was useful in the early stages of development, but in recent years has become markedly less so. In fact, the Ninth Five Year Plan may well signal an attempted transition from the traditional Soviet extensive growth model to a new intensive model of economic growth. Why this shift in emphasis?

First, Soviet growth performance in the future will increasingly depend upon increases in factor productivity rather than upon simple expansion of factor inputs. In the case of the labor force, for example, we noted the remarkably rapid flow of labor out of the rural and into the urban sector during the 1930s. That type of movement is now minimal, and in addition, the remaining rural labor force is largely unsuited for industrial employment. Also the labor force participation rates of the Soviet population can no longer be raised dramatically as they were during the earlier stages of development. In fact, rising prosperity may make it difficult to maintain the high participation rates of Soviet women. In short, Soviet planners can no longer rely upon significant increases in the industrial labor force to generate economic growth as they could in the past. It is noteworthy that the Ninth Five Year Plan projects relatively slow rates of growth of the labor force, thus making the fulfillment of the moderate overall growth targets quite dependent upon raising labor productivity.[7]

Second, Soviet planners are, in large measure, constrained by the prevailing utilization of national income. To the extent that consumption is to be increased to enhance labor participation and effort, certainly it will not be possible to achieve a rapid expansion of the capital stock, at least not with the prevailing level of defense spending, in which no significant decline can be forecast in the immediate future. In fact, the traditional Soviet model that calls for highly unbalanced growth in favor of capital investment cannot be continued indefinitely, for to do so would require over half of GNP devoted to investment after a while. Thus there are natural limits to the Soviet model. With capital as with labor, therefore, the emphasis will have to be upon raising its productivity, and this presents Soviet leaders with a significant challenge in the economic sphere.

Third, and possibly most important to future economic growth

---

[7] J. Noren and F. Whitehouse, "Soviet Industry in the Ninth Five Year Plan," in *Soviet Economic Prospects for the Seventies, op. cit.,* p. 237.

will be the nature of technological change. Soviet leaders have always expressed great faith in the existence of hidden "reserves," and especially in the ability of organizational change to bring those reserves to the surface. We have noted a number of important barriers to technological change in the Soviet economy. The removal of these barriers will be at best a slow and difficult task. The general implication here is a need for economic reform and essentially for change in the managerial system. There is some evidence that ongoing economic reform begun in 1965 is not being implemented according to the original blueprint, and there is certainly no evidence of significant economic reforms in the offing. If anything, the signs point to a gradual return to administrative controls at the expense of the "economic levers" stressed in the reform proposals. We have noted that even a theoretical blueprint of reform is a most complex matter, and yet should such a blueprint be developed, its practical implementation would be even more difficult. Despite the apparent need for significant change in the Soviet command system, we envision little prospect for this to actually happen. The reason is that one of the basic functions of those in authority in the Soviet Union is the direction of resource allocation. To have this allocation proceed according to economic levers means a loss of authority for them.

Two factors external to the Soviet economic system will likely play an important role in determining future performance: the development of economic relations with the West and the magnitude of the perceived external military threat. Despite rather massive efforts to develop new technology at home, much of the Soviet success in this area will probably depend upon the Soviets' ability to acquire advanced technology from the West.[8] This can only proceed from the further expansion of commercial relations with the capitalist world. The external military threat is important in that it will determine the size of future Soviet defense expenditures, and the tradeoff between defense spending and economic growth has been substantial in the past.[9]

---

[8] Raymond Hutchings, "Soviet Technology Policy," in *Soviet Economic Prospects for the Seventies, op. cit.,* p. 82.
[9] Stanley Cohn, "Economic Burden of Defense Expenditures," in *Soviet Economic Prospects for the Seventies, op. cit.,* pp. 147–162.

A NEW SOVIET
ECONOMIC MODEL?

The study of alternative economic systems is an exciting venture and no less so now than in the past. While much of our effort has been devoted to understanding what we have called the Soviet development model, this model is itself undergoing change. However crudely and with whatever social, economic, and other costs, the SDM has worked its will, and by most standards of judgement the Soviet Union is today a developed economy. Cast in this light, the important challenge for the future will be the ability of Soviet leaders to manipulate, and most important, for the system itself to adapt to the demands of economic maturity. Many of the issues raised in this work, for example, appropriate levels of decision-making, use of mathematical methods, the proper combination of plan and market, and so on, will be the important issues of the future.

The important implication here is the likelihood of a new Soviet economic model not geared to rapid mobilization of resources under severe economic backwardness, but rather capable of improving economic efficiency to maintain respectable growth and improvement of economic well-being in a relatively developed economic system.

Selected Bibliography

Norton T. Dodge, ed., *Analysis of the USSR's 24th Party Congress and 9th Five-Year Plan* (Mechanicsville, Md.: Cremona Foundation, 1971).

Joint Economic Committee, *Soviet Economic Prospects for the Seventies* (Washington, D.C.: U.S. Government Printing Office, 1973).

M. Yves Laulan, ed., *Prospects for Soviet Growth in the 1970s* (Brussels: NATO Directorate of Economic Affairs, 1971).

H. Linnemann, J. P. Pronk, and J. Tinbergen, "Convergence of Economic Systems in East and West," in Emile Benoit, ed.,

Disarmament and World Economic Interdependence (New York: Columbia University Press, 1967), pp. 246–260.

James R. Millar, "On the Merits of the Convergence Hypothesis," *Journal of Economic Issues,* vol. 2, no. 1 (March 1969), 60–68.

Jan S. Prybyla, "The Convergence of Market-Oriented Systems: A Critical Estimate," in Jan S. Prybyla, ed., *Comparative Economic Systems* (New York: Appleton-Century-Crofts, 1969), pp. 467–476.

Robert C. Stuart and Paul R. Gregory, "The Convergence of Economic Systems: An Analysis of Structural and Institutional Characteristics," in *Yearbook of East-European Economics* (Munich: Günther Olzog Verlag, 1971), pp. 425–442.

Index

79 80   10 9 8